T0323648

Collective Skill Formation in the Knowledge Economy

Collective Skill Formation in the Knowledge Economy

Edited by
Giuliano Bonoli
Patrick Emmenegger

OXFORD
UNIVERSITY PRESS

OXFORD
UNIVERSITY PRESS

Great Clarendon Street, Oxford, OX2 6DP,
United Kingdom

Oxford University Press is a department of the University of Oxford.
It furthers the University's objective of excellence in research, scholarship,
and education by publishing worldwide. Oxford is a registered trade mark of
Oxford University Press in the UK and in certain other countries

© Oxford University Press 2022

The moral rights of the authors have been asserted

Impression: 1

Published in the United States of America by Oxford University Press
198 Madison Avenue, New York, NY 10016, United States of America

British Library Cataloguing in Publication Data
Data available

Library of Congress Control Number: 2022935509

ISBN 978-0-19-286625-7

DOI: 10.1093/oso/9780192866257.001.0001

Printed and bound by
CPI Group (UK) Ltd, Croydon, CR0 4YY

Acknowledgements

Like other large collaborative projects, this volume would not have been possible without the support of various individuals and institutions. The book was developed within the GOVPET Leading House project, which is generously financed by the Swiss State Secretariat for Education, Research and Innovation (SERI). The book benefited greatly from the enthusiasm and the commitment of the whole GOVPET team and of the members of the scientific advisory board, many of whom are authors or co-authors of the book's chapters. They are the first to be thanked.

Gratitude is also due to the scientific advisory board and GOVPET team members who are not part of the book, but whose advice throughout the preparation of the project was extremely precious: Pepper Culpepper, Anke Hassel, Cathie Jo Martin, and Justin Powell from the scientific advisory board, and Scherwin Bajka, Carmen Baumeler, Sonja Engelage, Flavia Fossati, Cecilia Ivardi Ganapini, Margarida Matos, Ihssane Otmani, Delia Pisoni, Alexandra Strebel, and Linda Wanklin from the GOVPET team. Finally, we would like to thank Chantal Kamm, Emily Murphy, and Matthias Pilz for helpful feedback on earlier versions of the chapters.

A very important contribution was made by Alyssa Taylor, who proofread and formatted the entire manuscript and greatly helped us improve the quality of our English. Finally, at Oxford University Press, we are very grateful to Adam Swallow for managing this project from start to finish in an efficient and friendly way.

Table of Contents

List of Figures

List of Tables

List of Contributors

Annatina Aerne is a postdoctoral researcher at the University of Lausanne at the Swiss graduate school of public administration (IDHEAP). Her current research focuses on migration and labour markets. Previously, she researched organization and culture, focusing on the art scene in Bogotá, Colombia.

Nadine Bernhard is a postdoctoral researcher at the Centre for Comparative and International Education at Humboldt Universität zu Berlin in Germany. Using institutional, organizational, comparative, discourse analytical, and/or ethnographical approaches she works on questions of institutional change, educational transfer, internationalization, organizational evolutions, educational practices, social inequality, and diversity in education (with the main focus on vocational education and training and higher education).

Giuliano Bonoli is a professor of social policy at the Swiss graduate school of public administration, University of Lausanne. His main research focus is on social and labour market policies, with an interest in international comparisons, the politics and the transformation of welfare regimes.

Regula Bürgi works at the education ministry of the canton of Lucerne, Switzerland. Her research interests are international organizations, history of education, vocational and higher education.

Marius R. Busemeyer is a full professor of political science with a focus on comparative political economy at the University of Konstanz and speaker of the Excellence Cluster 'The Politics of Inequality' in Germany. He is also an affiliated senior researcher at the WSI, Düsseldorf. His research focuses on comparative political economy and welfare state research, education and social policy, public spending, theories of institutional change and public opinion on the welfare state.

Martin B. Carstensen is professor with special responsibilities in public administration and politics in the Department of Social Science and Business, Roskilde University, in Denmark. His work focuses on the dynamics of institutional and ideational change in key policy areas of advanced economies like labour market policy, education policy, and financial regulation.

Gina Di Maio is a project and quality manager in higher education at the Zurich University of the Arts in Switzerland. In her dissertation, she investigated how to get employers to cooperate and collectively provide vocational training. She focused on inclusiveness-enhancing training programmes for disadvantaged candidates as well as continuing vocational training.

Niccolo Durazzi is a lecturer in the political economy of social policy in the

School of Social and Political Science at the University of Edinburgh in Scotland. His research takes a comparative political economy approach to examine advanced capitalist countries' transition in the knowledge economy, with a particular focus on education, skills, and labour market policy.

Christian Ebner is a professor of sociology at the Technische Universität Braunschweig, Germany, where he specializes in work and organizational research. He is also a research fellow at the Bundesinstitut für Berufsbildung. His research interests comprise vocational education and training, the transformation of the working world, and how occupations shape social inequalities.

Philipp Eigenmann is head of research and a lecturer in education at Thurgau University of Teacher Education (PHTG) in Kreuzlingen, Switzerland. His research interests are history of education, higher education, vocational education, and teacher education.

Patrick Emmenegger is a professor of comparative political economy and public policy at the University of St. Gallen in Switzerland. His research focuses on education, skills, and labour market policies, industrial relations, democratization, state building, and institutional theory.

Leonard Geyer is a researcher at the European Centre for Social Welfare Policy and Research in Vienna, Austria. His research interests comprise comparative political economy, (active) labour market and skills policies, and the role of social partners in determining policy outcomes, wages, and working conditions.

Philipp Gonon is recently retired (in 2021) but is still working at the Institute of Education at the University of Zurich in Switzerland. His research focuses on Swiss vocational education and training, history and comparative international VET and digitalization at a Secondary II level.

Lukas Graf is an assistant professor of educational governance at the Hertie School, The University of Governance in Berlin. He works at the intersection of political economy, sociology, educational science, and public policy. He combines comparative, institutional, and organizational approaches to analyse questions of educational governance, labour markets, social inequalities, institutional changes, and internationalization processes.

Sandra Hirtz is a research associate at the Bundesinstitut für Berufsbildung Forschungsdatenzentrum (BIBB Research Data Centre (BIBB-FDZ)) in Bonn, Germany. The focus of her research is on the German vocational and education training system. Her research interests cover wage inequality in the German labour market, especially with regard to occupational and sectoral stratification.

Christian Lyhne Ibsen is an associate professor at FAOS, Department of Sociology, University of Copenhagen in Denmark. His research focuses on collective bargaining, vocational education and training, and the future of work and employment relations.

Markus Maurer is a professor of vocational education at the Zurich University of Teacher Education in Switzerland. His research focuses on implementation of education and training policy reforms, on adults in vocational education, as well as on comparative analysis of education and training systems.

Dennie Oude Nijhuis is a lecturer at the Institute for History at Leiden University, in the Netherlands. He specializes in the comparative political economy of labour markets and welfare states and the political economy of European integration. He is also the editor of *Business Interests and the Development of the Modern Welfare State*.

Daniela Rohrbach-Schmidt is a research associate at the Bundesinstitut für Berufsbildung Forschungsdatenzentrum (BIBB Research Data Centre (BIBB-FDZ)) in Bonn, Germany. Her fields of research are vocational education and training, occupations, and social inequality.

Lina Seitzl is a member of the German parliament. Previously, she worked as a postdoctoral researcher at the School of Economics and Political Science of the University of St. Gallen, Switzerland and was part of GOVPET, a centre of excellence for research on the governance of vocational and professional education and training. Her research examines the effects of digitization and the knowledge economy on dual training systems.

Kathleen Thelen is Ford professor of political science at the Massachusetts Institute of Technology in the United States and a permanent external member of the Max Planck Institute for the Study of Societies in Germany. Her work centres on the origins, evolution, and contemporary political economies of the rich democracies. Her current work focuses on the American political economy and on the political economy of platform capitalism.

Christine Trampusch is a professor of comparative political economy at the Cologne Center for Comparative Politics (CCCP), University of Cologne in Germany. Her research includes models of capitalism, labour–business–government relationships and the change of institutions and policies.

Daniel Franz Unterweger is a researcher and consultant at 3s: Research & Consulting for Lifelong Learning, based in Vienna. He is involved in several projects for Cedefop and the European Commission, and has previously consulted the OECD on the governance of skills policies. He is a former member of GOVPET at the University of St. Gallen (Switzerland).

Anna Wilson is a postdoctoral researcher with the International Postdoctoral Fellowship (GFF-IPF) at the School of Economics and Political Science, University of St. Gallen in Switzerland. Her research interests lie mainly in firms' strategies to address skill mismatches in the knowledge economy, firms' role in including disadvantaged young people in VET, and the institutional, internal, and external conditions enabling and constraining them.

1

Collective Skill Formation in a Knowledge Economy

Challenges and Dilemmas

Giuliano Bonoli and Patrick Emmenegger

1.1 Introduction

Skill formation has been subject to rapidly increasing attention in the last decades, both in academic debates as well as politics. Generally, skill formation systems are expected to provide individuals with access to high-quality training and the economy with a well-trained workforce. Yet skill formation systems display important differences with regard to the division of tasks between firms, intermediary associations, and the state in providing and financing skill formation.[1]

Based on Busemeyer and Trampusch (2012: 11–15), we can distinguish between liberal, segmentalist, statist, and collective skill formation systems (see Table 1.1). In liberal regimes, the general education system and market-based transactions are the primary providers of education and training. Public commitment to skill formation is limited and firms are rarely involved apart from basic on-the-job training. In contrast, segmentalist regimes rely on internal labour markets and lifelong employment to retain employees. In this way, large firms provide newly recruited employees with a considerable amount of high-quality training, for instance in firm-specific vocational schools. However, public commitment to skill formation is low and small firms are rarely involved. Most training therefore focuses on firm-specific skills. Statist regimes feature a strong public commitment to skill formation and full-time vocational schooling. However, since training is part of the

[1] We thank Christian Lyhne Ibsen and Christine Trampusch for helpful comments on an earlier draft of this chapter.

Giuliano Bonoli and Patrick Emmenegger, *Collective Skill Formation in a Knowledge Economy*. In: *Collective Skill Formation in the Knowledge Economy*. Edited by Giuliano Bonoli and Patrick Emmenegger, Oxford University Press.

Table 1.1 Skill formation systems in advanced economies

		Involvement of firms in VET	
		Low	High
Public commitment to VET	High	Statist (e.g. Sweden)	Collective (e.g. Germany)
	Low	Liberal (e.g. United Kingdom)	Segmentalist (e.g. Japan)

Source: Busemeyer and Trampusch (2012: 12).

general education system, firm involvement remains limited. These systems therefore often struggle to facilitate a smooth transition from training into employment.

This book focuses on collective skill formation systems, which are characterized by a strong public commitment to and high involvement of firms in the training effort. Four specific features distinguish collective systems from the other regimes. First, they are based on dual training combining school-based and work-based learning—increasingly also at the post-secondary level (Graf 2018). Second, employers and their associations are involved in the financing and administration of training, meaning that collective skill formation regimes presuppose inter-firm cooperation and employers' willingness to engage in collective action. Third, intermediary organizations, including trade unions, play an important role in the administration and development of these systems. Finally, collective systems lead to certified and standardized occupational skills that are portable between firms. The most prominent examples are the vocational education and training (VET) systems of Austria, Denmark, Germany, the Netherlands, and Switzerland. Yet elements of collective systems are increasingly adopted in other countries as well (Busemeyer and Trampusch 2012: 14–15).

Collective skill formation systems have been long hailed for their capacity to straddle the twin demands of supplying relevant skills to employers and offering a point of access for large groups of the population (including working-class youth) to stable and relatively well-paid jobs (Thelen 2014). Unsurprisingly, then, the European Union (EU) is strongly pushing its member states to develop and strengthen dual training in the framework of collective skill formation systems. Based on the Copenhagen Process (started in 2002) and further enhanced with the 2010 Bruges Communiqué (European Union 2010) and the 2015 Riga Conclusions (European Union 2015), the EU is actively promoting work-based learning, in particular with regard to dual apprenticeships and by involving the social partners in the governance of these systems.

Yet the rise of the knowledge economy has put a question mark over whether such solidaristic outcomes are still possible to sustain (Anderson and Hassel 2013; Thelen 2014; Bonoli and Emmenegger 2021; Carstensen and Ibsen 2021). Increasingly knowledge-intensive forms of production lead to demands for new, higher, and ever-changing skills, which creates a number of challenges for skill formation systems, both with regard to their ability to supply relevant skills to employers and offering a point of access for large groups of the population. For instance, labour market polarization created by automation processes is reducing the pool of mid-skilled jobs that in the past have greatly contributed to middle-class well-being and that were made accessible through vocational training (Autor 2010).

These challenges are compounded by a number of concomitant developments, in particular growing social inequality and the emergence of multicultural societies. Social inequality has been rising in most advanced economies in recent decades (OECD 2008; Piketty 2013; Atkinson 2015). Inequalities in income and resources are associated with inequality in the ability to learn and school achievement (OECD 2019a), generating problems of access to demanding VET programmes for those at the bottom of the distribution. Such inequalities are further exacerbated by the emergence of multicultural societies that result from mass migration to advanced economies. For individuals with a migration background, access to dual VET can be problematic, as they may suffer from disadvantages both in the education system and in the labour market side of dual VET.

Clearly, changing levels of social inequality are in part also related to the shift towards a knowledge economy. Labour market polarization created by automation processes is a case in point (Kristal and Cohen 2017; Murphy and Oesch 2018). Yet macro-structural pressures such as technological change do not automatically translate into levels of social inequality. Instead, they are mediated by social and political institutions, most notably education and skill formation systems that have the potential to both accentuate and weaken the effects of these structural trends (Emmenegger et al. 2012).

The shift to a knowledge economy and the concomitant expansion of social inequalities are pulling collective skill formation systems in opposite directions. Vocational training must remain competitive *and* integrative in a context that changes and makes both functions more challenging. Adopting a political economy perspective, the contributions to this book examine how collective skill formation systems cope with and are adapted to a knowledge economy in the context of growing social inequalities. This perspective implies that, in addition to changes in the socio-economic context, we highlight the power of actors and conflicts of interest, emphasize the role of institutions in structuring political and economic processes, and stress the challenges of cooperation and collective action (Streeck 2009; Thelen 2014; Busemeyer 2015).

In this introductory chapter, we first review structural economic, social, and macro-political trends that challenge collective skill formation systems. Our focus is on the growing relevance of knowledge-intensive production processes. However, we also emphasize other macro-trends that, as argued above, are crucial for these systems' ability to perform an integrative function: the rise in social inequality and the emergence of multicultural societies. Subsequently, we discuss what we argue to be the two main dilemmas collective skill formation systems face in a knowledge economy: (1) balancing efficiency and inclusiveness in an increasingly knowledge-intensive economy and (2) collective action in the age of de-collectivization. The final section reviews the contributions to this volume.

1.2 Challenges

Collective skill formation systems have managed to produce appreciable outcomes both in terms of efficiency and inclusiveness (Busemeyer 2015). However, a number of ongoing socio-structural and macro-political trends have the potential to disrupt the successful operation of these systems. In this book, we focus on the key trends that are part of the overall transition to a knowledge economy. On the one hand, increasingly knowledge-intensive forms of production are likely to lead to demands for new, higher, and ever-changing skills. This puts pressure on collective skill formation system's ability to provide industry with the necessary skills and contributes to the decline of collectivism as a form of coordination in advanced economies. On the other hand, trends that are happening concomitantly amplify these challenges. These include the rise in social inequality and the emergence of multicultural societies, which are reinforcing inequalities in terms of skill acquisition and making it harder for collective skill formation system to fulfil their integrative function.

Our focus on these challenges is not meant to deny the relevance of other structural trends. However, macro-trends often interact and accentuate each other. For instance, digitalization, deindustrialization, and globalization all create pressure on low-skilled work in advanced economies and demand a stronger focus on more knowledge-intensive forms of production. We argue that it is not productive to try to isolate these structural trends to create some artificial conceptual separation. Instead, we subsume these structural economic, political, and social trends under the label 'knowledge economy', which captures well how economic activity is increasingly skill and knowledge intensive.

The knowledge economy pushes firms to increasingly require new, higher, and ever-changing skills. Yet it does so in a context of increasingly diverse and unequal societies. In the following, we discuss how these developments challenge collective skill formation systems.

1.2.1 The growing relevance of knowledge-intensive production processes

Technological change that goes under the broad rubric of digitalization is transforming the world of work (Thelen 2018; Crouch 2019; Grundke et al. 2018). Digitalization refers to the phenomenon of replacing analogue or physical processes through digital ones (Loebbecke and Picot 2015). It denotes how production processes are automatized (computerization) and how different parts of the producing equipment may be able to communicate among themselves (internet of things). Digitalization does not only imply the use of big data and digital technologies (machine learning, artificial intelligence) in the production of goods, it also refers to the rise of platform firms which provide digital services (online marketplaces, social media, app stores), which lead to new labour market structures (gig economy).

These developments create a number of challenges for skill formation systems (Gonon 2019; Achtenhagen and Achtenhagen 2019; Rolandsson et al. 2019). Most of these challenges have to do with the growing importance of knowledge-intensive production in advanced economies and with an accelerated pace of change due to technological innovation. These processes lead to changing and higher skill needs as well as labour market polarization since change is skill-biased and empowers multinational companies that are more capital-intensive and less labour-intensive (Acemoglu and Autor 2011). Moreover, these developments are accentuated by ongoing processes of globalization and deindustrialization. Less knowledge-intensive and more routine-task-intensive occupations—precisely the traditional focus of collective skill formation systems—are at the highest risk of suffering from international trade (Owen and Johnston 2017). In addition, the decline of the industrial sector and the expansion of the service economy challenge collective skill formation systems, because these systems were originally anchored in the craft and industrial sectors and depend on neo-corporatist institutions more prevalent in the industrial sector to function (Culpepper and Thelen 2008; Strebel et al. 2021).

In the context of knowledge-intensive production processes, we identify three main challenges. First, the growing relevance of knowledge-intensive production processes leads to *new, higher, and ever-changing skill demands.* While predictions are difficult to make, the literature estimates that between 9 per cent (Arntz et al. 2016) and 47 per cent (Frey and Osborne 2013) of all jobs are at risk of automation. However, in the same period, a similar number of new jobs will be created. Yet these new jobs require different skills, which implies that a large part of the labour force will have to be re-skilled in this period (see also OECD 2017; Cedefop 2018; McKinsey Global Institute 2018).

However, as technological change and globalization make investments into new equipment more attractive, production processes for most businesses may benefit from automation and different parts of the producing equipment may be able to communicate among themselves. Therefore, it is possible that in production processes, digital technologies and infrastructure are increasingly substituting labour (Kemmerling and Trampusch 2021). As investments into capital and technology become more attractive alternatives, firms may reduce investment in training (OECD 2017: 8). At the same, digitalization is also related to offshoring processes (Brown et al. 2011; Goos et al. 2014).

In any case, technological change is skill biased, thus substituting for workers performing routine tasks, while complementing workers performing non-routine tasks (Autor 2010; Kristal and Cohen 2017). As a result, recent studies suggest that the impact of technological change on skill demands leads to a trend towards labour market polarization, with technological change strengthening demand for non-routine cognitive jobs carried out in high-end jobs and having little impact on demand for non-routine personal services carried out in low-end jobs (Murphy and Oesch 2018). This development has been clearly observed in the United States but also in several European countries (Autor 2010; Autor and Salomons 2017), with demand sometimes being skewed towards the upper end of the skill distribution (Oesch and Menés 2010; Oesch 2013).

Given the increase in demand for high-skill labour, we can expect firms to require an overall upskilling of training, which all else equal, is more likely to exclude weaker students. As training curricula are revised so that they comply with the requirements of technological innovation, they may become less accessible for academically weaker students (Martin and Knudsen 2010). Moreover, collective skill formation systems have historically been good at providing a well-trained workforce for mid-skilled occupations first in industry and then in the services. They have thus contributed to providing access to good quality mid-level jobs to individuals for whom tertiary education is not accessible. In this respect, collective skill formation systems have been able to perform a socially integrative function also thanks to the existence of a strong demand for labour in the middle of the skill distribution (Thelen 2014). With labour market polarization and the decline of demand for mid-skilled professionals, this integrative function may be put at risk.

Second, digitalization, globalization, and deindustrialization increase the pace of economic change (e.g. due to accelerated production processes, radical technological innovation, or changing product markets) and thus create *uncertainty about the skills firms will require in the future*. Put differently, training decisions for firms might become riskier since they are increasingly unsure about their future skill demands. Similarly, because skill formation requires young individuals to 'accept the long deferral of gratifications that is the essence of investing', for them, skill formation 'presupposes a degree of certainty as to what one is likely to need and value in the future' (Streeck 1989: 92). If there is growing uncertainty about future value of (occupational) skills, talented youth might increasingly opt for general education, which is considered the 'safer' and more flexible option, thus further contributing to academic drift (Iversen and Soskice 2001). Research has not yet answered the question whether collective skill formation systems can adapt (fast enough) to the needs of a knowledge economy, and whether and how they differ in meeting this challenge from liberal or statist training systems (but see Anderson and Hassel 2013; Chuan and Ibsen 2021). If they cannot, firms may no longer turn to collective skill formation systems to meet their training needs.

In addition, in the light of previous adaptation processes, it is unclear whether technological change will complicate the reconciliation of social inclusiveness and economic efficiency (Bonoli and Emmenegger 2021). More ambitious and knowledge-intensive programmes may need stricter entry requirements, thereby de facto becoming inaccessible to academically less inclined students (Martin and Knudsen 2010; Carstensen and Ibsen 2021). At the same time, prospective apprentices increasingly face the risk of learning an occupation, which the labour market of the future will not demand. Consequently, having insufficient or obsolete skills has emerged as a new social risk (Bonoli 2005). Given these uncertainties, apprentices might increasingly opt for training opportunities that focus on transferable and more general skills (Estevez-Abe et al. 2001), which could contribute to a devaluation of vocational education.

Third, by removing constraints (e.g. geographical restrictions on business activities), digitalization, globalization, and to a lesser extent deindustrialization also increase the structural power of business and *weaken the ability of collective actors to integrate firms* (Thelen and Busemeyer 2012; Emmenegger and Seitzl 2019)—a 'dualization' process that can also be observed in other parts of the economy (Emmenegger 2014; Thelen 2014). As Brown et al. (2011) highlight, due to new possibilities of high-speed data transfer and further standardization of production processes ('Digital Taylorism'), it might matter increasingly less where jobs are performed. If firms are not dependent on a specific institutional environment (characterized, for example, by egalitarian wage setting or employment protection legislation), firms might refrain from collective training due to the uncertainty of pay-offs in the provision of collective training (Streeck 2009; Sorge and Streeck 2018). Importantly, de-collectivization processes can also be observed among trade unions, which further reduces firms' motivation to organize collec-tively. At the same time, due to increased capital mobility, digitalization also increases the share of multinational corporations, which are often harder to integrate into collective governance than more traditional corporations (Edwards 2004).

Moreover, digitalization advances new forms for corporations, thus mak-ing their organization more difficult and increasing the heterogeneity of their skill needs (Thelen 2018). Particularly relevant for training is the role of e-business and the rise of platform business models. As the cost for com-munication and computing has decreased, new digital forms to create and deliver value have emerged. These processes have encouraged new forms of transaction and transformed the way businesses interact with customers and suppliers, which may also affect employment relationships. For instance, the gig economy makes it easier and less costly to contract freelancers for small jobs, making it less attractive for firms to train in order to address skill gaps (Crouch 2019).

1.2.2 Rising social inequality and the emergence of multicultural societies

Over the last few decades, we have witnessed a large increase in social inequality across the developed world. This trend has been documented in a large number of studies, which confirm the view that income inequality has been increasing over the last three to four decades in a majority of advanced countries (OECD 2008; Emmenegger et al. 2012; Atkinson 2015). The trend in wealth inequality has followed an even sharper rise (Piketty 2013). There is some cross-national variation in the pace of this trend, with English-speaking countries and particularly the United States being at the forefront. However, countries with collective skill formation systems are not immune. Between the 1980s and the 2010s, Germany, Austria, and the Netherlands experienced a more or less constant increase in inequality in disposable incomes (but not Denmark and Switzerland).

Studies on inequality have tended to focus on income inequality, i.e. on inequality of outcomes. With regard to the integrative capacity of collective skill formation systems, however, equality of opportunity seems just as important. In any case, the two types of inequality are related, since success in education is highly dependent on the socio-economic conditions in which people grow up (Atkinson 2015). Educational sociologists have long known that household income and social class are key determinants of educational success. In their seminal study, Shavit and Blossfeld (1993) showed that social origin, measured for example by fathers' profession or educational level, remains a powerful predictor of educational trajectories in most countries. Even though this conclusion has been challenged by subsequent studies, showing that a trend towards equalization is more pervasive, social background remains a powerful determinant of educational success (Breen and Jonsson 2005). In a well-known survey of school performance of fifteen-year-old youths, the OECD (2019b: 58) found that the socio-economic status related performance gap remained stable in the vast majority of countries between 2009 and 2019. Large educational inequalities at the end of compulsory schooling constitute a challenge for skill formation systems that typically target the low to middle part of the skill distribution because it affects their level of preparedness. PISA surveys also show that, on average, the proportion of 'low achievers' has increased in several countries (OECD 2019a: 138).

Scholars of skill formation systems are not the only ones who are interested in these developments. The link between inequality of outcomes and the skill distribution is at the centre of the perspective taken in the social investment literature, which emphasizes the need for policies that enhance individuals' capabilities, not least by means of educational investments at all stages of the life cycle, in order to allow people to participate in the labour market and maximize their social welfare (Morel et al. 2012; Garritzmann et al. 2021). Preserving (and developing) the integrative capacity of collective skill formation systems in a knowledge economy is an objective that is perfectly in line with the strategy put forward in this literature.

Inequality of opportunities is driven by inequality of outcomes but also by another important trend: mass migration and the advent of multicultural societies. Large-scale immigration and the management of multicultural societies are major societal and political issues in Western democracies. Migration is not a new development, but migration flows have been on the rise over the last few years. In 2017, some five million individuals migrated to OECD countries (OECD 2018). Current demographic and geopolitical trends suggest that the trend towards increasingly multicultural societies is unlikely to revert. Migration is a multifaceted phenomenon and raises a number of issues in relation to skill formation. In general, immigrant children and youth tend to face more difficulties in terms of school performance. Research has repeatedly shown that having a migration background is a major factor of disadvantage in most school systems (Heath et al. 2008; OECD 2019b: 180–98).

The integration of immigrants into the labour market is a major public and policy preoccupation. Western European countries' response to the emergence of multicultural societies has been the adoption of 'integration' policies that are meant to improve social cohesion and reduce potential tensions between immigrants and natives (Geddes and Scholten 2016). Immigrants are obviously a very diverse group and the issue of integration concerns above all low-skilled immigrants, many of whom come as asylum seekers. However, the success of integration policies remains mitigated. In spite of the efforts made, in virtually all European countries immigrants, however defined, are overrepresented among the disadvantaged and are often excluded from the labour market (Kogan 2006; Fleischmann and Dronkers 2010). In addition, immigrants are more likely to be dependent on welfare state support (Barret and Maître 2013).

Collective skill formation systems, because of the involvement of employers, are a promising tool to promote the economic and the social integration of low skilled and unskilled immigrants (Dahlstedt and Bevelander 2010; OECD 2016; Joyce 2018). Many young immigrants who arrive in Western countries as asylum seekers lack the basic skills required to succeed in an academic education. In addition, training provided at the firm level can be a very effective way to teach non-cognitive skills that are essential to succeed in the labour market and difficult to acquire for immigrants coming from culturally distant places (Kautz et al. 2014).

Another challenge concerns skilled immigrants who struggle to get their skills recognized. Among the various immigrant groups, refugees are one of the main targets of training policies, also because in various occupations the recruitment of apprentices has become extremely difficult. Over the last few years, several European countries have accepted large numbers of young refugees, often fleeing war-torn countries. Yet refugees often lack education or possess limited educational credentials. What is more, these credentials are generally not known to employers in receiving countries. For refugees, skill formation systems, and particularly dual VET, seem a promising tool to promote integration. It is therefore not surprising that various collective skill formation systems have developed dedicated programmes (Aerne and Bonoli 2021). Yet, it remains unclear to what extent these programmes succeed in integrating immigrants.

Next to questions concerning integration, large-scale immigration has also the potential to influence collective skill formation systems in other ways. Most notably, immigration of individuals, in particular skilled ones, might be in competition with VET systems, as firms increasingly opt to recruit from this pool of workers rather than train themselves. As a result, immigrants might provide an alternative to trained domestic workers (Røed and Schøne 2012). In turn, occupation-specific regulations and access restrictions might be used to protect domestic workers from competition from immigrants and thereby accentuate labour market integration problems (Busemeyer and Trampusch 2019; Trampusch 2019).

These ongoing transformations will undoubtedly require the reform of skill formation systems. At the same time, though, the growing relevance of knowledge-intensive production processes is likely to complicate the inclusion of disadvantaged youth, which accentuates the tension between the logic of selectivity, which is inherent in the labour market, and the logic of inclusiveness, which governs (public) education systems (Bonoli and Emmenegger 2021). The presence of large numbers of individuals with weak educational records challenge skill formation systems that already struggle to cope with macro-structural pressures, such as technological change, globalization, and deindustrialization. In this knowledge economy, which puts a premium on high and transferable skills and in which well-paid low-skill jobs are all but gone, skill formation systems are increasingly tasked with the inclusion of disadvantaged youth. Little surprise, then, that collective skill formation systems are dealing with two dilemmas, which we discuss in the next section.

1.3 Dilemmas

The challenges that we outlined above generate two main dilemmas that collective skill formation systems face in the current context. These two dilemmas form the core interest of this book's contributions. The first dilemma concerns the balancing between efficiency and inclusiveness, while the second dilemma focuses on the struggle to act collectively despite increasingly heterogenous interests.

1.3.1 Balancing efficiency and inclusiveness

Collective skill formation systems are supposed to provide an economy with a well-trained and competitive workforce (related to concerns about efficiency) *and* are supposed to integrate young people into the production system, including academically weaker students (related to concerns about inclusiveness). Inevitably, there is a trade-off between these two functions (Thelen 2014; Bonoli and Emmenegger 2021; Carstensen and Ibsen 2021). An efficiency-oriented system is likely to be selective and demanding and thus to exclude academically weaker youth. In contrast, an inclusive training system is by definition less demanding and as a result less suited to the requirements of highly competitive firms. In theory, collective skill formation systems could be located anywhere on this efficiency–inclusiveness continuum. In reality, however, since they require the voluntary participation of firms, the extent to which they can directly promote inclusiveness is limited (Bonoli and Emmenegger 2021).

Given the above, we can expect employers to resist inclusiveness, if they perceive inclusiveness-enhancing interventions to have negative consequences for economic efficiency. Such negative consequences include the declining prestige of certain forms of training, which might make it more difficult to recruit promising youth for such activities. Following Carstensen and Ibsen (2021), we are not arguing that employers always know what is best for them and therefore always push for 'efficient' policies. Instead, we define efficiency as the *perceived* political-economic effect. In addition, we do not argue that employers mind inclusiveness per se. In fact, employers are happy to transfer this responsibility to the state. However, we expect employers to object to two kinds of pro-inclusiveness measures: (1) those that force them to play a social policy role and (2) those that shift the overall objective of skill formation systems too much towards inclusion.

How do collective skill formation systems balance the twin objectives of efficiency and inclusion? In general, governments will prioritize measures that can be defined as 'external', i.e. interventions targeting academically weaker students aiming to improve their ability outside of the collective skill formation system, so that they will be better able to enter it. External measures are to a large extent 'invisible' to employers and do not require them to adapt the way they train. Such external measures are by far the most common approaches collective skill formation systems use to improve inclusiveness. Examples of external measures are an additional year of schooling or the provision of supervision and coaching in the search for an apprenticeship position (Bonoli and Wilson 2019). Yet external measures have only limited inclusion potential. As a result, governments regularly try to push the inclusiveness logic further by developing tools that intervene more directly into the functioning of the VET systems, such as subsidies for firms who train disadvantaged youth or less ambitious short-track vocational degrees (Di Maio et al. 2019; Durazzi and Geyer 2022). We call these measures 'internal' because they are part of the VET system and require active involvement by employers.

Internal measures, however, are tricky and sometimes resisted by employers. If governments try to impose internal measures against the will of employers, they are unlikely to succeed. Since collective skill formation systems rely on the voluntary participation of firms, employers can easily resist measures they feel inappropriate, first in the political arena, and then if unsuccessful, simply by not using them. In a way, the interaction between governments and employers regarding the definition of the appropriate balance between efficiency and inclusiveness can be conceptualized as a two-level game. First, on the system level, governments and employers share a common objective of keeping a functioning collective skill formation system. They are likely to agree that this is an asset for a country's economy. Second, on the firm level, individual firms can decide autonomously whether or not to contribute to government-induced efforts to increase inclusiveness. Here firms clearly have the upper hand. If governments are too intrusive with their demands, firms will simply pull out of the system. Since governments want to avoid this outcome, they will refrain from being too intrusive (see Bonoli and Emmenegger 2021).

In addition, the balance between efficiency and inclusiveness preferences is also decisively shaped by the particular makeup of governance institutions. Carstensen and Ibsen (2021) argue that the degree of firm, union, and state involvement in VET governance affects which actors are involved in specific aspects of the skill formation system. For instance, Busemeyer and Trampusch (2012) highlight five main areas of conflict: (a) who provides training (is the dominant venue of training the workplace or in public schools?), (b) who finances training (how much of the funding comes from companies and the state, respectively?), (c) who controls access to training (the state, firms, or the social partners?), (d) who is involved in the administration of the system (do social partners play an active role in the day-to-day administering of training programmes?), and (e) who controls the content and quality of training (is training monitored by firms, social partners, or the state?). For each area of conflict, actor composition might be different. Importantly, however, these governance questions do not neutralize the tension between efficiency and inclusiveness in collective skill formation systems. Yet they are likely to shape how the politics of skill formation systems ultimately play out (Durazzi and Geyer 2020; Carstensen et al. 2022).

Moreover, as we argue below, these challenges take place in a context in which collective solutions are increasingly difficult to adopt. This is arguably why in some countries we see the development of inclusive training solutions outside the realm of collective training. For example, since the late 1990s, Austria has been developing public training workshops, which constitute an alternative, state-based access route to skill formation (Durazzi and Geyer 2020; Carstensen et al. 2022). Collective skill formation systems always have the opportunity to 'de-collectivize' and turn to state-provided training. However, this option means losing many of the benefits of collective skill formation systems (Bonoli and Emmenegger 2021). As a result, most countries try to adapt their collective systems, so that they can cope with the changing socio-economic context (Busemeyer et al. 2021; Graf et al. 2021). However, the trade-off between efficiency and inclusiveness is in our view an intrinsic feature of any such system. This means that balancing these two objectives is likely to remain a key dilemma for many years to come.

1.3.2 Collective action in the age of de-collectivization

Collective skill formation systems face the challenges associated with the rise of a knowledge economy in a period of constant de-collectivization. These systems rely on cooperation between several actors, most notably firms, in order to produce a collective good: a skilled workforce. While skills are tied to an individual, their acquisition is costly and marred by uncertainty because individuals cannot know whether these skills will be in high demand in the future. Unless this uncertainty can be reduced, individuals are likely to be reluctant to bear the costs of financing their own skill acquisition (Crouch 2005).

Similarly, employers benefit from a skilled workforce, which is why we could expect employers to co-finance skill acquisition. Yet employers might be equally reluctant to do so. The economic literature on labour markets has repeatedly shown that skill formation systems are vulnerable to cooperation dilemmas (Marsden 1999; Johansen 2002; Culpepper 2003), with the employers' decision to train or recruit skilled workers corresponding to a prisoners' dilemma with the collective under-provision of training as a Nash equilibrium (Emmenegger and Unterweger 2021). Firms participate in training activities only if they expect to benefit from their involvement. Whether they do is dependent on the behaviour of other firms. If other firms do not train, if the quality of training is low, or if competition for prospective trainees increases its cost, firms are unlikely to train themselves.

The literature has emphasized how employers' organizations, serving as intermediaries between firms, can help 'to restrain free-riding on training costs' (Marsden 1999: 223). In addition, these systems are also dependent on the collective organization of labour, which serves an important counterweight to business and provides many of the (beneficial) constraints that facilitate employer collective action (Streeck 1992). In any case, cooperation in collective skill formation systems is not self-sustaining but depends on public policies and capable intermediary organizations (Ryan 2000; Culpepper 2003; Emmenegger et al. 2019; Graf et al. 2021).

Yet the rise of a knowledge economy has the potential to fatally undermine the collective action necessary to keep these skill formation systems going because the knowledge economy may destabilize the fragile institutional arrangements that facilitate cooperation. Moreover, these structural changes are likely to trigger adjustment processes, which have to be collectively negotiated and agreed upon. In this context, complicated and time-consuming negotiation processes, delays (or outright failures) to adapt to new challenges, or the exit of dissatisfied firms may lead to a creeping collapse of collective skill formation systems (Anderson and Hassel 2013).

The most visible indicators of collective action on both sides of the class divide are employer associations and trade unions, which also play important roles in VET governance (Emmenegger and Seitzl 2020). These collective organizations have been under constant pressure in recent decades and suffer from processes of de-collectivization (Baccaro and Howell 2017). This is most visible in the case of trade unions, which have seen their membership numbers dwindle in recent decades (Donado and Wälde 2018) due to the joint pressures of deindustrialization and digital technologies increasingly substituting workers (Kemmerling and Trampusch 2021). Yet unions are key actors in providing the constraints to push employers to consider skill investments (Streeck 1992; Acemoglu and Pischke 1999). As unions lose power, these constraints disappear or must be replaced by other actors, most notably the state (Martin and Thelen 2007; Thelen 2014), although there is much debate whether the state is able to fill this void (Howell 2016, 2019; Busemeyer et al. 2021; Carstensen et al. 2022).

In addition, recent structural economic, social, and macro-political trends have also made employer collective action harder. For various reasons related to globalization, deindustrialization, and technological change, the diversity of both firms and their skill needs have increased. Today's collective skill formation systems must also try to integrate multinational corporations with no previous experience in local skill formation systems (Unterweger 2020), have to deal with new business models that defy conventional logics of employer–employee relationships (Thelen 2018), and have to serve economic sectors that have little tradition in collective skill formation, never mind the necessary organizational infrastructure (Graf et al. 2021; Strebel et al. 2021). Internationally exposed firms demand additional and ever-changing training to have the necessary skilled workforce to compete, but not all firms are able or willing to keep up with these developments (Emmenegger and Seitzl 2019). In addition, post-secondary training has gained in importance, but here collective action and coordination problems seem even more vexing (Johansen 2002; Bowman 2005; Trampusch and Eichenberger 2012). It thus seems evident that collective action is getting more challenging.

Less noticed, but equally important are the organizational struggles of employer associations, which have tended to lose sway over their members and have seen their membership numbers decline (Woll 2006). Facing an increasingly internationalized economic environment, firm interests are becoming increasingly heterogeneous. In addition, large firms have begun to pursue lobbying strategies independent of employer associations (Streeck et al. 2006). Although it is debated whether the representativeness of employer and business associations is declining, there can be no doubt that they are under stress and must adapt their organizational structure as well as activities to the changing needs of firms (Brandl and Lehr 2019; Strebel et al. 2021). However, in the case of employers' associations, there are also important organizational interests that may make employers' associations rally in defence of collective skill formation systems. These intermediary associations are often concerned with their organizations' prestige and autonomy, which is often predicated on the collective nature of training (Emmenegger and Seitzl 2019; Trampusch 2010). Moreover, as membership numbers dwindle, these organizational interests might gain in importance (Davidsson and Emmenegger 2013).

In the context of collective skill formation systems, such developments linked to de-collectivization and changing skill requirements are often related to processes of segmentalism, which refer to how the content and governance of training increasingly focuses on the needs of large firms, resulting in a less encompassing and thus more segmented labour market with limited occupational mobility for employees (Busemeyer 2012; Thelen 2014; Emmenegger and Seitzl 2019). This literature argues that firms increasingly exit from collective skill formation because training becomes too costly for them. In order to motivate the other (larger) firms to remain in the system, the state agrees to their demands for a more fragmented (i.e. segmented) skill formation system. However, by doing so, the collective nature of these skill formation systems is increasingly undermined. Hence, segmentalism describes how the collective nature of collective skill formation systems is being increasingly compromised.

Obviously, these developments have implications for power dynamics in the politics of training. For instance, these developments strengthen the position of large firms at the expense of intermediary associations. However, there are also less obvious effects related to the 'power of inaction' (Woll 2016). For instance, de-collectivization trends might strengthen the power of actors who do not want any policy interventions. This is most likely the case for business and in particular large firms, which may benefit from structural changes, as they can increasingly turn to firm-specific training solutions. Such developments are related to forms of gradual institutional change such as drift (Hacker 2004) but also the problem that the state is dependent on the cooperation with employers in the context of training reform (Busemeyer and Thelen 2020), which is, however, increasingly difficult, as the intermediaries lose influence over their members (Bonoli and Emmenegger 2021).

There is plenty of evidence of struggles to act collectively. For instance, in several countries, we observe declining numbers of firms participating in training activities and of youth starting apprenticeships (Strebel et al. 2021). In addition, we observe an increasing number of youths struggling to enter the training system (Durazzi and Geyer 2020, 2021). In Germany, for example, every year between 250,000 and 300,000 youths who have failed to obtain an apprenticeship position enter the so-called transition system, a vast range of programmes that help them re-integrate the standard training system (BMBF 2019: 25). In Denmark, before the 2014 reform, the number of VET students without an apprenticeship position kept increasing, reaching 13,000 (i.e. one third) in 2013 (Carstensen and Ibsen 2021). In Switzerland, every year between 10 and 12 per cent of those finishing compulsory education fail to enter the general education or VET system (Bonoli and Emmenegger 2021).

In sum, recent structural economic, social, and macro-political trends have made employer collective action considerably harder, which is, however, a necessary condition for collective skill formation systems to thrive. Moreover, these developments have led to segmentalism, which describes how collective action is becoming less inclusive, moving away from the cooperation of a large number of heterogeneous firms to the cooperation of a small number of more homogeneous ones. In this book, we are particularly interested in understanding the conditions that weaken or possibly even prevent such tendencies.

1.4 This volume

The book begins with a focus on structural changes. First, Christian Ebner, Sandra Hirtz, and Daniela Rohrbach-Schmidt adopt a market segmentation approach to examine the extent to which apprenticeships remain a promising way to integrate workers into the employment system (with quality being measured primarily by wages and working conditions). Using a representative survey of the German collective skill formation system, they show that in some lower-skilled occupations, the premium associated with obtaining a vocational degree is rather low or inexistent. Overall, there is a high degree of heterogeneity within the system. This result represents a break with the history of occupations in Germany and their connection with the VET system that played the role of a gatekeeper and guaranteed good working conditions. While still true for many occupations, there are integration problems for specific occupations and occupational segments.

Turning to adaptation processes, Regula Bürgi, Philipp Eigenmann, and Philipp Gonon explore how the challenges of a knowledge economy, in particular rapidly changing skill profiles, alter collective governance in the Swiss skill formation system. Focusing on an important reform adopted in the early 2000s, they show how VET institutions are being adapted to the new context, for example by making provision for regular updates of VET curricula through dedicated commissions. Yet some of these provisions have unintended effects, e.g. undermining employer collective action and stifling innovation in other areas. The chapter also shows that institutional adaptation is made difficult by the role of traditional and macro-political institutions such as federalism that limit the ability of the VET system to adapt to the fast-changing needs of firms.

Martin B. Carstensen and Christian Lyhne Ibsen argue that obtaining both equality and efficiency in either collectivist or state-led skill formation systems is an increasingly untenable policy position in a knowledge economy. Based on a comparative analysis of Danish and Swedish VET reforms since the 1990s, the chapter finds that both systems ended up more focused on employers' interests in the 2010s, despite their different starting points. Thus, what used to be a balance between efficiency and equality seems increasingly lopsided in favour of efficiency. In Sweden, the reforms of the 2010s focused on limiting mobility between VET and higher education, while reforms in Denmark instead focused on keeping out the very weakest students to attract stronger ones. In both systems, the chapter thus observes institutional reforms aimed at bolstering the mid-level skill space that traditionally enabled VET to produce egalitarian outcomes while satisfying the skill demands of employers. However, stubbornly low admission numbers in both systems indicate that this strategy is less than successful even in systems with a historically strong commitment to egalitarianism.

Adaptation processes were different in the Netherlands, though. Dennie Oude Nijhuis explores the transformations of the Dutch skill formation system in the face of macrostructural pressures variably associated with deindustrialization, increased international economic competition, and the growing importance of knowledge-intensive forms of production. The chapter shows that in contrast to Denmark and Sweden, Dutch employers supported the inclusive pathway towards VET reform followed since the 1980s. What explains this broad cross-class cooperation and the spirit of social partnership that characterized the reform process? The chapter shows that the informal and therefore flexible nature of the Dutch apprenticeship system as well as its low status made sure that employers did not view the introduction and expansion of full-time vocational schools as a threat to the apprenticeship system. Moreover, Dutch employers used their leverage to ensure that the social inclusion function did not impose major costs and constraints on firms.

In the emerging knowledge economy, unskilled individuals are subjected to an increased penalty and are exposed to a high risk of long-term reliance on the welfare state. The next four chapters focus on the social policy role that vocational training is sometimes asked to play. They show that governments face strong incentives to use skill formation systems as social policies aimed at integrating disadvantaged individuals, such as refugees, school dropouts, and unskilled unemployed people. However, firms' involvement in these systems and their requirements are likely to limit the extent to which VET can be used as a substitute for social policy.

Leonard Geyer and Niccolo Durazzi develop a theoretical framework for the analysis of actors' positions in relation to the inclusiveness dimension of collective skill formation systems. They consider the preferences of the main actors, i.e. employers, trade unions, and governments, in relation to three key dimensions of collective skill formation systems: efficiency, inclusiveness, and governance. The framework is then applied to the development of inclusiveness-oriented initiatives adopted in Germany and in Austria since the 1990s. They find that left-leaning governments and unions are most likely to show first-order preferences towards inclusive measures. However, inclusive measures are politically most feasible when they do not impinge on the efficiency and control dimension. Moreover, governments can soften employers' stance towards socially inclusive measures by granting them more control over the administration of the measures.

Under what conditions are employers more open to give a chance to disadvantaged applicants for apprenticeship positions? Anna Wilson uses original data collected in a survey experiment with Swiss employers to show that firms in the public sector as well as firms that are more recognized across Switzerland are more open to hire candidates with a mediocre school record, whereas employers in sectors with high skill demands are most reluctant. The chapter also shows that to some extent, hiring decisions are shaped by the personal values of the recruiting staff. The conclusion is that when it comes to assessing the function of a collective skill formation system as a promoter of social inclusiveness, the role of the state as an employer-trainer should not be underestimated. By giving a chance to less talented youth, state organizations can make a significant contribution to a system's inclusiveness.

Annatina Aerne examines the role of occupational prestige in the implementation of integration pre-apprenticeships in Switzerland. These pre-apprenticeships are meant to provide refugees with access to vocational education by preparing refugees to join a regular vocational education track after an additional training year. Professional training associations are key gatekeepers though as they shape the contours of the pre-apprenticeships or may even refuse to implement them. The chapter shows that in the initial stages of the programme, there was some resistance by employers, professional training associations, and by government departments overseeing the VET system. These actors all feared that the new programme, by including young refugees, would somehow reduce the value and attractiveness of given occupational tracks. However, the chapter shows that through careful negotiation, the authorities responsible for refugees were able to reassure these actors, although they had to make concessions that went in the direction of protecting occupational prestige and the value of diplomas. The chapter highlights a trade-off between the inclusiveness of VET systems and perceived occupational prestige.

Recognition of prior learning is a potentially promising tool to enhance the integration of people without certified skills who have been working in a profession for a given time. A new Swiss law on VET has introduced new provisions for recognition of prior learning. However, as Markus Maurer demonstrates this tool remains underdeveloped and is rarely used. The chapter shows that the limited expansion of recognition of prior learning is due to a strong commitment by several actors to preserve the perceived high credibility of VET qualifications associated with the standard certificate. The chapter thus illustrates the trade-off between occupational status protection and inclusiveness of collective skill formation systems.

The shift to a knowledge economy results among other things in a redefinition of actors' interests and structural power. The next four chapters show how the key actors of collective skill formation, i.e. the state, trade unions, and firms with different skill needs, are constantly renegotiating the settlement on which the system rests.

Marius R. Busemeyer and Kathleen Thelen explore employer responses to the dilemma the new knowledge economy poses. Firms are confronted simultaneously with two problems: the need to augment traditional occupational skills with a more general education and counteracting the drift on the part of youth away from vocational training towards more academic tracks. Germany's firm-based VET system is heavily oriented towards the acquisition of practical vocational skills, leaving advanced firms in particular with deficits in the more general theoretical skills that figure increasingly prominently in the new knowledge economy. Sweden's school-based system, conversely, has traditionally been stronger in the provision of general education at the upper-secondary level, leaving manufacturing firms, especially, short of the more practical skills on which they rely. Comparing these two contrasting cases, the chapter identifies a shared trend towards the growing involvement of employers in public educational institutions—in Germany at the level of higher education as a way of augmenting the country's heavily practical VET with more theoretical content, and in Sweden at the upper-secondary level to inject a practical component into school-based training in order to strengthen the connection to local firms. In both cases, changes are occurring less through outright reform of traditional educational institutions and more through the addition of new arrangements in and around existing institutions.

The knowledge economy has increased the importance of post-secondary vocational training. Gina Di Maio and Christine Trampusch explore the conditions that lead employers to co-finance and collectively provide transferable skills in post-secondary vocational training. Analysing four economic sectors with varying levels of employer cooperation in the provision and financing of transferable skills, this chapter finds that employers cooperate when they rely on internal labour markets for recruitment, when there are spill-over effects between employers' cooperation in initial and continuous vocational training, when large firms are committed to collective training, when there is a tradition of collective labour agreements, when employers' associations' logic of organization building includes training policies as an important means to attract members, and when employers do not prefer universities as an alternative and substitutive track to enhance the general skills of their employees.

Nadine Bernhard and Lukas Graf focus on the issue of permeability, i.e. the possibility that students can move across different parts of the education system. Of particular importance is the ability to continue after VET to academic education. The chapter starts from the observation that enhanced permeability is one way to respond to the increased skill needs associated with a knowledge economy. It then moves on to provide a conceptual framework for the analysis of permeability. The framework is subsequently applied to a reform that was meant to improve the permeability of the skill formation system in the German state of Saxony. The chapter shows that hybrid certificates, combining VET with academic education, are a promising avenue to improve permeability and strengthen collective skill formations systems. However, they also demonstrate that increasing permeability is by no means a trivial task.

Lina Seitzl and Daniel Franz Unterweger show how initially rather limited statist elements, layered onto the collective skill formation system, can lead to self-reinforcing dynamics that have the potential to gradually decrease and crowd out employer participation in collective training. Analysing the VET policy initiatives entailed in Austria's 1998 National Action Plan for Employment, this chapter shows how the initially limited public training workshops, which were part of a short-term 'rescue package' to combat the apprenticeship crisis, reduced training participation of firms at the lower end of the skill formation system, thereby facilitating a long-term expansion of training workshops. Moreover, such crowding out of the collective provision of training is not restricted to strategies aimed at increasing inclusiveness. The chapter also shows how in the case of occupations in the information and communications technology (ICT) sector, the school-based sector has crowded out employer participation in dual VET at the higher end of upper-secondary-level training. Thereby, it limited the adaptability and viability of collective training in a knowledge economy. In both cases, state interventions to deal with specific and focused challenges unintentionally contributed to a further decline of collective training, as employers learnt to appreciate the benefits that these statist VET schemes offer.

In a concluding chapter, Patrick Emmenegger and Giuliano Bonoli discuss the five main themes that help understand how collective skill formation systems adapt to a knowledge economy. First, they argue that one constant preoccupation of employers is to keep dual training attractive for talented youths and avoid academic drift. This is clearly visible in their support for measures aiming to protect the value of VET degrees, to improve permeability of the overall education system, and to develop new hybrid forms of training that combine academic and vocational training. Second, they show that in some countries, there are attempts to upskill collective skill formation systems. Such measures include investments in post-secondary VET or new forms of cooperation between firm-based training and higher-education institutions. However, in these attempts to upskill, forms of collective governance become more elusive. Instead, individual firms or the state play more prominent roles. Third, they observe that employers' attachment to collective skill formation remains strong, but they increasingly experience problems to act collectively, which fuels segmentalist tendencies. Fourth, they document that over the last decades, states have developed a multitude of measures to make collective skill formation systems more inclusive. These measures differ widely with regard to their degree of intrusiveness and the role dedicated to employers. Fifth, they argue that states put pressure on collective skill formation systems to make them more inclusive, which often—but not always—creates considerable frictions, especially if inclusion measures risk undermining the perceived quality of training. In contrast, employers are more open to inclusion measures that target the middle of the skill distribution and aim to increase social mobility.

References

Acemoglu, D., and D. Autor. 2011. 'Skills, Tasks and Technologies: Implications for Employment and Earnings'. In *Handbook of Labor Economics*, Vol. 4b, edited by O. Ashenfelter, and D. E. Card, pp. 1043–171. Amsterdam: Elsevier.

Acemoglu, D., and J.-S. Pischke. 1999. 'Beyond Becker: Training in Imperfect Labour Markets'. *Economic Journal 109* (453): 112–42.

Achtenhagen, C., and L. Achtenhagen. 2019. 'The Impact of Digital Technologies on Vocational Education and Training Needs: An Exploratory Study in the German Food Industry'. *Education and Training 61* (2): 222–33.

Aerne, A., and G. Bonoli. 2021. 'Integration through Vocational Training: Promoting Refugees' Access to Apprenticeships in a Collective Skill Formation System'. *Journal of Vocational Education and Training*: 1–20. Published online 15 March 2021.

Anderson, K., and A. Hassel. 2013. 'Pathways of Change in CMEs: Training Regimes in Germany and the Netherlands'. In *The Political Economy of the Service Transition*, edited by A. Wren, pp. 171–94. Oxford: Oxford University Press.

Arntz, M., T. Gregory, and U. Zierahn. 2016. *The Risk of Automation for Jobs in OECD Countries: A Comparative Analysis.* OECD Social, Employment and Migration Working Papers No. 189. Paris: OECD.

Atkinson, T. 2015. *Inequality: What Can Be Done?* Cambridge, MA: Harvard University Press.

Autor, D. H. 2010. *The Polarization of Job Opportunities in the U.S. Labor Market. Implications for Employment and Earnings.* Washington, DC: Center for American Progress.

Autor, D. H., and A. Salomons. 2017. *Does Productivity Growth Threaten Employment?* Paper prepared for the ECB Forum on Central Banking, June 2017.

Baccaro, L., and C. Howell. 2017. *Trajectories of Neoliberal Transformation: European Industrial Relations since the 1970s.* Cambridge: Cambridge University Press.

Barrett, A., and B. Maître. 2013. 'Immigrant Welfare Receipt across Europe'. *International Journal of Manpower 34* (1): 8–23.

BMBF. 2019. *Berufsbildungsbericht 2016.* Berlin: Bundesministerium für Bildung und Forschung.

Bonoli, G. 2005. 'The Politics of the New Social Policies: Providing Coverage against New Social Risks in Mature Welfare States'. *Policy and Politics 33* (3): 431–49.

Bonoli, G., and P. Emmenegger. 2021. 'The Limits of Decentralised Cooperation: The Promotion of Inclusiveness in Collective Skill Formation Systems?' *Journal of European Public Policy 28* (2): 229–47.

Bonoli, G., and A. Wilson. 2019. 'Bringing Firms on Board: Inclusiveness of the Dual Apprenticeship Systems in Germany, Switzerland and Denmark'. *International Journal of Social Welfare 28* (4): 369–79.

Bowman, J. R. 2005. 'Employers and the Politics of Skill Formation in a Coordinated Market Economy: Collective Action and Class Conflict in Norway'. *Politics and Society 33* (4): 567–94.

Brandl, B., and A. Lehr. 2019. 'The Strange Non-death of Employer and Business Associations: An Analysis of their Representativeness and Activities in Western European Countries'. *Economic and Industrial Democracy 40* (4): 932–53.

Breen, R., and J. O. Jonsson. 2005. 'Inequality of Opportunity in Comparative Perspective: Recent Research on Educational Attainment and Social Mobility'. *Annual Review of Sociology 31*: 223–43.

Brown, P., H. Lauder, and D. Ashton. 2011. *The Global Auction: The Broken Promises of Education, Jobs, and Incomes.* New York: Oxford University Press.

Busemeyer, M. R. 2012. 'Business as a Pivotal Actor in the Politics of Training Reform: Insights from the Case of Germany'. *British Journal of Industrial Relations 50* (4): 690–713.

Busemeyer, M. R. 2015. *Skills and Inequality: Partisan Politics and the Political Economy of Education and Training Reforms in Western Welfare States.* Cambridge: Cambridge University Press.

Busemeyer, M. R., M. B. Carstensen, and P. Emmenegger. 2021. 'Orchestrators of Coordination: Towards a New Role of the State in Coordinated Capitalism?'

European Journal of Industrial Relations, forthcoming. https://doi.org/10.1177/09596801211062556

Busemeyer, M. R., and K. Thelen. 2020. 'Institutional Sources of Business Power'. *World Politics 72* (3): 448–80.

Busemeyer, M. R., and C. Trampusch. 2012. *The Political Economy of Collective Skill Formation.* Oxford: Oxford University Press.

Busemeyer, M. R., and C. Trampusch. 2019. 'The Politics of Vocational Training: Theories, Typologies, and Public Policies'. In *The Wiley Handbook of Vocational Education and Training,* edited by D. Guile and L. Unwin, pp. 137–64. Hoboken: John Wiley & Sons.

Carstensen, M. B., P. Emmenegger, and D. F. Unterweger. 2022. 'Setting the Terms of State Intervention: Employers, Unions and the Politics of Inclusiveness in Austrian and Danish Vocational Education Institutions'. *European Political Science Review.* https://doi.org/10.1017/S1755773922000017

Carstensen, M. B., and C. L. Ibsen. 2021. 'Three Dimensions of Institutional Contention: Efficiency, Equality and Governance in Danish Vocational Education and Training Reform'. *Socio-Economic Review 19* (3): 1037–63.

Cedefop. 2018. *Less Brawn, More Brain for Tomorrow's Workers.* Cedefop Briefing Note (June 2018).

Chuan, A., and C. L. Ibsen. 2021. 'Skills for the Future? A Life Cycle Perspective on Systems of Vocational Education and Training'. *ILR Review,* Published online 7 June 2021.

Crouch, C. 2005. 'Skill Formation Systems'. In *The Oxford Handbook of Work and Organization,* edited by S. Ackroyd, P. Thompson, and P. Tolbert, pp. 95–114. Oxford: Oxford University Press.

Crouch, C. 2019. *Will the Gig Economy Prevail?* Cambridge: Polity Press.

Culpepper, P. D. 2003. *Creating Cooperation: How States Develop Human Capital in Europe.* Ithaca: Cornell University Press.

Culpepper, P. D., and K. Thelen. 2008. 'Institutions and Collective Actors in the Provision of Training'. In *Skill Formation,* edited by K. U. Mayer and H. Solga, pp. 21–49. Cambridge: Cambridge University Press.

Dahlstedt, I., and P. Bevelander. 2010. 'General versus Vocational Education and Employment Integration in Sweden'. *Journal of Immigrant and Refugee Studies 8* (2): 158–92.

Davidsson, J. B., and P. Emmenegger. 2013. 'Defending the Organization, Not the Members: Unions and the Reform of Job Security Legislation in Europe'. *European Journal of Political Research 53* (3): 339–63.

Di Maio, G., L. Graf, and A. Wilson. 2019. 'Torn between Economic Efficiency and Social Equality? Short-track Apprenticeships in Denmark, Germany and Switzerland'. *European Educational Research Journal 18* (6): 699–723.

Donado, A., and K. Wälde. 2018. 'How Trade Unions Increase Welfare'. *Economic Journal 122* (563): 990–1009.

Durazzi, N., and L. Geyer. 2020. 'Social Inclusion in the Knowledge Economy: Unions' Strategies and Institutional Change in the Austrian and German Training Systems'. *Socio-Economic Review 18* (1): 103–24.

Durazzi, N., and L. Geyer. 2022. 'Social Inclusion and Collective Skill Formation Systems: Policy and Politics'. *Journal of European Social Policy* 32(1): 105–116.

Edwards, T. 2004. 'The Transfer of Employment Practices across Borders in Multinational Companies'. In *International Human Resource Management*, edited by A.-W. Harzing and J. Van Ruysseveldt, pp. 389–410. London: Sage.

Emmenegger, P. 2014. *The Power to Dismiss: Trade Unions and the Regulation of Job Security in Western Europe*. Oxford: Oxford University Press.

Emmenegger, P., L. Graf, and C. Trampusch. 2019. 'The Governance of Decentralized Cooperation in Collective Training Systems: A Review and Conceptualization'. *Journal of Vocational Education and Training 71* (1): 21–45.

Emmenegger, P., S. Häusermann, B. Palier, and M. Seeleib-Kaiser. 2012. *The Age of Dualization: The Changing Face of Inequality in Deindustrializing Societies*. New York: Oxford University Press.

Emmenegger, P., and L. Seitzl. 2019. 'Collective Action, Business Cleavages and the Politics of Control: Segmentalism in the Swiss Skill Formation System'. *British Journal of Industrial Relations 57* (3): 575–98.

Emmenegger, P., and L. Seitzl. 2020. 'Social Partner Involvement in Collective Skill Formation Governance: A Comparison of Austria, Denmark, Germany, the Netherlands and Switzerland'. *Transfer 26* (1): 27–42.

Emmenegger, P., and D. Unterweger. 2021. 'Business and Training Policy'. In *The Edward Elgar Handbook on Business and Public Policy*, edited by A. Kellow, T. Porter, and K. Ronit, pp. 140–55. Cheltenham: Edward Elgar.

Estevez-Abe, M., T. Iversen, and D. Soskice. 2001. 'Social Protection and the Formation of Skills: A Reinterpretation of the Welfare State'. In *Varieties of Capitalism: The Institutional Foundations of Comparative Advantage*, edited by P. A. Hall and D. Soskice, pp. 145–83. Oxford: Oxford University Press.

European Union. 2010. *The Bruges Communiqué on enhanced European Cooperation in Vocational Education and Training for the period 2011–2020*. Retrieved from https://www.eqavet.eu/Eqavet2017/media/Documents/brugescom_en.pdf.

European Union. 2015. *Riga Conclusions*. Retrieved from https://www.izm.gov.lv/images/RigaConclusions_2015.pdf.

Fleischmann, F., and J. Dronkers. 2010. 'Unemployment among Immigrants in European Labour Markets: An Analysis of Origin and Destination Effects'. *Work, Employment and Society 24* (2): 337–54.

Frey, C. B., and M. A. Osborne. 2013. *The Future of Employment: How Susceptible Are Jobs to Computerization?* Oxford: University of Oxford.

Garritzmann, J., S. Häusermann, and B. Palier. 2021. *The World Politics of Social Investment: Welfare States in the Knowledge Economy.* Oxford: Oxford University Press.

Geddes, A., and P. Scholten. 2016. *The Politics of Migration and Immigration in Europe,* 2nd edition. London: Sage.

Gonon, P. 2019. 'Learning Skills in the Digital Age: In Schools or in the Workplace?' *Contemporary Apprenticeship Reforms and Reconfigurations 35*: 154.

Goos, M., A. Manning, and A. Salomons. 2014. 'Explaining Job Polarization: Routine-biased Technological Change and Offshoring'. *American Economic Review 104* (8): 2509–26.

Graf, L. 2018. 'Combined Models of Gradual Change: The Case of Academic Upgrading and Declining Collectivism in German Skill Formation'. *Socio-Economic Review 16* (1): 185–205.

Graf, L., A. Strebel, and P. Emmenegger. 2021. 'State-led Bricolage and the Extension of Collective Governance: Hybridity in the Swiss Skill Formation System'. *Regulation and Governance.* Published online 16 August 2021. https://doi.org/10.1111/rego.12436

Grundke, R., L. Marcolin, T. L. B. Nguyen, and M. Squicciarini. 2018. *Which Skills for the Digital Era? Returns to Skills Analysis.* OECD Science, Technology and Industry Working Papers. Paris: OECD.

Hacker, J. 2004. 'Privatizing Risk without Privatizing the Welfare State: The Hidden Politics of Social Policy Retrenchment in the United States'. *American Political Science Review 98* (2): 243–60.

Heath, A. F., C. Rothon, and E. Kilpi. 2008. 'The Second Generation in Western Europe: Education, Unemployment, and Occupational Attainment'. *Annual Review of Sociology 34:* 211–35.

Howell, C. 2016. 'Regulating Class in the Neoliberal Era: The Role of the State in the Restructuring of Work and Employment Relations'. *Work, Employment and Society 30* (4): 573–89.

Howell, C. 2019. 'Neoliberalism, Capitalist Growth Models and the State: An Agenda for Industrial Relations Theory'. *Journal of Industrial Relations 61* (3): 457–74.

Iversen, T., and D. Soskice. 2001. 'An Asset Theory of Social Policy Preferences'. *American Political Science Review 95* (4): 875–93.

Johansen, L. H. 2002. 'Transferable Training as a Collective Good'. *European Sociological Review 18* (3): 301–14.

Joyce, P. 2018. *Newcomers in the North: Labour Market Integration of Refugees in Northern Europe.* Migration Information Source, 27 February 2018.

Kautz, T., J. J. Heckman, R. Diris, B. T. Weel, and L. Borghans. 2014. *Fostering and measuring skills: improving cognitive and non-cognitive skills to promote lifetime success.* NBER Working Paper No. 20749. Cambridge, MA: NBER

Kemmerling, M., and C. Trampusch. 2021. 'Corporate Power Sources in Digital(ized) Capitalism'. Paper presented at 2021 SASE Conference 2021.

Kogan, I. 2006. 'Labor Markets and Economic Incorporation among Recent Immigrants in Europe'. *Social Forces* 85 (2): 697–721.

Kristal, T., and Y. Cohen. 2017. 'The Causes of Rising Wage Inequality: The Race between Institutions and Technology'. *Socio-Economic Review* 15 (1): 187–212.

Loebbecke, C., and A. Picot. 2015. 'Reflections on Societal and Business Model Transformation Arising from Digitization and Big Data Analytics: A Research Agenda'. *The Journal of Strategic Information Systems* 24 (3): 149–57.

Marsden, D. 1999. *A Theory of Employment Systems: Micro-foundations of Societal Diversity.* Oxford: Oxford University Press.

Martin, C. J., and J. S. Knudsen. 2010. 'Scenes from a Mall: Retail Training and the Social Exclusion of Low-skilled Workers'. *Regulation and Governance* 4 (3): 345–64.

Martin, C. J., and K. Thelen. 2007. 'The State and Coordinated Capitalism'. *World Politics* 60 (1): 1–36.

McKinsey Global Institute. 2018. *The Future of Work: Switzerland's Digital Opportunity.* McKinsey Global Institute.

Morel, N., B. Palier, and J. Palme. 2012. *Towards a Social Investment Welfare State? Ideas, Policies and Challenges.* Bristol: Policy Press.

Murphy, E., and D. Oesch. 2018. 'Is Employment Polarisation Inevitable? Occupational Change in Ireland and Switzerland, 1970–2010'. *Work, Employment and Society* 32 (6): 1099–117.

OECD. 2008. *Growing Unequal: Income Distribution and Poverty in OECD Countries.* Paris: OECD.

OECD. 2016. *Making Integration Work: Refugees and Others in Need of Protection.* Paris: OECD.

OECD. 2017. *Future of Work and Skills.* Paris: OECD.

OECD. 2018. *International Migration Outlook 2018.* Paris: OECD.

OECD. 2019a. *PISA 2018 Results: What Students Know and Can Do, Volume I.* Paris: OECD.

OECD. 2019b. *PISA 2018 Results: Where All Students Can Succeed, Volume II.* Paris: OECD.

Oesch, D. 2013. *Occupational Change in Europe: How Technology and Education Transform the Job Structure.* Oxford: Oxford University Press.

Oesch, D., and R. J. Menés. 2010. 'Upgrading or Polarization? Occupational Change in Britain, Germany, Spain and Switzerland, 1990–2008'. *Socio-Economic Review 9* (3): 503–31.

Owen, E., and N. P. Johnston. 2017. 'Occupation and the Political Economy of Trade: Job Routineness, Offshorability, and Protectionist Sentiment'. *International Organization 71* (4): 665–99.

Piketty, T. 2013. *Capital in the Twenty-first Century*. Cambridge, MA: Harvard University Press.

Røed, M., and P. Schøne. 2012. *The Impact of Immigration on Investment in Vocational Skills*. Institute for Social Research Working Paper May 2012.

Rolandsson, B., J. E. Dölvik, A. Hedenus, J. R. Steen, A. Ilsöe, T. P. Larsen, and T. Alasoini. 2019. *Digitalization in Nordic Manufacturing: Some Case-study Illustrations*. Nordic Future of Work Project 2017–2020, Working Paper No. 3.

Ryan, P. 2000. 'The Institutional Requirements of Apprenticeship: Evidence from Smaller EU Countries'. *International Journal of Training and Development 4* (1): 42–65.

Shavit, Y., and H. P. Blossfeld. 1993. *Persistent Inequality: Changing Educational Attainment in Thirteen Countries*. Boulder: Westview Press.

Sorge, A., and W. Streeck. 2018. 'Diversified Quality Production Revisited: Its Contribution to German Socio-economic Performance over Time'. *Socio-Economic Review 16* (3): 587–612.

Strebel, A., P. Emmenegger, and L. Graf. 2021. 'New Interest Associations in a Neo-corporatist System: Adapting the Swiss Training System to the Service Economy'. *British Journal of Industrial Relations 59* (3): 848–73.

Streeck, W. 1989. 'Skills and the Limits of Neo-liberalism: The Enterprise of the Future as a Place of Learning'. *Work, Employment and Society 31* (1): 89–107.

Streeck, W. 1992. *Social Institutions and Economic Performance*. London: Sage.

Streeck, W. 2009. *Re-forming Capitalism: Institutional Change in the German Political Economy*. Oxford: Oxford University Press.

Streeck, W., J. Grote, V. Schneider, and J. Visser. 2006. *Governing Interests: Business Associations Facing Internationalization*. London: Routledge.

Thelen, K. 2014. *Varieties of Liberalization and the New Politics of Social Solidarity*. Cambridge: Cambridge University Press.

Thelen, K. 2018. 'Regulating Uber: The Politics of the Platform Economy in Europe and the United States'. *Perspectives on Politics 16* (4): 938–53.

Thelen, K., and M. R. Busemeyer. 2012. 'Institutional Change in German Vocational Training: From Collectivism toward Segmentalism'. In *The Political Economy of Collective Skill Formation*, edited by M. R. Busemeyer and C. Trampusch, pp. 68–91. Oxford: Oxford University Press.

Trampusch, C. 2010. 'Co-evolution of Skills and Welfare in Coordinated Market Economies? A Comparative Historical Analysis of Denmark, the Netherlands and Switzerland'. *European Journal of Industrial Relations 16* (3): 197–220.

Trampusch, C. 2019. 'Social Partners' Policy Reactions to Migration in Occupational Labour Markets: The Case of the Swiss Construction Industry'. *European Journal of Industrial Relations 26* (2): 157–72.

Trampusch, C., and P. Eichenberger. 2012. 'Skills and Industrial Relations in Coordinated Market Economies: Continuing Vocational Training in Denmark, the Netherlands, Austria and Switzerland'. *British Journal of Industrial Relations 50* (4): 644–66.

Unterweger, D. 2020. 'Unconstrained Capital? Multinational Companies in Collective Skill Formation Systems'. *Socio-Economic Review*: 1–21. Published online 2 October 2020. https://doi.org/10.1093/ser/mwaa035

Woll, C. 2006. 'National Business Associations under Stress: Lessons from the French Case'. *West European Politics 29* (3): 489–512.

Woll, C. 2016. *The Power of Inaction: Bank Bailouts in Comparison*. Ithaca: Cornell University Press.

2
Occupations and Collective Skill Formation in the Knowledge Economy

Exploring Differential Employment Integration for the German Case

Christian Ebner, Sandra Hirtz, and Daniela Rohrbach-Schmidt

2.1 Introduction

Macro-trends such as globalization, technological change, digitalization, and the shift to a knowledge economy demand ever new skills from employees and thus put considerable pressure on national qualification systems (see Chapter 1 in this volume). Comparative research shows that countries with *collective skill formation systems* (Busemeyer and Trampusch 2012) have the capacity to successfully integrate large numbers of their graduates into employment. This is reflected in low youth unemployment rates, high shares of permanent contracts, decent wages, and graduates being employed in skilled occupations (e.g. Breen 2005; Gangl 2004; Ebner 2015). When reviewing the 'school-to-work-transitions' literature these general findings can be attributed to several typical features of collective skill formation systems (Allmendinger 1989; Müller and Shavit 1998; Greinert 2005; Brzinsky-Fay 2007; Ebner 2013). First, in contrast to liberal market economies with on-the-job training systems, people in countries with collective skill formation systems spend several years in the training system and thus invest intensively in their skills before they are employed. Second, in contrast to countries with full-time school-based vocational training, the duality of learning locations (firm and vocational school) allows the acquisition of both theoretical-abstract and practical knowledge. Third, training in a firm alongside vocational school enables trainees to enter employment directly after graduation and thus reduces search unemployment. Fourth, the involvement of the economy (employers' associations and trade unions) in vocational training guarantees

Christian Ebner, Sandra Hirtz and Daniela Rohrbach-Schmidt, *Occupations and Collective Skill Formation in the Knowledge Economy*. In: *Collective Skill Formation in the Knowledge Economy*. Edited by Giuliano Bonoli and Patrick Emmenegger, Oxford University Press. © Oxford University Press (2022). DOI: 10.1093/oso/9780192866257.003.0002 the labour market relevance of training courses. Fifth, the standardization of vocational training and training certificates by state regulations enables firms to (more or less) correctly assess the skills of training graduates in the process of labour recruitment. And sixth, by providing trainees with skills specific to certain occupations, these skills are portable between firms and graduates can easily change firms.

In this chapter we will take a closer look at the latter point, i.e. *occupations and employment integration* of vocational education and training (VET) graduates. In our view, the often-cited advantage that occupational skills can be used in different firms might overshadow one major disadvantage: while occupation-specific skills allow individuals to move between firms, empirical evidence from social mobility research underscores that changing occupations can be difficult to impossible (Haupt and Ebner 2020; Vicari and Unger 2020). In other words: people who have been trained as bakers will find it difficult to work as car mechanics; car mechanics are usually denied access to the occupation of tax clerk; tax clerks will very unlikely be employed as nurses, etc.

High barriers surrounding individual occupations may not be seen as a problem if the opportunity for successful employment were similarly high for different training occupations. However, if this is not the case it has severe consequences on two different levels of reasoning: first, it would imply that employment chances of graduates from vocational training are unequally distributed according to training occupations questioning the creed of equality of opportunity. Second, from the perspective of collective skill formation systems, this would indicate that it makes little sense to speak of an integrative effect of the system as such, but that we need to take a much more differentiated approach and pay more attention to the concept of occupation or occupational segments within the system.

Against this background, the aim of this chapter is to examine the occupation-specific integrative capacity of collective skill formation systems by analysing the prototypical case of Germany. The German system of dual VET enjoys a strong international reputation. It is said to contribute to high product quality through market-oriented standardized training of skilled workers (Streeck 1991)—'Made in Germany' is still regarded as a seal of excellence. The dual system has great quantitative significance in Germany today. By the end of 2017, there were 1.32 million trainees nationwide (Bundesinstitut für Berufsbildung 2019, 9). Nevertheless, it is an open question how well the training system is adapted to current developments in the employment system. Besides the expansion of service activities, the increased use of computers is evident (Jovanovic and Rousseau 2005). Many activities that have been described as 'routine' can in principle also be performed by computers and robots, so that the substitution of workers has already occurred or is at least imminent (Autor et al. 2003). It is also apparent that non-routine activities are in greater demand by companies and that the sector of knowledge-intensive services has been booming for decades (Hope and Martelli 2019; Rohrbach 2009).

These developments certainly require specific skills on the labour supply side (Liu and Grusky 2013). In collective skill formation systems, trainees acquire very diverse skills or to be more precise 'skill bundles' depending on the occupation they were trained for. Against the background of ongoing changes in the employment system and a higher prevalence of knowledge-intensive services, different occupation-specific skill bundles should therefore also be associated with varying opportunities and risks for graduates in the employment system.

Drawing on up-to-date representative employment data, we examine the integrative (in)capacity of the German dual training system by analysing the employment status of dual VET graduates with different occupational specializations. A weak integration of VET graduates into the employment system can be reflected in three indicators that we examine in more detail in this study: (1) earning low wages, (2) working in low-skilled jobs, and (3) working on a fixed-term contract. The German VET system was traditionally specialized in the training of craftsmen and industrial workers. Therefore, it is of further interest whether systematic differences between training occupations for certain fields such as manufacturing or services occur. Our results show that VET graduates are exposed to heterogeneous risks depending on the occupation and occupational segment to which their training occupation belongs. In particular, VET graduates from the primary service sector are exposed to comparatively high labour market risks measured via low wages, unskilled work, and temporary employment. Manufacturing graduates, on the other hand, are generally quite well off, although there are exceptions for some training occupations in this segment. Training in one of the secondary service occupations (knowledge work) also mostly insures graduates against the labour market risks studied here. Collective skill formation systems thus appear to be fundamentally capable of training people for future fields of employment and offering them a certain degree of security against typical risks on the labour market. The results of our analyses should be of interest to the scientific community, because analysing training occupations and occupational segments is complementary to studies addressing firm-specific differences and industries in the field of dual vocational training (e.g. Thelen and Busemeyer 2012); for example, Avent-Holt et al. (2020)

show that occupations can statistically explain employees' wages to a significant extent, over and above establishment characteristics. From a policy perspective, which focuses on the inclusiveness dimension of collective skill formation (see Chapter 6 in this volume), targeted interventions related to individual occupations and occupational segments may be particularly effective.

Our contribution is structured as follows. In the next section (2.2), we describe the historical roots of occupations. Indeed, occupations have been a crucial element of vocational training in Europe since the Middle Ages, and they continue to be essential for collective skill formation systems today. Then (section 2.3), from a theoretical point of view, the interplay between the training system and the employment system is discussed, with occupations taking on a key role. This is followed (section 2.4) by a detailed description of the data used, central variables, and statistical methods of analysis. The results (section 2.5) show that integrative problems within the framework of dual VET are obvious for specific occupations, but not for the system as a whole. We finish (section 2.6) by discussing these results and draw a conclusion.

2.2 The historical roots of occupations in European vocational training

Even before industrialization had its breakthrough, the cities of Europe institutionalized a well-organized vocational training system. Apprentices were taught by a master craftsman and took part in the family life of the master's household (Stratmann 1993). Already at this time occupations (e.g. baker, blacksmith, carpenter, shoemaker, weaver) played a central role for vocational training. Now as before, they have determined individuals' activities, status, and identity (Stooß 1985). Guilds—occupational associations of craftsmen—regulated the practical training and accomplished final examinations. Most occupations were only allowed to be practised by members of the according guild (Greinert 2005: 23).

Over time, craft businesses came under increasing pressure (Volti 2008). Manufactories in which the division of labour had already been established were highly productive and the crafts could not keep up with them in many places. Furthermore, liberal currents and ideas of free competition called the rigid guild system into question. With the legal anchoring of freedom of occupation and freedom of trade in Europe, the traditional vocational training model finally came to an end (Henning 1996).

From then on, the organization of vocational training in Europe followed very different paths (Greinert 2005; Thelen 2004). While a liberal 'training-on-the-job' model was established in England, France opted for a state-controlled vocational training model. Following the establishment of freedom of trade (Stein-Hardenberg reforms in Prussia), Germany reacted in a rather traditionalistic manner. The Handwerkerschutzgesetz [Trades Protection Act] of 1897 once again assigned the regulation of apprentice training to the chambers of trade as occupational associations (Rinneberg 1985). German industry followed this model. Eventually, the state regulated German vocational training via the Handwerksordnung (HwO) [Crafts Code] of 1953 and the Berufsbildungsgesetz (BBiG) [Vocational Training Act] of 1969 (Greinert 2006). From then on, training was governed uniformly throughout Germany and the second training location besides the firm, the state vocational school, was legally anchored. This 'dual training system', which is still very prominent in Germany today, is also common in other European countries like Austria, Denmark, the Netherlands, and Switzerland.

Just as in the Middle Ages, the occupation is a central element of the German training system today. For each of the 325 German training occupations (2019), training content and training conditions are listed in an occupation-specific Ausbildungsordnung [training regulation]. In accordance with §5 of the BBiG and §26 of the HwO, the following five points are regulated:

1. the title of the training occupation
2. the duration of the training, which shall not exceed three years and shall not be less than two years
3. the professional skills, knowledge, and abilities covered by the vocational training
4. guidelines on how to structure the teaching of professional skills, knowledge, and abilities
5. the examination requirements.

The very different skills of trainees are thus anchored in law, i.e. they are formally institutionalized. Whether this institutionalization not only reflects a diversity of skills but is also linked to social inequality in that it is associated with different opportunities and risks of graduates will be discussed in more detail below.

2.3 Occupations and the integrative capacity of collective skill formation systems

International comparative studies underscore the integrative capacity of collective skill formation systems. In countries with dual vocational training youth unemployment is comparatively low (Breen 2005; Brzinsky-Fay 2007; Gangl 2001) and the vocational placement of training graduates is favourable (Allmendinger 1989; Müller and Shavit 1998; Wolbers 2003; DiPrete et al. 1997; Scherer 2001; Gangl 2002, 2004; Longhi and Brynin 2010; Saar et al. 2008; Quintini and Manfredi 2009; Andersen and van de Werfhorst 2010). These findings are related to the systemic design of dual vocational training. The dual mode of training (vocational school and firm) is one crucial element in this respect: apprentices gain theoretical-abstract knowledge, but also very practical, 'tacit knowledge' (Polanyi 1966) which makes them competitive against incumbent employees with good working conditions so-called labour market insiders (Lindbeck and Snower 2002). With the firm as one of the two training places, the dual vocational training system is already linked to the employment system. This linkage reduces search unemployment. As discussed above, the state sets general quality standards (Allmendinger 1989), which are described in the BBiG and the HwO. Such standards include the rights and obligations of trainees, minimum standards for training institutions and training personnel, or regulations on final examinations. The economy (economic associations and unions) defines contents and conditions of individual training occupations, which are then described in official training regulations. The aim is to ensure that there is a match between the skills and abilities acquired during training on the one hand and the need for skills on the employer's side on the other.

Still, employment opportunities and employment risks of VET graduates may vary considerably by *training occupation*. Theories of market segmentation state that markets such as the training market or the labour market fall into distinct parts ('segments'). Market segments are permanent, stable, and can be regarded as 'non-competing groups' (Cairnes 1874). The market divide manifests itself in segment-specific institutions, supply and demand conditions, and limited mobility between segments.

For the German labour market, a conceptual distinction between three market segments has been established (Lutz and Sengenberger 1974: 43–70): (1) a non-specific labour market segment, where general skills such as dedication to performance and certain basic physical and mental requirements are needed; (2) a firm-specific labour market segment, which describes internal career ladders and where firm-specific knowledge and skills play an important role, and (3) a skilled labour market segment, where skills and knowledge needed are mainly occupation specific. The great importance of occupations for processes of training and employment in Germany has been explicitly emphasized in a number of studies. Germany has consequently been described as an 'occupational labour market' (Marsden 1990; cf. also Gangl 2001).[1]

Possible reasons for differential effects of training occupations on the employment integration of VET graduates are manifold. On the one hand, training occupations might differ in the degree to which the training regulations keep up with the changes in the labour market; although training regulations are constantly being revised, in some cases this process takes a long time so that codified knowledge is outdated. Moreover, even though all training occupations are somewhat specific, the broadness of the occupations and the degree to which VET graduates compete with unskilled workers or academically trained workers differs (e.g. Menze 2017). Finally, both different training behaviour of firms (e.g. training above demand) and changes in demand on the labour market can influence the career opportunities of graduates. It is quite possible that the skills and abilities taught in training may not fit recent requirements in the employment system, because the demand for some specific skill bundles is declining while it is increasing for others. Digital literacy has become ever more important with the growing use of computers in the workplace (Autor et al. 2003). In addition, sectoral shifts are associated with an increasing need for synthesis, critical thinking, and related analytical skills (Liu and Grusky 2013).

A major challenge lies in measuring the integrative capacity of the vocational training system with the help of empirical data. This integrative capacity can then be broken down to the level of single training occupations. Our assumption is that the integrative capacity of the dual VET system can be classified as 'intact' if training graduates find themselves in favourable employment positions or they can at least prevent precarious employment. In this chapter, we identify integration problems in employment by referring to three indicators. First, integration can be viewed as not successful if graduates work in low-wage employment. Low wages are a major threat to the training system as young people in the future might decide to go to university or directly enter the labour market after general education instead of investing in long-term VET programmes (cf. also

---

[1] Very similar to the concept of 'occupational labour markets' Maurice et al. (1986) speak of 'qualificational spaces'.

Estevez-Abe et al. 2001). Second, employment integration is defined to be not successful if training graduates do not work as skilled workers but are employed in low-skilled jobs. This is reasonable, as the purpose of the VET system is by definition to train skilled workers. Third, integration cannot be seen as successful if training graduates' employment is limited in time (fixed-term work contract); a high prevalence of fixed-term employment contradicts the core principle of employment stability within collective skill formation systems. The subsequent empirical analyses aim at exploring occupation-specific differences between VET graduates when it comes to risks of employment integration (low wages, low-skilled job, temporary employment).

2.4 Data and methods

2.4.1 Dataset and study population

The study draws on data from the 2018 Employment Survey (Hall et al. 2020) carried out by the Federal Institute for Vocational Education and Training (BIBB) and the Federal Institute for Occupational Safety and Health (BAuA). The sample of around 20,000 employees is representative for the German working population. It comprises people in employment (i.e. paid work), aged fifteen years and over, with a regular working time of at least ten hours per week. The data were collected via computer-assisted telephone interviews (CATI). The 2018 Employment Survey is the seventh survey of its kind since 1979 and has become established in the scientific community as a central survey in the field of qualification and vocational (education) research in Germany. The strength of the data for the given purpose is that it not only allows the analysis of individual levels of qualification but also carries exact information on the occupation employees were trained for. Such training occupations are coded in the most recent German Klassifikation der Berufe 2010 (KldB 2010) [German Classification of Occupations 2010, see Paulus and Matthes 2013].

For the analyses in this chapter, we restrict the sample to persons with a degree attained in dual vocational training, according to the BBiG and the HwO, as their highest attainment. We thus exclude persons who earned an academic or advanced training degree (masters/technicians/other). Moreover, we exclude persons who attained a degree in full-time vocational schools. Even though the formal level of qualification is the same as with dual VET, this educational sector differs from dual VET in several ways (e.g. access requirements, organization of training, labour market prospects). Importantly, both systems train for different occupations.[2]

In addition, we further exclude civil servants, the self-employed, and freelancers because we are interested in the occurrence of temporary employment which is virtually not possible for the self-employed and civil servants in Germany. By focusing on workers and salaried employees with dual training as their highest attainment the sample size reduces to 6,147 (13,264 cases have no dual training degree as highest attainment; a further 601 cases are self-employed, civil servants, or freelancers). Finally, to be able to estimate robust coefficients for single occupations, we only consider five-digit occupations[3] with at least forty observations.[4] The final sample of analysis consists of 3,460 cases in 35 five-digit occupations. It is important to stress that with this statistically reasonable selection we only focus on the largest occupations in the dual VET system. As mentioned earlier, currently the dual VET system encompasses more than 300 training occupations, and thus a much larger number than considered here. Nevertheless, these thirty-five occupations cover a large share of the total population in the training system (around 70%).

2.4.2 Concepts and variables

The *independent variable* in our analysis is the occupation employees were trained for within the German dual VET system.[5] The occupational titles used in the results tables represent the official titles of training occupations in Germany (Bundesinstitut für Berufsbildung 2020).

As *dependent variables* we consider three measures possibly indicating a weak integrative capacity of dual training occupations: low wages, a low-skilled job, and a temporary work contract. Among labour market returns, wages are one of the central outcomes and play a decisive role in determining life chances. To analyse restricted earning opportunities, we

---

[2] The main focus of the school-based training courses is on the subject of person-related service occupations. Social occupations (e.g. educator) and health occupations (e.g. nurses) alone account for more than half of all school-based occupations. In the dual system, industrial and technical professions in industry and crafts are strongly represented.

[3] The fifth level is the most detailed level in the German classification of occupations 2010. At this level, training occupations can be identified.

[4] The number of observations per occupation varies between forty cases (e.g. occupations in metalworking: cutting (24232) or occupations in the production of clothing, hat, and cap making (28222)) to 367 cases (office clerks and secretaries (without specialization), 71402). The average number of observations per occupation in the sample is 155. The predictive margins reported in the results section are estimated more imprecisely for the smaller occupational groups.

[5] In the Employment Survey up to five vocational degrees are surveyed. In cases with more than one dual training degree attained we use the occupation that has been learnt last in the educational biography.

focus on low-wage employment. One challenge is to define an appropriate low-wage threshold. In line with (relative) poverty research where the at-risk-of-poverty threshold is set at 60 per cent of national median equalized disposable income (Eurostat 2020) we speak of low-wage employment when the gross hourly wage is below the 60 per cent threshold of the gross median hourly wage.[6] This gives us a critical value of 9.66 euros. We compute an indicator variable for 'low-wage employment' with value 1 if the dual VET graduates earn less than 9.66 euros per hour and value 0 otherwise. As a first orientation: in 2018, the year in which our study was conducted, the national minimum wage in Germany was 8.84 euros and was thus slightly lower.

The German system of vocational education and training aims at guaranteeing its graduates a qualified employment, i.e. employment that requires at least a degree at the level of vocational education and training. Employment in low-skilled jobs, i.e. positions that do not require a VET degree, can be judged as unfavourable, both from the perspective of the individual as well as from a training systems perspective. In the BIBB/BAuA Employment Survey, respondents are asked whether their current position requires no qualification, vocational education and training, advanced further training (master/technicians and other degrees) or an academic degree. With this information we compute an indicator variable for 'low-skilled job' with value 1 if the dual VET degree earners in our sample work in positions that do not require any qualification and 0 otherwise.

Our third measure is a temporary work contract. This information was directly asked from respondents and equals 1 if the worker states that the current position is temporary and 0 if he or she has a permanent contract. Table 2.1A (appendix) shows descriptive statistics for the selected sample with non-missing cases on all variables of interest. Regarding the three dependent variables of interest the table shows that 13 per cent of the sample earns low wage, 15 per cent work in a low-skilled job, and 8 per cent have signed a temporary work contract. Reflecting the known structure of VET degree holders in Germany, with 50 per cent most of the cases in the sample have a medium-level schooling degree (Realschule), 34 per cent have a Hauptschulabschluss (lowest German schooling certificate) and further 16 per cent have an Abitur (university entrance qualification). The sample is slightly male dominated (57%).

---

[6] We use the imputed values for missing wages (Alda and Rohrbach-Schmidt 2011). Wage is measured as gross monthly wage (without taxes and the like). To consider full and part-time employment we use average weekly working time and contractually agreed working time to compute hourly wages.

2.4.3 Analytical strategy

We estimate logistic regression models as our dependent variables are binary coded. In a first step (Model 1), only the training occupations are included as dummy variables, with occupations in wood construction, furniture and cabinet making, and interior finishing as the reference category. Since logit coefficients cannot be interpreted meaningfully, we calculate predictive margins from the logistic model. The predictive margins (times 100) report the probability of earning low wages, working in low-skilled jobs, or performing a temporary job, in a particular training occupation.

Up to this point it is an open question whether occupation-specific effects are caused by genuine differences between occupations or whether it is typical compositions of occupations that drive these results. A high prevalence of low wages for a specific occupation could for instance have less to do with the occupation 'as such' but be related to a lower level of schooling of occupational incumbents, which might indicate lower general skills. We are aware that the allocation of individuals to (training) occupations is a result of self-selection (people striving for certain occupations) and other selection (firms looking for personnel who are particularly suitable for certain occupations) (e.g. Weeden and Grusky 2005). In this respect, observable heterogeneity can be distinguished from unobservable heterogeneity. Due to measurability issues and the data basis, we are not able to consider unobservable characteristics such as individual preferences, abilities, or affinities directly, but use proxies for those in our models. To account for selection effects as much as possible, we extend our logistic regression models in a second step (Model 2). Additional variables that enter the equation are the highest school-leaving certificate and school-leaving grades as proxy for competence and the career orientation of individuals as proxy for motivation. In order to capture self-selection and possible discrimination in the labour market we include the two crucial variables: gender and migration background. As further biographical and structural variables which can be related to the dependent variables we add to the model: employees' labour market experience and cohort, region (east and west Germany), the size of the firm as well as the sector people are working in.

2.5 Empirical results

The tables in this section show the predicted probabilities to earn low wages (Table 2.1), work in a low-skilled job (Table 2.2), and have signed a temporary

Table 2.1 Predicted probabilities in per cent for the risk of earning low wages by occupation

KldB2010	Training Occupation	Model 1	Model 2
63302	Restaurant specialist	35.00%	37.84%
28222	Custom tailor	37.50%	36.11%
82312	Hairdresser	33.33%	35.38%
51312	Warehouse logistics operator	23.08%	23.53%
33212	Painter and varnisher	22.22%	22.22%
81112	Qualified dental employee	20.97%	20.97%
62102	Management assistant for retail services	18.35%	18.61%
63222	Specialist in the hotel business	17.39%	17.91%
29302	Cook	17.65%	17.82%
32122	Mason	15.91%	16.67%
22342	Joiner	14.86%	15.07%
29222	Baker	15.52%	14.04%
24412	Construction mechanic	11.84%	12.68%
72132	Insurance and financial services broker	12.50%	12.50%
71402	Office manager	12.26%	12.40%
72302	Tax clerk	11.11%	11.11%
34212	Plant mechanic for sanitary, heating, and air conditioning	8.75%	8.86%
25212	Motor vehicle mechatronics technician	8.93%	8.81%
27212	Technical product designer	8.70%	8.70%
73112	Legal assistant	8.33%	8.45%
81102	Medical assistant	8.33%	8.41%
71302	Industrial clerk	8.30%	8.37%
24232	Milling machine operator	7.50%	7.89%
51622	Freight forwarding and logistics services clerk	7.55%	7.55%
26212	Electronics technician for building and infrastructure systems	6.06%	5.65%
61212	Management assistants in wholesale and foreign trade	4.58%	4.61%
25102	Industrial mechanic	3.89%	3.98%
72112	Bank clerk	3.98%	3.98%
43102	Information technology specialist	3.92%	3.92%
26312	Electronics technician for devices and systems	3.16%	3.16%
26252	Electronics technician for industrial engineering	1.19%	1.19%
73202	Clerk in public administration	1.15%	1.15%
24522	Tools mechanic*	0%*	0%*
41322	Chemical laboratory technician*	0%*	0%*
73212	Insurance management assistant*	0%*	0%*
N		3,312	3,251

Source: Own calculations based on the BIBB/BAuA-Employment Survey 2018. * All cases in the dataset with the training occupations tools mechanic (n = 40), chemical technical laboratory occupations (n = 42), and insurance management assistant (n = 66) do not practice low-wage employment.
Note: Results from Model 1 without control variables. Results from Model 2 with control variables. The predictive margins for each training occupation (Model 2) are sorted in descending order.

Table 2.2 Predicted probabilities in per cent for the risk of performing a low-skilled job by occupation

KldB2010	Training Occupation	Model 1	Model 2
28222	Custom tailor	42.50%	41.67%
82312	Hairdresser	31.88%	32.31%
62102	Management assistant for retail services	27.34%	27.01%
29222	Baker	25.86%	26.32%
32122	Mason	27.27%	26.19%
63302	Restaurant specialist	22.50%	24.32%
29302	Cook	22.55%	22.77%
81112	Qualified dental employee	20.97%	20.97%
51312	Warehouse logistics operator	19.23%	19.61%
24232	Milling machine operator	17.50%	18.42%
33212	Painter and varnisher	16.67%	16.67%
63222	Specialist in the hotel business	15.94%	16.42%
25212	Motor vehicle mechatronics technician	16.67%	16.35%
27212	Technical product designer	13.04%	13.04%
71402	Office manager	13.08%	12.95%
24412	Construction mechanic	11.84%	12.68%
34212	Plant mechanic for sanitary, heating, and air conditioning	12.50%	12.66%
26312	Electronics technician for devices and systems	12.63%	12.63%
61212	Management assistants in wholesale and foreign trade	11.76%	11.84%
72132	Insurance and financial services broker	10.71%	10.71%
71302	Industrial clerk	10.94%	10.27%
24522	Tools mechanic	10.00%	10.00%
43102	Information technology specialist	9.80%	9.80%
26212	Electronics technician for building and infrastructure systems	11.36%	9.68%
22342	Joiner	10.81%	9.59%
51622	Freight forwarding and logistics services clerk	9.43%	9.43%
25102	Industrial mechanic	9.44%	9.09%
73112	Legal assistant	8.33%	8.45%
72112	Bank clerk	6.82%	6.82%
81102	Medical assistant	5.56%	5.61%
73202	Clerk in public administration	4.60%	4.60%
73212	Insurance management assistant	4.55%	4.55%
72302	Tax clerk	2.47%	2.47%
26252	Electronics technician for industrial engineering	1.19%	1.19%
41322	Chemical laboratory technician	0%*	0%*
N		3,418	3,357

Source: Own calculations based on the BIBB/BAuA-Employment Survey 2018. * All cases in the dataset with the training occupation chemical technical laboratory occupations (n = 42) do not practice low-skilled employment.
Note: Results from Model 1 without control variables. Results from Model 2 with control variables. The predictive margins for each training occupation (Model 2) are sorted in descending order.

work contract (Table 2.3) by training occupation.[7] Two things become evident: first, the risks of unfavourable employment differ substantially between different training occupations. In our sample the probabilities of low-wage employees within occupations (Model 1) ranges from 0 per cent to 37.5 per cent, that of low-skilled employment from 0 per cent to 42.5 per cent and the share of temporary contracts ranges from 0 per cent to 19.2 per cent. A concrete example of less favourable occupations is the production of clothing (custom tailor) scoring high with 37.5 per cent in low-wage employment and 42.5 per cent in low-skilled work. With 33.3 per cent (low-pay) and 31.8 per cent (low-skilled), hairdressers as well belong to the high-risk occupations, which score high on two risk dimensions. At the more favourable end of the distribution, we can find workers in insurance management or workers installing and maintaining electrical machines. Warehouse logistics operator is one example for high shares of temporary employment (19.2%) and clerk in public administration is one example for low shares of temporary employment (2.3%). Another finding is that occupations with high (low) shares on one risk dimension also tend to have high (low) shares on the other risk dimensions. This holds especially for low-wages and low-skilled jobs and is reflected in their high bivariate correlation coefficient (i.e. r = 0.8).[8]

Second, the results are pretty robust, when controlling for selection effects and structural conditions as can be seen from Model 2. The order of occupations hardly differs. The multivariate results thus strengthen the observation that the integrative capacity of dual vocational training differs systematically between occupations, even if compositional effects concerning education, gender, migration background, cohort, firm size, or sector are considered.

Systematic differences can be observed when focusing on broader occupational segments. We find that training occupations in manufacturing fare pretty well in general (with some exceptions such as production of clothing). This is remarkable in light of a diminishing quantitative importance of such occupations in the employment system. The demand for service occupations has been increasing steadily over the last decades (Zika et al. 2012).

Within the services sector, it seems reasonable to further differentiate between 'primary service occupations' and 'secondary service occupations' (Klauder 1990; Tiemann et al. 2008; Hall 2007). Primary service occupations comprise activities that maintain the flow of production in the economy as a

---

[7] We only report the predicted probabilities for the occupations. The logit coefficients for occupations and the control variables can be requested from the authors. The model goodness (Nagelkerke's pseudo R2) is for low-wage employment M1: 7.7%; M2: 22.0%, for low-skilled employment M1: 6.1%; M2: 11.5%, and for temporary employment M1: 3.6%; M2: 12.2%.

[8] The coefficient is significant at the 5% level.

Table 2.3 Predicted probabilities in per cent for the risk of having a temporary contract by occupation

KldB2010	Training Occupation	Model 1	Model 2
51312	Warehouse logistics operator	19.23%	19.61%
63222	Specialist in the hotel business	15.94%	16.42%
24232	Milling machine operator	12.50%	13.16%
63302	Restaurant specialist	12.50%	10.81%
29222	Baker	10.34%	10.53%
62102	Management assistant for retail services	9.71%	9.85%
41322	Chemical laboratory technician	9.52%	9.52%
82312	Hairdresser	10.14%	9.23%
29302	Cook	8.82%	8.91%
26312	Electronics technician for devices and systems	8.42%	8.42%
43102	Information technology specialist	7.84%	7.84%
24522	Tools mechanic	7.50%	7.50%
73112	Legal assistant	6.94%	7.04%
24412	Construction mechanic	7.89%	7.04%
71402	Office manager	6.54%	6.61%
51622	Freight forwarding and logistics services clerk	5.66%	5.66%
25212	Motor vehicle mechatronics technician	5.36%	5.66%
81102	Medical assistant	5.56%	5.61%
33212	Painter and varnisher	5.56%	5.56%
22342	Joiner	5.41%	5.48%
61212	Management assistants in wholesale and foreign trade	5.23%	5.26%
71302	Industrial clerk	4.91%	4.94%
81112	Qualified dental employee	4.84%	4.84%
32122	Mason	4.55%	4.76%
27212	Technical product designer	4.35%	4.35%
25102	Industrial mechanic	3.89%	3.98%
26252	Electronics technician for industrial engineering	3.57%	3.57%
72112	Bank clerk	3.41%	3.41%
73212	Insurance management assistant	3.03%	3.03%
34212	Plant mechanic for sanitary, heating and air conditioning	2.50%	2.53%
72302	Tax clerk	2.47%	2.47%
26212	Electronics technician for building and infrastructure systems	2.27%	2.42%
73202	Clerk in public administration	2.30%	2.30%
72132	Insurance and financial services broker	1.79%	1.79%
28222	Custom tailor	0%*	0%*
N		3,420	3,363

Source: Own calculations based on the BIBB/BAuA-Employment Survey 2018. * All cases in the dataset with custom tailor occupation (n = 36) do not practice temporary employment.
Note: Results from Model 1 without control variables. Results from Model 2 with control variables. The predictive margins for each training occupation (Model 2) are sorted in descending order.

whole. Such activities include purchasing and selling, preparing food, driving vehicles, or waste disposal.

Secondary service occupations are predominantly provided intellectually and are also referred to as 'mental work' or 'knowledge work'. Typical work tasks are consulting, controlling, doing research, applying laws, or managing people. In fact, the services occupations in our study provide a differentiated picture. VET graduates, who have chosen one of the secondary services occupations are pretty well integrated into the employment system, whereas the opposite is the case for primary services occupations (e.g. salesperson, gastronomy, hairdressers). However, there are also examples for a successful integration of VET graduates in the latter area such as public administration, hinting at some advantages the public sector might offer.

2.6 Summary, discussion, and outlook

Social scientists and policymakers typically stress that VET graduates from countries with collective skill formation systems have particularly favourable employment prospects. In this chapter we have examined to what extent the integrative capacity of the dual training system might vary if the system is broken down to the level of training occupations.

Whereas dual VET seems to be intact as a whole, the empirical findings point to a high degree of heterogeneity within the system. An individual's decision to opt for a particular training occupation can entail quite different employment opportunities and risks (low-wages, unskilled work, temporary employment). A rough differentiation of occupations as manufacturing occupations, primary services occupations, and secondary services occupations provides initial evidence as to whether the dual training system can cope with ongoing changes in the employment system. In general, it seems that the dual training system can offer good employment opportunities for graduates of secondary, knowledge-intensive service occupations. This is despite the fact that the training system's roots lie in the medieval crafts sector and secondary, knowledge-intensive service occupations are dominant in higher education.

Integration difficulties of training graduates are still most evident in the primary service segment, whereas graduates from the manufacturing sector are all in all well integrated. At this point we can only speculate about why VET graduates from the primary service segment are exposed to comparatively high risks in the labour market. On the *macro level*, at least two explanations seem plausible to us. One explanation refers to market forces. It is possible that supply and demand relationships have shifted to the disadvantage of the primary service occupations because the transformation towards a knowledge economy is strengthening secondary services occupations; it is also possible that there will be increased competition for VET graduates from unqualified employees in the primary services segment. A second explanation is that institutional support (e.g. involvement of employers' associations and trade unions) for the primary service segment is rather weak. This would also explain the relatively low risk for VET graduates in manufacturing occupations, despite the fact that the latter might carry higher risks of labour substitution (Autor et al. 2003). Even though we cannot exclude the possibility that there are unobserved factors at the *individual level* too that are responsible for the differences between occupational segments, we have taken into account several crucial variables such as motivation, educational background, gender, and migration background in our statistical models.

Nevertheless, our study faces some limitations. Firstly, it should be emphasized that the study is based on thirty-five rather large training occupations. Although these thirty-five occupations cover around 70 per cent of trainees, it would make sense for future research to expand the set of occupations. Also, to increase the precision of the estimates for the training occupations with smaller case numbers in this sample, pooling several Employment Surveys would be an important extension. However, this procedure is subject to the assumption that the employment opportunities by occupation have not noticeably changed over the years. Secondly, we see an opportunity for future research to develop a more detailed segmentation approach of training occupations than the established distinction between manufacturing occupations, primary service occupations, and secondary service occupations. A more detailed approach would make sense because we find rather high occupational heterogeneity *within* those broad occupational segments. The employment opportunities of trainees *by individual occupation* may differ due to occupation-specific competences taught and the duration of the training period—the time trainees invest in their skills differs between two and three-and-a-half years. Furthermore, occupation-specific considerations of firms should be taken into account. Some occupational titles might carry higher reputation or signal higher productivity to firms (Spence 1973). Moreover, varying investment costs for firms which supply specific apprenticeships programmes should be considered.

Some implications can be derived from our study. At the political level, it seems reasonable to talk less about the training system as such, but to take a more differentiated perspective that addresses the level of training occupations or occupational segments. While some training occupations seem to have little need for policy intervention, other occupations from where people largely enter precarious employment do. Targeted interventions therefore seem to make more sense than across-the-board reform. For future research on collective skill systems, it is worthwhile to further elaborate the segmentation lines within the system. This applies not only to divisions between firms, but also to occupational divisions. A more differentiated view may also advance research that deals with the competitive relationship between vocational secondary education and tertiary education (Graf 2018). Which occupations will the dual system and universities compete for in the future?

References

Alda, H., and D. Rohrbach-Schmidt. 2011. 'BIBB-FDZ Daten- und Methoden-berichte. Nr. 2/2011. Imputation fehlender Werte für die Einkommensvariable in der BIBB/BAuA-Erwerbstätigenbefragung 2006'. Bonn: Bundesinstitut für Berufsbildung.

Allmendinger, J. 1989. 'Educational Systems and Labor Market Outcomes'. *European Sociological Review 5* (3): 231–50.

Andersen, R., and H. G. van de Werfhorst. 2010. 'Education and Occupational Status in 14 Countries: The Role of Educational Institutions and Labour Market Coordination'. *British Journal of Sociology, 61* (2): 336–55.

Autor, D., F. Levy, and R. Murnane. 2003. 'The Skill Content of Recent Technological Change: An Empirical Exploration'. *The Quarterly Journal of Economics 118* (4): 1279–333.

Avent-Holt, D., L. Henriksen, A. Hägglund, J. Jung, N. Kodama, S. Melzer, E. Mun, A. Rainey, and D. Tomaskovic-Devey. 2020. 'Occupations, Workplaces or Jobs? An Exploration of Stratification Contexts Using Administrative Data'. *Research in Social Stratification and Mobility 70*: 1–14.

Bundesinstitut für Berufsbildung. 2019. *Datenreport zum Berufsbildungsbericht 2019.* Informationen und Analysen zur Entwicklung der beruflichen Bildung, Bonn: BIBB.

Bundesinstitut für Berufsbildung. 2020. *Informationen zu Aus- und Fortbildungsberufen.* Available at: https://www.bibb.de/dienst/berufesuche/de/index_berufesuche.php/certificate_supplements/de [Accessed 16 October 2020]

Breen, R. 2005. 'Explaining Cross-national Variation in Youth Unemployment: Market and Institutional Factors'. *European Sociological Review 21* (2): 125–34.

Brzinsky-Fay, C. 2007. 'Lost in Transition? Labour Market Entry Sequences of School Leavers in Europe'. *European Sociological Review 23* (4): 409–22.

Busemeyer, M. R., and C. Trampusch. 2012. *The Comparative Political Economy of Collective Skill Systems*. Oxford: Oxford University Press.

Cairnes, J. E. 1874. *Some Leading Principles of Political Economy Newly Expounded*, New York: Harper & Brothers.

DiPrete, T. A., P. M. De Graaf, R. Luijkx, M. Tahlin, and H. P. Blossfeld. 1997. 'Collectivist versus Individualist Mobility Regimes? Structural Change and Job Mobility'. *American Journal of Sociology 103* (2): 318–58.

Ebner, C. 2013. *Erfolgreich in den Arbeitsmarkt? Die duale Berufsausbildung im internationalen Vergleich*. Frankfurt/ New York: Campus.

Ebner, C. 2015. 'Labour Market Developments and their Significance for VET in Germany: An Overview'. *Research in Comparative and International Education 10* (4): 576–92.

Estevez-Abe, M., T. Iversen, and D. Soskice. 2001. 'Social Protection and the Formation of Skills: A Reinterpretation of the Welfare State'. In *Varieties of Capitalism: The Institutional Foundations of Comparative Advantage*, edited by P. Hall and D. Soskice, pp. 145–83. Oxford: Oxford University Press.

Eurostat. 2020. 'Living Conditions'. In *Eurostat Regional Yearbook*, 2020 edition. Luxembourg: Publications Office of the European Union.

Gangl, M. 2001. 'European Patterns of Labour Market Entry: A Dichotomy of Occupationalized vs. Non-occupationalized Systems?' *European Societies 3* (4): 471–94.

Gangl, M. 2002. 'Changing Labour Markets and Early Career Outcomes: Labour Market Entry in Europe over the Past Decade'. *Work, Employment and Society 16* (1): 67–90.

Gangl, M. 2004. 'Institutions and the Structure of Labour Market Matching in the United States and West Germany'. *European Sociological Review 20* (3): 171–87.

Graf, L. 2018. 'Combined Modes of Gradual Change: The Case of Academic Upgrading and Declining Collectivism in German Skill Formation'. *Socio-Economic Review 16* (1): 185–205.

Greinert, W. 2005. *Mass Vocational Education and Training in Europe: Classical Models of the 19th Century and Training in England, France and Germany during the First Half of the 20th*. Cedefop Panorama series 118, Luxembourg: Office for Official Publications of the European Communities.

Greinert, W. 2006. 'Geschichte der Berufsausbildung in Deutschland'. In *Handbuch der Berufsbildung*, edited by A. von Rolf and A. Lipsmeier, pp. 499–508. 2.

überarbeitete und aktualisierte Auflage. Wiesbaden: VS Verlag für Sozialwissenschaften.

Hall, A. 2007. 'Tätigkeiten, berufliche Anforderungen und Qualifikationsniveau in Dienstleistungsberufen—Empirische Befunde auf Basis der BIBB/BAuA-Erwerbstätigenbefragung 2006 und des Mikrozensus'. In *Qualifikationsentwicklung im Dienstleistungsbereich. Herausforderungen für das duale System der Berufsausbildung*, edited by G. Walden, pp. 153–208. Bielefeld: Bundesinstitut für Berufsbildung.

Hall, A., L. Hünefeld, and D. Rohrbach-Schmidt. 2020. 'BIBB/BAuA Employment Survey of the Working Population on Qualification and Working Conditions in Germany 2018. SUF_1.0, SV_1.0'; Research Data Center at BIBB (ed.); doi:10.7803/501.18.1.1.10, doi:10.7803/501.18.1.5.10.

Haupt, A., and C. Ebner 2020. 'Occupations and Inequality: Theoretical Perspectives and Mechanisms'. *Kölner Zeitschrift für Soziologie und Sozialpsychologie 72*: 19–40.

Henning, F.-W. 1996. *Handbuch der Wirtschafts- und Sozialgeschichte Deutschlands. Band 2: Deutsche Wirtschafts- und Sozialgeschichte im 19. Jahrhundert*. Paderborn, Munich, Vienna, Zürich: Ferdinand Schöningh.

Hope, D., and A. Martelli 2019. 'The Transition to the Knowledge Economy, Labor Market Institutions, and Income Inequality in Advanced Democracies'. *World Politics 71*(2): 236–88.

Jovanovic, B., and P. Rousseau. 2005. *General Purpose Technologies*. NBER Working Paper No. 11093. Available at http://www.nber.org/papers/w11093.

Klauder, W. 1990. *Ohne Fleiß kein Preis. Die Arbeitswelt der Zukunft*. Zürich: Edition Interfrom.

Lindbeck, A., and D. Snower. 2002. 'The Insider-Outsider Theory: A Survey'. IZA Discussion Paper No. 534.

Liu, Y., and D. Grusky 2013. 'The Payoff to Skill in the Third Industrial Revolution'. *American Journal of Sociology 118* (5): 1330–74.

Longhi, S., and M. Brynin. 2010. 'Occupational Change in Britain and Germany'. *Labour Economics 17* (4): 655–66.

Lutz, B., and W. Sengenberger. 1974. *Arbeitsmarktstrukturen und öffentliche Arbeitsmarktpolitik*. Göttingen: Verlag Otto Schwartz & Co.

Marsden, D. 1990. 'Institutions and Labour Mobility: Occupational and Internal Labour Markets in Britain, France, Italy and West Germany'. In *Labour Relations and Economic Performance*, edited by R. Brunetta and C. Dell'Arringa, pp. 414–38. London: Palgrave Macmillan.

Maurice, M., F. Sellier, and J.-J. Silvestre. 1986. *The Social Foundations of Industrial Power: A Comparison of France and Germany*. Cambridge, MA: MIT Press.

Menze, L. 2017. 'Horizontale und vertikale Adäquanz im Anschluss an die betriebliche Ausbildung in Deutschland. Zur Bedeutung von Merkmalen des Ausbildungsberufs'. *Kölner Zeitschrift für Soziologie und Sozialpsychologie 69*: 79–107.

Müller, W., and Y. Shavit 1998. 'The Institutional Embeddedness of the Stratification Process: A Comparative Study of Qualifications and Occupations in Thirteen Countries'. In *From School to Work: A Comparative Study of Educational Qualifications and Occupational Destinations*, edited by Y. Shavit and W. Müller, pp. 1–47. Oxford: Calderon Press.

Paulus, W., and B. Matthes, 2013: The German Classification of Occupations 2010 - Structure, Coding and Conversion Table. FDZ-Methodenreport, 08/2013, Bundesagentur für Arbeit: Nürnberg. Available at: https://doku.iab.de/fdz/reporte/2013/MR_08-13_EN.pdf

Polanyi, M. 1966. *The Tacit Dimension*. Chicago: University of Chicago Press.

Quintini, G., and T. Manfredi. 2009. *Going Separate Ways? School-to-work Transitions in the United States and Europe*. OECD Social, Employment and Migration Working Paper No. 90. Paris: OECD.

Rinneberg, K.-J. 1985. *Das betriebliche Ausbildungswesen in der Zeit der industriellen Umgestaltung Deutschlands*. Cologne: Böhlau.

Rohrbach, D. 2009. 'Sector Bias and Sector Dualism: The Knowledge Society and Inequality'. *International Journal of Comparative Sociology 50* (5–6): 510–36.

Saar, E., M. Unt, and I. Kogan 2008. 'Transition from Educational System to Labour Market in the European Union: A Comparison between New and Old Members'. *International Journal of Comparative Sociology 49* (1): 31–59.

Scherer, S. 2001. 'Early Career Patterns: A Comparison of Great Britain and West Germany'. *European Sociological Review 17* (2): 119–44.

Spence, M. 1973. 'Job Market Signaling'. *The Quarterly Journal of Economics 87* (3): 355–74.

Stooß, F. 1985. 'Verliert der "Beruf" seine Leitfunktion für die Integration der Jugend in die Gesellschaft?' *Mitteilungen aus der Arbeitsmarkt- und Berufsforschung (MittAB) 18* (2): 198–208.

Stratmann, K. W. 1993. *Die gewerbliche Lehrlingserziehung in Deutschland. Modernisierungsgeschichte der betrieblichen Berufsbildung. Band 1: Berufserziehung in der ständischen Gesellschaft (1648–1806)*. Frankfurt: Gesellschaft z. Förd. Arbeitsorient. Forsch. u. Bild.

Streeck, W. 1991. 'On the Social and Political Conditions of Diversified Quality Production'. In *Beyond Keynesianism*, edited by E. Matzner and W. Streeck, pp. 21–61. Cheltenham: Edward Elgar.

Thelen, K. 2004. *How Institutions Evolve. The Political Economy of Skills in Germany, Britain, the United States, and Japan*. Cambridge: Cambridge University Press.

Thelen, K., and M. Busemeyer. 2012. 'Institutional Change in German Vocational Training: From Collectivism toward Segmentalism'. In *The Comparative Political Economy of Collective Skill Systems*, edited by M. Busemeyer and C. Trampusch, pp. 68–100. Oxford: Oxford University Press.

Tiemann, M., H.-J. Schade, R. Helmrich, A. Hall, U. Braun, and P. Bott 2008. *Berufsfeld-Definitionen des BIBB auf Basis der Klassifikation der Berufe 1992*. Wissenschaftliche Diskussionspapiere 105. Bonn: Bundesinstitut für Berufsbildung. Available at https://www.bibb.de/veroeffentlichungen/de/publication/show/2080 [Accessed 29 March 2017].

Vicari, B., and S. Unger. 2020. 'No Way out or No Way in? The Effect of Standardization, Licensing, and Skills Specificity of the Initial and Target Occupations on Status Mobility'. *Kölner Zeitschrift für Soziologie und Sozialpsychologie 72*: 135–56.

Volti, R. 2008. *An Introduction to the Sociology of Work and Occupations*. Thousand Oaks: Pine Forge Press.

Weeden, K., and D. Grusky 2005. 'The Case for a New Class Map'. *American Journal of Sociology 111* (1): 141–212.

Wolbers, M. 2003. 'Job Mismatches and their Labour-market Effects among School-leavers in Europe'. *European Sociological Review 19* (3): 249–66.

Zika, G., R. Helmrich, T. Maier, M. Hummel, M. Kalinowski, C. Hänisch, M. Wolter, and T. Drosdowski. 2012. 'In der Arbeitszeit steckt noch eine Menge Potenzial. Qualifikations- und Berufsfeldprojektionen bis 2030'. *IAB-Kurzbericht* 18: 1–11. Nürnberg: Institut für Arbeitsmarkt- und Berufsforschung.

Appendix

Table 2.1A Descriptive sample statistics

Dependent variables	
Low-wage employment	0.125 (0.331)
Low-skilled job	0.154 (0.361)
Temporary employment	0.081 (0.273)
Control variables	
School-leaving certificate	
Hauptschule	0.337 (0.473)
Realschule	0.502 (0.500)
Abitur	0.161 (0.368)
School-leaving grade	2.439 (0.649)
Labour market experience (in years)	21.79 (11.77)
Male	0.567 (0.496)
Migration background	0.156 (0.363)
Career orientation (strong = 1/not strong = 0)	0.322 (0.467)
Graduate cohorts	
Cohort 1960–1989	0.395 (0.489)
Cohort 1990–2018	0.605 (0.489)
Cohort 1960–1989 (West Germany)	0.325 (0.469)
Cohort 1960–1989 (East Germany)	0.069 (0.253)
Cohort 1990–2018 (West Germany)	0.490 (0.500)
Cohort 1990–2018 (East Germany)	0.116 (0.320)
Region	
Work place region (West Germany)	0.833 (0.373)
Sectors	
Public service	0.136 (0.343)
Industry	0.267 (0.442)
Crafts	0.157 (0.364)
Trade	0.145 (0.352)
Other services	0.236 (0.425)
Other economic sector	0.044 (0.205)
Trade unions, interest groups, associations, chambers, clubs	0.015 (0.122)

Continued

Table 2.1A *Continued*

Dependent variables	
Firm size classes	
1–9 employees	0.135 (0.342)
10–49 employees	0.270 (0.444)
50–249 employees	0.260 (0.439)
250–1000 employees	0.336 (0.472)
N	3,460

Source: BIBB/BAuA-Employment Survey 2018.
Note: Mean coefficients are reported and the standard deviation (sd) is shown in parentheses.
Mean values are weighted by sample weight.

3
Reshaping the Role of Professional Associations and the Federal State in Swiss VET

Ambiguous Reactions to the Knowledge Economy

Regula Bürgi, Philipp Eigenmann, and Philipp Gonon

3.1 Introduction

'Is the dual system of vocational education and training with its standard-ised vocations an outdated model impeding the transition to a knowledge society or is it the secret that will secure Germany's future competitiveness?' (Bosch 2014: 1). This question asked by Gerhard Bosch, an internationally renowned vocational education researcher, is by no means new. The 'erosion of professions' and the vocational education and training system (VET) has been a recurring topic in debates since the 1960s (Baethge and Baethge-Kinsky 1998: 461; Seifried et al. 2019). While recent studies have criticized those sceptical of VET's future for their narrow focus on the economy (e.g. supply for a qualified workforce) and point out the multiple dimensions contained within the concept of a profession (such as socialization and identity formation) (Jørgensen 2013; Ziegler 2015), Bosch (2014: 1) pins the survival of vocational training on how 'open to reform the social partners sustaining the system are'.

It is precisely the governance level that this chapter addresses, although it is less interested in the intentions of the social partners than in their responses to the reforms necessitated by the knowledge economy. While there is considerable research studying the macro governance level in Germany (e.g. Graf 2012; Thies 2015), Austria (Ebner and Nicolai 2011), and Switzerland (Emmenegger and Seitzl 2019; Renold et al. 2019; Berner 2013), there is a dearth of systematic studies examining the responses and changes on the

Regula Bürgi, Philipp Eigenmann, and Philipp Gonon, *Reshaping the Role of Professional Associations and the Federal State in Swiss VET*. In: *Collective Skill Formation in the Knowledge Economy*. Edited by Giuliano Bonoli and Patrick Emmenegger, Oxford University Press. © Oxford University Press (2022). DOI: 10.1093/oso/9780192866257.003.0003 micro level (individual firms) and on the meso level, namely among the professional associations (Strebel et al. 2021).

Our study aims to provide a meso-level perspective by focusing on professional associations in Switzerland, a country that exemplifies collective skill formation (CSF). In contrast to liberal and statist skill formation systems, collective systems organize professional knowledge and skills cooperatively, bringing together both state and private actors (Busemeyer and Trampusch 2012; see also Bonoli and Emmenegger (Chapter 1), in this volume). In Switzerland, state actors consist of the federal authorities (responsible for strategic governance) and the cantons (responsible for the implementation of VET). The private actors belong to intermediary associations, such as professional associations that are in charge of determining the structure and curricula of vocational training. Each occupation (approximately 230) has—approved by the federal state—at least one responsible intermediary or professional association (Emmenegger et al. 2019a: 5–7).[1]

The central questions of this chapter are: how have the challenges of the knowledge economy, such as rapidly changing skill profiles or ever-rising demands for upskilling (SBFI 2017; see Bonoli and Emmenegger (Chapter 1), in this volume), altered Swiss collective governance in VET and, in particular, what implications do the reforms have for professional associations? We argue that the changes in the VET system include both self-preserving and transformative elements, thus are ambiguous in character. While some elements have transformative effects, others express continuity due to path-dependent developments (Thelen 2004).

In his seminal work *Institutional Change and Globalization*, John Campbell (2004) discusses the problem of institutional change and offers a differentiated view on diverse modes of change and the temptation of the researchers to overstate disrupting changes on the one hand and evolutionary developments on the other hand. He characterizes changes as 'constrained innovation' (Campbell 2004: 173), which means that institutions include bundles of dimensions, which contain contradictory and conflicting logics. Thus, inconsistency in the light of stability and instability is often part of changing institutions. That is why researchers stress either the self-preserving elements or the more transformative ones. We argue in this chapter that both elements are crucial. Furthermore, the knowledge economy requires transformative measures in order to keep the existing system stable.

---

[1] For the sake of readability, we use in the following only the term professional associations since all responsible intermediary associations in our case studies are professional associations.

In our case the relation between professional associations and the federal state was modified. The transformative developments increase standardization as well as the influence of the state. The self-preserving and path-dependent elements become evident by leaving the lead for the single occupations with the professional associations. In this case, decentralized organization of VET—as it is characteristic for CSF—continues. This results in a variety of governance modes depending upon established or path-dependent practices of cooperation and institutionalized ways of thinking within the professional associations (Bürgi and Gonon 2021). In a nutshell, we argue that the reactions to the knowledge economy circle around the conflicting poles of standardization (read centralization) on the one hand and persistent diversity (read continued differences) on the other.

To develop this argument, the chapter focuses on the processes that accompany the reforms that emerged in the wake of the 2002 Berufsbildungsgesetz (Federal Act on Vocational and Professional Education and Training). The legislation was passed in response to a shortage of apprenticeship positions in the 1990s and sought to improve, amongst other things, permeability and flexibility. Its goal was to optimize vocational education along with its collective governance. The reforms were designed to ensure that vocational training could keep pace with the rapid technological changes of the ever-expanding knowledge economy (Berner 2013).

While our consideration of the macro level draws primarily on secondary literature, our analysis of the meso level is based on the Kommissionen Berufsentwicklung und Qualität (B&Q commissions, enabling 'vocational development and quality'). These commissions are considered the 'heart' of collective governance in Switzerland. In the aftermath of the new legislation in 2002, every professional association responsible for a vocation has created a B&Q commission bringing together private and state actors in ways specific to the respective vocations. A commission's main task is to periodically evaluate the vocational training in the respective vocation and adapt it to the changing demands of the world of work. B&Q commissions are key for shaping the vocations' structure and regulations because they define and negotiate the standards required for the respective professions, which are then laid down in a training regulation for each profession. They represent a distinctive feature of collective governance in Switzerland since other countries with CSF lack such entities. Their functions are in Germany, for example, most likely to be performed by the chambers (Emmenegger et al. 2019a). Based upon an analysis of B&Q commissions' composition and their ways of working, the chapter sheds light on the implications of knowledge-economy reforms for professional associations.

The study draws upon the professions' regulations produced by the B&Q commissions as well as eleven in-depth expert interviews with the chairwomen (n = 1) and chairmen (n = 10) of the commissions.[2] We focus on the two occupational fields of food services and electrotechnology.[3] Both fields operate regionally and internationally and are undergoing considerable technological changes. Furthermore, the occupations represented in those fields are quite heterogeneous with regard to the required skills and the number of trainees.[4] In the field of food services, there are six responsible associations and in the field of electrotechnology, there are five different associations that are accountable for the respective occupations, and accordingly for the compositions and tasks of the B&Q commissions. The associations differ in terms of size and also in terms of professionalization—some have up to twenty-one full-time employees, others are staffed on an entirely part-time basis.

This chapter consists of four sections. In the first, we present the theoretical assumptions of our argument. In the second, we focus on the reform effects the knowledge economy has had at the macro level before analysing in the next section the changes' implications at the meso level of the B&Q commissions. We show that the reform processes have paradoxical effects, which we call 'standardized diversity'. Finally, we conclude with a discussion of the most important implications for both the macro and meso levels when it comes to Swiss vocational training and the knowledge economy.

3.2 Institutional paths and incremental changes in collective skill formation systems

The knowledge economy poses a challenge for VET. The notion of apprenticeship and VET is changing not only in countries that have adopted CSF systems, but everywhere in Europe (Markowitsch and Wittig 2020). The knowledge economy strengthens state-based and standardized regulation

[2] Each interview lasted between one and one-and-a-half-hours. Interviews took place between March and December 2018 in the premises of the associations or companies. One was conducted at the University of Zurich. The interviews were semi-structured and consisted of open questions (to get information on the characteristics of cooperative practices) as well as problem-oriented sequences (in order to extract information on the underlying reasonings) (Kruse 2015; Helfferich 2011). The interviews are fully transcribed and coded.

[3] All certified occupations in Switzerland are categorized in an occupational field, see Schweizerisches Dienstleistungszentrum Berufsbildung / Berufs-, Studien und Laufbahnberatung SDBB (2018). The occupational field 'food services' (n = 6) includes occupations from the sub-fields of nutrition and food technology. The occupational field 'electrotechnology' (n = 5) includes occupations from the sub-fields of electrical installation and electronics.

[4] In total there are six occupations in the occupational field of nutrition (n) and ten in the occupational field of electrotechnology (e). In 2016, four (1n + 3e) of them had more than 600 apprentices, seven (2n + 5e) had 100 to 600 and five had less than 100 apprentices (3n + 2e) (SBFI 2020).

to make VET systems more permeable within comprehensive educational frameworks. As Iversen and Soskice (2019) argue, the knowledge economy has reoriented capitalism towards more uncertainty, calling for greater flexibility and education. In this respect, the knowledge economy endorses academic drift. This affects VET, which has to adapt to individuals seeking higher-skill career choices. Rising skill demands and the call for greater flexibility has made it more difficult for small- and medium-sized enterprises as well as professional associations to maintain their dominant role in VET. Large enterprises have much more resources to address these changes. Thus, a growing divide between big firms and professional associations becomes visible. Learning a profession, long a goal of many, has lost its allure along with its specificity. In Switzerland, the traditional model of VET is being 'optimized' to fit changing conditions (Gonon 1998: 321).

Another challenge to CSF systems is technological change. As Hall and Soskice (2001: 40) state more generally, these systems are better in supporting 'incremental innovation' due to the highly coordinated relationships between industries and corporate structures, which rely on strategic alliances. This governance model provides a mix of company-specific and general technical skills. Nevertheless, technological change increases the complexity of the governance in CSF systems: while a strong state is still required, professional associations are defining new tasks and organizing collective cooperation as they modify the curricula. At the same time, permeability within the education system is being fostered to shore up the existing model.

In this chapter, we argue that VET has changed in response to the knowledge economy, as the actors within it have started to modify its institutional core. These adaptation processes are important to stave off greater reform pressures and perhaps the fading out of VET itself. We examine how the professional associations moderate the challenges of the knowledge economy to find a compromise between governing diverse employers' claims and implementing new regulations within a common framework for a more flexible VET system. Thus, such a reinterpretation and redefinition of existing institutions aims to respond to the ongoing technological and economic change, trying to avoid or minimize inefficiencies or dysfunctionality (Mahoney and Thelen 2010). In Switzerland, the creation of B&Q commissions, which includes federal and cantonal state actors as well as professional associations, represents precisely such a decisive compromise (GPK NR 2015: 6896).

VET as an institution in Switzerland has changed gradually over time. From a historical perspective, the aims of the changes were less about modifying the core framework than reproducing or reinforcing it (Van der Heijden 2013: 7). The path of VET in Switzerland began with the first vocational education act in 1930 and has strengthened ever since. Hence, actors in VET have a basic interest in maintaining this model. It is based on processes of learning that value apprenticeships and partnership between educational institutions and professional trades (Arnold 2013: 41). Nevertheless, the 'golden age' of apprenticeship, when workers went on to have careers at the company that trained them, is coming to an end. What is emerging in its place is a hybrid model that integrates occupation-oriented professional training combined with more formal classroom education. Hence, feedback effects do not necessarily reproduce the original system (Thelen 2003: 295). Whether this new governance will lead to a segmentalist system, as Thelen and Buse-meyer (2008) argue for the German case, is another question. As we show below, the more likely scenario for Switzerland is that more standardized governance structures will administer diverse fields of vocational education, though the principle of collective management will remain quite stable.

3.3 Reshaping governance driven by knowledge economy

The development of vocational education in Switzerland is based on incremental reforms. In particular, the changes to the vocational educational law from 2002 were far more gradual than disruptive. Swiss legislators did not question the principle of CSF when figuring out how to adapt VET to the new economic and technological demands of the knowledge economy. The latest reforms confirmed the strong role of professional associations to determine the curricula for individual vocational programmes while standardizing strategic executive authority at the federal level. Yet the framework defined at the federal level produced very different responses among the individual professional associations.

In describing these different responses to the changing demands of vocational education and federal guidelines, we will first outline and classify the measures taken at the macro level. The main macro-level change in the last decades was the reform of the Swiss vocational educational law in 2002. It had three objectives: make vocational education more attractive by increasing its permeability, ensure the compatibility of vocational qualifications in Europe, and prepare VET for the knowledge economy. In the negotiations leading up to the reforms, legislators aimed to improve the existing dual system so that it could meet the demands of economic and technological change, in particular rising skill demands and changing skill profiles within occupations. The main way of achieving this was to create more demanding VET

programmes for skilled occupations with a large share of classroom education (Berner 2013: 44), but not to abandon the path of dual apprenticeship
and collective responsibilities on skill formation.

The literature is ambiguous about the question whether the Swiss reforms
have strengthened the role of the federal state in VET governance or have
helped maintain the collective governance model. On the one hand, the
2002 legislation enhanced federal responsibilities, especially the strategic
governance of VET (Berner 2013: 47). Moreover, the law puts the VET programmes in care, social work, and the arts under the strategic governance of
the federal VET authorities (Trampusch 2010: 199). Though federal authorities took on elements of strategic governance, the professional associations
on the other hand continue to be responsible for shaping existing curricula
and creating new ones. In particular, professional associations in the sectors
of care, social work, and the arts had to be established to meet the governance principles for new VET programmes in their sectors according to the
federal law. This process supported collective governance by strengthening
the responsibility of the professional associations for VET in their occupations. In the case of new professions, such as in the field of information and
communications technology (ICT), the reforms have led to the creation of
new professional associations responsible for initial VET (Maurer 2013). The
reforms affected the cooperation between federal authorities and the social
partners, as it streamlined strategic components at the federal level while
entrusting the design of VET to the professional associations. According to
these ambiguous findings, Christine Trampusch thus classifies the reform as
an 'incremental and self-preserving change' (Trampusch 2010: 198).

The reform of the vocational education law in 2002 was ultimately a reform
of VET governance. At its core, the reform established a quality assurances
system and thus a new steering element in Swiss VET governance. In the
following, we discuss this quality assurance system at the macro and meso
levels. In the spirit of New Public Management—typical for the political
reforms in the public sector at the time—quality assurance was accompanied by an emphasis on outputs and outcomes (Bolder et al. 2017). Since
the 1990s, quality has represented one of the central modes of governance
in education (Klieme and Tippelt 2008; Gonon 2017). The specific quality
assurance instrument we address here was no external quality monitoring.
Rather it was a call by the federal authorities to the professional associations
to advance quality assurance from the bottom up. These instruments were
meant to meet the challenges of rising skill demands and changing skill profiles within occupations as they promise to respond faster to new realities and
challenges.

Hence, it was designed to strengthen responsibility both at the federal level and in the individual professional associations. Federal authorities strove to standardize the basic principles of vocational education (e.g. the dual system in basic vocational education) and defined the formal guidelines for ensuring quality assurance. It placed responsibility for evaluating and regulating VET curricula with the professional associations and put the monitoring of those evaluations in the hands of the federal authorities. Leaving the regulation of VET programmes to the professional associations and supervising their action is paradigmatic of how a state organizes a collective governance of skill formation. Nevertheless, it is also much more a core element of a new governance in education that arose in the 1990s.

The processes of quality assurance in education are paradigmatic for the logic of new governance in education. The higher-level governance defines the strategic objectives and concepts, which provides a standardized framework within which lower-level governance can determine specific forms of implementation. This is especially true for the question of how to prepare the great variety of VET programmes for the economic and technological demands of the future. Giving leeway to professional associations is conceptually meant to help adapt the occupations and professions faster and more accurately to technological changes than in a top-down process.

Accordingly, the vocational education law of 2002 does not specify how the professional associations should implement the quality assurance objectives (BBG 2002 Art. 8). It is only the directive on vocational education that names specific 'commissions for vocational development and quality' (B&Q commissions), each of which must have at least one federal representative on its board and respect the different language areas of the country (BBV 2003 Art. 12). The function and operation of the commissions were determined by guidelines jointly developed by the federal authorities, the cantons, and employer associations. These guidelines extended the pool of B&Q participants to the VET schools and the cantons[5] and entrust the B&Q commissions with periodically adapting VET programmes to the demands of the world of work (SGV et al. 2014: 3). All other aspects are defined in the educational directives of the individual professions. However, they are surprisingly uniform with regard to the rules governing evaluation: in each case, the educational regulations of the individual professions must be evaluated

---

[5] The VET schools and the cantons are not within the focus of this article. However, the governing role of both actors changed with the new federal act, issued in 2002. First insights indicate that the influence of the schools was shrinking for the benefit of the professional associations. On the contrary, the voices of the cantons were strengthened by integrating them into the B&Q commissions (Bonoli and Notter 2016; Fleischmann 2012).

every five years. The federal authorities determine the formal structures and standardize how the B&Q commissions are to complete their tasks. But this still leaves much room for the various ways in which these commissions carry out their work based on the institutional traditions of their professional associations.

In this sense, the case of the B&Q commissions contrasts with the general tendency towards a gradual de-collectivization of CSF systems (see Bonoli and Emmenegger (Chapter 1), in this volume). Indeed, the B&Q commissions represent an attempt to stabilize collective governance in Switzerland, implying a continued reliance on decentralized collective governance by institutionalizing close cooperation between the federal authorities, the cantons and professional associations for every profession. However, the B&Q commissions are at the same time a sign of standardization (every professional association has to convene the meetings) and the mandatory inclusion of a federal state's representative also implies a moment of centralized control of the professional association's work. Hence, the creation of the B&Q commissions epitomizes the ambiguous reactions—standardization and persisting diversity—in VET governance to the challenges of knowledge economy. How this ambiguity is implemented by professional associations' creations of B&Q commissions and their ways of working is outlined in the following sections.

3.4 Standardized diversity among professional associations

It is argued in this section that the B&Q commissions have to negotiate between two conflicting poles, namely standardization and persistent diversity. As federal regulations prescribe certain aspects of the B&Q commissions, VET governance has become on the one hand more standardized. On the other hand, in particular with regard to the heterogenous composition of the B&Q commissions and their different ways of working, a remarkable diversity within VET governance persists. These two strands are outlined in the following.

3.4.1 The standardization of governance approaches

In the wake of the 2002 legislation and in response to the challenges of the knowledge economy, the federal authorities introduced processes to structure and standardize VET governance, such as the B&Q commissions, five-year evaluations, and guidelines for vocational development. Although the constellation of actors that make up the collective governance did not change per se, these newly introduced elements had a transformative effect. Many interviewees stressed the positive sides of the new instruments—such as more strategic planning and assistance, the regular rethinking of education, a rejuvenation of quality assurance commissions, and a stronger nationwide network. But in both fields, B&Q experts maintained that the standardization, resulting in short reform cycles, growing amount of paperwork, and growing federal authority, challenges professional associations, in particular the ones relying mostly on voluntary participation, i.e. non-professional structures.

Neither the vocational education act nor the vocational education directive stipulates that the VET programmes must be assessed (and if needed adjusted) every five years. Nevertheless, an informal consensus has emerged that it is the task of the B&Q commissions to evaluate the educational structures and curricula over a five-year cycle. The federal authorities can steer this process by providing financial incentives. For example, they have decided to discuss professional associations' funding for quality assessment only every five years.

The interviewed experts believed that this has altered the direction from which pressure to change or adapt flows. Before, the pressure came more from within the branch, while today it comes from outside the branch, specifically from the federal authority (SBFI; that has the power to issue the educational regulations) to the professional associations (Interview G). This reversal also expresses itself in the fact that the federal representatives only welcome changes every five years, and not before (SBBK 2017: 19). Most associations in the field report difficulties in coping with the five-year assessment cycle, in involving the firms that carry out the vocational training, and thus, in ensuring the implementation of educational reforms. One expert stressed: 'Some people just refuse to participate. It's as if before finishing the house one starts drawing up new plans. This leaves us feeling overwhelmed' (Interview G). The same person reports that the pressure has doubled as the knowledge economy has expanded:

The wheel is spinning faster and faster. It is clear that technology changes. We have the same thing in our firm. Industry 4.0. This is chasing us. Do we have to put the entire education programme on its head each time? Is this necessary for the profession? (Interview G)

Thus the reform cycle is a challenge, especially in B&Q commissions whose professional associations still rely on volunteer participation without a professionalized structure. Assessment and vocational development processes require numerous steps, including an extensive, time-consuming survey of the training companies and trainees:

> And we know how it is today with work. And we have enough to do in our *job*. And then on the side I am supposed to spend *days* outside work and say 'I have to work for the association' and then I can complete this stuff. [. . .] One person with a small business [. . .] was totally overwhelmed. (Interview H)

More and more, the professional associations rely on professionalized administrative structures. Along with the effort required, the paperwork assumes specialized knowledge, which is why most professional associations outsource assessment and vocational development tasks to external experts. Since the plans detailing the methods of education have gone from being heterogenous to following a standardized regime, the professional associations have been required to use pedagogical support in order to complete their work (Maurer and Pieneck 2013: 90).

The specific knowledge that requires the outsourcing of certain tasks and the specific terminology that goes along with it complicates the communication between the state and professional associations as well as the exchange with trainers in the firms. For instance, one interviewee noted that some of the wording in the template of the federal questionnaires for the professional association's representatives was incomprehensible. As a result, the interviewee expected a lack of understanding and acceptance in the companies and feared a low volume of returned questionnaires (Interview G). The specific knowledge, the language codes, and the large time demands have restricted the circle of actively involved individuals, leading to an accumulation of influence of certain associations and firms (Bürgi and Gonon 2019).

Overall, the interviewees characterized the federal specifications and rules as extremely detailed ('everything is prescribed' [Interview F]), rigid, and authoritarian: 'Good, we of course know if the federal representative says no, then [laughter] . . . then we have to repack it again, that's for sure' (Interview E). As a result, the experts criticized the lack of attention given to the specific needs of the respective professions, and the way large and small professions are handled in the same way.

The closely set, standardized evaluation phases for ensuring that education keeps pace with technological developments is at odds with the bottom-up governing approach and runs the risk of preventing professional associations from responding quickly to the specific needs of their professions. That's why some professional associations think of a more modular approach to VET that does not require federal approval and increases the scope and authority of the professional associations (Interview D), hence circumventing the standardized procedures.

3.4.2 Persistent diversity

Despite the increasing levels of standardization and federal authority, we have identified areas of freedom in the professional associations for the two occupational fields we examined resulting in diverse compositions and ways of working of the B&Q commissions. These differences are due to path dependencies at the meso level, i.e. traditional cooperative practices and ways of thinking of the professional associations. This affects the form and regulations of the respective occupations. Recognizing these effects and their causes is crucial for adjusting vocations to meet the demands of the knowledge economy. The path-dependent diversity is outlined in the following by introducing first the heterogenous composition of the B&Q commissions and second their diverse ways of working.

In contrast to the detailed process guidelines for assessing and developing vocations, the determination of the tasks, voting procedures, and composition of the B&Q commissions is mostly left to the professional associations. Several of the interviewed experts characterized the B&Q commissions as continuations of the vocational development commissions, which were already in place in most cases (Interviews D, E, H, K).

The differing composition of the B&Q commissions is an example of their variety and how traditional cooperative practices are maintained. The vocational training directive requires that one federal representative sit on each B&Q commission and that its composition appropriately reflects the Swiss language areas. But the professional associations are otherwise free to determine the number of commission members and who serves on the commission. As a result, the commissions differ in central aspects, such as the number of persons and associations, the integration of personnel and union representatives, school representatives, number of cantonal representatives and individual companies (most being larger). The same goes for voting procedures, which range from majority decisions to restriction of voting to branch representatives (i.e. excluding school representatives and state delegations), to giving one vote per actor from collective governance—from the federal level, from the canton level, and from the professional association (Bürgi and Gonon 2021).

With regard to the composition of the commissions, what stands out most is the diverging representation of the unions. Compared to Germany, Swiss unions are less integrated into the vocational training policy processes, which is reflected in the low wages received by trainees and in the fewer number of classroom hours (Emmenegger et al. 2019b). More academic training is crucial for the 'upskilling' demanded by the knowledge economy (SBFI 2017; Bonoli and Emmenegger (Chapter 1), in this volume). A look at the meso level of the B&Q commissions shows that the unions shape the individual professions to various degrees. Some B&Q commissions have up to four different unions as members and some have none. For example, one interviewee, when asked whether unions were represented in the commission, said: 'No. What do we need them for?' (Interview A). The differences are attributable to different historical practices. This becomes visible if we consider a profession that includes both traditional trades and industries. In this profession's B&Q commission, the members discussed the issue of unions' participation. Two fronts formed—one from traditional trades and the other from industrial representatives: 'Yes, the trades don't like it, they aren't happy . . . about these things . . . Yes, and the industry is used to working with unions' (Interview F). In other words, different traditional forms of cooperation can fill the standardized B&Q 'glass' with momentous effects on vocational training.

In addition to their composition, the various approaches and decision-making rationales of the B&Q commissions are also important for the design and regulation of the training of the different occupations. Like in the case of the trade unions, these processes are shaped by traditional paths, i.e. cooperative practices and specific rationales. In the following we discuss three examples of such path-dependent diversities in B&Q commissions' ways of working: the merger of professions, changes to the qualification system, and legislative history.

The merger of professions, as a first topic discussed within B&Q commissions, was part of the 2002 reforms. Broader skill profiles through, among other things, the merger of various occupations were expected to be more in line with the quickly developing knowledge economy (Bundesrat 2000; Strebel et al. 2019). The success or failure of such mergers, which entails a division or loss of influence for the respective professional associations, is based only in part on the functional logic of VET; it is also significantly shaped by the institutional legacy of professional associations, as we show in the following.

The interviews with the B&Q expert showed that professional associations are more likely to merge VET programmes when they are taught in the same training facility. One interviewee, explaining the reasons for the merger of two professions, said: 'Historically these professions were taught in the same . . . school' (Interview I). At the forefront of the decision was the availability of infrastructural 'synergies' (Interview I) rather than criteria on a content level. Moreover, the facilities of the professional associations were themselves decisive. For example, one professional association owning a large training site, was not ready to cooperate with another professional association and merge professions until they experienced a massive decline in trainees and needed the cooperation to ensure the continued existence of the training facility (Interview H).

While these examples show how infrastructural circumstances shaped cooperation, the traditional cooperative practices of a branch also play a crucial role as discussions within the B&Q commission reveal. The professional associations aim to strengthen their respective branch and seek collaborations based more on whether professions belong to their branch than on similarities between professional activities. One interviewee describes the merger of two professions: 'The professions had the choice of coming together or weakening our branch' (Interview F). The merger occurred even though one of the professions had more in common with another profession located outside the branch.

Over the course of many years of cooperation, specific rationales emerge that complicate or restrict the possibilities of collaboration:

> But in every branch and we of course are no different, one wants primarily to tend to his own garden, and as *soon* as one shows *too much* openness, there is danger that afterward everything is open. Unless one says, 'Yes, we will join *you*.' But not necessarily when one says, 'Yes, we have decided to think out of the box and are considering doing something on a green field.' Behind that are many structures, much *history*, and staffing details. (Interview F)

Professional associations tend to be cooperative when others are ready to go beyond their own professional identity and 'join', whereas functional cooperation from scratch is limited by historical constraints.

Similar findings that point towards specific styles of reasoning within the different B&Q commissions can be found in the change to the qualification system. The knowledge economy needs skilled workers and at the same time the state has to guarantee an inclusive system. The 2002 reform took this need into account by an 'external measure' (see Bonoli and Emmeneg-ger (Chapter 1) in this volume), i.e. by promoting the creation of a further qualification stage below the most frequent degree known as the Eidgenössis-ches Fähigkeitszeugnis (Federal VET Diploma, or EFZ). It is not mandatory that the professional associations introduce this lower stage, which is called the Eidgenössisches Berufsattest (Federal VET Certificate, or EBA). The professional associations discuss this possibility in the B&Q commissions. Rationales in the form of professional pride shape these decisions in a piv-otal way. EBA learners are considered to have fewer abilities and reduced social skills. One interviewee said that the decision to introduce an EBA is less about ability than about the fact that the historically constructed 'we' makes no place for 'socially weak people' (Interview D). Professional pride and identity—as the example made visible—were mentioned again and again in the interviews, and even cemented with the metaphor of the vocational 'family' (Interview G) that prevents, in this case, a socially inclusive system (see Aerne (Chapter 8), in this volume).

A further institutional legacy that expresses the different ways of work-ing and thinking within the B&Q commissions is legislative history. This category only applies to the field of food services since some professions in the food branch were not integrated into the federal vocational educational law until 2002. Previously, some of the professions were governed in agri-culture law. With the uniform legislation, comprehensive economic reforms such as those required by the knowledge economy can be addressed more quickly. Nevertheless, different legislative histories continue to reverberate in the B&Q design of vocational training (Graf et al. 2021):

> Agricultural professions have a special history in the vocational training world because until the new [legislation came] . . . the cantons were responsible, not the federal authorities, and often it was not with the VET office but with the economy or agriculture. And for this reason, a few differences exist today between let us say *normal* vocational training and vocational training in agriculture. (Interview I; emphasis added)

The differences show themselves in, say, the distribution of training sites. Hence, in these professions it is a tradition (not a requirement) for trainees to visit multiple training sites. To enable this, the classroom hours follow a pro-gressive logic: at the beginning of their vocational training, trainees spend less time in the classroom to make it easier for them to switch from train-ing facility to facility, especially when they are located in different language regions. Trainees then make up the classroom time in the third year of their education. These particularities were explained and justified by traditional rationales, as it was explained: the old regulations for the profession are 'still in people's heads' (Interview F).

These considerations show that although the standardized elements were introduced into the governance architecture of Switzerland, they are performed and interpreted within the B&Q commissions based on the professional associations' institutional legacy, thus in different ways—resulting in a standardized diversity. Hence B&Q commissions centre around two conflicting poles of more state intervention while maintaining at the same time the influence of professional associations.

3.5 Implications and challenges for adapting vocational education and training to the knowledge economy

The question of how Swiss CSF has responded to the challenges of the knowledge economy is twofold: on the one hand, the power of the federal authority has grown via increased standardization processes. On the other, the professional associations have maintained their responsibility and influence resulting in heterogenous modes of governance that become visible in the composition and ways of working of the B&Q commissions. What are the implications of these diametrically opposed processes for adapting VET to the knowledge economy? Where do these trends mark decisive challenges?

As is clear from the analysis of the macro perspective, Swiss VET has not experienced a radical change or break in response to the challenges of the knowledge economy. It retained the three-part structure of actors (professional associations, cantons, federal authority) and with it the collective mode of governance. In this respect, there is no sign of de-collectivization in Swiss VET. Nevertheless, the standardized guidelines and conditions have gathered the strategic processes at the federal level. This standardization is not governed by 'hard laws'. Rather it corresponds to developments caused by 'soft-law' instruments, such as detailed guidelines with regard to vocational development or the quality assessment funding provided ever five years. The introduction of these elements does little to change governance relations prima facie. But it has changed the relationship between the involved actors, i.e. between the federal authorities and the professional associations as we have shown by analysing the B&Q commissions. Although they are informally governed, these 'soft' standardizing developments have produced invasive effects on the workings of professional associations.

The first challenge that accompanies standardization is increasing professionalization. The knowledge economy is a phenomenon that is not restricted to the economy. This is shown not least by the parallel and equally prominent term *knowledge society*. The professional associations thus face within the B&Q commissions a double challenge: on the one hand, they must modify vocational training to prepare graduates for the technological changes at companies. On the other hand, they must generate, process, and implement a specific form of data-based knowledge. The demand for the professionalization of governance presents a difficulty for professional associations, which strongly rely on volunteer participation or non-professional structures, as it is typical for Switzerland. The newly introduced instruments are demanding with regard to time and knowledge (on the level of governance and curricula). Both developments threaten to lower the number of voluntary and broad-based participants. As a result, medium- and large-sized companies, which often have professionalized educational structures, have an easier time participating in B&Q commissions (Bürgi and Gonon 2021). Against the background of small companies providing the majority of training positions (see Wettstein et al. 2017: 109), these dynamics are key challenges for VET in Switzerland.

A second tension associated with the standardization concerns the flexibility of the professional associations. The 2002 legislation was passed to ensure that vocational training can keep pace with the rapid developments of the knowledge economy by evaluating it at regular intervals. Indeed, while the five-year rule motivates professional associations to rethink their training programmes regularly, at the same time it lowers their flexibility to coordinate the instruments and assessment times with the specific needs of their professions.

Finally, the standardization obscures the fact that the professional associations—as it became visible by means of the B&Q commissions—still show a great degree of diversity in governing their training programmes. Any adaptation of VET to the knowledge economy must consider these differences. Traditional cooperative practices and established rationales (i.e. path dependencies) shape the reforms and lead to reinterpretations.

This persistent variety gives a clue to the question we posed at the beginning with regard to the survival of 'standardized professions'. Similar to the answer provided by those who stress the social and psychological importance of professions, we argue that the path to dissolving occupational profiles and introducing 'individual professions' (Voss 2001) cannot be taken even in the face of the knowledge economy, at least as long as professional associations have the task of determining the curricula of vocational training. This stance owes less to their willingness to reform than to their particular institutional legacy.

References

Arnold, Judith. 2013. *Die pfadabhängige Entwicklung im schweizerischen Bildungswesen: der Einfluss des Kulturkampfes auf das Zentralschweizer Bildungssystem, 1882 bis heute.* Zürich: Universität Zürich. Retrieved from https://doi.org/10.5167/uzh-164216.

Baethge, Martin, and Volker Baethge-Kinsky. 1998. 'Jenseits von Beruf und Beruflichkeit? Neue Formen von Arbeitsorganisation und Beschäftigung und ihre Bedeutung für eine zentrale Kategorie gesellschaftlicher Integration'. *Mitteilungen aus der Arbeitsmarkt- und Berufsforschung 31*: 461–72.

Berner, Esther. 2013. '"Verbundpartnerschaft"—Schlagwort oder Erfolgsrezept? Zur Steuerung der schweizerischer Berufsbildung'. In *Herausforderungen für die Berufsbildung in der Schweiz*, edited by Markus Maurer and Philipp Gonon, pp. 37–60. Bern: hep Verlag.

Bolder, Axel, Helmut Bremer, and Rudolf Epping. 2017. *Bildung für Arbeit unter neuer Steuerung.* Wiesbaden: Springer VS.

Bonoli, Lorenzo, and Patricia Notter. 2016. 'Länderstudie Schweiz (Endbericht)'. Projekt 'Entwicklung nationaler Ausbildungsstandards—Akteure, Verfahren und Gestaltung im europäischen Vergleich' geleitet von Philipp Ulmer und Marthe Geiben (Bundesinstitut für Berufsbildung—BIBB). Zollikofen: EHB.

Bosch, Gerhard. 2014. 'Facharbeit, Berufe und berufliche Arbeitsmärkte'. *WSI Mitteilungen 1*: 5–13. Retrieved from https://www.boeckler.de/wsimit_2014_01_bosch.pdf.

Bundesrat. 2000. *Botschaft zu einem neuen Bundesgesetz über die Berufsbildung.* Bern: Bundesblatt.

Bürgi, Regula, and Philipp Gonon. 2019. 'Zwischen Steuerungsoptimierung und Ämterkumulation: Analyse der Kommissionen Berufsentwicklung und Qualität (B&Q)'. SGAB-Newsletter 2. Retrieved from https://www.sgab-srfp.ch/de/newsletter/zwischen-steuerungsoptimierung-und-aemterkumulation.

Bürgi, Regula, and Philipp Gonon. 2021. 'Varieties within a Collective Skill Formation System: How VET Governance in Switzerland Is Shaped by Associations'. *International Journal for Research in Vocational Education and Training 8* (1): 46–64. Retrieved from https://doi.org/10.13152/IJRVET.8.1.3.

Busemeyer, Marius, and Christine Trampusch (eds). 2012. *The Political Economy of Skill Formation.* Oxford: Oxford University Press.

Campbell, John L. 2004. *Institutional Change and Globalization*. Princeton: Princeton University Press.

Ebner, Christian, and Rita Nicolai. 2011. 'Duale oder schulische Berufsausbildung? Entwicklungen und Weichenstellungen in Deutschland, Österreich und der Schweiz'. *Swiss Political Science Review 16* (4): 617–48.

Emmenegger, Patrick, Lukas Graf, and Christine Trampusch. 2019a. 'The Governance of Decentralized Cooperation in Collective Training Systems: A Review and Conceptualization'. *Journal of Vocational Education and Training 71* (1): 21–45.

Emmenegger, Patrick, Lukas Graf, and Alexandra Strebel. 2019b. 'Social versus Liberal Collective Skill Formation Systems? A Comparative-historical Analysis of the Role of Trade Unions in German and Swiss VET'. *European Journal of Industrial Relations 26* (3): 1–16.

Emmenegger, Patrick, and Lina Seitzl. 2019. *Expertenbericht zur systemischen Steuerung der Berufsbildung in der Schweiz*. St. Gallen: SEPS HSG.

Fleischmann, Daniel. 2012. 'Gelebte Verbundpartnerschaft'. *Folio 2:* 22–35.

Gonon, Philipp. 1998. *Das internationale Argument in der Bildungsreform. Die Rolle internationaler Bezüge in den bildungspolitischen Debatten zur schweizerischen Berufsbildung und zur englischen Reform der Sekundarstufe II*. Bern: Peter Lang.

Gonon, Philipp. 2017. 'Quality Doubts as a Driver for Vocational Education and Training (VET) Reforms—Switzerland's Way to a Highly Regarded Apprenticeship System'. In *Vocational Education and Training in Times of Economic Crisis*, edited by Matthias Pilz, pp. 341–54. Basel: Springer.

GPK NR—Geschäftsprüfungskommmission des Nationalrats. 2015. *Qualität der Verbundpartnerschaft in der Berufsbildung*. Bern.

Graf, Lukas. 2012. 'Wachstum in der Nische. Mit dualen Studiengängen entstehen Hybride von Berufs- und Hochschulbildung'. *WZB-Mitteilungen 138*: 49–52.

Graf, Lukas, Alexandra Strebel, and Patrick Emmenegger. 2021. 'State-led Bricolage and the Extension of Collective Governance: Hybridity in the Swiss Skill Formation System'. Regulation *and* Governance. Published online 16 August 2021. Retrieved from https://doi.org/10.1111/rego.12436.

Hall, Peter, and David Soskice. 2001. 'Introduction'. In *Varieties of Capitalism— The Institutional Foundations of Comparative Advantage*, edited by Peter Hall and David Soskice, pp. 1–71. Oxford: Oxford University Press.

Heijden, Jeroen van der. 2013. 'Institutional Layering: A Review of the Use of the Concept'. *Politics 31* (1): 9–18.

Helfferich, Cornelia. 2011. *Die Qualität qualitativer Daten. Manual für die Durchführung qualitativer Interviews*. Wiesbaden: Springer VS.

Iversen, Torben, and David Soskice. 2019. *Democracy and Prosperity: Reinventing Capitalism through a Turbulent Century*. Princeton: University Press.

Jørgensen, Christian H. 2013. 'The Role and Meaning of Vocations in the Transition from Education to Work'. *International Journal of Training Research* 11 (2): 166–83.

Klieme, Eckhard, and Rudolf Tippelt. 2008. *Qualitätssicherung im Bildungswesen. Eine aktuelle Zwischenbilanz*. Weinheim: Beltz.

Kruse, Jan. 2015. *Qualitative Interviewforschung. Ein integrativer Ansatz*. Weinheim: Beltz.

Mahoney, James, and Kathleen Thelen. 2010. 'A Theory of Gradual Institutional Change'. In *Explaining Institutional Change: Ambiguity, Agency, and Power*, edited by James Mahoney and Kathleen Thelen, pp. 1–37. New York: Cambridge University Press.

Markowitsch, Jörg, and Wolfgang Wittig. 2020. 'Understanding Differences between Apprenticeships in Europe: Towards a New Conceptual Framework for the Changing Notion of Apprenticeship'. *Journal of Vocational Education and Training*. Published online 27 July 2020. Retrieved from https://doi.org/10.1080/13636820.2020.1796766.

Maurer, Markus. 2013. 'Berufsbildung und Arbeitsmarkt zwischen Tertiarisierung und Fachkräftemangel'. In *Herausforderungen für die Berufsbildung in der Schweiz*, edited by Markus Maurer and Philipp Gonon, pp. 15–36. Bern: hep Verlag.

Maurer, Markus, and Silke Pieneck. 2013. 'Die Reform von Berufsbildern als ständige Auseinandersetzung über Form und Inhalt'. In *Herausforderungen für die Berufsbildung in der Schweiz*, edited by Markus Maurer and Philipp Gonon, pp. 81–100. Bern: hep Verlag.

Renold, Ursula, Katherine Caves, and Maria E. Oswald-Egg. 2019. *Governance im Berufsbildungssystem der Schweiz. Systemische Steuerung des schweizerischen Berufsbildungssystems*. Zürich: KOF ETH.

SBBK 2017. *Arbeitsdossier 2017 für bildungssachverständige Personen der SBBK in Reformkommissionen und in Schweizerischen Kommissionen für Berufsentwicklung und Qualität*. Bern: SBBK Sekretariat.

SBFI. 2017. *Berufsbildung 2030. Vision und strategische Leitlinien. Hintergrundbericht zum Leitbild*. Bern: SBFI.

SBFI. 2020. 'Datenbank Berufsentwicklung auf Sekundarstufe II [Database for VET development]'. Available online at https://www.sbfi.admin.ch/sbfi/de/home/bildung/berufliche-grundbildung/datenbank-berufsentwicklung-auf-sekundarstufe-ii.html.

Schweizerisches Dienstleistungszentrum Berufsbildung/Berufs-, Studien und Laufbahnberatung SDBB. 2018. Die 22 Berufsfelder nach Zihlmann. Retrieved from https://edudoc.ch/record/106589/files/Berufsfelder.pdf?version=1.

Seifried, Jürgen, Klaus Beck, Bernd-Joachim Ertelt, and Andreas Frey (eds). 2019. *Beruf, Beruflichkeit, Employability*. Bielefeld: wbv.

SGV, SBFI, and SBBK. 2020. 'Orientierungshilfe für die Schweizerischen Kommissionen für Berufsentwicklung & Qualität [Guideline for the Swiss commissions for VET development and quality]'. Available online at https://www.berufsbildung.ch/dyn/bin/20504-20516-1-orientierungshilfe_sgv_deutsch_def.pdf.

Strebel, Alexandra, Patrick Emmenegger, and Lukas Graf. 2021. 'New Interest Associations in a Neo-corporatist System: Adapting the Swiss Training System to the Service Economy'. *British Journal of Industrial Relations* 59: 848–73. Retrieved from https://doi.org/10.1111/bjir.12581.

Strebel, Alexandra, Sonja Engelage, and Carmen Baumeler. 2019. 'Der Beitrag der institutional work-Perspektive zu Educational Governance. Dezentrale institutionelle Arbeit in der Berufsbildung'. In *Handbuch Educational Governance Theorien*, edited by Roman Langer and Thomas Brüsemeister, pp. 201–18. Wiesbaden: Springer Nature.

Thelen, Kathleen. 2003. 'How Institutions Evolve: Insights from Comparative-historical Analysis'. In *Comparative Historical Analysis in the Social Sciences*, edited by James Mahoney and Dietrich Rueschemeyer, pp. 208–40. New York: Cambridge University Press.

Thelen, Kathleen. 2004. *How Institutions Evolve: The Political Economy of Skills in Germany, Britain, the United States, and Japan*. Cambridge: Cambridge University Press.

Thelen, Kathleen, and Marius Busemeyer. 2008. *From Collectivism towards Segmentalism: Institutional Change in German Vocational Training*. Cologne: MPfG.

Thies, Lars. 2015. *Ländermonitor berufliche Bildung*. Bielefeld: Bertelsmann.

Trampusch, Christine. 2010. 'The Politics of Institutional Change: Transformative and Self-preserving Change in the Vocational Education and Training System in Switzerland'. *Comparative Politics 42* (2): 187–206.

Voss, Günter G. 2001. 'Auf dem Wege zum Individualberuf? Zur Beruflichkeit des Arbeitskraftskraftunternehmers'. In *Aspekte des Berufs in der Moderne*, edited by Thomas Kurtz, pp. 287–314. Opladen: Leske und Budrich.

Wettstein, Emil, Evi Schmid, and Philipp Gonon. 2017. *Swiss Vocational and Professional Education and Training (VPET). Forms, System, Stakeholders*. Bern: hep Verlag.

Ziegler, Birgit. 2015. 'Verallgemeinerung des Beruflichen—Verberuflichung des Allgemeinen?' In *Verallgemeinerung des Beruflichen—Verberuflichung des Allgemeinen?* edited by Birgit Ziegler, pp. 9–19. Bielefeld: Bertelsmann.

4

Still Egalitarian? How the Knowledge Economy Is Changing Vocational Education and Training in Denmark and Sweden

Martin B. Carstensen and Christian Lyhne Ibsen

4.1 Introduction

Comparative political economists have eagerly debated if the rise of the knowledge economy spells the demise of egalitarian capitalism, or whether a broadly solidaristic organization of the economy remains tenable even when faced with structural pressures like deindustrialization and globalization (Ibsen and Thelen 2017; Iversen and Soskice 2019; Baccaro and Howell 2017; Thelen 2014; Hall 2020; Busemeyer et al. 2021). One area that has received considerable scrutiny is skill formation, where particularly the capacity of vocational education and training (VET) institutions to produce solidaristic outcomes is increasingly questioned (see Bonoli and Emmenegger, in this volume). Long considered a hallmark of coordinated capitalism (Hall and Soskice 2001; Streeck 1992), collective skill formation systems were hailed for their capacity to straddle demands for efficiency, notably supplying relevant skills to employers, and equality, in this literature typically understood as the inclusion of working-class youth into relatively well-paid and stable employment (Iversen and Soskice 2001; Estevez-Abe et al. 2001). The link between equality and efficiency, however, seems increasingly strained by shifts in the demands of employers towards the upper and lower ends of the skill spectrum (Autor et al. 2003; Solga and Kohlrausch 2013; Durazzi and Geyer 2020). Extant scholarship shows that collectivist skill formation systems have tended to cater to the interests of large employers (Busemeyer 2012; Thelen and Busemeyer 2012; Emmenegger and Seitzl 2020), in some cases leading

Martin B. Carstensen and Christian Lyhne Ibsen, *Still Egalitarian? VET in Denmark and Sweden.* In: *Collective Skill Formation in the Knowledge Economy.* Edited by Giuliano Bonoli and Patrick Emmenegger, Oxford University Press.
© Oxford University Press (2022). DOI: 10.1093/oso/9780192866257.003.0004

to dualization (Emmenegger et al. 2012; Thelen 2014), while in other cases the state has taken over key inclusionary measures (Bonoli and Wilson 2019; Durazzi and Geyer 2020; see also Seitzl and Unterweger, in this volume).

While considerable attention has been paid to the dynamics of institutional change in Continental European collective VET systems that traditionally have accepted significant levels of social stratification, less is known about how dilemmas related to equality and efficiency play out in Nordic political economies focused more squarely on maintaining and increasing social equality. In this chapter, we focus on trajectories of change in two egalitarian economies, Denmark and Sweden (see also chapter by Busemeyer and Thelen, in this volume, for an analysis of Sweden). Although both countries are broadly similar in their overall approach to social welfare (Esping-Andersen 1990) and education (Antikainen 2006; Virolainen and Thunqvist 2017), they differ in important ways in the role employers play in the two systems. Specifically, while the Swedish system is school-based and employers play a very limited role in its governance, the Danish system is dual and depends on the involvement of the social partners in its governance (see Dobbins and Busemeyer 2015). Our case selection thus allows us to explore the importance of employer involvement in the governance of VET for negotiating the balance between equality and efficiency in economies strongly committed to social equality.

Based on our analysis of key reform developments in Danish and Swedish VET since the 1990s, we argue that obtaining both equality and efficiency in either collectivist or state-led skill formation systems is increasingly an untenable policy position. We find that both systems ended up more focused on employers' interests in the 2010s, despite their different starting points. Thus, what used to be a balance between efficiency and equality, seems increasingly lopsided in favour of efficiency. In Sweden, the reforms of the 2010s focused on limiting mobility between VET and higher education, while reforms in Denmark instead focused on keeping out the very weakest students to attract stronger students. However, stubbornly low admission numbers in both systems indicate that the strengthened focus on efficiency so far has not translated into increasing demand for VET from strong students.

The story of how the two egalitarian systems responded to the rise of the knowledge economy, then, is one of diversity within common trajectories. Thus, we find that in both Denmark and Sweden policymakers have sought to first increase equality. However, when employers increasingly expressed their frustration with equality-enhancement, policymakers limited inclusion in their VET systems. The countries differ, however, as they have focused their policies for equality on two different groups of VET students. In Sweden, reforms implemented in the early 1990s aimed to strengthen equality of opportunity for working-class youth by boosting mobility between VET and higher education. This involved an increase in general and less directly applicable subjects in VET programmes and served to strengthen educational mobility among the strongest and most academically oriented VET students. In contrast, reforms in the Danish system focused on attracting the weakest students to the system and retaining them once they were admitted. This too meant the introduction of more generalist subjects in the curriculum but focused on increasing students' ability to study rather than enabling them to access higher education. That is, reforms were directed at students with different educational capacities: top of the working class in Sweden, and bottom of the working class in Denmark. And, indeed, owing to waning support from employers during the 1990s and 2000s, neither of them successfully built a sustainable combination of equality and efficiency in their VET institutions.

The diversity within common trajectories in important ways hinges on differences in the institutional setup of the respective systems. In Sweden, VET and gymnasiums are placed within the same institutional structure, and the social partners only take up an advisory position in the governance structure. Thus, while employer demands made an impact in the Swedish trajectory, implementing a socially progressive policy of enabling VET students to continue into higher education was relatively easily done because employers have a less central role in governing VET. In Denmark, by contrast, the central role social partners play in the governance of the Danish system enable them to oppose ideas of generally qualifying VET students for higher education by replacing specific skills with general ones. However, under the pressure of maintaining their central position in the VET system, and Danish labour market policy more generally, employers still had to accept some twenty years of VET deployed as social policy.

4.2 Balancing equality and efficiency in the knowledge economy

The institutional perspective on vocational education in coordinated market economies takes as its starting point a classic puzzle of education research (Becker 1964): how is it possible for firms to agree on training their employees to obtain skills that are useful beyond the specific production taking place in that company? With the advent of the knowledge economy, this conundrum now plays out in a new context. Changing skill needs of employers are thus putting a question mark over the resilience of the institutions that in the Fordist manufacturing economies enabled firms to effectively cooperate in addressing the collective action problems involved in producing portable skills (Thelen 2004).

The classic statement of Hall and Soskice (2001) in *Varieties of Capitalism* (VoC) focused on the competitive advantages companies using diversified quality production derived from collective action in firm-based training (Streeck 1997). Subsequent scholarship has stressed the central role of the state for sustaining cooperation (Busemeyer and Trampusch 2012; Culpepper 2003; Martin and Thelen 2007; Thelen 2004). This is an important conceptual advance, since it puts us on firmer ground to detail the different trajectories taken by the broad group of advanced economies placed under the rubric of coordinated market economies. Importantly, these include both collective skill formation systems heralded for their ability to undergird the high-wage and high value-added equilibrium of the Fordist manufacturing model, as well as statist VET systems, where training takes place in schools and employers are much less involved in the funding, provision, and governance of training (Busemeyer and Trampusch 2012).

The recognition among VoC scholars that the state may play an important role in the setup of skill formation is especially important for analysing the balance between efficiency and equality within VET systems. This argument has been made with particular force by Thelen (2014). She suggests that 'embedded flexibilization' of VET—which Denmark and Sweden are key examples of—sustains solidaristic outcomes by combining decollectivization on the part of employers and liberalization of the economy while the state takes over key inclusionary functions. This requires a relatively high level of state capacity, which incentivizes the state to provide equality-enhancing measures and enables it to pressure employers to maintain an inclusive training system (Martin and Thelen 2007).

We submit that the notion of embedded flexibilization gives rise to an overly optimistic assessment of the potential of maintaining broadly solidaristic outcomes in egalitarian economies like the Danish or Swedish. Here we focus specifically on the continued ability of vocational education systems to balance demands for efficiency and equality. Our less than benign conclusion is reached by placing centrally Streeck and Thelen's (2005) contention that the institutional setup surrounding vocational education—or any other sphere of the economy—typically is characterized by considerable heterogeneity. This implies that institutions directed at different purposes and potentially answering to competing logics exist side by side, but also that tensions between what we refer to as dimensions of institutional contention have the potential to negatively affect employer support for the system.

From the perspective of vocational education, we consider the issues of equality, efficiency, and governance as the three principal dimensions of contention in vocational education institutions (Carstensen and Ibsen 2021). The efficiency dimension ranges from highly efficient systems based on perceived cost-effective matching of supply and demand for skilled workers to highly inefficient systems with costly and poor matching. The governance dimension ranges from a perceived high degree of self-governance to a high degree coercion by the state. The equality dimension ranges from perceived high degree of inequality effects through tight entry requirements, low apprenticeship income, and strong tracking-effect of VET to high degree equality through open entry, high apprenticeship incomes, and permeability of VET to higher education. Employing these three dimensions of contention enables identification of how reform processes are fuelled by contending objectives and instruments related to VET institutions, putting in view how political battles are structured by efforts of coalitions to change the existing configuration of the three principal dimensions (see Carstensen and Ibsen 2021 for further elaboration).

Particularly relevant for analysing tensions within coordinated market economies that undergo 'embedded flexibilization' is how the state's effort to increase the inclusiveness of the VET system may clash with employers' focus on strengthening skill match. It is broadly recognized within VoC scholarship that employers' continued support is central for explaining institutional stability (Thelen 2004; Busemeyer and Thelen 2020), making it even more important to understand how the effort of the state to boost equality through VET may trigger processes of institutional change. This may happen as dissatisfaction among companies reaches a tipping point that sets in motion a weakening support for the system among employers (Bonoli and Emmenegger 2021).

Our argument points to severe strains on the ability of the state to counter the decreasing solidarity following de-collectivization in advanced economies. Notably, this applies to both statist and collectivist systems, i.e. neither governance structure is particularly suited to bolstering inclusiveness of VET in the knowledge economy. In a state-led VET system, policymakers do not share authority over the system with the social partners and thus enjoy significant leeway in reforming the systems in ways that match the preferred balance between concerns about social inclusion and skill match. However, despite this freedom of manoeuvre, the state will not be well placed to identify what are in fact the specific skill demands of employers. In a context with rapidly shifting skill needs among companies—and employers reluctant to make a greater commitment without increased influence—statist systems, which exhibit significant ambitions for enhancing equality, lack the information from employers and the institutional agility to satisfy fast-changing skill demands of companies. This, in turn, is likely to push up youth unemployment and hurt the equality that it sought to boost, particularly among the weakest of students (Busemeyer 2014).

In a collectivist system, the state enjoys the support of employers and unions in the governance and funding of the system, which helps it develop the system to satisfy the skill demands of employers. Concomitantly, the state is also more strained in its effort to make the VET system more inclusive and might have to develop parallel systems for training that are inferior to the typical dual-training track (Bonoli and Wilson 2019). The involvement of employers in these options for weaker students is not guaranteed. And even if employers engage, they might be dissatisfied with the quality of students and eventually opt out of training given the voluntarist nature of collectivist systems (Carstensen and Ibsen 2021; Ibsen and Thelen n.d.). In turn, the threat of employers opting out of training gives employers considerable power vis-à-vis the state and trade unions wanting to introduce more equality (Bonoli and Emmenegger 2021; Durazzi and Geyer 2020).

As we show below, the common challenge of balancing efficiency and equality has become more severe for the state regardless of governance structure. Both countries have embarked on common trajectory of reforms in the 2010s to strengthen efficiency by aligning VET more and more with employer demands. This trajectory was taken as a response to reforms in the 1990s and 2000s that had increased social inclusiveness, i.e. the trajectory in the 2010s represent a rebalancing. However, the nature of the challenge and policies to sustain or increase social inclusiveness differ across statist and collectivist systems. The Swedish system was in the early 1990s reformed in a significantly more socially progressive way, most notably by making qualification for higher education a right for VET graduates. In contrast, reforms in Denmark focused on making VET more inclusive for the weakest learners by providing school-based alternative access to VET for students who could not obtain an apprenticeship. While the Swedish state thus exercised its authority to change the system with little explicit support from employers, the Danish state was significantly more limited in its ambitions to breed social inclusion, but also more successful in keeping youth unemployment at bay. Despite the more limited ambitions of Danish VET, it was still too much for employers who for well over a decade now have been complaining that the inclusionary measures to bring on board the weakest pupils have severely hurt the quality of VET students.

4.3 Denmark

The Danish VET system is based on the dual-training principle, i.e. a sandwich model where periods in schools are combined with periods of training in companies (apprenticeships). Students can enter VET either via an apprenticeship contract with an employer or directly through a vocational school. Owing to the continuing high involvement of employers and unions and extensive government funding, the VET system in Denmark is considered a collectivist skill formation system (Busemeyer and Trampusch 2012). Although the central position of the social partners in the governance of Danish VET institutions underlines the collectivist nature of the system, there is also little doubt that there are strong statist elements in the system. Simply put, while regulation of apprenticeships has to a very large extent been the purview of self-governance by the social partners, the influence that the state has over schools, has long been used to pursue shifting political agendas. Since the early 1990s, a key policy priority reaching across party lines has been the 95-per-cent goal, i.e. that 95 per cent of a youth cohort graduate at least from secondary education. A key motivation for this policy was to prepare for the advent of the knowledge economy, both by ensuring the supply of relevant skills, and to maintain a broadly egalitarian society. From the beginning, vocational education played a central role realizing this ambition, because it was employed as an inclusionary measure for the weakest learners that also, unsurprisingly, remained the major stumbling block for reaching the 95-per-cent goal.

4.3.1 VET as social policy

An important institutional background for the social policy role allotted to VET in preparing for the knowledge economy was that the state took on a more active role in the system (Juul and Jørgensen 2011). The watershed 1991 reform set the stage for this transformation by bringing together the apprenticeship-based system and the school-based system. Up until the reform, Danish VET had been structured in two separate programmes—one placed in vocational schools with a significant apprenticeship element, another focused around an apprenticeship with significant periods of time in school. After the 1991 re-organization these were instead two different access points to VET: one starting with an apprenticeship contract, the other commencing in school (Nelson 2012). This meant that the Danish apprenticeship system, with roots in the guilds' apprenticeships, principally was replaced with a dual VET system that involved learning alternating between the workplace and school (Bøndergaard 2014). Common for both tracks, however, was that the 1991 reform increased the number of general subjects taught in school. The reform had a strong focus on combining vocational knowledge with general formative development objectives, and the reform introduced the pedagogical principle of interdisciplinary and holistic teaching (Cort 2008).

A key inclusionary measure in the reform was the creation of school-based apprenticeships. As a response to the lack of apprenticeship positions offered by employers during the economic downturn in the late 1980s, it was decided to offer apprenticeship training in a school setting. This made students less dependent on the current economic situation and removed a sorting mechanism, which in other systems—like, for example, the German one—led the less resourceful students into the transition system rather than real, qualifying VET education (Protsch and Solga 2016). It also made employers less powerful, but they reluctantly accepted it as a response to the lack of apprenticeship positions (Koudahl 2005). It is worth noting that although the school-based apprenticeship option could be perceived as a threat to the dual system, the option of a school-based apprenticeship has remained less attractive in terms of pay than regular apprenticeships (see Martin 2012 for a historical explanation of the Danish combination of schools and firm-based training). Students are also obliged to seek out regular apprenticeship positions when they are in a school-based apprenticeship. In that sense, the system has not become a threat to the regular dual system (Carstensen et al. 2022), and it has made it possible to include weaker students without the abilities, resources, and networks to secure an apprenticeship position that would have been stopped in their tracks in the older system. School-based apprenticeships became more and more important in the 1990s as vocational schools were incentivized by the productivity-based funding model—also implemented as part of the 1991 reform—to increase their uptake of students, which they then could guarantee the possibility of graduating.

As the Social Democrats and the Social Liberals took over government reigns in 1993, VET came to play a prominent role in the effort to battle youth unemployment and prepare for the knowledge economy. The government's policy mantra of 'Education for all'—where the 95-per-cent goal figured as a prominent policy aim—became a creed for Danish education policy in the following twenty-five years. The focus in the 1991 reform on holistically adjusting teaching to the particular strengths and weaknesses of students was further strengthened in the 2000 reform, which explicitly sought to increase the inclusiveness of VET (at both the top and bottom of the class) by differentiating teaching according to the abilities of the students. The reform was based on the notion that in a knowledge society, the most important competency is an ability to learn and adapt. It thus took individualization even further by considering students not as part of a group with specific expectations or needs, but rather as individuals without common characteristics (Koudahl 2005).

The reform was based on ideas about the skill needs necessary to succeed in post-industrial society and how education could be used to include weaker groups in society. Thelen (2014) considers this reform liberalizing in that it enabled students to set up a more individualized and flexible education path, but it is important to recognize that its primary motivation was to enable more effective inclusion of the weakest learners. Beyond boosting general competencies, a key aim of the reform was through modularization and increased flexibility to enable students to set up their own education according to their interests. The reform thus entailed that the pendulum swung decisively towards a focus on the individual away from earlier emphasis on the more specific skills that employers demanded (Cort 2010; Koudahl 2005).

It is well worth noting that the reforms of VET in the 1990s and 2000s were created with broad support in parliament. The largely non-partisan nature of the Danish reform trajectory (see also Carstensen et al. 2022) is not least seen in the fact that the 2007 reform, which once again had inclusion and the 95-per-cent goal as its main focus, was created under the auspices of a Liberal-Conservative government. The overall motivation for the reform was to harness VET as part of a strategy for Denmark in the global economy. This included a strengthened focus in teaching and curriculum on holistic perception, flair for business, flexibility, self-management, the ability to acquire and apply new knowledge, to communicate, and to take initiatives. The 2007 reform also continued the focus of earlier reforms on increasing inclusion. Although in theory the flexibility of the system catered to both strong and weak students, it was clear that most of the initiatives in the reforms were aimed at supporting weaker students in graduating. This included the development of 'basic course packages' that could help students with additional needs, including improving language skills and knowledge of Danish culture, but also the gradation of courses at different levels, enabling students to choose the right level for them.

The 2000s witnessed significant increases in students with low grades from basic school that more often struggled with other social issues (e.g., drug use, housing problems, etc.) (Jørgensen 2018: 182). This was to a great extent the result of two intersecting unintended consequences from previous reforms.

On one hand, the productivity-based funding model implemented as part of the 1991 reform meant that the schools were heavily incentivized to admit as many students as possible, including those with social problems that made it more than difficult for them to participate productively in school. Second, from the perspective of students, the activation turn in labour market policy in the 1990s had as a consequence that young people were increasingly being asked to educate themselves rather than receive benefits. Particularly important was the requirement, established in policy in 1996, for young people under twenty-five seeking unemployment benefit to seek out education. VET was considered the obvious choice for this group (Jørgensen 2018). In this way, institutional changes in labour market policy and social policy, together with a consensus around the belief that education was the route for everyone, congealed to produce new patterns in the uptake of students to VET.

4.3.2 Excluding the weakest students

Taken together, in the 1990s and 2000s, the Danish VET system increasingly took on a social policy role of integrating the so-called residual group of the most challenged learners to reach the overall goal of 'Education for all'. Following this institutional logic, reforms of the VET system, particularly large reforms in 2000 and 2007, sought to enhance the capacity of Danish VET to accommodate the needs of these weaker learners. This overall approach to VET only changed in 2014, when the social partners all but forced through a reform that implemented grade requirements that kept out a large part of the 'residual group'. This is a very significant change, which was brought on by growing scepticism among employers. For the 2000 reform, both unions and employers were still enthusiastic about the notion of individualization and flexibilization of VET. For example, the Danish Chamber of Commerce joined forces with the Danish Metalworkers' Union to produce a proposal for flexible and individualized VET programmes (Politiken 1998). Notably, the actual 2000 reform was negotiated between peak associations for labour and business and the state. For the 2007 reform, employers started to voice concerns about whether inclusion had gone too far. The Danish Employers Association found a significant risk that firms would stop offering training positions in the VET system, because 'they are not interested in all that inclusion', and so the reform was argued to be a threat to the VET system (Berlingske 2006).

After years of high drop-out rates, fewer apprenticeships, and a declining intake of young students in VET vis-à-vis general upper-secondary education *(gymnasium)*, the social partners and a majority of the political parties agreed that using VET as social policy was no longer viable and that a rebalancing of VET towards efficiency-enhancing objectives was needed. Nonetheless, it was only after pressure from the social partners—especially the Confederation of Danish Industry and the Danish Metalworkers' Union—that the government agreed to expand their focus to also include stricter admission requirements (Carstensen and Ibsen 2021). Due to the legacy of inclusiveness through VET, the centre-left government was afraid to include elements, like grade requirements, that could exclude certain groups of young people. Moreover, their parliamentary support party, the Unity List *(Enhedslisten)*, were in principle against grade requirements. However, with even the general workers' union, 3F, on board, the government's reform proposal of August 2013 was clearly in line with social partners. In parliament, only the left-wing Unity List did not vote in favour of the reform, referring to the inequality effects of introducing grade requirements.

The reform also added efficiency-enhancing elements that cater to talented students and increase permeability between VET and tertiary education. VET schools are required to implement methods for differentiated teaching taking into account the different abilities and skills of students. Moreover, schools are required to create and expand the number of courses at different levels in order to challenge more skilled students. In this vein, 'talent tracks' were established to prepare particularly ambitious students for relevant higher education and international competition. Regarding permeability, there already exist possibilities for combining VET with general secondary education *(gymnasiel eksamen)* that give access to higher secondary education, called the EUX *(erhvervsfaglig studentereksamen)*. In contrast to the Swedish system, where qualifying for higher education was a right for all students enrolled in VET, the Danish EUX was created to attract the strongest students and is also generally considered much more demanding than normal VET programmes. The reform expands EUX to all relevant VET programmes and makes it available for both young students and students above twenty-five years of age. The reform also qualifies VET programmes with a duration of a minimum of three years for enrolment in business academies and equates higher-level courses in VET with general upper-secondary school courses to enable access to higher education. To make the reform as appealing as possible for the social partners, the governance dimension was left largely intact and the central role of social partners was even reinforced. Indeed, the national trade commissions (FU) are given more influence on determining educational requirements for the second part of the basic course that concludes with a test, the content of which is decided by the FUs.

The 2015 reform was a clear break with the use of VET for social policy purposes. For example, while a reform in 2007 focused on social inclusion through more effective retention of the weaker students who became part of VET, the 2015 reform made it impossible for the weakest students to access the system. The message was that students who are not qualified to be in VET should find something else to prepare for further education—in most cases the 'transition system' (*Forberedende Grunduddannelse*) where it is possible to obtain the necessary grade level—and that taking care of these students was the responsibility of the state and municipalities, not employers. Once again, policymakers changed the school-based part of vocational education, leaving employer discretion in the apprenticeship system untouched (Nyen and Tønder 2020), thereby following the wishes of both employers and labour unions.

Ultimately, as part of a reform of the transition system, the 95-per-cent goal was given up and replaced instead with a 90-per-cent goal. Consequently, it was accepted that the last part of the residual group, who until then VET had been tasked with including in the labour market, could instead legitimately remain unskilled labour. What had been considered a 'creed' of Danish education policy since the early 1990s was given up without a struggle from the left wing parties who had initiated it three decades earlier. In exchange, in an agreement with unions and the state made in 2016, the employers committed to provide 8–10,000 more apprenticeship positions than then current levels. Moreover, the transition system was reformed to deal more effectively with residual groups struggling to progress into further education or employment (Di Maio et al. 2019). Hence, the refusal on the part of employers that VET should continue to be used as social policy does not indicate an all-out rejection of equality-enhancing measures. But it indicates a growing vigilance on the part of both social partners to counter policies that threaten to undermine employers' privileged position in accessing skilled labour.

Implementation of the VET reform began in 2015, and so far, results have been less than impressive (see KORA 2017). The main goal of the reform was to increase the uptake of (qualified) students directly from primary education, specifically by bringing the percentage of applicants to 25 per cent in 2020 and 30 in 2025. In 2019 the number was 20.1 per cent (Ministry of Education 2019), which is very close to pre-reform levels (e.g. 18.8% and 19.6% in 2013 and 2014, respectively), although it is worth noting that the students who were accepted in the first year of the reform have somewhat higher grades. Additional goals were a decrease in drop-outs, but here too numbers remain stagnant. As mentioned, the number of apprenticeship positions has been increased through an agreement between the state and the social partners, and has for many sectors remained high following a general increase labor demand in the economy. According to the agreement, employers agreed to provide at least 8–10,000 more training positions in 2025 than in 2016. In 2018 a total extra of 3,000 positions were created compared to 2016. This indicates that although employers have successfully turned the political focus towards VET providing relevant skills rather than inclusion of the 'residual group', it has still a long way to go in dealing with the consequences of twenty-five years of VET as social policy.

4.4 Sweden

Since the landmark 1968 reform which integrated general and vocational upper-secondary programmes into one unified school (*gymnasieskolan*), Swedish VET has been heralded for its social inclusiveness (Nelson 2012). Students in Sweden entered VET through standardized admission procedures at unified schools and the emphasis on general skills and permeability to higher education made Swedish VET a highly inclusive system with a low degree of stratification. Owing to its high level of public funding and state-led curriculum and governance, the Swedish system is often characterized as a statist system, where social partners play a marginal role (Busemeyer 2014) with apprenticeships and workplace-based learning taking up very limited space compared to countries such as Denmark and Germany.

However, the Swedish system has changed in multiple ways since the 1990s marking gradual departures from social inclusion and school-based teaching towards efficiency concerns and workplace learning. In both the 1991 and 2011 reforms, the main objective was to improve VET students' chances in a context of changing skill needs in the knowledge economy. However, the substantive content of reforms went in opposite directions owing to different interpretations of how to reach this objective. In the former reform, focus was on establishing links to higher education for strong students and giving more general skills to VET students. In the latter reform, the strong link to higher education was severed and focus shifted towards the immediate skill needs of employers. In both reforms, however, the legacy of a statist governance limited aspirations for fundamental change.

4.4.1 VET as a source of social mobility

The 1991 reform (finalized in 1994) was conceived during increasing distress in the Swedish economy and a 'stronger awareness of a trade-off relation between equality and efficiency, and a greater concern than previously with efficiency' (Lauglo 1993: 26). Swedish VET programmes—while popular among the youth—were increasingly seen as expensive and not fulfilling the conflicting interests of employers and trade unions. Above all, employers were dissatisfied with the labour market relevance of the VET programmes. Studies showed that three to four years after graduating only one-third of VET students were in an occupation for which their training had prepared them (Nilsson 1986, cited in Lauglo 1993: 25). To solve this problem, employers wanted to increase their influence over the content of VET, for example by letting trade councils with representatives from trade unions and employer associations decide more. Employers were less positive about strengthening apprenticeships and vehemently opposed taking on apprentices as employees (Lundahl et al. 2010). In contrast, unions were dissatisfied with the social mobility of VET programmes arguing that too few VET students went on to higher education—something which the 1968 reform had envisioned. While not opposed to more workplace learning, their concern was first and foremost that the reform would contribute to more stratification rather than reducing it (Thunqvist et al. 2019).

The original reform proposal by the centre-right government in 1991 contained ideas about strengthening apprenticeships and bringing the content of programmes much closer to employer needs (Lundahl et al. 2010). Foreshadowing the upper-secondary education reform in 2011—the so-called Gy11 reform—the government argued that a key problem with the VET system was the poor match between student ability and the unified upper-secondary schools. Specifically, it thought that severing the link to higher education could lead to better matching of 'school-tired' students with programmes and eventually employment (Lundahl et al. 2010). The actual reform did not reflect these ideas—on the contrary. As the Swedish economy worsened in the first years of the 1990s, employers were increasingly incapable of providing apprenticeships. Moreover, as youth unemployment soared to over 22 per cent in 1993, the idea of introducing more specialization to specific jobs that were not there and cutting off links to higher education (and a later graduation year) was untenable (Lauglo 1993). Instead, union-supported ideas took over and further galvanized the Swedish approach to VET: high inclusiveness through integrated schools, focus on general skills, and, importantly, permeability.

When the incoming social democratic government took over in 1994, the reform was launched and contained elements that catered to the social mobility of the strongest VET students. All VET programmes were extended to last three years and the extension allowed for more general education that qualified VET students for higher education. Hereby, much to the satisfaction of trade unions, the social democratic goal of social mobility was prioritized. Employers for their part welcomed the extra year, seeing it as upgrade of VET programmes which enabled labour market mobility in times of economic restructuring. Moreover, they were relieved of the training burden that an expansion of apprenticeships would have entailed (Lauglo 1993; Olofsson and Thunqvist 2014). VET programmes were reduced to fourteen programmes and made broader to enable more flexibility within each programme. While at least 15 per cent of the scheduled time should be for instruction at places of work, the crux of VET programmes was general subjects, project work, and optional courses. Like the Danish reforms in the 1990s, individual students should tailor learning to individual preferences whilst receiving a strong foundation in general skills. In contrast, workplace learning through apprenticeships was not expanded due to the historical weak link between schools and employers.

The elements of choice and flexibility dovetailed with the general trend in Swedish educational policies during the 1990s (Nylund and Virolainen 2019). Governance of schools was being decentralized to the local level and private schools could enter the educational market (Lundahl 2016). For VET, this trend meant that upper-secondary schools were given the responsibility of designing programmes to fit students' wishes, and schools could compete for students. Furthermore, as we show below, local social partnerships between companies, trade unions, and schools later developed and over time created an additional more stratified system on top of the otherwise egalitarian model of public VET education in Sweden. The size of this extra system could make the Swedish system more stratified over time (see Lundahl 2016). However, at the time, the 1991 reform cemented the statist VET system, and by boosting permeability to higher education it introduced more inclusiveness for strong VET students.

The reform, however, did not solve some of the fundamental problems in the Swedish economy: weak links between VET programmes and employer skill demands. Increasingly, policymakers, employers, and some trade unions argued that this weak link was in part to blame for the persistent high youth unemployment rate in Sweden (consistently over 9% since 1992, see World Bank Data 2021). Moreover, critics echoed critiques from the 1980s and 1990s that the emphasis of getting VET students through to higher education produced high drop-out rates because it only favoured strong learners (Lauglo 1993; Thunqvist et al. 2019). Thus, old ideas of bringing VET closer to the labour market began to resurface in the 2000s, leading to the Gy11 reform.

4.4.2 Increasing employability at the expense of mobility

A major goal of Gy11 was to improve employability of VET students, whereas goals such as citizenship and social mobility were downplayed (Nylund and Rosvall 2016). Many observers of Swedish VET regarded the reform as a break with the traditionally inclusive social democratic educational policy (Lundahl et al. 2010; Nylund 2012; Thunqvist and Hallqvist 2014). The centre-right government—at the time of the reform in a much stronger parliamentary situation—wanted to realize what it had not been able to in the 1990s: reduce the permeability and bring VET content closer to employers' immediate skill demands. The final reform in 2011 had three major components: cutting off direct access to higher education, introducing an apprenticeship track, and reducing general theoretical subjects.

First, cutting off direct access to higher education was arguably the most controversial departure from the objectives in the 1991 reform. The government argued that the general subjects qualifying VET students for higher education were a distraction that demotivated 'school-tired' learners. Thus, the logic of the Swedish government went in the opposite direction of many collectivist skills formation systems, e.g. Germany, which have made VET more permeable to attract students (see Bernhard and Graf, in this volume). To qualify for higher education, students now needed to take additional courses and extend the studying time. By cutting off the automatic link, the government hoped that students would make better choices that would decrease drop-out rates and fast-track students to employment.

The move was highly controversial as it introduced unprecedented stratification into Swedish upper-secondary education. The left-wing parties, unions, and even some employer associations complained that VET programmes would become dead ends (Thunqvist and Hallqvist 2014: 27–8) and that the change would severely reduce the social status of VET among youth and their parents (see Billett 2014). They were right. Almost immediately, the share of youth going into VET programmes dropped from 34 per cent in 2010 to 28 per cent in 2012 and continued to drop until its lowest point of 22 per cent in 2016 (Skolverket 2019: 18). The most recent share was 25 per cent (Skolverket 2019: 18). The reaction was so negative that the government in 2013 made it possible to acquire basic eligibility for higher education within the framework of all upper-secondary vocational programmes without having to choose an extended curriculum. Some schools also began including the optional courses to be eligible for higher education in their standard offerings (Thunqvist and Hallqvist 2014). Nonetheless, the signal in the reform was clear; VET was no longer an obvious choice for students who wanted to go on to higher education.

Second, the reform introduced a new apprenticeship track with at least 50 per cent of time spent in apprenticeship. While some programmes, especially in the building trades, had retained a strong element of apprenticeships throughout the twentieth century, this new track was a radical departure for many programmes and schools. The government explicitly wanted to use the track to attract and retain students who were discouraged by the theory-heavy school-based teaching in the typical vocational tracks. Like the 1991 reform, the Gy11 reform was preceded by pilot projects and governmental inquiries. Particularly important in the preparations for the reform were experiments with apprenticeships (SOU 2008, 2010, 2011). In their final report of the governmental inquiry on apprenticeships (SOU 2011: 13–23), the expert group highlighted the enormous potential for workplace learning but warned that government needed to ensure quality through supporting employers in taking on apprenticeships. This recommendation to some extent summarized the inherent contradiction in the Gy11 reform: introducing apprenticeships top-down by government decree (Thunqvist and Hallqvist 2014).

To be sure, apprenticeship-based training did not replace school-based VET in Sweden. While the track has grown from 3 per cent of VET students in 2011 to 12 per cent in 2018 (Skolverket 2016: 90; 2019: 24), it is still modest compared to dual-training countries like Germany and Denmark. Moreover, critically missing in the implementation of the apprenticeship track is the heavy hand of employers in the funding and governance of apprenticeships. This missing piece makes the integration between school-based education and apprenticeship training difficult (Thunqvist and Hallqvist 2014: 12). Moreover, since the social partners cannot agree on whether to employ students as apprentices or not, the connection between students and specific employers is marginal compared to collectivist countries. The exceptions to this rule are the so-called TeknikColleges (see later).

Third, in accordance with the new emphasis of employer-relevant skills, Gy11 reduced general subjects by one-fifth and narrowed the set of competences specific to each programme, in contrast to the broadening of the curriculum found in the 1991 reform (Nylund and Rosvall 2016: 697). Alongside this curriculum change, workplace-based learning (*Arbetsplatsbaserat Lärande, APL*) was included in all vocational programmes for a minimum period of fifteen weeks (Thunqvist and Hallqvist 2014: 12). Thus, rather than preparing students for changing skill demands through broad and flexible education, the GY11 sought to teach students specialized competences that would be immediately relevant for employers. And instead of educating 'citizens', 'entrepreneurship' became a recurrent issue across programmes (Nylund and Rosvall 2016: 697). Schools were required to include social partners in local councils for each programme to ensure that the knowledge and demands from employers (and trade unions) could be transmitted to schools. At the national level, each programme also got a council with relevant employer representatives and trade unions. Despite these formal innovations, anecdotal evidence suggests that government officials still to a large extent dominate curriculum-setting (Thunqvist and Hallqvist 2014).

Compared to the 1991 reform, the interpretation of social inclusion in the knowledge economy has changed with Gy11. From focusing on flexibility and social mobility due to changing skill demands, the focus is now on getting students the skills that will get them a job in the occupation that they trained for. This new focus does not cater for the strongest students who would typically go on to higher education through VET, but it could help weaker students into jobs they would not otherwise have gotten. The apprenticeship track epitomized this new interpretation. However, the emphasis on employability in the Gy11 reform contains a significant contradiction because employers are not driving the programmes, which are still very much under the control of the state (Thunqvist and Hallqvist 2014). Thus, one of the crucial ingredients of the success of dual-training systems is missing. Perhaps for this reason, Swedish employers are increasingly in favour of industrial schools, e.g. TeknikColleges, that they govern more independently (Thunqvist and Hallqvist 2014: 11; see also Busemeyer and Thelen, in this volume). Despite its high ambitions, the Gy11 reform seems to have fallen short of delivering.

4.5 Conclusion

This chapter has explored how the state has tried to rebalance efficiency in equality in two egalitarian countries—Denmark and Sweden—since the 1990s. As shown by numerous contributions in this book, the balance between equality and efficiency in VET is increasingly strained by shifts in the demands of employers towards the upper and lower ends of the skill spectrum. Whereas the skill demands in the Fordist economy inherently supported the link between efficiency and equality (Iversen and Soskice 2015; Hall 2020), the knowledge economy puts pressure on policymakers to redress the link between efficiency and equality (Durazzi and Geyer 2020; Cedefop 2018; Thelen 2014).

We argue that the Swedish and Danish cases exhibit diversity within common trajectories. Both systems pursued equality, albeit in different ways in the 1990s. In Sweden, reforms implemented in the early 1990s aimed to boost mobility between VET and higher education. In contrast, reforms in the Danish system focused on attracting the weakest students to the systems and retaining them once they were admitted. Despite these differences, both systems ended up more focused on employers' interests in the 2010s. In Sweden, the Gy11 reform limited mobility between VET and higher education, while reforms in Denmark instead focused on excluding the weakest students to attract stronger students and employers. In both systems, we thus see institutional reform aimed at bolstering the mid-level skill space that traditionally enabled VET to produce egalitarian outcomes while satisfying the skill demands of employers. However, stubbornly low admission numbers in both systems indicate that this strategy is less than successful even in systems with a historically strong commitment to egalitarianism. The chapter indicates that obtaining both equality and efficiency in either the collectivist Danish system or state-led Swedish system is increasingly an untenable policy position.

To be sure, the Danish and Swedish systems are still comparatively inclusive due to their high degree of public funding and free access to education. Nonetheless, our study supports the view that VET systems increasingly rely on the state for equality (Thelen 2014). Moreover, we show that equality enhancement is increasingly problematic and that the state can be forced to lessen equality measures given the power of employers to withdraw from VET (Bonoli and Emmenegger 2021; Carstensen and Ibsen 2021). That being said, the power of employers to limit or reduce inclusiveness is not pre-determined. For example, evidence from Austria suggests that employers can be 'cajoled' into supporting or at least accepting more inclusive measures, and that they can be convinced about the quality of training on offer from the state (Carstensen et al. 2020; Seitzl and Unterweger, in this volume). The recent tripartite agreement in Denmark on bonuses and penalties for over- and undertraining, respectively, relative to the share of VET workers in the company points in this direction. However, the question remains if bonuses and penalties will really make a difference. In Sweden, the challenge is how to get employers engaged in training in the first place. As we argue, this might entail that the state gives up some control over the content of training—something which has proven difficult despite the intentions in the Gy11 reform. Similarly, students at the top end might not be interested in employer-driven education and will prefer general upper-secondary programmes to access university (Ibsen and Thelen n.d.).

While speculative at present, our findings suggest the following scenarios for egalitarian outcomes in Denmark and Sweden. First, the mid-level skill space may be hollowed out over time, leading to more job polarization rather than upgrading. At the moment, the evidence of polarization in Denmark and Sweden is scant (Oesch and Piccitto 2019; FH—Danish Trade Union Confederation 2019; Tåhlin 2019) owing to strong collective bargaining systems, free education, plentiful opportunities for lifelong learning, and second-chance education in both countries. Indeed, VET in both countries increasingly seems to deliver an equality-enhancing function for adult VET students (Ibsen and Thelen n.d.; Thunqvist and Hallqvist 2014). However, this 'second-chance' approach to education is expensive and might not enjoy political support in the long run. Furthermore, policymakers may adjust their standards for what constitutes acceptable levels of educational inequality. For example, in 2017 the Danish government decided to give up the goal that 95 per cent of the population under forty years should achieve at least upper-secondary education. The new goal is 90 per cent of youth under twenty-five years. What happens to the remaining 10 per cent is unclear. It is possible that policymakers and social partners in Denmark and Sweden will tacitly accept that this group is destined for the growing number of unskilled and low-paid jobs in the service sector or for becoming welfare-state clients.

Second, over time, some employers might adjust their skill needs away from VET and increasingly opt out, forcing the state to take over even more. This scenario seems most problematic for the Danish system, whereas the Swedish state-led system does not require extensive employer involvement. However, in both countries, employers may develop their parallel systems by which they can tailor training to their own needs. To some extent, this has already happened in Sweden with the Industrial Schools and TeknikColleges (see Busemeyer and Thelen, in this volume). These schools attract strong students and transitions into jobs are typically very smooth. From an equality perspective, these parallel systems are problematic as they could fuel stratification in the otherwise free and public skill formation systems. In contrast, a more benign interpretation would be that these programmes are integrated innovations to the public system and thus perform the required efficiency functions to shore up the system as a whole (see chapter by Unterweger and Seitzl, in this volume).

References

Antikainen, A. 2006. 'In Search of the Nordic Model in Education'. *Scandinavian Journal of Educational Research* 50 (3): 229–43.

Autor, D. H., F. Levy, and R. J. Murnane. 2003. 'The Skill Content of Recent Technological Change: An Empirical Exploration'. *The Quarterly Journal of Economics* 118 (4): 1279–333.

Baccaro, L., and C. Howell. 2017. *Trajectories of Neoliberal Transformation: European Industrial Relations since the 1970s.* Cambridge: Cambridge University Press.

Becker, G. 1964. *Human Capital: A Theoretical and Empirical Analysis, with Special Reference to Education.* Chicago: University of Chicago Press.

Berlingske. 2006. 'Reform er en bombe under erhvervsuddannelserne'. *Berlingske*, 21 Juni 2006.

Billett, S. 2014. 'The Standing of Vocational Education: Sources of its Societal Esteem and Implications for its Enactment'. *Journal of Vocational Education and Training* 66 (1): 1–21.

Bøndergaard, G. 2014. *The Historical Emergence of the Key Challenges for the Future of VET in Denmark.* Oslo: NordForsk.

Bonoli, G., and P. Emmenegger. 2021. 'The Limits of Decentralized Cooperation: Promoting Inclusiveness in Collective Skill Formation Systems?' *Journal of European Public Policy* 28 (2): 229–47.

Bonoli, G., and A. Wilson. 2019. 'Bringing Firms on Board: Inclusiveness of the Dual Apprenticeship Systems in Germany, Switzerland and Denmark'. *International Journal of Social Welfare* 28 (4): 369–79.

Busemeyer, M. 2012. 'Business as a Pivotal Actor in the Politics of Training Reform: Insights from the Case of Germany'. *British Journal of Industrial Relations* 50 (4): 690–713.

Busemeyer, M. 2014. *Skills and Inequality: Partisan Politics and the Political Economy of Education and Training Reforms in Western Welfare States.* Cambridge: Cambridge University Press.

Busemeyer, M. R., M. B. Carstensen, and P. Emmenegger. 2021. 'Orchestrators of Coordination: Towards a New Role of the State in Coordinated Capitalism?' *European Journal of Industrial Relations*, DOI: https://doi.org/10.1177/09596801211062556

Busemeyer, M. R., and K. Thelen. 2020. 'Institutional Sources of Business Power'. *World Politics* 72 (3): 448–80.

Busemeyer, M. R., and C. Trampusch. 2012. 'Introduction: The Political Economy of Collective Skill Formation'. In *The Political Economy of Collective Skill Formation*, edited by M. R. Busemeyer and C. Tampusch, pp. 3–40. Oxford: Oxford University Press.

Carstensen, M. B., and C. L. Ibsen. 2021. 'Three Dimensions of Institutional Contention: Efficiency, Equality and Governance in Danish Vocational Education and Training Reform'. *Socio-Economic Review 19* (3): 1037–63.

Carstensen, M. B., P. Emmenegger, and D. Unterweger. 2022. 'Setting the Terms of State Intervention: Employers, Unions and the Politics of Inclusiveness in Austrian and Danish Vocational Education Institutions'. *European Political Science Review*, DOI: https://doi.org/10.1017/S1755773922000017.

Cedefop. 2018. *The Changing Nature and Role of Vocational Education and Training in Europe, Volume 3: The Responsiveness of European VET Systems to External Change (1995–2015)*. Luxemberg: Publications Office.

Cort, P. 2008. *The Danish Approach to Quality—in Vocational Education and Training*, 2nd edition. Copenhagen: Danish Ministry of Education.

Cort, P. 2010. 'Europeanisation and Policy Change in the Danish Vocational Education and Training System'. *Research in Comparative and International Education 5* (3): 331–43.

Culpepper, P. D. 2003. *Creating Cooperation: How States Develop Human Capital in Europe*. Ithaca: Cornell University Press.

Di Maio, G., L. Graf, and A. Wilson. 2019. 'Torn between Economic Efficiency and Social Equality? Short-track Apprenticeships in Denmark, Germany and Switzerland'. *European Educational Research Journal 18* (6): 699–723.

Dobbins, M., and M. R. Busemeyer. 2015. 'Socio-economic Institutions, Organized Interests and Partisan Politics: The Development of Vocational Education in Denmark and Sweden'. *Socio-Economic Review 13* (2): 259–84.

Durazzi, N., and L. Geyer. 2020. 'Social Inclusion in the Knowledge Economy: Unions' Strategies and Institutional Change in the Austrian and German Training Systems'. *Socio-Economic Review 18* (1): 103–24.

Emmenegger, P., S. Häusermann, B. Palier, and M. Seeleib-Kaiser (eds). 2012. *The Age of Dualization: The Changing Face of Inequality in Deindustrializing Societies*. New York: Oxford University Press.

Emmenegger, P., and L. Seitzl. 2020. 'Social Partner Involvement in Collective Skill Formation Governance: A Comparison of Austria, Denmark, Germany, the Netherlands and Switzerland'. *Transfer 26* (1): 27–42.

Esping-Andersen, G. 1990. *The Three Worlds of Welfare Capitalism*. Princeton: Princeton University Press.

Estevez-Abe, M., T. Iversen, and D. Soskice. 2001. 'Social Protection and the Formation of Skills: A Reinterpretation of the Welfare State'. In *Varieties of Capitalism: The Institutional Foundations of Comparative Advantage*, edited by P. Hall and D. Soskice, pp. 145–83. New York: Oxford University Press.

FH—Danish Trade Union Confederation. 2019. *Klinger polarisering af det danske arbejdsmarked af? [Is the polarisation of the Danish labour market receding?]*. Copenhagen: FH—Danish Trade Union Confederation.

Hall, P. A. 2020. 'How Growth Strategies Evolve in Developed Democracies'. In *Growth and Welfare in the Global Economy: How Growth Regimes Evolve*, edited by A. Hassel and B. Palier, pp. 57–97. Oxford: Oxford University Press.

Hall, P., and D. Soskice. 2001. *Varieties of Capitalism: The Institutional Foundation of Comparative Advantage*. New York: Oxford University Press.

Ibsen, C. L., and K. Thelen. 2017. 'Diverging Solidarity: Labor Strategies in the New "Knowledge" Economy'. *World Politics 69* (3): 409–47.

Ibsen, C. L., and K. Thelen. n.d. *Vocational Education and Training as a Second Chance: Firm-based Training for Young Adults in Denmark and Sweden.* Unpublished working paper.

Iversen, T., and D. Soskice. 2001. 'An Asset Theory of Social Policy Preferences'. *American Political Science Review 95* (4): 875–93.

Iversen, T., and D. Soskice. 2015. 'Democratic Limits to Redistribution: Inclusionary versus Exclusionary Coalitions in the Knowledge Economy'. *World Politics 67* (2): 185–225.

Iversen, T., and D. Soskice. 2019. *Democracy and Prosperity: Reinventing Capitalism through a Turbulent Century.* Princeton: Princeton University Press.

Jørgensen, C. H. 2018. 'The Modernization of the Apprenticeship System in Denmark 1945–2015'. In *Vocational Education in the Nordic Countries: The Historical Evolution*, edited by S. Michelsen and M. L. Stenström, pp. 171–89. Abingdon: Routledge.

Juul, I., and C. H. Jørgensen. 2011. 'Challenges for the Dual System and Occupational Self-governance in Denmark'. *Journal of Vocational Education and Training 63* (3): 289–303.

KORA. 2017. *Grundforløb på erhvervsuddannelserne efter reform.* Copenhagen: Det Nationale Institut for Kommuners og Regioners Analyse og Forskning.

Koudahl, P. 2005. 'Den gode erhvervsuddannelse? En analyse af relationerne mellem uddannelsespolitisk tænkning og elever i erhvervsuddannelse'. PhD dissertation, Roskilde University.

Lauglo, J. 1993. *Vocational Training: Analysis of Policy and Modes. Case studies of Sweden, Germany and Japan.* Paris: International Institute for Educational Planning.

Lundahl, L. 2016. 'Equality, Inclusion and Marketization of Nordic Education: Introductory Notes'. *Research in Comparative and International Education 11* (1): 3–12.

Lundahl, L., I. Erixon Arreman, U. Lundström, and L. Rönnberg. 2010. 'Setting Things Right? Swedish Upper Secondary School Reform in a 40-year Perspective'. *European Journal of Education 45*: 49–62.

Martin, C. J. 2012. 'Political Institutions and the Origins of Collective Skill Formation Systems'. In *The Political Economy of Collective Skill Formation,* edited by R. Busemeyer and C. Trampusch, pp. 41–67. Oxford: Oxford University Press.

Martin, C. J., and K. Thelen. 2007. 'The State and Coordinated Capitalism'. *World Politics 60* (1): 1–36.

Ministry of Education. 2019. *Hvad vælger eleverne, når de forlader grundskolen efter 9. og 10. klasse i 2019?* Copenhagen: Ministry of Education.

Nelson, M. 2012. 'Continued Collectivism: The Role of Trade Self-management and the Social Democratic Party in Danish VET and Training'. In *The Political Economy of Collective Skill Formation*, edited by M. Busemeyer and C. Trampusch, pp. 179–204. Oxford: Oxford University Press.

Nilsson, L. 1986. 'Fackdidaktik ur yrkespedagogiskt perspektiv' 'Teaching Methods in Vocational Education'. In *Fack didaktik del I [Teaching Methods Part I]*, edited by F. Marton, pp. 191–212. Lund: Akademiforlaget.

Nyen, T., and A. H. Tønder. 2020. 'Capacity for Reform: The Changing Roles of Apprenticeship in Three Nordic Countries'. *Transfer 26* (1): 43–56.

Nylund, M. 2012. 'The Relevance of Class in Education Policy and Research: The Case of Sweden's Vocational education'. *Education Inquiry 3* (4): 591–613.

Nylund, M., and P. Å. Rosvall. 2016. 'A Curriculum Tailored for Workers? Knowledge Organization and Possible Transitions in Swedish VET'. *Journal of Curriculum Studies 48* (5): 692–710.

Nylund, M., and M. Virolainen. 2019. 'Balancing 'Flexibility' and 'Employability': The Changing Role of General Studies in the Finnish and Swedish VET Curricula of the 1990s and 2010s'. *European Educational Research Journal 18* (3): 314–34.

Oesch, D., and G. Piccitto. 2019. 'The Polarization Myth: Occupational Upgrading in Germany, Spain, Sweden, and the UK, 1992–2015'. *Work and Occupations 46*: 441–69.

Olofsson, J., and D. P. Thunqvist. 2014. *The Swedish Model of Vocational Education and Training—Establishment, Recent Changes and Future Challenges*. Oslo: NordForsk.

Politiken. 1998. Erhvervsuddannelser strømlines' [*Vocational education is being streamlined*], *Politiken 1*. Section, p. 8.

Protsch, P., and H. Solga. 2016. 'The Social Stratification of the German VET System'. *Journal of Education and Work 29* (6): 1–25.

Skolverket. 2016. *Samlad redovisning och analys inom yrkesutbildningsområdet. Rapport 442*. Stockholm.

Skolverket. 2019. *Uppföljning av gymnasieskolan 2019. Rapport 480*. Stockholm.

Solga, H., and B. Kohlrausch. 2013. 'How Low-achieving German Youth Beat the Odds and Gain Access to Vocational Training—Insights from Within-group Variation'. *European Sociological Review 29* (5): 1068–82.

SOU. 2008. *Framtidsväge—en reformerad gymnasieskola. Betänkande av gymnasieutredningen*. Stockholm: Utbildningsdepartementet.

SOU. 2010. *Gymnasial lärlingsutbildning—utbildning för jobb. Erfarenheter efter två års försök med lärlingsutbildning*. Delbetänkande av Nationella Lärlingskommittén. Stockholm.

SOU. 2011. Gymnasial lärlingsutbildning—med fokus på kvalitet! Hur stärker vi kvaliteten i gymnasial lärlingsutbildning? Slutbetänkande av Nationella lärlingskommittén. Stockholm.

Streeck, W. 1992. *Social Institutions and Economic Performance*. London: Sage.

Streeck, W. 1997. 'Beneficial Constraints: On the Economic Limits of Rational Volumtarism'. In *Contemporary Capitalism: The Embeddedness of Institutions*, edited by J. R. Hollingsworth and R. Boyer, pp. 197–219. Cambridge: Cambridge University Press.

Streeck, W., and K. Thelen. 2005. 'Introduction: Institutional Change in Advanced Political Economies'. In *Beyond Continuity: Institutional Change in Advanced Political Economies*, edited by W. Streeck and K. Thelen, pp. 1–39. New York: Oxford University Press.

Tåhlin, M. 2019. Polariseringsmyten. Försvinner verkligen de medelkvalificerade jobben? Stockholm: Arena Idé. http://urn.kb.se/resolve?urn=urn:nbn:se:su:diva-169610.

Thelen, K. 2004. *How Institutions Evolve: The Political Economy of Skills in Germany, Britain, the United States, and Japan*. New York, Cambridge University Press.

Thelen, K. 2014. *Varieties of Liberalization and the New Politics of Social Solidarity*. Cambridge: Cambridge University Press.

Thelen, K., and M. Busemeyer. 2012. 'Institutional Change in German Vocational Training: From Collectivism toward Segmentalism'. In *The Political Economy of Collective Skill Formation*, edited by M. Busemeyer and C. Trampusch, pp. 68–91. Oxford: Oxford University Press.

Thunqvist, D. P., and A. Hallqvist. 2014. *The Current State of the Challenges for VET in Sweden*. Oslo: NordForsk.

Thunqvist, D. P., A. H. Tønder, and K. Reegård. 2019. 'A Tale of Two Reforms: Institutional Change in Vocational Education and Training in Norway and Sweden in the 1990s'. *European Educational Research Journal* 18 (3): 298–313.

Virolainen, M., and D. P. Thunqvist. 2017. 'Varieties of Universalism: Post-1990s Development in the Initial School-based System Model of VET in Finland and Sweden and Implications for Transitions to the World of Work and Higher Education'. *Journal of Vocational Education and Training* 69 (1): 47–63.

World Bank Data. 2021. *Unemployment, Youth Total (% of Total Labor Force Ages 15–24) (National Estimate)—Sweden*. Available at https://data.worldbank.org/indicator/SL.UEM.1524.NE.ZS?locations=SE. Accessed on 8 November 2021.

5
Efficiency, Social Inclusion, and the Dutch Pathway towards Vocational Education and Training Reform

Dennie Oude Nijhuis

5.1 Introduction

Collective skill formation systems have long been admired for their ability to simultaneously deliver high-quality skills that bolster firms' competitiveness and perform an integrative function by offering access to stable and relatively well-paid jobs for large groups of the population, including working-class and less academically inclined youth (Soskice 1994; Iversen 2005). According to recent scholarly work, however, it may have become increasingly difficult for collective skill formation systems to combine these two goals of delivering economic efficiency and social inclusion in recent decades (Bonoli and Emmenegger, in this volume). Broad socio-economic trends such as deindustrialization, increased international economic competition, and the growing importance of knowledge-intensive production are all believed to have undermined firms' willingness to participate in collective skill formation on a voluntary basis and accept pro-inclusiveness measures that impose costs on them. In addition, they are believed to have forced employers to become more selective in the apprenticeship application process, thereby making it more difficult for low achievers to obtain training positions (Thelen 2014; Carstensen and Ibsen 2021; Bonoli and Emmenegger, in this volume).[1]

As observed in various cross-national comparative studies, these challenges have prompted rather diverse national responses. In some of the

[1] I would like to thank Marc van der Meer, Jeroen Onstenk, Wim Nijhof, Chiel Renique, and Marlou Min for their input and comments on an earlier version of this chapter. In addition, I would like to thank the interviewees for their willingness to share their insights on the trajectory of Dutch VET reform in recent decades.

Dennie Oude Nijhuis, *Efficiency, Social Inclusion, and the Dutch Pathway towards Vocational Education and Training Reform.*
In: *Collective Skill Formation in the Knowledge Economy.* Edited by Giuliano Bonoli and Patrick Emmenegger,
Oxford University Press. © Oxford University Press (2022). DOI: 10.1093/oso/9780192866257.003.0005

countries where collective skill formation systems have come under pressure in recent decades, attempts to stem their decline and preserve their integrative function have been lacklustre or have simply failed (Thelen 2007; Kupfer 2010; Durazzi and Geyer 2019; see also Geyer and Durazzi, in this volume). In other countries, however, deliberations between the social partners and the state have succeeded in setting inclusive pathways to reform that bolstered collective skill formation systems or resulted in the creation of state-administered alternatives that offer equally certified skills (Durazzi and Geyer 2019; Bonoli and Wilson 2019; Seitzl and Unterweger, in this volume). This chapter looks at events in one such country, the Netherlands, where a series of reforms that started in the early 1980s effectively did both, creating a mixed system of vocational education and training (VET) with separate workplace-based and school-based pathways that provide equally certified skills (Anderson and Oude Nijhuis 2012; Cedefop 2016; De Bruijn et al. 2017).

The success of this inclusive pathway towards reform is of broad academic interest because it seems to defy existing trends. Despite being subjected to the same socio-economic trends as other countries classified as having collective skill formation systems, the Netherlands has not only managed to strengthen the 'dual nature' of its VET system in recent decades; it has also ensured that this system has become considerably more inclusive (Nijhof 2004; Bronneman-Helmers 2006; Westerhuis 2007; Hövels et al. 2006; De Bruijn et al. 2017). The reform process that successfully strengthened both the efficiency and social inclusion functions of the Dutch VET system culminated in the late 1990s, when both preparatory and upper-secondary level vocational education, which respectively cater for roughly 60 and 50 per cent of all school-attending youth in their respective age groups (Inspectie van het Onderwijs 2019), were completely overhauled.

One of the most striking features of this inclusive pathway towards reform, and an important reason for its success, is that it could count on broad support from the employer community. Contrary to their counterparts in countries such as Austria, Denmark, and Germany (Wiborg and Cort 2009; Nelson 2012; Busemeyer 2012; Durazzi and Geyer 2019), the main employer federations in the Netherlands for instance supported the introduction of a non-firm-based alternative to the apprenticeship system when it became clear that the latter lacked the capacity to offer sufficient training positions. After some hesitancy, and despite the fact that this school-based alternative was open to youth without any prior qualifications, Dutch employers also consented to making sure that both training methods were to produce the same skill certifications. In addition, they actively supported a series of other initiatives that served to broaden access, improve the ability of weaker students to complete their programmes, and increase mobility within the VET system as well as between the VET system and general education system.

As employers that are used to working with well-developed firm-based training systems are generally expected to oppose the introduction of alternative, non-firm-based pathways to skill formation (Busemeyer 2012) as well as measures that may 'shift the overall objective of skill formation systems too much towards inclusion' (Bonoli and Emmenegger, in the volume: XX; Carstensen and Ibsen 2021), the supportive stance of Dutch employers for these inclusive measures forms an interesting academic puzzle that this chapter seeks to tackle. This chapter does so by highlighting the importance of two distinctive historical features of the Dutch VET system: the informal and therefore flexible nature of the apprenticeship system, and the low status of both preparatory-secondary vocational education and apprenticeship training compared to respectively secondary general education and upper-secondary vocational education (which was non-firm based). These two features, which will be outlined in the following section, crucially ensured that Dutch employer groups did not view the introduction of a school alternative as a threat to the existence of the apprenticeship system—as many of their foreign counterparts did (Esser 2006). On the contrary, and as we will see, over time they genuinely came to appreciate the benefits of having two separate but equal pathways to skill formation that alternately contracted and expanded depending on economic circumstances (see also Cedefop 2016).

In line with conventional approaches on the development of collective skill formation institutions (Busemeyer and Trampusch 2012), the chapter highlights the central role played by employer groups in determining the direction of Dutch VET reform. It places particular emphasis on the asymmetry between the influence of employer groups and that of the unions in recent decades. It shows that the consequences of this asymmetry have become particularly clear in discussions over the financing, provision, and treatment of workplace training, where the unions have been forced to scale down their ambitions and come to accept employer positions in recent years. At the same time, it shows that this growing asymmetry has not undermined the willingness of Dutch employers to support measures that serve to strengthen the social inclusion function of the VET system. The chapter explains this apparent contradiction by showing how Dutch employers effectively used their leverage to ensure that this social function was largely to be performed outside of the collective skill formation framework, which meant that it did not impose major costs and constraints on firms.

The chapter is structured as follows. Given the importance of institutional legacies in shaping Dutch employer and union preferences on VET reform, it opens with a short overview of the main institutional features of the Dutch VET system during the early 1980s. The following two sections cover the series of reforms that started in this period and culminated in a major overhaul of both preparatory and upper-secondary level vocational education around the turn of the century. The fourth part analyses more recent efforts to improve the integrative nature of the skill formation system. The analysis is based on secondary readings, a reading of internal memos of the main employer federation in the Netherlands and its successors, the Federation of Dutch Industries-Christian Employers Federation (VNO-NCW), and fourteen background interviews (see appendix) with representatives of labour unions, employer organizations, and corporatist institutions.

5.2 The setting: vocational training in the Netherlands in the 1980s

Like with many of its other economic and social institutions, the Dutch VET regime has long defied a clear classification. While frequently classified as a dual system that combines high levels of workplace training with instruction at school (Eurostat 2003; OECD 2004), the importance of work-based training through apprenticeships (or work-based pathway) has actually consistently decreased since the 1970s. As shown in Table 5.1, this decline has primarily been a relative phenomenon. As the number of participants in upper-secondary vocational education began to rapidly increase from

Table 5.1 Number of youths participating in upper-secondary vocational education as part of a school-based and workplace-based pathways, 1970–2020

	School-based pathway	Workplace-based pathway
1970	77,000	61,593
1980	158,000	58,425
1990	284,000	82,421
2000	344,000	153,000
2010	358,096	172,174
2020	372,382	129,520

Sources: Ganga (1992); CBS (2020).
Note: The numbers for the years 1970, 1980, and 1990 relate to the number of participants in MBO schools and number of apprenticeships, which can be viewed as the precursors to respectively the school-based pathway and work-based pathway.

the 1970s on, the number of apprenticeship positions lagged behind, both because the availability of apprenticeship offerings was determined by market conditions and because many youth preferred upper-secondary vocational (MBO) schools (the school-based pathway) to the apprenticeship system.

These youth did so in turn because, contrary to many neighbouring countries, the school-based pathway did not have a reputation for being of poorer quality than the apprenticeship pathway. On the contrary, it had—and continues to have—a reputation among students and their parents for offering better labour market prospects than the apprenticeship pathway (Wolthuis 1999; Anderson and Oude Nijhuis 2012; Christoffels et al. 2016; Karsten 2016).

The weak reputation of the apprenticeship pathway in turn is related to the general structure of the education system (see Figure 5.1). As the Netherlands never succeeded in introducing a comprehensive middle school, students were forced to choose between various general and vocational education pathways at the age of twelve. While the choice for either the preparatory-general secondary education system—which initially consisted of three hierarchically ranked pathways: pre-university education (VWO), upper-general secondary education (HAVO), and middle-general secondary education (MAVO)—and preparatory secondary vocational education system—which consisted of one pathway called lower-professional education (LBO)—was

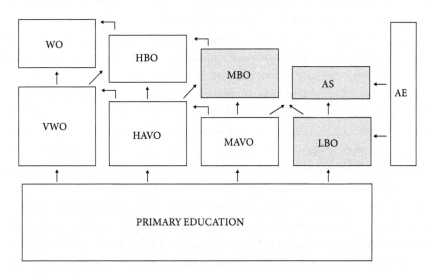

Fig. 5.1 The structure of the Dutch educational system in the early 1980s

Notes: AE, adult education; LBO, lower-professional education; MAVO, middle-general secondary education; HAVO, upper-general secondary education; VWO, pre-university education; AS, apprenticeship system; MBO, upper-secondary vocational education; HBO, higher-vocational education; WO, university education.

not necessarily supposed to be based on academic merit, it did naturally work out this way (Meijers 1983; Wolthuis 1999). As a result, LBO schools increasingly came to be viewed as the lowest ranking of four hierarchically ranked pathways, rather than as a separate but equal educational pathway. And as the apprenticeship system mostly catered for LBO graduates, while MBO schools were also open to students who had completed the secondary education system and became increasingly popular among MAVO graduates, the apprenticeship option consequently came to be viewed as lower ranking than the 'school pathway' as well.

The result was a highly stratified skill regime that offered increasingly poor labour market prospects for large groups of youth. The early age of selection meant that the social background of students played a major role in deciding whether they ended up in one of the three pathways of the secondary general education system or LBO schools. Moreover, once students ended up at LBO schools there were few opportunities for upward mobility for them. The apprenticeship system generally did not prepare them for high-paying jobs; in fact, as MBO schools became more popular among the youth, large firms in particular increasingly turned to their graduates for managerial and office work and more complex technical functions (Interviews NLD 2 and 3). And while LBO graduates could in principle participate in MBO schools, they were often ill-prepared to participate in the more theoretical, four-year programmes offered by these schools. Moreover, in response to the economic stagnation that followed the outbreak of the second oil crisis, firms increasingly scaled down their collective and individual training efforts, which meant that an increasing number of LBO graduates could not even find apprenticeship positions (Van Dijk et al. 1987).

In addition, the system was increasingly seen as performing poorly in terms of meeting firms' skill demands. Initially this criticism mostly focused on one of the consequences of the low status of the apprenticeship system and corresponding growth of MBO schools, namely, that the social partners lacked direct control over the content of an increasingly important component of professional skill formation. Whereas employer and labour union representatives jointly ran the apprenticeship system independent of government interference, including its theoretical component that was mostly organized through regional schools, the content of LBO and MBO schools was determined by school boards with little industry involvement.[2] The

---

[2] Up until the 1963 Act on Secondary Education that established the LBO, MAVO, HAVO, and VWO pathways, vocational education had largely been run by industry, although regulated and funded by the government, in the form of craft schools. The newly established LBO schools were by contrast run by school boards without industry involvement, as was the case with MBO schools, which would become

result, according to industry and an increasing number of policymakers, was a growing disconnect between the supply of and demand for skilled labour (Hövels et al. 2006). In later years, the employer federations also increasingly worried that the low status of LBO schools and the apprenticeship system would lead to a shortage of skilled workers—especially in the more technical industries (SER 1988).

By the early 1980s, discontent over the low labour market prospects of LBO graduates and the lack of direct industry influence over the content of non-apprenticeship vocational education served to trigger a series of reforms that would lead to a complete overhaul of the Dutch VET system. Because of its technical nature, importance for industry, and possibly also the low level of voter salience and absence of strong partisan cleavages, the direction of reform was heavily influenced by the preferences of the social partners. To improve the labour market prospect of LBO graduates, two groups of proposals were put forward. The first centred on ways to address the crisis of the apprenticeship system. The second involved the creation of a new non-firm-based alternative to the apprenticeship system. Like in most other countries, discussions on the first of the proposals were characterized by considerable disagreement. On the matter of the introduction of a non-firm-based alternative to the apprenticeship system, agreement by contrast proved easy to reach, as contrary to many of their foreign counterparts in more recent years, both employers' groups and the labour unions supported this initiative. The following section outlines the reasons for this support.

5.3 Dealing with the apprenticeship crisis and the introduction of a school-based alternative to firm-based training

As collective skill formation systems have come under pressure in recent decades, employer groups and labour unions have tended to develop rather different views on how to address this decline (Thelen 2007; Thelen and Busemeyer 2012). The Netherlands has been no exception to this rule. As the number of apprenticeship offerings decreased during the early 1980s, the unions initially insisted on dealing with this problem through compulsory offerings of apprenticeship positions by firms, a view that the employer federations naturally opposed. As noted by union representatives who were involved in

increasingly important as the government raised the age of compulsory education during the 1970s and 1980s (see Anderson and Oude Nijhuis 2012).

discussions over apprenticeship reform during this period, their lobbies for compulsory apprenticeship positions immediately fell flat, however, as even their political allies on the left were unwilling to support this position (Interviews NLD 7 and 9). As a result, employers merely pledged to do their best to increase the number of apprenticeship positions in future years. In addition, they insisted on the need for deregulation and lower levels of remuneration (Van Dellen 1984; Geurts 1989). These pleas eventually proved somewhat successful: in the mid-1980s, a centre-right government for instance introduced legislation that allowed individual firms to pay apprenticeship wages that were below the youth minimum wage under certain circumstances, although doing so required sectoral-level union consent (Van Dijk et al. 1987; Hövels et al. 2006: 15).

In addition, negotiations between the state and social partners resulted in an agreement to introduce and expand collective training funds to deal with the problem of poaching. These funds, which were jointly financed by workers and employers, already existed in some sectors and set at a certain percentage (generally between 0.2% and 0.5%) of the wage sum. As the development of these funds was linked to discussions on wage moderation, they were initially largely financed by workers themselves (Van Dijk et al. 1987). To stimulate their development, the government in turn increased the level of employer subsidies for apprenticeship positions and allocated them towards these funds rather than to individual firms (Geurts 1989). The existence of these funds provided a strong stimulus to firms to create new apprenticeship positions. After all, while payment was obligatory (the bargaining agreements that regulated these funds were generally subjected to statutory extension), the receipt of a subsidy depended on firms' training efforts. As a result, but partly also because the economy improved in the second half of the decade, the number of apprenticeship positions increased by roughly 30 per cent during the 1980s (see Table 5.1).

Since the number of students increased by much more than 30 per cent in this period, this expansion was not nearly sufficient to make sure that all LBO graduates were able to find apprenticeship positions though. And as MBO schools continued to be out of reach for many of these graduates, so was further educational advancement for them. Partly in response to this problem, government officials suggested the idea of creating a two-year school-based alternative to both the apprenticeship system and the four-year MBO schools, called 'short track-MBO' (KMBO) programmes. As these programmes were primarily designed for LBO graduates, they were meant to produce skills that were similar to and as equally valued as those provided by the apprenticeship system. Moreover, to ensure that everyone in this age group could obtain access to upper-secondary education, government officials proposed that youths without any prior qualifications should also be able to register for them; the only condition was to be that participants were at least sixteen years of age (Karstanje 1988).

As longstanding proponents of measures to improve access and permeability, the union federations naturally supported the initiative. Perhaps more surprisingly, so did the employer federations. Contrary to their counterparts in countries such as Austria, Denmark, and Germany when faced with similar non-firm-based training initiatives in later years (Wiborg and Cort 2009; Busemeyer 2012; Nelson 2012; Durazzi and Geyer 2019), and despite initially professing doubts as to whether it clearly served industry's skill needs, the employer federations raised no objections to the KMBO initiative (Van Dijk et al 1987). Nor did they object to the scheme's open nature. In fact, in later years representatives of the largest employer federation in the Netherlands, the Federation of Dutch Industries (VNO), would come to describe the absence of admission requirements as 'one of the great strengths' of the KMBO programmes (VNO-NCW, Archief Chiel Renique, Beroepsonderwijs 1987–1991, 19 February 1987).

The employer federations did object to the unions' suggestion to structure some of these programmes as de facto apprenticeships, and thus to provide their participants with a status and treatment that was similar to that of apprentices. While supporting the notion that KMBO participants obtained some workplace experience, the employer federations were adamant that they were regarded as school participants. This insistence was obviously motivated by cost concerns and the desire to retain control over who entered the apprenticeship system. As had been the case with discussions on how to revive the apprenticeship system, the employer federations once more negotiated from a position of strength and found it easy to impose their views on this matter (Interviews NLD 3, 7, and 9). Unlike participants in the apprenticeship system, KMBO participants were therefore to be treated as school-goers with no clear link to individual firms; nor were they to receive wages and benefits (Geurts 1989).

As employers who are used to working with well-developed firm-based training systems are generally expected to oppose the introduction of alternative, non-firm-based pathways to training (Busemeyer 2012; Busemeyer and Trampusch 2012) and given that the KMBO initiative so clearly served a social purpose, the employer federations' supportive stance may nevertheless be viewed as remarkable. So how are we to explain their support? The answer to this question seems to lie foremost in the informal and therefore relatively flexible approach towards apprenticeship training in the Netherlands at the time. Unlike in countries such as Germany, apprenticeship certifications were for instance not codified into labour law. Instead, they were determined by the industry associations on a voluntary basis, with employer groups generally taking a leading role (Willemse 2011). These associations, which also ran the regional schools that provided the theoretical component of the apprenticeship system, were also given responsibility for running the KMBO programmes. As a result, employers not only controlled the content of KMBO programmes; they also had significant leeway to determine whether KMBO programmes were to develop the same learning goals and award the same skill certificates as the apprenticeship pathway.

This latter feature was important as the social partners initially disagreed on the extent to which KMBO programmes could deliver skills that were equal to those delivered by the apprenticeship system. Whereas labour union representatives immediately emphasized the necessity of treating them as delivering equal skills, many employers, in particular in construction, were sceptical as to whether this would be possible (Interviews NLD 7, 8, and 9). Yet crucially, this stance seems to have evolved over time. When the employer-dominated Wagner committee in the early 1980s published a report on VET reform, it merely recommended that KMBO programmes should have a legal status that was 'similar' to that of the apprenticeship system (Van Dellen 1984: 138). By the late 1980s, VNO representatives noted that there was still debate within certain sectors as to whether KMBOs could achieve the same qualification levels as the apprenticeship pathway, but also argued that industry should strive to achieve this aim (VNO-NCW, Archief Chiel Renique, Beroepsonderwijs 1987–1991, 19 February 1987). Another couple of years later these representatives had firmly concluded that it was indeed possible to develop the same learning goals and certificates for both pathways in most sectors (VNO-NCW, Archief Chiel Renique, Beroepsonderwijs 1992–1997, 11 May 1993).

This evolutionary stance seems to have been partly tied to a growing appreciation among employers of the complementary nature of the KMBO and apprenticeship pathways. In that respect the KMBO initiative differed crucially from similar attempts to create school-based alternatives to the apprenticeship system, such as the initiative to temporarily upgrade the system of school-based vocational training in Germany in the early 2000s: where German employer groups viewed this initiative as a potential threat that could undermine firms' willingness to participate in apprenticeship training (Esser 2006), their Dutch employer counterparts never expressed similar concerns. Instead, they emphasized the advantages of having an alternative training route under circumstances that made it difficult for particular sectors to train sufficient workers through the apprenticeship system (Interviews NLD 2 and 3). It is for this reason also that they developed an interest in making sure that KMBO programmes developed the same learning goals and offered the same certificates as the apprenticeship system. Thus, when a centre-right government in the mid-1980s suggested barring KMBOs from providing final qualifications, which would effectively have turned them into a preparatory route for the apprenticeship system, the employer federations among others rejected this idea by referring to the benefits of having two pathways towards skill formation that alternately expanded or contracted based on economic circumstances (Geurts 1989). This feature would later come to be viewed as one of the main strengths of the Dutch VET system (Cedefop 2016)—including by the social partners (Interviews NLD 1–13). The 1995 Act on professional education (Wet educatie en beroepsonderwijs, or WEB) would formalize this principle by integrating the three existing pathways for VET (MBO, KMBO, and the apprenticeship system) into a single organizational structure.

In addition to providing an accessible pathway towards improving the labour market prospects of less academically inclined LBO graduates, KMBO programmes thus increasingly came to be appreciated by industry as providing an equivalent route towards meeting their skill needs. To be sure, in certain sectors there remained discussion as to whether KMBO programmes offered skills that were equal to that of the apprenticeship system (Interviews NLD 8, 9, and 10). Yet when the 1995 introduction of the WEB formally equalized the two routes by creating an integrated system with separate school-based and workplace-based pathways that delivered the same skill certifications at all levels of secondary vocational education, the employer federations raised no objections (Interviews NLD 2, 3). According to union representatives who were involved in the act's introduction, this acceptance foremost reflected the growing appreciation of KMBO programmes among employers (Interviews NLD 7, 8, and 9). In addition, they emphasized a more strategic consideration: as the WEB created equal school- and workplace-based pathways at *all* levels of secondary vocational education, it also served to raise the status of the apprenticeship system vis-à-vis MBO programmes. Any objections to the equalization of school-based and workplace-based pathways at the former KMBO level might possibly have jeopardized the latter goal (Interviews NLD 8 and 9).

In sum, unlike their counterparts in many other countries with well-established firm-based training systems, Dutch employers did not oppose the introduction of a school-based alternative to the apprenticeship system. In fact, they increasingly came to appreciate the benefits of having two separate but equal pathways towards skill formation. At the same time, they opposed any attempt to impose constraints on the operation of the apprenticeship system. As we will see in the following section, they would continue to do so in subsequent years when confronted with proposals to improve the efficiency function of the VET system by completely reorganizing it along dual lines. Because of their opposition to doing so, the major WEB reform of the 1990s instead created a hybrid system that imposed a much lower burden on industry than traditional dual systems tended to do (Nijhof 2004; Cedefop 2016; De Bruijn et al. 2017). And because the system consequently retained the open nature of school systems while internal mobility simultaneously increased, the WEB also improved the system's integrative function.

5.4 The introduction of the current 'dual system'

The introduction of the WEB can best be viewed as the culmination of a series of reforms that started with the above-mentioned introduction of KMBO schools and agreements to stem the decline of the apprenticeship system during the 1980s. While these measures had certainly been successful, they were not designed to solve two other aforementioned problems that were increasingly viewed as urgent. The first of these was the perceived lack of 'fit' between the skill demands of industry and the skill set provided by the school system (Van der Klink 1999; Hövels et al. 2006). The second was the low status of LBO schools, which accordingly found it increasingly difficult to attract and retain students, and, by extension, the apprenticeship system (Wolthuis 1999; Bronneman-Helmers 2006). By the end of the decade, employers had become so concerned about the latter problem that they publicly expressed fears about the emergence of skill shortages in the future (VNO 1989). This fear not only provided them with a strong interest in raising the status of the apprenticeship system, as we will see below, it also prompted them to become early proponents of a merger between MAVO and LBO schools.

To improve the fit between the supply of and demand for skilled labour, two solutions were put forward. The first of these imposed few constraints on employers while greatly increasing their control over the content of vocational education. As a result, they received broad employer support (Interviews NLD 2, 3, and 11). Following recommendations of the aforementioned Wagner Committee to create a procedure to enable industry and school representatives to consult on a regular basis to investigate how MBO programmes could best meet industry needs, a procedure was set up to create sectoral-designed learning outcomes and professional qualifications that were to be used by MBO schools to determine the content of their courses. The process of devising sectoral-designed learning outcomes would later be formalized with the introduction of the WEB, which made existing national sectoral bodies run by representatives of education and the social partners responsible for the framework of certification by instructing them to define professional profiles, design skill requirements for these profiles, and doing quality checks (Van der Meijden et al. 2009).

The second proposal by contrast threatened to impose a major burden on employers and consequently received a much more cautious response from them. From the early 1980s on, various government officials and committees came to argue for a complete reorganization of the upper-secondary vocational system on a dual basis or even—as was the case with the 1990 Rauwenhof Committee—the entire educational system. Government officials and the representatives of these committees often motivated their proposals by pointing to the operation of the German dual system and its success in adequately preparing youths for the labour market (Tijdelijke Adviescommissie Onderwijs-Arbeidsmarkt 1990; Westerhuis 2007). In addition, they pointed out that an increase in on-the-job learning would not only make it easier for students to meet the skill demands of industry; it might also help to motivate more practically oriented students to continue their education—an argument that carried much weight because of the high level of early leaving at the time (Karsten 2016).

While certainly appreciative of the strengths of the German dual system, the employer federations nevertheless realized that its introduction in the Netherlands would impose an immense organizational burden on industry (Interview NLD 3). After all, the number of KMBO and MBO students was nearly three times as large as the number of apprentices during the 1980s (see Table 5.1). In addition, the employer federations suspected that the government's interest in reorganizing upper-secondary vocational education on a dual basis was partly motivated by financial considerations, which meant that it could very well result in a partial shift in the costs of education from the state to industry (Wolthuis 1999). And indeed, during discussions over the introduction of the WEB, the government did initially link proposals for a partial shift from school to workplace training to plans for cost reductions (Interviews NLD 2 and 7).

As they simultaneously recognized the benefits of reorganizing the VET system on a dual basis, the employer federations nevertheless expressed their support for emerging plans to do so. At the same time, however, they sought to ensure that the burden that such a move would place on industry was to be as limited as possible—and with much success. The previous section already mentioned how earlier union pleas for compulsory offerings of apprenticeship positions had fallen flat on their face after they were resisted by the employer federations. On the latter's insistence, government representatives similarly refrained from expressing any interest in putting pressure on employers to ensure that there would be sufficient training positions. Instead, governments of various political persuasions always proceeded from the assumption that voluntary cooperation by industry would be sufficient. They did so even though the labour unions and various government officials voiced strong doubts as to whether this would indeed be the case (Interviews NLD 7 and 9).

Following long tripartite consultations, parliament eventually also shied away from introducing a 'pure' dual training system under which all students were to be treated as apprentices. This decision was not only supported by the employer federations, but also by the unions. Whereas the employer federations did so because of the potential costs that such a system would impose on firms, the labour unions did so out of fear that it might lead to a lack of training positions for all students—especially during economic downturns and for weaker students (Interviews NLD 8 and 9). The latter fear was undoubtedly reinforced by the governments' voluntary approach towards the provision of apprenticeship positions. In addition, the unions had a strong interest in preserving the gains that had been made in previous years with the introduction of KMBO programmes, which granted access to all youths aged sixteen and over and did not require these youths to obtain a contract with an employer first. In other words, both sides of industry wanted to preserve a more open school-based pathway in addition to the existing apprenticeship pathway—although they did so for partly different reasons.

As a result, the 1995 WEB introduced a mixed system that differentiated between a school-based pathway under which workplace training amounted to between 20 and 60 per cent of student activity and a workplace-based pathway under which workplace training amounted to at least 60 per cent of student activity. Students who undertook workplace training as part of the school-based pathway were to be treated as interns rather than as apprentices with a work contract and union attempts to regulate their treatment in collective bargaining agreements were mostly unsuccessful (Interviews NLD 7 and 9). Moreover, whereas the quality of training as part of the workplace-based pathway remained subject to extensive guidelines and strong scrutiny, the regulation and supervision of internships as part of the school-based pathway was to be relatively light. In other words, the act ensured that workplace training as part of the school-based pathway imposed as light a burden on industry as possible.

The benefits of this system included its ability to offer high levels of work-place training—by the mid-2000s workplace training on average amounted to roughly 50 per cent of total curriculum time for the school-based pathway (Onstenk 2010), while being less vulnerable than regular dual training systems to shortages in the availability of training slots. Students in the school-based pathway did of course have to find internship positions, but as these were unpaid and their duration was generally limited to three to six months, finding such positions was viewed as less challenging than finding apprenticeship positions for all participants in upper-secondary-level vocational education. And indeed, while there have consistently been concerns about the availability of training positions for both the school-based and workplace-based pathways, in particular for minority youths, these problems are generally viewed as being less severe than in countries with more 'pure' dual systems (Interviews NLD 1, 5, and 6).

In addition to agreeing on the need to maintain separate school- and apprenticeship-style pathways, the social partners jointly pushed for a full integration of all existing programmes into a single integrated system of upper-secondary-level vocational training. The WEB realized this ambition by creating separate but equally certified school- and workplace pathways that both offered programmes which were mostly organized by large regional training centres (ROCs),[3] and categorizing the programmes offered by both pathways into four hierarchical levels. Most of the programmes that ranked at the highest two levels (levels 3 and 4) corresponded to former MBO programmes, although some of these programmes also corresponded to former apprenticeship programmes. All programmes ranked at the second-lowest level (level 2) corresponded to either former KMBO or apprenticeship programmes. All programmes were categorized as MBO programmes and to make sure that the new system remained broadly accessible, entry into all level 1 and 2 programmes (a new category that trained for assistant-level jobs) and level 2 programmes of the school-based pathway were open to youth without prior qualifications; access to the workplace-based pathway of level 2 programmes and all level 3 and 4 programmes did require the completion of a lower-secondary-level education programme—or a lower-level upper-secondary education programme.

By maintaining separate but equally certified school- and workplace-based pathways, the system maintained its accessible nature. Moreover, by integrating all existing programmes the WEB also greatly increased mobility within the VET system. The completion of a programme at a particular level enabled

---

[3] While most MBO programmes were organized through regional training centres, some sectors (agriculture, shipbuilding, furniture, and the graphical sector) preserved the right to organize their own sectoral schools, which meant that they remained separate from the multi-sectoral approach of regional training centres.

students to continue their education at a higher level and do so at an accelerated pace; completion of the highest level (level 4) furthermore gave access to participation in higher professional education (HBO) schools—as had previously been the case with the completion of MBO programmes. Finally, by grouping programmes into large regionally organized school centres, it proved easier to facilitate students when they wanted to switch between pathways and different types of programmes—as long as these were on the same level. As these 'inclusive' features imposed no constraints on employers and had various benefits they were fully supported by them. The preservation of a separate open school-based pathway meant that there would continue to be two 'communicating vessels' that alternately contracted and expanded based on economic circumstances, thus ensuring the continuation of skill formation during economic downturns (Interviews NLD 3, 10). Moreover, as it facilitated skill development, employer representatives furthermore appreciated the new system's ability to facilitate mobility within the VET system. Finally, the integration of all forms of upper-secondary-level education into a single school under the name MBO school primarily helped to realize their long-standing ambition of raising the status of the apprenticeship pathway (Interviews NLD 2, 3, 10, 12, 13).

In consecutive years, employer representatives consequently put considerable effort into expanding the number of workplace-based level 3 and 4 programmes. These efforts have not been fully successful, however, in part as a consequence of a major concession the social partners had been forced to make during the WEB's introduction: where they previously controlled the content and organization of the apprenticeship system, ROCs—which are run by independent school boards—now determine which courses are to be offered as part of both the school- *and* workplace-based pathways. And for a variety of reasons, ROCs have generally displayed a preference for creating programmes that are offered as part of the school-based pathway (Onstenk and Blokhuis 2007). Employer and union representatives view this loss of control as the price they had to pay for the responsibility they gained in a more important area, that of determining professional profiles and skill requirements for all ROC programmes. Moreover, as the share of participants in the workplace-based pathway initially increased, they did not immediately regard the lack of newly created workplace-based level 3 and 4 programmes as a major problem. This changed as the share of participants in the workplace-based pathway began to decline in recent years, however (see Table 5.1). According to many actors involved, the failure to radically increase the number of workplace-based level 3 and 4 programmes constitutes a major reason for the continuation of the low status of this pathway and its decreasing popularity among students in recent years (Interviews NLD 2, 3, 8, and 9).

A few years after the WEB's introduction, parliament embarked on another major reorganization of the educational system by merging MAVO and LBO schools into large preparatory vocational education (VMBO) schools. This reform was viewed as complementary to the WEB's introduction, which had after all merged the programmes for which MAVO and LBO schools prepared, creating the structure shown in Figure 5.2.

By embarking on this reform parliament fulfilled a longstanding wish of the social partners, which had jointly argued for a merger between these two types of education since the late 1980s (SER 1988). The employer federations had done so by arguing that such a merger offered 'the best possibility to increase the status of LBO schools' (VNO-NCW, Archief Chiel Renique, Beroepsonderwijs 1987–1991, 24 November 1987). As a result, they opposed initial calls for a 'vertical' integration wherein these two types of education were offered in the same location but remained separate in practice. Instead, they argued that differentiation at VMBO schools should start in the third year only (VNO-NCW, Archief Chiel Renique, Beroepsonderwijs 1987–1991, 23 February 1988; 15 June 1990).

That it would take more than a decade for the joint lobby of the social partners to result in actual reform may partly be attributed to the priority given to the reform of upper-secondary-level education. More important, however,

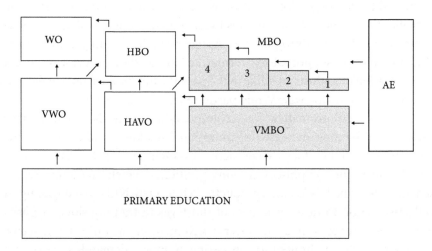

Fig. 5.2 The current structure of the Dutch educational system

Notes: AE, adult education; VMBO, preparatory vocational education; HAVO, upper-general secondary education; VWO, pre-university education; MBO, upper-secondary vocational education; HBO, higher-vocational education; WO, university education.

was that MAVO schools and other interests strongly resisted a merger with VBO schools, fearing that it would lower the status and quality of education for future MAVO-level students. And to some extent these fears do seem to have materialized. As had been the case with LBO schools in the past, VMBO schools suffer from a poor reputation, with some parents going to great lengths to make sure their children do not attend these schools. As a result, the share of Dutch youth attending VMBO schools has declined slightly since their introduction while the share attending HAVO and VWO schools has grown somewhat (CBS 2019). In response to this development the Educational Council (Onderwijsraad), an advisory council that mainly consists of educational experts, published a report in 2015 in which it advised the government to re-organize lower-secondary-level education into two pathways, a 'MAVO' and 'craftmanship' pathway (Onderwijsraad 2015).

5.5 Recent initiatives to improve the system's social inclusion function

As the reforms of the 1990s constituted such a major overhaul of the VET system, consecutive reform mostly amounted to incremental changes that were often taken in response to existing problems that had not been sufficiently addressed by previous reforms. Most of these measures served to ensure the availability of sufficient training positions and encourage weaker VET students to complete their programmes. As had been the case in previous years, Dutch employers supported the former as long as these did not impose a strong burden on industry. Unlike in the past, the unions have not challenged this stance in a major way. While partly reflecting past experience of their weak position on this matter, this accommodating stance also seems to have been guided by their increased organizational weakness and resulting tendency to redirect their focus to core activities (Interview NLD 9). Thus, rather than lobbying for compulsory training positions—which one union representative described as 'counterproductive' (Interview NLD 5)—engaging in collective action to raise awareness of shortages in training slots, or pushing for measures to combat employer discrimination, the unions' role seems to have been mostly limited to supporting employer demands for external supervision, government funding, and making sure that the number of participants in VET programmes and content of these programmes are in line with industry demand (Interview NLD 1, 5, 6, and 11).

As a result, most initiatives echoed the voluntary approach taken in the past. These included stimulating ROCs to improve their contacts with individual firms and sectoral associations, which resulted in various sectoral- and regional-level initiatives. Some of these agreements also included 'declarations of intent' by employers to specifically offer training positions for vulnerable groups and youths living in deprived areas (Bokdam et al. 2015). In addition, the government aimed to facilitate employers by providing tax facilities (which have, however, been reduced in the wake of the 2009 crisis) and providing external coaching for students in need of heavy supervision. In addition, initiatives such as the 2013 'Tech Pact' aimed to facilitate the use of digital counters to connect schools, students, and firms that offer training slots and employment. These measures also extended to school leavers: a 2009 report produced by a taskforce on youth unemployment for instance resulted in an agreement to create 25,000 jobs for school leavers who could not find a job within three months (Ministerie van Sociale Zaken en Werkgelegenheid 2009).

The unions' weakness on this matter is also reflected by the recent weakening of the financial position of collective training funds in several sectors. This development has been particularly severe in construction, traditionally one of the strongholds of these funds, where two major collective funds have recently been liquidated after employer organizations in the sector proved unwilling to continue to finance them (Blijleven et al. 2016). While the more rapid growth in non-standard labour in this sector makes the situation in construction unique, employers in other sectors have in recent years also become more reluctant to continue to finance sectoral training funds. This reluctance is due to a variety of different factors, including the rapid depletion of these funds in some sectors and the worsening of the position of individual firms in the wake of the 2009 crisis, and the transfer of some legal tasks that were initially performed by these funds to the national level (Interviews NLD 6, 7, and 8). As the weakening of sectoral training funds is a relatively recent development, it is hard to say whether it will continue or be reversed in the future—and what consequences this will have for the development of the workplace-based pathway.

Recent discussions on how to encourage weaker VET students to complete their programme and move up in the skill ladder have similarly been characterized by strong agreement among labour unions and employers. This consensus has been facilitated by a common interest in increasing the workplace training component of the school-based pathway, which they, as noted earlier, view as crucial for both improving the skill set of VET participants and enabling low academic achievers to complete their education

(Onstenk 2010; Interviews NLD 3, 7, and 8). For partly similar reasons, both employer groups and the labour unions also supported the introduction of a new 'learn–work trajectory' for practically oriented VMBO students in 2001, which provides access to comparable MBO-programmes at level 2. This new trajectory is generally viewed as having played a crucial role in decreasing the early leaving rate, which declined significantly in recent decades from 17.6 per cent in 1996 to 7.5 per cent in 2019—which is lower than the rate in most neighbouring countries (Eurostat 2020).

At the same time, agreement has been facilitated by the fact that responsibility for the content of both the school- and workplace-based pathway now lie with ROCs, which means that efforts to encourage mobility and the ability of weaker VET students to complete their programme mainly places a burden on ROC school boards—rather than on employers. These efforts included rewarding ROCs for fast programme completion and compulsory monitoring of early leavers for at least a year after they leave school. At the same time, it has become easier for the government to cancel programmes when a higher percentage of graduates remains unemployed for a long period (OCW 2015). In addition, the government has increased funding for students with weak prospects of programme completion, job coaching facilities for vulnerable groups, and orientation programmes, which have become obligatory for the practical VMBO pathways.

To encourage students to further improve their skill set, various initiatives furthermore aimed to facilitate ROCs in their efforts to persuade their students to continue schooling at a higher level after they had completed a lower-level programme. In addition, and as noted earlier, with limited success, the social partners have attempted to increase the number of workplace-based level 3 and 4 programmes. Moreover, in 2008 parliament passed a law stating that youths aged 16 and 17 without a basic vocational qualification at the upper-secondary level (VWO, HAVO, MBO-2, or up) are required to continue learning (the qualification requirement). Finally, to improve the overall quality of VET education and better prepare VET students for participation in the labour market, basic skill requirements—in particular with regards to the use of language and elementary-level mathematics—at both the preparatory and secondary level have been made stricter in recent years.

These latter two initiatives have received some criticism in recent years from school representatives and educational experts who have pointed to a well-known dilemma that affects both school-based and dual VET systems: initiatives that aim to improve the quality of education may serve to prepare students more adequately for the labour market but do so at the risk of reducing inclusiveness. After all, they tend to present an additional hurdle to programme completion while not improving the relative position of weaker students in the educational system. For similar reasons, another measure has also received some criticism in recent years: in 2013, parliament ended the possibility of non-qualified enrolment in MBO level 2 programmes, which are now only open to those who have obtained VMBO, HAVO, or VWO certificates. This policy change was prompted by a growing increase in the number of students who entered level 2 programmes without a previous qualification, and who often required intensive supervision. To make sure that this measure did not reduce access in a major way, ROC and other MBO schools were required to create entry-level programmes separate from MBO level 1 programmes.

5.6 Conclusion

For a variety of reasons that are outlined in this volume, collective skill formation systems have in recent decades found it increasingly difficult to deliver on the twin goals of meeting firms' skill demands and offering access to stable and relatively well-paid jobs for large groups of the population, including the working class and less academically inclined youths. Moreover, in many countries, attempts at progressive reform have faltered because of employer—and sometimes also union—resistance to the two main conceivable solutions to this problem. First, employer groups have tended to oppose measures that impose additional costs and constraints on their members. Because of their reliance on firm-based training, it has consequently proven to be very difficult to improve the operation and preserve the integrative function of collective skill formation systems. At the same time, employer groups, and sometimes also labour unions, used to working with well-established apprenticeship systems have tended to resist the introduction of non-firm-based alternatives to firm-based training. By focusing on VET reform in the Netherlands, this chapter, however, has shown that the latter is by no means inevitable.

The main purpose of this chapter was to show how the unusual stance of Dutch employers' groups facilitated the coming about of an inclusive pathway towards VET reform in the Netherlands in recent decades. Like their counterparts in neighbouring countries, Dutch employers have in recent decades consistently resisted all attempts to improve the operation of the apprenticeship system by imposing additional obligations on their members. To limit the costs of apprenticeship training to industry, they also resisted suggestions to reorganize the entire VET system along the lines of traditional dual systems. At the same time, they did not resist the coming about of a new school-based alternative to the apprenticeship system. Nor did they oppose the equalization of firm-based and non-firm-based pathways to skill formation. As a result, they played a key role in making sure that the reform process started in the 1980s resulted in a hybrid system of VET provision that effectively combines the open nature of school-based systems with the close involvement of industry that characterizes apprenticeship-based or 'dual' systems.

In addition to reaffirming the pivotal role of employers' groups in shaping the direction of VET reform, the chapter offers various broader insights. First, it shows that employer groups do not necessarily have to view the introduction of non-firm-based pathways towards skill formation as a threat to the operation of the apprenticeship system. In fact, neither the employer nor union representatives who were involved in the introduction of KMBO programmes and the WEB (which after all created separate school- and workplace-based pathways at all levels of VET) displayed much concern about the impact of these initiatives on firms' willingness to offer apprenticeship positions. Nor, it should be added, is there much evidence of such an impact. While the share of participants in the workplace-based pathway has declined in recent years, there is broad agreement that this decline is primarily the result of the low appreciation of this pathway by youths and their parents—rather than of firms' unwillingness to offer apprenticeship positions (Onstenk and Blokhuis 2007; De Bruijn et al. 2017).

In addition, the findings of this chapter confirm the importance of institutional legacies in shaping the positions and preferences of major actors on important aspects of VET reform. Like their counterparts in other countries with well-developed collective skill formation systems when faced with similar initiatives, Dutch employers for instance initially displayed some doubts as to the ability of KMBO programmes to deliver the same skills as existing apprenticeship programmes. As a result of the flexible nature of the apprenticeship system and their control over the content and certification of KMBO programmes, these doubts did not, however, lead them to oppose the introduction of these programmes or insist on formally designing them as a preparatory route for the apprenticeship system—as their German counterparts did, for instance. Instead, they adopted a flexible approach under which the manner of skill certification was determined at the sectoral level— as was already the case with apprenticeship programmes. And crucially, this flexible approach enabled industry groups to change the manner of skill certification over time. The latter is important, as employers over time became increasingly confident that KMBO programmes could develop the same learning goals and produce the same skill certifications as apprenticeship programmes.

Finally, the chapter showed how difficult it is to disentangle the many factors that determine the policy positions of collective actors. Take for instance the consent of the Dutch employer federations for the formal equalization of KMBO and apprenticeship programmes that came about with the introduction of the WEB. This consent can be explained in two ways. First, the employer federations seem to have displayed a genuine appreciation of KMBO programmes and increasingly came to view them as able to provide equal skills to those delivered by apprenticeship programmes. At the same time, there can be no doubt that strategic considerations played a role: as the WEB integrated all existing pathways towards vocational skill formation it also served employers longstanding goal of raising the status of the apprenticeship system by creating workplace-based alternatives to existing MBO programmes, and resistance to the formal equalization of KMBO and apprenticeship programmes might very well have jeopardized that goal.

References

Anderson, K., and D. Oude Nijhuis. 2012. 'The Long Road to Collective Skill Formation in the Netherlands'. In *The Political Economy of Skill Formation*, edited by M. Busemeyer and C. Trampusch, pp. 101–25. Oxford: Oxford University Press.

Blijleven, R., F. Marcelissen, A. Weel, and J. Golsteijn. 2016. 'Een nieuwe organisatie, een nieuwe aanpak'. *Tijdschrift Bedrijfs- en Verzekeringsgeneeskunde 24*: 225–9.

Bokdam, J., I. van den Ende, and A. Gelderblom. 2015. *Monitoring en evaluatie vsv-beleid 2012–2015: overkoepelende samenvatting*. Zoetermeer: Panteia.

Bonoli, G., and A. Wilson. 2019. 'Bringing Firms on Board: Inclusiveness of the Dual Apprenticeship Systems in Germany, Switzerland and Denmark'. *International Journal of Social Welfare 28* (4): 369–79.

Bronneman-Helmers, R. 2006. *Duaal als ideaal? Leren en werken in het beroeps- en hoger onderwijs*. The Hague: SCP.

Bruijn, E. de, S. Billet, and J. Onstenk. 2017. *Enhancing Teaching and Learning in the Dutch Vocational Education System: Reforms Enacted*. New York: Springer.

Busemeyer, M. 2012. 'Business as a Pivotal Actor in the Politics of Training Reform: Insights from the Case of Germany'. *British Journal of Industrial Relations 50* (4): 690–713.

Busemeyer, M., and C. Trampusch. 2012. 'The Comparative Political Economy of Collective Skill Formation'. In *The Political Economy of Collective Skill Formation*, edited by M. Busemeyer and C. Trampusch, pp. 3–40. Oxford: Oxford University Press.

Carstensen, M. B., and C. L. Ibsen. 2021. 'Three Dimensions of Institutional Contention: Efficiency, Equality and Governance in Danish Vocational Education and Training Reform'. *Socio-Economic Review 19* (3): 1037–63.

CBS—Centraal Bureau voor de Statistiek. 2019. *Jaarrapport 2019 Landelijke jeugdmonitor*. Den Haag: CBS.

CBS—Centraal Bureau voor de Statistiek. 2019. Statline. Den Haag: CBS.

Cedefop. 2016. *Vocational Education and Training in the Netherlands: Short Description*.Luxembourg: Cedefop.

Christoffels, I., J. Cuppen, and S. Vrielink. 2016. *Verzameling notities over de daling van de bbl en praktijkleren. Interne rapportage in opdracht van het ministerie van OCW, directie MBO*. Den Bosch: ECBO.

Dellen, H. van. 1984. *Een nieuw elan*. Deventer: Kluwer.

Dijk, C. van, T. Akkermans, and B. Hövels. 1987. *Sociale partners en het beroepsonderwijs in Nederland*. Luxemburg: Cedefop.

Durazzi, N., and L. Geyer. 2019. 'Social Inclusion in the Knowledge Economy: Unions' Strategies and Institutional Change in the Austrian and German Training Systems'. *Socio-Economic Review 18* (1): 103–24.

Esser, F. H. 2006. 'Vollzeitschulische Berufsausbildung: Bedrohung oder Herausfordering für das duale System?' In *Vollzeitschulische Berufsausbildung: Eine gleichwertige Partnerin des dualen Systems?* edited by A. Zöller, pp. 91–8. Bielefeld: Bertelsmann–Verlag.

Eurostat. 2003. *Key Figures on Vocational Education and Training*. Luxembourg: European Centre for the Development of Vocational Training.

Eurostat. 2020. Education and Training in the EU. Luxembourg: European Centre for the Developmetn of Vocational Training.

Ganga, V. 1992. *Deelname, uitval en rendement van het leerlingwezen*. Zoetermeer: Ministerie van Onderwijs en Wetenschap.

Geurts, J. 1989. *Van niemandsland naar beroepenstructuur: een studie over de aansluiting tussen onderwijs en arbeid op het niveau van aankomend vakmanschap*. Nijmegen: Instituut voor Toegepaste Sociale Wetenschappen.

Hövels, B., K. Visser, and H. Schuit. 2006. *Over 'hamers' en 'vasthouden' gesproken. Vijfentwintig jaar middelbaar beroepsonderwijs in Nederland: terug- en vooruitblik*. Nijmegen: Kenniscentrum Beroepsonderwijs Arbeidsmarkt.

Inspectie van het Onderwijs. 2019. *De staat van het onderwijs*. Den Haag: Ministerie van Onderwijs, Cultuur en Wetenschap.

Iversen, T. 2005. *Capitalism, Democracy and Welfare*. New York: Cambridge University Press.

Karstanje, S. 1988. *Beleidsevaluatie bij controversiële onderwijsvernieuwing.* Amsterdam: Stichting Centrum voor Onderwijsonderzoek.

Karsten, S. 2016. *De hoofdstroom in de Nederlandse onderwijsdelta. Een nuchtere balans van het mbo.* Antwerpen: Maklu Uitgevers.

Klink, M. van der. 1999. *Effectiviteit van Werkplek-Opleidingen.* Universiteit Twente: Academisch Proefschrift.

Kupfer, A. 2010. 'The Socio-political Significance of Changes to the Vocational Systems in Germany'. *British Journal of Sociology of Education 31* (1): 85–97.

Meijden, A. van der, A. Westerhuis, J. Huisman, J. Neuvel, and R. Groenenberg. 2009. *Beroepsonderwijs in verandering: op weg naar competentiegericht onderwijs.* Den Bosch: ECBO.

Meijers, F. 1983. *Van ambachtsschool tot LTS.* Nijmegen: Socialistische Uitgeverij Nijmegen.

Ministerie van Sociale Zaken en Werkgelegenheid. 2009. *Actieplan jeugdwerkloosheid.* Den Haag: Ministerie van Sociale Zaken en Werkgelegenheid.

Nelson, M. 2012. 'Continued Collectivism: The Role of Trade Self-management and the Social Democracy Party in Danish Vocational Education and Training'. In *The Political Economy of Skill Formation*, edited by M. Busemeyer and C. Trampusch, pp. 179–204. Oxford: Oxford University Press.

Nijhof, W. 2004. 'The Process of Shaping a Responsive VET System: A Reconstruction'. In *Unravelling Policy, Power, Process and Performance: The Formative Evaluation of the Dutch Adult and Vocational Education Act*, edited by W. Nijhof and W. van Esch, pp. 13–43. Den Bosch: Cinop.

OCW—Ministerie van Onderwijs, Cultuur en Wetenschap. 2015. *Actieplan MBO Focus op Vakmanschap 2011–2015.* Den Haag: OCW.

OECD. 2004. *Education at a Glance: OECD Indicators 2004.* Paris: OECD.

Onderwijsraad. 2015. *Herkenbaar VMBO met sterk vakmanschap.* Den Haag: Onderwijsraad.

Onstenk, J. 2010. 'Coaching and Collaborative Work-based Learning in Dutch VET: The 'TEAMstages' Project'. In *Rediscovering Apprenticeship: Research Findings of the International Network on Innovative Apprenticeship (INAP)*, edited by F. Rauner and E. Smith, pp. 161–70. Heidelberg: Springer.

Onstenk, J., and F. Blokhuis. 2007. 'Apprenticeship in the Netherlands: Connecting School- and Work-based Learning'. *Education and Training 49* (6): 489–499.

SER—Sociaal-Economische Raad. 1988. *Advies over de aanpassing van de vakopleiding aan de automatisering.* Den Haag: SER.

Soskice, D. 1994. 'Reconciling Markets and Institutions: The German Apprenticeship System'. In *Training in the Private Sector: International Comparisons*, edited by L. Lynch, pp. 25–60. New York: NBER.

Thelen, K. 2007. 'Contemporary Challenges to the German Vocational Training System'. *Regulation and Governance 1* (3): 247–60.

Thelen, K. 2014. *Varieties of Liberalization and the New Politics of Social Solidarity.* New York: Cambridge University Press.

Thelen, K., and M. Busemeyer 2012. 'Institutional Change in German Vocational Training: From Collectivism towards Segmentalism'. In *The Political Economy of Collective Skill Formation*, edited by M. Busemeyer and C. Trampusch, pp. 68–100. Oxford: Oxford University Press.

Tijdelijke adviescommissie Onderwijs-Arbeidsmarkt. 1990. *Onderwijs Arbeidsmarkt: Naar een werkzaam traject.* Alphen aan den Rijn: Samsom Tjeenk Willink.

VNO—Verbond van Nederlandse Ondernemingen. 1989. *Onderwijs, Pijlers onzer welvaart.* Den Haag: VNO.

Westerhuis, A. 2007. 'The Role of the State in Vocational Education: A Political Analysis of the History of Vocational Education in the Netherlands'. In *Vocational Education: International Developments and Systems*, edited by I. Clarke and C. Winch, pp. 21–33. London: Routledge.

Wiborg, S., and P. Cort. 2009. 'The Vocational Education and Training System in Denmark: Continuity and Change'. In *Vocational Training: International Perspectives*, edited by G. Bosch and J. Charest, pp. 84–109. New York: Routledge.

Willemse, P. 2011. *Historische schets examinering in het MBO.* Tilburg: IVA Onderwijs.

Wolthuis, J. 1999. *Lower Technical Education in the Netherlands 1798–1993: The Rise and Fall of a Subsystem.* Leuven: Garant.

Appendix

List of interviews

1. Interview NLD 1, secretary of education VNO-NCW, 20 May 2020.
2. Interview NLD 2, former secretary of education VNO-NCW, 9 June 2020.
3. Interview NLD 3, former secretary of education VNO-NCW, 28 May 2020.
4. Interview NLD 4, policy officer Labour Foundation (Stichting van de Arbeid), 26 May 2020.
5. Interview NLD 5, policy officer labour market and education FNV, 29 May 2020.
6. Interview NLD 6, policy officer CNV, 3 June 2020.
7. Interview NLD 7, former policy officer labour market and education FNV, 12 June 2020.
8. Interview NLD 8, former policy officer labour market and education FNV, 3 June 2020.
9. Interview NLD 9, former policy officer labour market and education FNV, 9 June 2020.
10. Interview NLD 10, senior policy officer Cooperation Vocational Education and Business (Samenwerking Beroepsonderwijs en Bedrijfsleven), 1 July 2020.
11. Interview NLD 11, senior policy officer Social-Economic Council (Sociaal-Economische Raad), 18 July 2020.
12. Interview NLD 12, former chair VNO, 24 February 2020.
13. Interview NLD 13, former chair VNO-NCW, 25 May 2020.
14. Interview NLD 14, Former chair VNO-NCW, 22 June 2020.

6

The Politics of Social Inclusion in Collective Skill Formation Systems

Actors, Coalitions, and Policies

Leonard Geyer and Niccolo Durazzi

6.1 Introduction

This chapter analyses policy initiatives aimed at expanding access to the collective skill formation systems of Austria and Germany since the 1990s. We cover examples of both policies that were implemented and policies that were proposed, debated, but ultimately quashed. We thus ask questions about the political destiny of policies aimed at increasing the social inclusion of training systems: why do they sometimes find broad political support and sometimes only lukewarm reactions? Why are they sometimes underpinned by cooperation between key actors and sometimes by stark conflict? Why do the very same actors forge coalitions on some measures while they firmly stand apart on others? By theorizing and scrutinizing empirically the preference formation process of trade unions, firms, employers' organizations, and governments, we shed light on the multifaceted and variable coalitional politics of socially inclusive measures, ultimately highlighting the political constraints towards fostering social inclusion through vocational training in the knowledge economy. Thereby, this chapter contributes to elucidating the dilemma of balancing inclusiveness and efficiency goals (see Bonoli and Emmenegger, in this volume).

Collective skill formation systems, like the Austrian and German dual apprenticeship systems, are famous for their ability to combine economic efficiency and social equality (Busemeyer 2015; Durazzi and Geyer 2021; Iversen 2005; Soskice 1994). This social inclusion function, however, has come under increasing pressure since the 1990s (Busemeyer 2012; Thelen 2014). Deindustrialization shrunk the number of jobs in manufacturing, leading to a

Leonard Geyer and Niccolo Durazzi, *The Politics of Social Inclusion in Collective Skill Formation Systems*. In: *Collective Skill Formation in the Knowledge Economy*. Edited by Giuliano Bonoli and Patrick Emmenegger, Oxford University Press. © Oxford University Press (2022). DOI: 10.1093/oso/9780192866257.003.0006 decline of apprenticeship slots offered in this sector, which have not been offset by a corresponding increase in the supply of apprenticeships in the service sector (Culpepper and Finegold 1999; Thelen and Busemeyer 2012; Thelen and Culpepper 2007). Technological changes and the rise of knowledge economies increased employers' skill demands (Durazzi 2019; Durazzi and Benassi 2020), making it more difficult for low-achieving young pupils to land an apprenticeship place (Thelen 2014). Migration has made societies more diverse and multiple barriers have been found to prevent young people with a migration background from entering and hence benefiting from the apprenticeship system (Tjaden 2017). In sum, while in the past apprenticeships offered disadvantaged young people—meaning less academically gifted and young people with lower socio-economic status—a route into well-paid and stable employment, pupils without (or with less valuable) school-leaving certificates have been facing increasing difficulties in landing a training position over the last two decades (Jacob and Solga 2015; Kupfer 2010).

Yet, governments and social partners did not stand still in the face of these secular developments. Actions have been taken to buck the trend as several countries deployed a range of policies to preserve the social inclusion function of their training systems (Bonoli and Wilson 2019; Di Maio et al. 2018; Durazzi and Geyer 2020, 2021). Some of these reforms were successfully implemented and backed by broad political coalitions, others have been politically contested, and others have been effectively vetoed by trade unions, employer organizations, or both (Durazzi and Geyer 2020). We find evidence of both class conflict and cross-class coalitions in favour and against inclusionary measures. However, left-leaning governments and trade unions are the actors most likely to show first-order preferences for social inclusion policies. Inclusionary measures are most likely to attract the support of a winning political coalition if they do not reduce the efficiency of training and do not impinge on the social partners' control over the training system. Lastly, governments can soften employer opposition to inclusionary policies by offering employers' organizations concessions in the control dimension.

This chapter is an investigation into the politics of such reforms and it enfolds as follows: section 6.2 provides a theoretical framework to analyse the politics of social inclusion in collective skill formation systems; section 6.3 provides the empirical evidence by tracing and comparing reform processes of similar measures aimed at increasing the socially inclusive nature of collective skill formation systems in Austria and Germany; section 6.4 discusses the findings and provides the conclusions.

6.2 The politics of social inclusion: theoretical framework

Our starting point in outlining a theoretical framework is a simple observation: the politics of social inclusion in collective training systems is inherently messy for three main reasons. Firstly, the policy space is populated by several actors with potentially divergent preferences: trade unions, firms, business associations, as well as centre-left and centre-right parties in government. Secondly, the preference formation of these actors takes place over multiple 'dimensions of contention' (Carstensen and Ibsen 2021). Thirdly, more than one policy option can be simultaneously negotiated and/or be in place, opening up the opportunity for political exchange and for strategic preferences to be at least as relevant as first-order preferences. Having acknowledged this complexity at the outset, this section proceeds in two steps: firstly, it provides a theorization of actors' preferences; secondly, it discusses how actors' preferences can coalesce in different ways, leading to variable coalitions underpinning different types of socially inclusive measures.

6.2.1 Actors' preferences along the three dimensions of contention

To outline a framework of actors' preferences, we build on recent work on institutional change in collective skill formation systems, and in particular on Durazzi and Geyer (2020) and Carstensen and Ibsen (2021). Both articles highlight the centrality of social inclusion and equity concerns in collective skill formation systems but they also showed that these concerns dynamically interact with two other dimensions that are of no less importance, namely: (1) the efficiency of the system (chiefly its ability to provide high quality skills); and (2) the governance of/control over the system (encompassing, for instance, control over how many apprenticeships should be offered and control over the content of training). We therefore outline the set of preferences that the main actors that populate this policy space—trade unions, firms, business associations, and governments—are expected to display along the three dimensions of social inclusion, efficiency, and control.

Trade unions are expected to assign high importance to all three dimensions. They will stand by the social inclusion function of the system because expanding access to high-quality certified training is conducive to a smoother transition into permanent/standard forms of employment, which in turn translates into higher rates of unionization as permanently employed are more likely to join trade unions than non-standard workers (OECD 2019). Furthermore, trade unions will support measures to increase training access for disadvantaged young people for ideological reasons as social inclusion is a core value of labour organizations (Durazzi 2017).[1] They will stand by the efficiency aims of the system because an effective school-to-work transition is more likely to occur if the skill formation system provides training for which there is demand in the labour market, which in turn will increase employment rates and wages of young people (Durazzi and Geyer 2020). They will finally have a vested interest in the control and governance of the system for at least two reasons: firstly, because it is a way to retain a role in public policymaking (Davidsson and Emmenegger 2013); secondly, because through their presence in the governance mechanisms, unions can have a say on the skill content, which has important implications, for example, on the transferability of skills between occupations and, therefore, on the relative power relationship between labour and capital. Thus, unions will support the development of socially inclusive measures, if they expect the measures to provide quality training, and there are no negative spillovers in the efficiency and control dimension on the rest of the training system. This means that unions are expected to support any increase in regular apprenticeship positions. However, they may oppose a reduction of training standards even, if this could create additional opportunities for disadvantaged young people.[2] Similarly, unions may oppose the creation of training opportunities outside the regular system, if they have no control over how the training is administered and how its quality will be ensured (Durazzi and Geyer 2020). Given that a trade-off between social inclusion and efficiency/control is not inevitable, unions will only turn against socially inclusive measures if these come with a consequential decrease in control over or the quality of the training system.

Firms will have a different set of preferences. We expect employers to rank both efficiency and control higher than social inclusion. Employers' crucial interests lie in the efficiency dimension to ensure that there are no skill mismatches or shortages (Durazzi and Geyer 2020) and the supply of apprenticeship positions meets firms' demand for skilled labour. Similar to

---

[1] From a dualization perspective (Rueda 2005), one might argue that insider-oriented trade unions oppose inclusive measures to limit the labour supply and create upward pressure on wages. This argument has been qualified by several studies that found differences in the level of support for inclusionary policies between trade unions, depending on types of unions. For example, Gordon (2015) finds that encompassing and centralized trade unions are more likely to empower weaker groups (see also Benassi and Vlandas 2016; Durazzi 2017; Durazzi et. al. 2018). However, while union fragmentation seems to contribute to exclusionary preferences in the field of labour market policy, this does not seem to be the case—at least as strongly—in the field of VET (Durazzi and Geyer 2020).

[2] See, for example, Busemeyer (2012) on German trade unions' opposition to the introduction of shorter, 'theory-reduced' two-year apprenticeships.

unions, employers' organizations also have a vested interest in the control of the system. However, employers do not strive for social inclusion (Durazzi and Geyer 2020). While we expect unions to fight against the stratification of the labour market (Benassi and Dorigatti 2015; Durazzi 2017; Durazzi et al. 2018), employers might in fact welcome it, as that weakens unions' power resources and allows for lower salaries and cost-cutting (Baccaro and Benassi 2016). Hence, companies will not have an interest in training skilled workers above and beyond what they strictly need, and they will be adamant at having exclusive control over the number of young people that enter the apprenticeship system. We therefore expect firms to be broadly against socially inclusive measures and they will at best consent to them if these do not enter into conflict with governance or efficiency dimensions. They might, however, support them in those instances in which socially inclusive measures lead to gains in either the governance or efficiency dimension (cf. Swenson 2002). Think for instance of a situation of skill shortages: this may be due to rapid economic expansion, whereby businesses are keen to expand their employment base, or it might be a structural condition for some businesses (e.g. small ones) who are typically less attractive to school-leavers (see e.g. Benassi et al. 2021 on the 'liability of smallness' in training policy). Skill shortages will be more severe if the full skill potential of young people does not come to fruition. In these situations, firms that are affected by skill shortages (as well as the organizations representing them) might support *socially inclusive* measures that improve the skills endowment of otherwise disadvantaged young people, i.e. they might think of them as *efficient* measures to avoid skill shortages.

Business associations will have a more nuanced position compared to that of their members. Seminal work by Schmitter and Streeck (1999) shows how associations are torn between a 'logic of membership', i.e. satisfying the needs of their members, and a 'logic of influence', i.e. pursuing their 'own' political objectives which may at times be in conflict with the interests of their members. In the field of training policy, this distinction appears particularly relevant in the relationship between business associations and their members. Business associations might have an eye for the long-term viability of the training system which their members are not expected to have. This might mean, for instance, that associations are keen to ensure that the number of young people entering the training system does not go below a certain level. There are organizational self-interests motivating this behaviour: for instance, associations participate in the development of training curricula and they provide examinations—hence they thrive financially from the very operations of the training system. Such strong interest in the long-term viability of the system makes business associations more open than their members towards the establishment of socially inclusive solutions that might increase the number of young people enrolled in the system. Moreover, we expect associations with *mandatory* membership (e.g. Austrian Economic Chamber (WKÖ) or the German Chamber of Industry and Commerce (DIHK)) to be more open to socially inclusive measures compared to associations with voluntary membership (e.g. the Confederation of German Employers' Associations (BDA)). The former are more likely to develop policy preferences that deviate from the interests of individual firms, while the latter are expected to be more heavily influenced by them—given that their very existence rests upon the continued willingness of their members to be part of the association.

Governments will display yet another set of preferences. Regardless of partisan composition, governments will *not* prioritize—in relative terms—the control dimension. At the end of the day, collective skill formation systems have been traditionally celebrated for their ability to provide agile responses to labour market needs thanks to decentralized cooperation among social partners (Culpepper 2001, 2003). And governments are aware that decentralized cooperation is a strength of collective skill formation systems (Culpepper 2003). More broadly, while it is plausible to think of vocational training as a crucial policy area for social partners in the context of their relatively narrow policy portfolio, it is less plausible to think of governments fighting hard to gain further control over a relatively minor policy area—especially when the full range of public policies handled by governments is considered. But clearly governments do have an interest in the social inclusion and efficiency function of their education and training systems. Social inclusion and efficiency are important to maintain the respective commitment of young people and employers to firm-based training. Furthermore, drop-outs and youth unemployment create high costs (Eurofound 2012) that governments are eager to avoid. Finally, progress on the inclusion and efficiency dimensions can be beneficial for politicians' core constituencies and therefore translate into electoral gains. We therefore hypothesize that governments at both ends of the political spectrum are concerned about both efficiency and inclusion. At the margins, however, left-leaning governments will prioritize social inclusion over efficiency, while right-leaning governments will do the opposite.

6.2.2 Coalitional dynamics and expected policy outcomes

Based on such a multiplicity of actors and dynamically interactive dimensions, we follow Busemeyer (2012) as we posit that coalitions will be variable.

Given the set of preferences hypothesized in the previous subsection, we expect a coalition between unions and left-leaning governments to be the most common pro-social inclusion coalition. Conversely, we expect firms and their associations to be the most common coalition militating against social inclusion. This is a classic scenario of class conflict in the politics of training (cf. Durazzi and Geyer 2020).

However, cross-class coalitions are also possible (Busemeyer 2012), in at least three ways. Firstly, we identified the joint interest of unions and employers (both firms and associations) in the control dimension. Hence, if governments seek to unilaterally introduce socially inclusive measures that weaken the control of social partners over the system, we expect to see a cross-class coalition forming against such measures. Secondly, we have seen how employer associations might depart from a narrow logic of membership and embrace a long-term-oriented logic of influence. Thus, if levels of training decrease to a point perceived by associations as threatening the long-term viability of the system, business associations and unions might form a coalition with the government—against individual firms—that favour the expansion of the training system, which is likely to have a socially inclusive effect. Finally, Carstensen and Ibsen (in this volume) show that employers, the government, and trade unions may form pro-efficiency coalitions to increase the attractiveness of VET programmes for higher-skilled students. This might happen for similar reasons as outlined under the previous point, i.e. if the VET system gradually becomes unattractive to perspective applicants.

Having linked preferences to coalitions, the final point that deserves attention to complete the theoretical framework is to link coalitions to policy outcomes. In other words, when different coalitions confront each other, what kind of power dynamics are at play? Here we point at three broad dynamics that might unfold. Firstly, we expect that major socially inclusive reforms cannot be pushed unilaterally by the government against the joint opposition of unions and employers. Because of the strong and highly institutionalized role of social partners in collective training systems, governments will not be willing to push major reforms unilaterally. Secondly, any reform that threatens to lower firms' control over the system—be it pushed by government and unions or by unions and business associations—can be credibly counteracted by firms through their threat of disinvestment from the system (Busemeyer 2012; Bonoli and Emmenegger 2020). Hence, it is unlikely that such reforms (think of a training levy) will be successful because proponents will be concerned that this might cause a breakdown of the system and lead to an even bigger problem.

Pro-inclusion coalitions, however, might be more successful under two particular circumstances: firstly, when they promote policy measures whose implementation does not weaken employers' control over the number of apprenticeship positions to be offered, i.e. measures that do not intrude in the underlying logic of the system (cf. Bonoli and Wilson 2019); and secondly when the implementation of these measures does not require employers' participation, making employers' threat of disinvestment less credible (see Bonoli and Emmenegger 2020 on the underling theoretical logic). So-called preparatory measures are an example of the former: these are training programmes that prepare disadvantaged young people for an apprenticeship and as such they do not intrude into the governance mechanisms of the apprenticeship system. Another example is support services which help apprentices (e.g. through tutoring) or companies (e.g. by supporting managers in training young people). In this case, individual firms might soften their stance because these measures do not change the underlying logic of the apprenticeship system, i.e. they do not force firms to offer apprenticeship positions they would not otherwise offer. Training outlets jointly run by unions and governments, catering to disadvantaged young people and sitting alongside the regular apprenticeship system are an example of the latter. In this case employers' participation is not needed because training takes place outside the firm, hence employers' threat of disinvestment is weaker and less credible, given that training does not structurally depend on firms providing it.

Having outlined actors' preference and having formulated broad expectations as to how these preferences might coalesce and subsequently shape policy outcomes, we now turn to the empirical evidence.

6.3 The politics of social inclusion: empirical evidence

We illustrate the theoretical framework by means of selected case studies encompassing both positive and negative cases of socially inclusive measures across two most-similar countries—Austria and Germany. The two countries have similar systems of collective training and since the late 1990s both have tried to introduce a number of similar measures to increase social inclusion albeit with different support coalitions and varying levels of success. To maximize the analytical gains of the comparison, we focus primarily on measures that were successfully introduced in both countries or successfully introduced in one country and attempted to be introduced in the other. In contrast, we do not discuss measures or reforms which were debated and/or introduced in one of the two countries only (for a comprehensive overview on the latter see Bonoli and Wilson (2019), Durazzi and Geyer (2020), and Geyer (2021)).

6.3.1 Germany: aiming for the core, getting at the edges?

The German apprenticeship system has seen re-occurring shortages of training positions since the 1970s (Thelen 2004; Busemeyer 2009) and gained renewed policy salience in the early 2000s. During this period, Germany experienced a continuous decline in the number of apprenticeships and rising youth unemployment. In response, the Red-Green government led by Gerhard Schröder considered a number of actions to make the training system more inclusive.

First, Schröder committed to the introduction of a training levy if employers did not increase their training efforts voluntarily (Busemeyer 2012). The levy was championed by the political left and most strongly by the metalworking union IG Metall, the trade union confederation DGB, and the left-wing of the governing social democratic party (SPD) (Busemeyer 2012). Schröder himself as well as more centrist members of his party, however, were open about the fact that they saw the levy primarily as a threat to extract concessions from employers—rather than as a policy objective per se.[3] Employers' organizations strongly opposed the levy claiming that it would not help increase employers' willingness to train apprentices and that it would lead to the increase of the role of the state in the dual system (*Verstaatlichung*) (Busemeyer 2012). It would, in other words, lower employers' control over the system as the levy would have intruded on the prerogative of employers to decide on the number of apprenticeships to be offered. Opposition politicians echoed these concerns and promised to veto the bill (Busemeyer 2012).

Eventually, the introduction of the levy failed as employers' credible threat of disinvestment and the likely veto in the Bundesrat led the government to settle for a voluntary 'training pact'[4] between employers and the federal government in 2004. As part of the pact, employers committed to providing 30,000 new apprenticeship positions in 2005 as well as 25,000 positions for a newly introduced form of firm-based pre-apprenticeship training called 'Initial Qualifications' (see Eurofound (2004)). Under the Initial Qualifications

---

[3] In his speech to the Bundestag on 14 March 2003 Schröder declared, 'I am not a fan of the levy. But without a sustainable improvement of the apprenticeship market, the federal government will be obliged to act.' See also Busemeyer (2012).
[4] Nationaler Pakt für Ausbildung und Fachkräftenachwuchs.

programme, employers offer six to twelve months' firm-based training to prepare young people for an apprenticeship. The training content is based on the curriculum of training in the dual system and the training itself is monitored by the monitoring institutions of the dual system. Young people participating in the programme receive a wage which is reimbursed up to 231 euros by the public employment service which also covers social insurance contributions (Bundesagentur für Arbeit 2016).

The Initial Qualifications and the new apprenticeship positions were 'offered' by employers' organizations to the Red-Green government in the context of the pact for apprenticeships and the related efforts to prevent the introduction of the training levy (Busemeyer 2012). However, not all employer groups were equally committed to the pact. While the president of the federal representation of the Chambers of Industry and Commerce (DIHK) promised the pact would be implemented 'meticulously', the president of the BDA clarified that he could not guarantee that the 30,000 positions would indeed be created (Eurofound 2004), suggesting that indeed a future-oriented logic of influence might manifest more likely among organizations less concerned with their membership numbers, while organizations relying on voluntary membership are more likely to gravitate towards their members' interests. Most trade unions initially opposed the Initial Qualification as part of their overall opposition to the voluntary training pact. They argued that a training levy was the only viable solution to the apprenticeship crisis—an option that from the unions' perspective would have been more beneficial in terms increasing the supply of high-quality skills, while decreasing employers' control over the training system. Over time, however, the position of the unions changed, and the Initial Qualifications programme is generally regarded as an effective tool for social inclusion (Geyer 2021). In 2016, German trade unions also advocated for the use of Initial Qualifications to support the integration of refugees into apprentices (DGB 2016).

An additional way of increasing training opportunities for disadvantaged young people considered by the government at the time was the creation of non-firm-based training positions by upgrading the school-based VET system. Specifically, the SPD-led government proposed that graduates from school-based VET should be admitted to the final examinations (*Kammerprüfung*) of the dual system. In addition, it was proposed that the Länder—who are in charge of education policy—should be allowed to develop school-based VET courses deliberately geared towards the exams of the dual system. This would have created an alternative system for young people who cannot find a firm-based apprenticeship to achieve the same qualifications as regular apprentices within the same period. However, the government's proposal was opposed by *both* social partners who effectively prevented its implementation (Busemeyer 2012). Unions and employers shared the concern that allowing students from the school-based system to achieve the same qualifications as apprentices would ultimately lead to an increased role of the state in the governance of the system. Moreover, unions considered the training provided outside of the apprenticeship system to be of considerably lower quality and they therefore sought to prevent an increasing share of young people from receiving low-quality training, which would have also watered down the attractiveness of the apprenticeship system (Durazzi and Geyer 2020).

In the second half of the 2000s, youth unemployment decreased but the lack of training opportunities for disadvantaged young people remained politically salient. In response, the grand coalition under Chancellor Merkel introduced two new measures in 2008: the 'Training Bonus' and counselling and orientation coaches (*Berufseinstiegsbegleitung—BerEb*). The Bonus had the declared goal of creating additional 100,000 apprenticeship positions by 2010 (Handelsblatt 2008). Through this programme, employers offering training to young people who had unsuccessfully applied for apprenticeships for a certain period of time would receive a financial bonus.[5] The Training Bonus was met with substantial scepticism by both unions and employers right from the start. The employers' organizations and the confederal union published a joint statement warning that any financial subsidy should be narrowly targeted at those young people most in need and that distorting incentives should be avoided at all costs (BDA, BDI, and DGB 2008). The employers' organizations were particularly concerned that a substantial and widely available bonus would create incentives for companies to profit from training itself rather than to develop skilled workers for the long-term benefit of the firm (Geyer 2021)—in other words, they feared that bonuses would weaken the efficiency of the system. The German trade union confederation (DGB) and its youth organization on the other hand voiced 'considerable concerns' over subsidizing firm-based training through public funds (Bundestag 2008). Against the background of ongoing criticism and with much fewer companies applying for the bonus than expected, the programme was discontinued in 2010 (Bundestag 2010).

Through the BerEb programme, coaches provide young people individualized and comprehensive counselling and support starting two years before their planned graduation from secondary education and lasting until the end of the first year in a regular apprenticeship. The aim of the programme is to

---

[5] Namely, 4,000 and 6,000 euros to be paid in equal shares at the start of the apprenticeship and once the apprentice registered to take the final examinations.

help young people without the necessary support infrastructure to identify career paths, apply for apprenticeship positions and, when necessary, help them navigate the various other support measures offered at the federal and state level to help young people in their transition from school to apprenticeships. This support is particularly valuable for individuals without strong family support networks or little familiarity with the training system, such as migrants (Ramboll 2014). In contrast to the Bonus, the BerEb programme was actively supported by trade unions and employers' organizations. The DGB welcome the government's efforts to help disadvantaged young people in making a direct transition from school to an apprenticeship (Bundestag 2008). On the employer side, the DIHK and the Chamber of Craftspeople (ZDH) supported the measure politically as well as in practice by cooperating with guidance counsellors at the local level motivated by concerns over (future) skills shortages (Geyer 2021). In particular, the ZdH, which represents mostly small companies, had warned already in 2007 that concerns over youth unemployment would soon be replaced by concerns over shortages of skilled labour. Against this background, the organization promoted orientation measures like the BerEB programme to bring underrepresented groups like women and people with a migration background into the dual system (ZdH 2007).

Other measures which received broad support from both social partners from the beginning are supportive measures (*Ausbildungsbegleitende Hilfen—AbH*) and assisted apprenticeships (*Assistierte Ausbildung—AsA*). AbH is a long-standing programme to provide additional tutoring and social support to apprentices during their training. In 2014, the grand coalition, again with active support from both employers and unions, decided to expand the target group of the programme to make the support services available to more young people. In addition, they decided to introduce the newly developed AsA programme which provides more intensive counselling and support to disadvantaged apprentices as well as support to the companies training them (Allianz für Aus- und Weiterbildung 2014). Similar to the BerEB programme, employers' organizations supported these reforms in an effort to fight skills shortages. However, while BerEB was mostly supported by the Chambers which tend to represent the interests of smaller employers, AbH and AsA were also heavily promoted by the BDA and the BDI which are dominated by large firms (cf. Trampusch 2010). In 2014 and 2015, the two organizations released several publications calling for additional efforts to enable lower-skilled youth to pursue firm-based apprenticeships too (BDA 2014, 2015; BDA, BDI, and Telekom 2014). In a call for action titled 'We need everybody!', employers' organizations specifically demanded that the Initial

Qualifications, the AbH, and the AsA should be used more widely to address skills shortages (BDA, BDI, and Telekom 2014).

The German case provides, therefore, a number of insights on the politics of social inclusion in training systems that are broadly in line with the expectations formulated in the theoretical framework. Firstly, the political left is indeed the main actor pushing for social inclusion: this was clear from the example of the training levy, where stark conflict along class lines took place. Secondly, it is politically highly difficult to push an inclusive reform that affects the core of the training system: to the extent that employers can threaten disinvestment, fundamental reforms seem difficult to achieve. Again, the training levy is a clear example here as it gathered significant political support from the left, but this proved ultimately insufficient against employers' threat of disinvestment. In the same vein, governments do not seem able to successfully push through unilateral solutions. This held true for policy measures as different as the upgrading of the school-based system and the introduction of the training bonus. In both instances, a cross-class coalition of unions and employers emerged against these measures and it proved too difficult for the government to overcome the opposition of such a coalition. Thirdly, the measures that gathered broader political support were measures that worked around the edges of the system, such as preparatory measures (Initial Qualifications) and support services (BerEb, AbH, AsA). Unions and governments appreciated, as expected, their socially inclusive nature, while employers did not see in these measures the risk of loosening their control over how many apprenticeships should be offered. And in a context of tight labour markets, employers not only consented to them, but they actively promoted them as they saw in these measures an effective way to plug skill shortages.

6.3.2 Austria: adjusting both the core and the edges?

Austria faced a peak in youth unemployment and an acute lack of training positions in the late 1990s. In response, a non-firm-based alternative to regular apprenticeships was introduced in 1998 by a government led by the social democratic SPÖ and based on active lobbying by the Chamber of Labour (AK) and the Austrian trade union confederation, ÖGB, in the form, at first, of a temporary 'safety net' (Durazzi and Geyer 2020). The safety net was a measure mimicking the apprenticeship system and providing both theoretical and practical training. However, different from a regular apprenticeship, the practical component was not carried out within firms but in training workshops organized by the public employment service. Nevertheless, the safety net would lead to the same certification as the apprenticeship system. The Austrian Economic Chamber (WKÖ) initially opposed the safety net but later agreed to it within a larger compromise on measures to support the training system. According to this compromise, a total of 4,000 publicly financed training positions co-manage the PES and labour organizations were provided for the cohort leaving school in 1998 (Durazzi and Geyer 2020).

Between 2000 and 2007, conservative coalitions between the conservative Austrian People's Party (ÖVP) and the populist Freedom Party (FPÖ/BZÖ[6]) were in office. In the context of persistently high rates of youth unemployment, the unions argued for the safety net to be made permanent. Conservative governments did not look upon this option with favour and refused to second these proposals. The trade unions managed nonetheless to extend the safety net with ad hoc measures every year, without, however, turning it into a permanent measure (Durazzi and Geyer 2019). The right-wing coalition rather favoured a more voluntaristic approach as it introduced the so-called Blum Bonus, a subsidy programme to increase the number of firm-based training positions—similar to the German Training Bonus. Companies creating new apprenticeship positions were paid a monthly subsidy of 400 euros in the first year of training, 200 euros in the second year and 100 euros per month in the third year. The goal of this measure was the creation of 2,000 additional apprenticeship positions (Der Standard 2006). The Bonus was perceived critically by various actors. The SPÖ, then in the opposition, criticized that more efforts were needed to address the lack of apprenticeship positions and that in particular that the country's safety net for unsuccessful apprenticeship seekers should be expanded. Furthermore, SPÖ politicians argued the Bonus would result in massive fraud with companies misusing the system (Bundesrat der Republik Österreich 2005). The unions were equally critical and shared the concern that the Bonus was open to misuse by employers and would do little to include academically weaker young people into apprenticeships (OE24 2007). Finally, the Austrian WKÖ was also not fully committed to the Bonus. As one representative of the employers' organization explained, they believed that the bonus did help improve the labour market for apprentices during the crisis years of 2007 and 2008. At the same time, he acknowledged that companies had abused the system by relabelling existing apprenticeship positions as 'new' to receive subsidies. Also, he shared

---

[6] In 2005, some members of the Freedom Party left the party to form the Alliance for the Future of Austria (BZÖ) which continued the coalition with the ÖVP.

the concern of the German employers and the Austrian labour organizations that financial incentives could turn training into a business model which the WKÖ strongly opposed.[7]

After the 2006 general election, a new grand coalition government led by the SPÖ replaced the right-wing coalition. In 2008, this new government implemented a wide-ranging package of reforms (*Jugendbeschäftigungspaket*) that significantly re-shaped the landscape of training in two main directions: firstly, the safety net was made permanent; secondly, the Blum Bonus was abolished and replaced with a new financing mechanism that amounts—in essence—to a training levy similar to the one which had been proposed—but not implemented—in Germany.

Once the newly elected government showed political will, the institution-alization of the safety net into a permanent 'supra-company state-financed training' (ÜBA) was rather straightforward: unions had always been its most fervent supporters and by 2008 employers' opposition had weakened. Indeed, after ten years of implementation, employers came to appreciate the good quality of training provided in the training workshop and they therefore became considerably more open towards its institutionalization out of the simple observation that it had worked reasonably well (Durazzi and Geyer 2019). In addition, Seitzl and Unterweger (in this volume) find that some companies learned to appreciate the ÜBA because it allows them to outsource the costly first year of training to the state and to hire ÜBA participants as cheap interns. Despite its possible crowding out of some firm-based training, the ÜBA retains an important social inclusion function which has been, if anything, heightened by the Covid-19 crisis: against the background of youth unemployment rate rising from 8.1 per cent in February to 12.7 per cent in April 2020, the AK has demanded that the number of training positions offered in the ÜBA double by the autumn of 2020 (AK 2020).

The introduction of a levy—or a functional equivalent thereof—comes across as a more puzzling development. The labour organizations had already briefly considered pushing for the introduction of a levy in 1998 at the onset of the apprenticeship crisis, but they quickly discarded this idea as they con-sidered it to be a non-starter in negotiations with employers (Durazzi and Geyer 2020). However, a de facto apprenticeship levy was introduced through a gradual re-purposing of the Austrian Insolvency Salary Fund (IEF) (*Insol-venz Entgelt Fonds*). The fund was established in 1978 to insure the salaries of employees of companies declaring bankruptcy. It is financed primarily by a

---

[7] Interview with a representative of the Austrian Economic Chamber (Wirtschaftskammer Österreich), January 2018.

surcharge on employers' unemployment insurance contributions. From 1999 until 2004, the fund generated substantially more income than it needed to fulfil its basic mission of guaranteeing the salaries of insolvent companies and the government reacted by using resources from the fund for other policies, including support for employers training apprentices from 2003 onwards (Verfassungsgerichtshof 2005). The 2008 reform institutionalizing the ÜBA incorporated the practice of using of IEF funds for policies supporting the dual system into the regular training code.[8] Based on this reform, all firms that engage in training receive an annual basic financing benefit for each apprentice, linked to the current salary and year of training of any given apprentice.[9] In addition, resources from the IEF are used to finance a wide range of measures to support integration into and equal access to firm-based training at the federal and Länder level (WKÖ 2021a, 2021b). Finally, the WKÖ was put in charge of administering the funds. While the use of funds is subject to review by the relevant ministries and the chamber of labour has a right to be consulted, the employers' organization has the power to decide which measures should be financed and it receives financial compensation for managing the funds.[10] Specifically, the administration of the funds was assigned to WKÖ Inhouse GmbH, a private company fully owned by the WKÖ. Payments from the fund account for a significant share of expenditure in Austria's labour market policy targeted at young people. In 2019, 229 million euros from the fund were used in this policy area compared to 620 million euros from the PES.[11]

The AK and ÖGB welcomed the introduction of additional means for inclusionary measures but strongly opposed the unilateral control of the WKÖ over these funds. Instead, the AK argued that the labour organizations too should be actively involved in all the activities of the levy—ranging from co-decision of what should be financed to evaluating these activities (ÖGB and AK 2008: 2). The WKÖ, for their part, eventually agreed to the reform and praised the final package as a set of 'effective measures to counter skills shortages' (WKÖ 2008). The support of SPÖ and the qualified support of the labour organizations for this reform are very much in line with the expected pro-inclusion stance of these actors. However, why did the employers agree to this reform as well? A crucial part of the explanation is certainly that, in contrast to Germany, the employer contribution to the funds already existed.

---

[8] See § 19c (1) Bundesausbildungsgesetz (BAG) and § 13e Insolvenz-Entgeldsicherungsgesetz (IESG) which were introduced by this reform.

[9] The support is currently three months' wages for apprentices in the first year, two months' wages in the second year and one month's wage in the third year (WKÖ 2021a).

[10] § 19c (3) and § 19c (5) BAG.

[11] Information provided to the authors by the Austrian Federal Ministry for Labour.

In fact, employer contributions were *reduced* alongside the reforms. In 2003, the unemployment insurance surcharge was abolished for apprentices[12] and the 2008 reform was accompanied by a reduction of the surcharge from 0.7 to 0.55 per cent.[13] Hence, it did not constitute a new tax or burden as it would have been in the German case, but it is rather a form of 'conversion' (Streeck and Thelen 2005). In addition, assigning to employers significant power in how to spend the revenue from the levy played an important role. While the use of the insolvency funds in Austria effectively constitutes a form of training levy, the way in which the levy is administered provides far-reaching power and it is a source of income to the Austrian chamber of commerce. In other words, it does not impinge on the control dimension but, if anything, it strengthens it relative to unions.

After the wide-ranging 2008 reforms, additional inclusionary policies were adopted in 2011. The SPÖ-led grand coalition introduced three policies in particular which are very similar to the German support services, namely: Youth Coaching (*Jugendcoaching*), Apprentice Coaching (*Lehrlingscoaching*) and Coaching for Companies (*Lehrbetriebscoaching*). Youth Coaching is an occupational counselling and career guidance programme similar to the German counselling and orientation coaches. The goal of the programme is to provide comprehensive support to young people who are likely to face problems in the transition from compulsory education into further education or training and to help drop-outs with the reintegration into education and training (Steiner et. al. 2013). Apprentice Coaching and Coaching for Companies are respectively akin to the German Support Measures and Assisted Apprenticeships. The first provides counselling and tutoring services to apprentices who struggle to keep up with training content and/or have personal problems including conflicts with their employers while the second provides counselling services to employers who employ apprentices (WKÖ 2020). Both programmes respectively put an emphasis on apprentices and employers with a migration background to increase their participation in the Austrian apprenticeship system (BMDW 2021). Apprentice Coaching and Coaching for Companies are financed through the IEF which also means that they are administered by the WKÖ Inhouse GmbH (BMDW 2021).

All three coaching programmes were supported by both the Employers Chamber and the Chamber of Employees (ÖGB and AK 2011; AK 2012;

---

[12] §12 (1)4 IESG introduced by BGBl. I Nr. 158/2002.
[13] Verordnung: Festsetzung des Zuschlags zum Arbeitslosenversicherungsbeitrag gemäß dem Insolvenz-Entgeltsicherungsgesetz. BGBl. II Nr. 431/2008.

WKÖ 2012).[14] Some labour organizations—although supporting the wider aims of the measures—renewed their criticism on the WKÖs control over the IEF funds. For example, the youth organization of the service sector union GPA-djp publicly opposed the implementation of Apprentice Coaching and Coaching for Companies through the WKÖ Inhouse GmbH (ÖGB 2011). The labour organizations continue to oppose the role of the WKO Inhouse GmbH but so far there has been no attempt by governments to change it. As one ministerial official explained, there is no desire to interfere with the implementation through the WKÖ Inhouse because 'objectively speaking, this arrangement works well'.[15]

In sum, the Austrian case shows that inclusionary reforms took place both at the core and at the edges of the training system. The latter are rather unsurprising and in line with both the theoretical discussion and the empirical developments that we have already traced in the German system: measures that work around the edges of the dual system like the coaching of apprentices and companies tend to find broad political support because they do not impinge on employers' control over the system and they serve the aim of inclusion, which is championed by the political left. In the case of Austria, the decision to assign a significant degree of control to employers over the funds that finance part of these measures guaranteed even stronger employer buy-in (compared to Germany) and some scepticism on the side of the unions. The latter—while supporting the aim of the measures—requested (albeit unsuccessfully) a greater voice in the administration of the funds.

Different from the German case, however, reforms in Austria also reached the core of the system through the ÜBA and the redeployment of the IEF into a quasi-training levy. The ÜBA provides young people who do not land an apprenticeship with the right—underwritten by the state—to a training place that will lead to the same certification as a regular apprenticeship. The introduction of this system was championed by unions and parties on the left. Its initial success was largely down to the fact that it side-stepped employers' opposition: as its implementation does not co-depend on them, employers found themselves in a relatively weak position for their preferences to prevail. Moving to the introduction of the levy, it is striking that it did not trigger in Austria the same fierce opposition that German employers waged against it. However, the Austrian levy did not amount to the introduction of a new tax altogether, instead it was rather a re-purposing of an existing tax contribution, which weakened employers' opposition at the outset. Yet,

---

[14] Interview with a representative of WKÖ—Austrian Economic Chamber (Wirtschaftskammer Österreich), June 2020.

[15] Interview with a representative of the Federal Ministry for Labour, Family and Youth, May 2020.

next to this rather idiosyncratic feature, it is worth noting from a broader theoretical standpoint how policymakers can play with the control dimension to achieve employer buy-in: charging the employer association with the administration of the funds raised through the levy has been key to softening the otherwise inevitably hard stance of business associations towards the establishment of a levy.

6.4 Conclusion

The analysis of measures to increase the socially inclusive nature of the German and Austrian training systems allow us to uncover several points of broader theoretical interest. By way of conclusion, we highlight four points in particular. First, socially inclusive measures are politically most feasible when they do not impinge on the efficiency and control dimensions of the system. This finding is perhaps most evident when zooming into preparatory training and support services. As they take place 'outside' of the system and they merely complement it, preparatory training and support services do not challenge the underlying logic of vocational training systems and they appear as a relatively unproblematic option to push through from a political point of view. Second, as expected, the cases show that the coalitions in favour of or against inclusive measures can feature both class conflict and cross-class alliances. Comparing the evolution of non-firm-based training in Austria and Germany illuminates this point: in Austria an alliance led by the unions and supported by centre-left parties led to the establishment (against the opposition of employers) of a parallel training system that provides equal certification to young people who cannot land an apprenticeship place. Unions were instrumental in setting up this system because in the Austrian institutional context they could do so without decreasing their control over the system and without lowering the quality of training. As neither condition applied in the German case, unions sided with employers as they jointly opposed the establishment of a parallel training system. Third, we find evidence that left-leaning governments and unions are the actors who will most likely display first-order preferences towards socially inclusive measures (e.g. unions supported a levy in both countries; centre-left governments and unions were the crucial actors in the broader inclusionary re-orientation of the training system in Austria). Employers, on the other hand, will either support some non-intrusive measures as a strategic choice to avoid more intrusive ones (e.g. German business consenting to some inclusive measures to ensure that the option of the levy was off the table) or they will support them for opportunistic reasons if and when social inclusion overlaps with efficiency motives (e.g. German business supporting preparatory measures only in the context of skill shortages). Fourth, government can play with the control dimension to soften employers' stance towards socially inclusive measures. This emerged clearly in the Austrian case: employers' stance towards a quasi-levy was softened by the fact that the employer association was charged with the administration of the funds raised by the levy. This is an interesting political option for governments: it triggers mild discontent among both unions and employers but probably not enough discontent to turn either of them against the proposed policy. Employers' buy-in for a policy that they would otherwise oppose is facilitated by increasing their control over the funds, while unions will be wary of opposing a policy that they have traditionally supported—although its implementation does not involve them as much as they would have wanted. Returning to the dilemma of balancing efficiency and inclusion described by Bonoli and Emmenegger (this volume), overall, the theoretical discussion and empirical evidence suggest that achieving greater inclusion in contemporary training systems requires a careful balancing act between actors' preferences not only regarding efficiency and inclusion, but also in the control dimension. Forging broad coalitions in favour of inclusionary policy measures to respond to the challenges posed by the knowledge economy is therefore difficult but not impossible.

References

AK—Arbeiterkammer. 2012. 'AK fordert Kurswechsel in der Arbeitsmarktpolitik' (press release).

AK—Arbeiterkammer. 2020. 'AK Oberösterreich fordert massives Jugendrettungspake' (press release).

Allianz für Aus- und Weiterbildung. 2014. *Allianz für Aus- und Weiterbildung 2015–2018.*

Baccaro, L., and C. Benassi. 2016. 'Throwing out the Ballast: Growth Models and the Liberalization of German Industrial Relations'. *Socio-Economic Review 15* (1): 85–115.

BDA—Bundesvereinigung der Deutschen Arbeitgeberverbände. 2014. *Mehr Jugendbeschäftigung durch praxisnahe Qualifizierung und gute wirtschaftliche Rahmenbedingungen.* Berlin: Bundesvereinigung der Deutschen Arbeitgeberverbände.

BDA—Bundesvereinigung der Deutschen Arbeitgeberverbände. 2015. *Fachkräfte-mangel bekämpfen, Wettbewerbsfähigkeit sichern*. Berlin: Bundesvereinigung der Deutschen Arbeitgeberverbände.

BDA, BDI, and DGB. 2008. *Ausbildungsbonus auf benachteiligte Altbewerber begrenzen!* Berlin: Bundesvereinigung der Deutschen Arbeitgeberverbände.

BDA, BDI, and Telekom. 2014. *Wir Brauchen Alle!* Berlin: Bundesvereinigung der Deutschen Arbeitgeberverbände.

Benassi, C., and L. Dorigatti. 2015. 'Straight to the Core—Explaining Union Responses to the Casualization of Work: The IG Metall Campaign for Agency Workers'. *British Journal of Industrial Relations* 53 (3): 533–55.

Benassi, C., N. Durazzi, and J. Fortwengel. 2021. 'Comparative Institutional Disadvantage: Small Firms and Vocational Training in the British Manufacturing Sector in Comparative Perspective'. *British Journal of Industrial Relations*. Published online 27 September 2021. https://doi.org/10.1111/bjir.12643.

Benassi, C., and T. Vlandas. 2016. 'Union Inclusiveness and Temporary Agency Workers'. *European Journal of Industrial Relations* 22 (1): 5–22. https://doi.org/10.1177/0959680115589485.

Bonoli, G., and P. Emmenegger. 2020. 'The Limits of Decentralized Cooperation: Promoting Inclusiveness in Collective Skill Formation Systems?' *Journal of European Public Policy* 28 (1): 229–47.

Bonoli, G., and A. Wilson. 2019. 'Bringing Firms on Board: Inclusiveness of the Dual Apprenticeship Systems in Germany, Switzerland and Denmark'. *International Journal of Social Welfare* 28 (4): 369–79.

BMDW—Bundesministerium Digitalisierung und Wirtschaftsstandort. 2021. 'Richtlinie gemäß § 19c Abs. 1 Z 8 Berufsausbildungsgesetz'. Available online at https://www.bmdw.gv.at/dam/jcr:38af8726-6f83-42e5-8957-6e33fbd36e5f/01072 021.richtlinie%20gem%C3%83%C2%A4%C3%83%C5%B8%20%C3%82%C2% A7%2019c%20abs.%201%20z%208_bag_barrierefrei.pdf.

Bundesagentur für Arbeit. 2016. *Brücke in die Berufsausbildung. Betriebliche Einstiegsqualifizierung (EQ)*.

Bundesrat der Republik Österreich. 2005. 'Stenographisches Protokoll 729. Sitzung des Bundesrates der Republik Österreich'. Wednesday 21 December 2005. (*Protocol of the 729 session of the Austrian parliament*). Available online at https://www.parlament.gv.at/PAKT/VHG/BR/BRSITZ/BRSITZ_00729/fname_059140.pdf.

Bundestag. 2008. 'Beschlussempfehlung und Bericht des Ausschusses für Arbeit und Soziales (11. Ausschuss) zu dem Gesetzentwurf der Bundesregierung–Drucksachen 16/8718, 16/9238'. Drucksache 16/9456. Available online at https://dserver.bundestag.de/btd/16/094/1609456.pdf.

Bundestag. 2010. 'Antwort der Bundesregierung auf die Kleine Anfrage der Abgeordneten Katja Mast, Anette Kramme, Petra Ernstberger, weiterer Abgeordneter und der Fraktion der SPD – Drucksache 17/3245 – Perspektiven und Konsequenzen aus dem ersten Bericht der Bundesregierung zur Wirkung des Ausbildungsbonus'. Drucksache 17/3384. Available online at dip21.bundestag.de/dip21/btd/17/033/1703384.pdf

Busemeyer, M. R. 2009. Wandel trotz Reformstau – Die Politik der beruflichen Bildung seit 1970. Campus: Schriften aus dem Max-Planck-Institut für Gesellschaftsforschung.

Busemeyer, M. R. 2012. 'Business as a Pivotal Actor in the Politics of Training Reform: Insights from the Case of Germany'. *British Journal of Industrial Relations 50* (4): 690–713.

Busemeyer, M. R. 2015. *Skills and Inequality: Partisan Politics and the Political Economy of Education Reforms in Western Welfare States*. Cambridge: Cambridge University Press.

Carstensen, M. B., and C. L. Ibsen. 2021. 'Three Dimensions of Institutional Contention: Efficiency, Equality and Governance in Danish Vocational Education and Training Reform'. *Socio-Economic Review 19* (3): 1037–63.

Culpepper, P. D. 2001. 'Employers, Public Policy, and the Politics of Decentralized Cooperation in Germany and France'. In *Varieties of Capitalism*, edited by P. A. Hall and D. Soskice, pp. 275–306. Oxford: Oxford University Press.

Culpepper, P. D. 2003. *Creating Cooperation: How States Develop Human Capital in Europe*. Ithaca: Cornell University Press.

Culpepper, P. D., and D. Finegold, (eds). 1999. *The German Skills Machine: Sustaining Comparative Advantage in a Global Economy*. New York: Berghahn Books.

Davidsson, J. B., and P. Emmenegger. 2013. 'Defending the Organisation, Not the Members: Unions and the Reform of Job Security Legislation in Western Europe'. *European Journal of Political Research 52* (3): 339–63.

Der Standard. 2006. *Mehr Lehrlingsförderung mit 'Blum-Bonus'*.

DGB—Deutscher Gewerkschaftsbund. 2016. *Integration und Ausbildung: Keine 'Insellösung' für eine Branche*. Berlin: Deutscher Gewerkschaftsbund.

Di Maio, G., L. Graf, and A. Wilson. 2018. Trajectories of Liberalization in Collective Governance: A Comparative Analysis of Short-track Apprenticeship Reforms in Denmark, Germany and Switzerland. Paper presented at the Political Economy of Education Workshop, Nuffield College, Oxford, 20–22 September 2018.

Durazzi, N. 2017. 'Inclusive Unions in a Dualized Labour Market?' *Social Policy and Administration 51* (2): 265–85.

Durazzi, N. 2019. 'The Political Economy of High Skills: Higher Education in Knowledge-based Labour Markets'. *Journal of European Public Policy 26* (12): 1799–817.

Durazzi, N., and C. Benassi. 2020. 'Going Up-skill: Exploring the Transformation of the German Skill Formation System'. *German Politics 29* (3): 319–38.

Durazzi, N., T. Fleckenstein, and S. C. Lee. 2018. 'Social Solidarity for All? Trade Union Strategies, Labor Market Dualization, and the Welfare State in Italy and South Korea'. *Politics and Society 46* (2): 205–33.

Durazzi, N., and L. Geyer. 2020. 'Social Inclusion in the Knowledge Economy: Unions' Strategies and Institutional Change in the Austrian and German Training Systems'. *Socio-Economic Review 18* (1): 103–24.

Durazzi, N., and L. Geyer. 2021. 'Social Inclusion and Collective Skill Formation Systems: Policy and Politics'. *Journal of European Social Policy*. Published online 12 August 2021.

Eurofound. 2004. 'Training levy avoided by pact'. Available online at https://www.eurofound.europa.eu/publications/article/2004/training-levy-law-avoided-by-pact.

Eurofound. 2012. *NEETs—Young People Not in Employment, Education or Training: Characteristics, Costs and Policy Responses in Europe*. Luxembourg: Publications Office of the European Union.

Geyer, L. 2021. 'The political economy of active labour market policies for young people—a comparative analysis of employers' influence on the use of youth ALMPs'. Unpublished PhD thesis, University of Bamberg.

Gordon, J. C. 2015. 'Protecting the Unemployed: Varieties of Unionism and the Evolution of Unemployment Benefits and Active Labor Market Policy in the Rich Democracies'. *Socio-Economic Review 31* (1): 79–99.

Handelsblatt. 2008. 'Bundestag beschließt "Ausbildungsbonus."' 5 June. https://www.handelsblatt.com/politik/deutschland/bundestag-beschliesst-ausbildungsbonus/2967070.html?ticket=ST-5013111-jfb1ZHNA7fEDE34G64uycas01.example.org (accessed on 11 November 2021).

Iversen, T. 2005. *Capitalism, Democracy, and Welfare*. New York: Cambridge University Press.

Jacob, M., and H. Solga. 2015. 'Germany's Vocational Education and Training System in Transformation: Changes in the Participation of Low- and High-achieving Youth over Time'. *European Sociological Review 31* (2): 161–71.

Kupfer, A. 2010. 'The Socio-political Significance of Changes to the Vocational Education System in Germany'. *British Journal of Sociology of Education 31* (1): 85–97.

OE24. 2007. *AK: Blum Bonus bringt wenig*. Available only at https://www.oe24.at/oesterreich/politik/blum-bonus-bringt-wenig/128557.

OECD. 2019. *OECD Employment Outlook 2019: The Future of Work*. Paris: OECD Publishing.

ÖGB and AK—Österreichischer Gewerkschaftsbund and Arbeiterkammer. 2008. 'Stellungnahme zum Bundesgesetz, mit dem das Berufsbildungsgesetz, das Jugendausbildungs-Sicherungsgesetz, das Insolvenz-Entgeltsicherungsgesetz, das Arbeitsmarktpolitik-Finanzierungsgesetz, das Arbeitsmarktservicegesetz, das Arbeitslosenversicherungsgesetz 1977, das Arbeitsmarktförderungsgesetz und das Einkommenssteuergesetz 1988 geändert werden' (18/SN-162/ME XXIII. GP - Stellungnahme zum Entwurf). Available only at https://www.parlament.gv.at/PAKT/VHG/XXIII/SNME/SNME_03344/imfname_104947.pdf.

ÖGB and AK—Österreichischer Gewerkschaftsbund and Arbeiterkammer. 2011. *Stellungnahme zur Novelle zum Berufsausbildungsgesetz (BAG) 2011* (6/SN-325/ME XXIV). Available online at https://www.parlament.gv.at/PAKT/VHG/XXIV/SNME/SNME_07696/index.shtml.

ÖGB—Österreichischer Gewerkschaftsbund. 2011. 'GPA-djp Jugend: Lehrausbildung braucht mehr als Sonntagsreden und Reförmchen!' Press release OTS0141, 7 October 2011. Available online at https://www.ots.at/presseaussendung/OTS_20111007_OTS0141/gpa-djp-jugend-lehrausbildung-braucht-mehr-als-sonntagsreden-und-refoermchen.

Ramboll. 2014. Externe evaluation der BMBF-initiative 'Abschluss und Anschluss – Bildungsketten bis zum Ausbildungsabschluss' Endbericht. Berlin: Ramböll Management Consulting. Available online at https://www.bildungsketten.de/bildungsketten/shareddocs/arbeitsmaterialien/de/Externe-Evaluation-der-BMBF-Initiative-Abschluss-und-Anschluss-Bildungsketten-bis-zum-Ausbildungsabschluss.pdf;jsessionid=A9E7757CD567E4B11C69CB4E167347D6.live471?__blob=publicationFile&v=2

Rueda, D. 2005. 'Insider–outsider Politics in Industrialized Democracies: The Challenge to Social Democratic Parties'. *American Political Science Review 99* (1): 61–74.

Schmitter, P. C., and W. Streeck. 1999. *The Organization of Business Interests: Studying the Associative Action of Business in Advanced Industrial Societies.* MPIfG Discussion Paper 99/1.

Soskice, D. 1994. 'Reconciling Markets and Institutions: The German Apprenticeship System'. In *Training and the Private Sector: International Comparisons*, edited by L. M. Lynch, pp. 25–60. Chicago: University of Chicago Press.

Steiner M., G. Pessl, E. Wagner, and J. Karaszek. 2013. *Evaluierung "Jugendcoaching"—Endbericht.* Studie im Auftrag des BMASK. Vienna.

Streeck, W., and K. Thelen (eds). 2005. *Beyond Continuity: Institutional Change in Advanced Political Economies.* New York: Oxford University Press.

Swenson, P. A. 2002. *Capitalist against Markets: The Making of Labor Markets and Welfare States in the United States and Sweden.* Oxford: Oxford University Press.

Thelen, K. 2004. How institutions evolve. The political economy of skill formation in the Germany, the United States and Japan. Cambridge: Cambridge University Press.

Thelen, K. 2014. *Varieties of Liberalization and the New Politics of Social Solidarity.* New York: Cambridge University Press.

Thelen, K., and M. R. Busemeyer. 2012. 'Institutional Change in German Vocational Training: From Collectivism towards Segmentalism'. In *The Political Economy of Collective Skill Formation,* edited by M. R. Busemeyer and C. Trampusch, pp. 68–100. Oxford: Oxford University Press.

Thelen, K., and P. D. Culpepper. 2007. 'Institutions and Collective Actors in the Provision of Training: Historical and Cross-national Comparisons'. In *Skill Formation: Interdisciplinary and Cross-national Perspectives,* edited by K. U. Mayer and H. Solga, pp. 21–49. Cambridge: Cambridge University Press.

Tjaden, J. D. 2017. 'Migrant Background and Access to Vocational Education in Germany: Self-Selection, Discrimination, or Both?' *Zeitschrift für Soziologie 46* (2): 107–23.

Trampusch, C. 2010. 'Employers, the State and the Politics of Institutional Change: Vocational Education and Training in Austria, Germany and Switzerland'. *European Journal of Political Research* 49 (4): 545–73.

Verfassungsgerichtshof. 2005. Decision in the joint cases G 39/05, V 25-31/05-12, G 40/05, V 32-37/05-10, and G 82/05, V 56-63/05-9. Available online at https://www.vfgh.gv.at/downloads/VfGH_G_39-05_ua__V_25-31-05_ua.pdf.

WKÖ—Wirtschaftskammer Österreich. 2008. 'Leitl: Jugendbeschäftigungspaket ist wirkungsvolle Maßnahme gegen Fachkräftemangel'. Press release OTS0067, 6 June 2008. Available online at https://www.ots.at/presseaussendung/OTS_20080606_OTS0067/leitl-jugendbeschaeftigungspaket-ist-wirkungsvolle-massnahme-gegen-fachkraeftemangel.

WKÖ—Wirtschaftskammer Österreich. 2012. *Österreich - ein Best practice Beispiel für geringe Jugendarbeitslosigkeit.* Press release OTS0184, 3. Dez. 2012. Available online at https://www.ots.at/presseaussendung/OTS_20121203_OTS0184/wkoe-oesterreich-ein-best-practice-beispiel-fuer-geringe-jugendarbeitslosigkeit.

WKÖ—Wirtschaftskammer   Österreich.   2020.   'Lehrlingscoaching—Lehrbetriebscoaching. Unterstützung von Lehrling und Lehrbetrieb bei Problemen in der Lehre'. Available online at https://www.wko.at/service/w/bildung-lehre/Lehrlingscoaching-Lehrbetriebscoaching.html.

WKÖ—Wirtschaftskammer Österreich. 2021a. 'Basisförderung—Förderung für Lehrbetriebe'. Available online at https://www.wko.at/service/bildung-lehre/Merkblatt_-_Basisfoerderung.html.

WKÖ—Wirtschaftskammer Österreich. 2021b. 'Laufende Projekte der Projektförderung Lehre'. Available online at https://www.wko.at/Content.Node/kampagnen/projektfoerderung-lehre/start.html#i-laufende-projekte.

ZdH—Zentralverband des deutschen Handwerks. 2007. *Ganzheitlich Passgenau Anschlussfähig: Grundzüge eines umfassenden und flexiblen Berufslaufbahnkonzepts im Handwerk*. Berlin.

7

Employer Visibility and Sectors as Predictors of Egalitarian Values in VET

A Mixed-method Study of Recruiters' Views on Apprentice Candidates

Anna Wilson

7.1 Introduction

One cornerstone for a successful transition into adulthood, economically, socially, and psychologically, is a solid education (Müller and Gangl 2003; Dieckhoff 2008; Protsch and Dieckhoff 2011; Dietrich 2012; Ryan 2012; Kriesi et al. 2012). This notion is even more pertinent in the face of a shift towards a knowledge economy (Powell and Snellman 2004; Hope and Martelli 2019). In most cases, a first step towards securing a stable life trajectory is finishing compulsory school and beginning an upper-secondary education (Kovacheva and Pohl 2007).

In countries where the dual apprenticeship is an established secondary-level-education option, in-firm apprentice recruiters act as gatekeepers for the youth who wish to follow the vocational education and training (VET) track (Imdorf 2017). The apprentice recruiters are in most instances free to select any candidate they wish based on criteria that they believe helps finding a suitable candidate (Wolter et al. 2006; Wolter and Ryan 2011).

This procedure sometimes leads to situations where shares of the candidates—especially those with low school qualifications—do not manage to obtain an in-firm apprenticeship. The reason is often that the firms or organizations where they applied considered them not trainable enough, or otherwise as a poor fit for the position (Hellan and Støren 2006; Di Stasio 2014; Jacob and Solga 2015; Protsch 2017). With the rise of the knowledge economy and the related surge in skill demands on the labour market (Murphy and Oesch 2018), the access to qualified vocational training for a broad

Anna Wilson, *Employer Visibility and Sectors as Predictors of Egalitarian Values in VET*. In: *Collective Skill Formation in the Knowledge Economy*. Edited by Giuliano Bonoli and Patrick Emmenegger, Oxford University Press.
© Oxford University Press (2022). DOI: 10.1093/oso/9780192866257.003.0007

share of the youth population is an increasingly pressing issue (see Bonoli and Emmenegger, in this volume).

Previous research has mapped the apprentice-hiring preferences of in-firm apprentice recruiters who provide vocational training and uncovered factors that seemingly improve low-qualified and socio-economically disadvantaged youths' hiring chances (Hupka-Brunner et al. 2010; Mohrenweiser 2012; Solga and Kohlrausch 2012; Protsch 2017; Imdorf 2017). A recent vignette survey experiment focusing on apprentice recruiters in commercial businesses asked what signals apprentice recruiters consider when hiring apprentices (see Fossati et al. 2020a) and showed, among others, that public-sector employers were more willing than private-sector employers to lower the hiring criteria for youth with lower academic qualifications (Wilson 2021).

Furthermore, research suggests that larger companies might be more willing to hire individuals with a migrant background compared to smaller ones (Imdorf 2017; Protsch 2017) and that the apprentice recruiters' individual values and beliefs impact their willingness to lower the threshold on school qualifications (Wilson 2021). What we lack to date is knowledge on which factors drive different attitudes towards low achievers, potentially resulting in improved hiring chances for this population.

This chapter addresses that gap in the literature by answering the following question: what factors drive the egalitarian and the non-egalitarian attitudes towards low-qualified apprentices in VET among apprentice recruiters? The aim is to pinpoint the underlying motives between hiring preferences in different sectors. With a more complete picture of the reasons behind employers' values and preferences, issues of applicant and apprenticeship mismatch can be better understood and perhaps even avoided.

The findings show that sectors with high-skill demands are less likely to have egalitarian hiring attitudes compared to sectors with lower-skill demands—even for recruitment to the same apprenticeship programme. Furthermore, they suggest that apprentice recruiters in firms with high visibility are more likely to have egalitarian hiring attitudes compared with firms with low visibility.

The chapter is organized as follows. In section 7.2, the theoretical framework that guides the study is presented and hypotheses to be tested are derived. The case selection, data, method, and operationalization are presented in section 7.3, followed by the results in section 7.4. The discussion and conclusion follow in section 7.5.

7.2 Theory

Recent research shows that egalitarian attitudes predict inclusive (stated) preferences for apprentice candidates (Wilson 2021). The following section reviews the strands of literature that attempt to explain what drives egalitarian attitudes.

7.2.1 Visibility and public image

In dual VET systems, employers are free to decide whether they want to participate as training providers or not (Wolter and Ryan 2011; Busemeyer and Trampusch 2012). The motivation to participate can perhaps best be described as a mix of economic interest and tradition (Juul and Jørgensen 2011; Nelson 2012; Deissinger and Gonon 2016). Employers in dual VET systems, thus, have a social pressure to 'fulfil their role' as apprenticeship-providers in countries with this tradition: much of which is due to the positive reactions from the public that can be expected when the firm assumes this 'duty' (Bonoli 2016).

For a few decades now, average school results and skill levels of school leavers appear to be falling; thus the training firms are often seen as a part of the solution to the problem of drop-out or failed transitions to upper-secondary education in VET systems (Van de Werfhorst 2014; Jørgensen 2014; Solga et al. 2014; Protsch 2017). In brief, there are not only cost–benefit reasons behind firms' apprenticeship provision but also a good measure of tradition and social norms (Bonoli 2012, 2016).

Naturally, there may be obstacles that hinder or make it less attractive for firms to offer apprenticeships. A small, local firm that faces sharp competition in its branch might simply not be able to afford to offer apprenticeships—let alone for weaker learners who may need more guidance and support (Wolter et al. 2006; Imdorf 2017). For a large and well-known firm, on the other hand, affording and offering apprenticeships to low-qualified candidates as well may be easier (Kis 2016; Kuczera 2017). Furthermore, with size and visibility, public expectations placed on the firm to profile itself as socially responsible rise (Bonoli 2016; Protsch 2017). A socially responsible 'image' could in turn generate public goodwill, which would also be beneficial for the firm (Vogel 2010).

One recent issue, targeted by both policymakers and educational researchers, is the decreasing qualities and academic capacities of school leavers: especially those with a migrant background or otherwise disadvantageous social origin (Davoli and Entorf 2018; SKBF CSRE 2018). The implications for apprenticeship-providing firms are higher costs of training since the apprentices are less prepared to follow the curriculum (Deissinger and Hellwig 2005; Solga et al. 2014). Consequently, some training firms which simply do not find it worthwhile providing training to low-qualified apprentices have opted out of apprenticeship provision (SERI 2019).

The size and training capacity (Mohrenweiser 2012) of the firm might, however, moderate the possibility and willingness for a training firm to consider hiring a low-qualified young person as apprentice. Furthermore, given that large and well-known firms generally receive more applications and thus have a larger pool of applicants to choose from (SERI 2019; Wettstein et al. 2017: 21, 191), they are aware that they can comfortably fill the positions with a 'good' applicant. This may make them more prone to also train low achievers without losing too much productivity (Kis 2016).

Another aspect often highlighted in the hiring literature is discrimination towards apprentice candidates with a migrant background (Imdorf and Leeman 2012; Schneider et al. 2014; Scherr et al. 2015; Imdorf 2017). Previous studies have shown a higher likelihood of aversion towards migrant candidates from some employers (especially small firms, see Imdorf 2017) who cannot 'risk' an atypical apprentice out of concern that these would not be accepted by customers (Holzer 1998; Imdorf 2017) or because of doubts regarding the language skills of the candidate (Gaugler et al. 1978; Hupka and Stalder 2004; Scherr et al. 2015). Studies showing an absence of migrant discrimination, however, have specifically underlined the public sector (Wilson 2021) and large employers (Holzer 1998) as key examples of *non-discriminating* employers. These two employer types also correspond with the literature connecting an inclusive hiring behaviour (with regards to low-qualified youth) with a concern for public image (Protsch 2017).

In sum, the expectation is that employers that are large and well known publicly have an interest in maintaining a positive and socially responsible image. Thus, their recruiters should be more inclined to give a chance to low-qualified youth compared with other firms. The first hypothesis, therefore, suggests that:

H1: The more well known and visible an employer is, other things being held equal, the more likely its apprentice recruiter is to have an egalitarian attitude towards low-qualified youth in VET.

7.2.2 Sectoral skill demands and apprentice preferences

The commercial training programme, the focus of this study, is provided by employers in a great variety of sectors, such as banking, construction, public administration, hotels and restaurants, etc. Although the programme leads to one common vocational certificate, the firm-based part of the commercial training is formed by the sectors offering this programme (SERI 2019). In that vein, recruitment and candidate selection is likely also influenced by the specific demands of the sector in which the training firm is active (Holzer 1998; Zuckerman 1999; Rivera 2011; Imdorf 2013; Castilla et al. 2013; Wilson 2021).

The literature proposes different logics that may govern the sectoral preferences for apprentices. One is the 'person–organization fit' logic, where the recruiters' hiring decision is based on estimates of the candidates' future career opportunities in the firm, the linkage to continued education in different fields (Adkins et al. 1994; Rivera 2015), or to other internal preferences that firms in different sectors have for their apprentice candidates (Castilla et al. 2013; Holzer 1998).

Similarly, recruiters might also follow a logic of homophily—i.e. preferring candidates who are like themselves—and look for apprentices that they think would fit well into the team, who seem suitable and easily integrated to the firm culture (Castilla et al. 2013; Daehlen 2017; Liechti 2020). Following this logic, recruiters in a firm operating in a sector that is highly demanding and where a strongly professional image is of great importance, would prefer hiring apprentices who the recruiter deems to fit into that profile. Vice versa, in a sector where other aspects are highlighted, for instance soft skills (Protsch and Solga 2015), candidates corresponding to such ideals would be prioritized.

There is evidence in the literature that the hiring decision in many sectors is influenced by the candidates' soft skills and other personality traits rather than school qualifications (Wettstein et al. 2017; Liechti et al. 2017; Auer et al. 2019; Fossati et al. 2020a). In a study of the hospitality and retail sectors in Sweden and Switzerland, the authors find that personal characteristics such as motivation to work hard sends a positive signal to employers, even in the event where the candidate has experienced long unemployment spells (Fossati et al. 2020b).

Although part of the scholarship on employer preferences has been focused on the supply side, such as the individual qualities of the apprenticeship applicants, another part is more oriented towards the sectoral specificities on the demand side. Previous studies focusing on Swiss commercial training in particular highlights the influence exerted by the banking and insurance sectors regarding the setup of the apprenticeship programme (Emmenegger and Seitzl 2019; Seitzl and Emmenegger 2019). The combination of high demands on sector-specific skills and influence in the commercial business field enabled the reform of the apprentice programme, granting the various industries involved the freedom to shape the firm-based training part according to industry needs (Emmenegger and Seitzl 2019; Pilz 2007). Thus, the banking and insurance sectors established a more demanding and industry-specific curriculum granting their graduates access to commercial employee work in all the other sectors but limiting the access for commercial employee graduates in other sectors (Emmenegger and Seitzl 2019). Thereby, the banking and insurance sectors have established themselves as highly demanding and selective in terms of skill requirements and trainability of their apprentices in order to preserve the status and high industrial integrity of these sectors (see also Aerne, in this volume). Against this background, the author formulates a second hypothesis:

> H2: Employers in sectors with high-skill demands are less likely to have an egalitarian hiring attitude towards low-qualified youth in VET than employers in sectors with lower-skill demands.

The two hypotheses presented in this theory section are tested in the results section 7.4. In section 7.3, the methodological considerations for this study are presented and discussed.

7.3 Methodology

7.3.1 Case selection

The object of study in this chapter is the three-year-long commercial employee vocational training programme (Employée de commerce CFC) in the canton of Vaud in Switzerland. The primary reason for choosing this vocational programme is its popularity and high participation rate among youth in all of Switzerland (Pilz 2007; Emmenegger and Seitzl 2019; OFS 2018). With collaborators the author was able to obtain the in-firm vocational trainers' contact details from the official centralized registry with help from the General Direction for Post-Mandatory Education (DGEP) in Lausanne, in the French-speaking canton of Vaud.

In terms of the generalizability of the results to the other, notably German-speaking regions, full-time vocational schools are more common in the French-speaking than in the German-speaking regions (Wettstein et al. 2017). This might generate fewer applicants per vacancy in the French region, but there were no reasons to believe the pool of applicants differs markedly between the linguistic regions. Furthermore, commercial training covers organizations operating in a wide variety of sectors and therefore provides a broad and heterogeneous sample of employers which enabled the possibility of cross-sectoral analyses.

7.3.2 Data

The objective in this study is to analyse the factors that drive egalitarian attitudes among vocational trainers and recruiters. Using a mixed-method approach by means of both quantitative and qualitative surveys and interviews, the author triangulates the research question and avoids biases that could potentially stem from the use of only one method or source of data. The hypotheses that were formulated in the previous section are preliminarily answered with the quantitative study and followed up with the qualitative study where the explanatory variables are investigated in detail.

The quantitative survey was sent via email, containing a link to the survey, to all approved in-firm vocational trainers in commercial training (N = 1,129) in the French-speaking Canton of Vaud (Switzerland). The data collection took place between March and May 2017. Data was obtained for 840 individual apprentice recruiters/in-firm vocational trainers reaching a response rate of circa 63 per cent.

The qualitative survey was administered, via email as well, to all respondents of the first, quantitative, survey who had agreed to be contacted for a follow-up study. Out of 355 contacted respondents, 208 took the survey and 181 completed it, yielding a response rate of circa 51 per cent (see Table 7.4A in the appendix).

Furthermore, eight interviews were carried out: three before the quantitative survey was launched and five after the data from the quantitative survey was collected. The first three interviews were carried out with the ambition to inform our survey questionnaire; the other five interviewees were selected randomly from the group of respondents from the quantitative survey who had agreed to be contacted for follow-up questions.

7.3.3 Operationalization

Egalitarian values. The 'egalitarian values' variable in the quantitative analysis is based on the respondents' rating on the following statement presented to them in the quantitative survey: *The firms* [in the Swiss VET system] *should provide all young people with a chance to obtain vocational training, regardless of their competence level or ambition.* This statement captures the respondents' attitude towards inclusion of weaker students in the dual system and is a suitable approximation of how they also view their own role as recruiters in the Swiss system. The response categories are gauged on a five-point scale ranging from 'completely disagree' to 'fully agree'. The author recoded this variable into a dummy by collapsing the 'completely disagree' and the 'disagree' categories into 'non-egalitarian' and the 'fully agree' and 'agree' into 'egalitarian'. The 'neither agree nor disagree' category was excluded from the analysis since it does not correspond with either value-orientation of interest.

Visibility. The first hypothesis expects that the level of visibility of an employer is positively associated with their inclination to have an egalitarian outlook on Swiss firms' role in providing training for youth regardless of the youths' skill level or ambition level. A variable capturing the visibility level of the firm ranges from 'locally recognized' to 'regionally recognized' (in this case, known on the cantonal level), 'Swiss-wide recognized' to 'internationally recognized'. The classification of the firms and organizations into the different categories was based on the size of the firm in terms of total number of employees together with number of locations. For example, a bank office might have only five employees in a smaller town, but the bank brand is internationally recognized and therefore benefits from the visibility that follows. Such an employer would therefore be coded as 'internationally recognized' (for more information about the coding, see Table 7.1A in the appendix).

Sector groups. The quantitative survey asked the respondents to indicate in which sector the firm or organization was active in. After the data were cleaned, the results yielded twenty-four different categories, including 'other', in which the sectors that only one or two employers had indicated that they belonged were placed (see Table 7.2A in the appendix). In the remaining twenty-three categories, some sectors had very few observations. Therefore, the author grouped them together with other businesses expected to have similar preferences regarding apprentice recruitment.

The following sector groups were created: 'Public administration', 'Tourism, hotel and restaurant, media, and events', 'Construction, crafts, industry, chemistry, and engineering', 'Education, charity, healthcare, service, and administration', 'Law and public notary, private insurance, and banking', 'Commerce and services' and 'Fiduciary and real estate'. Employers who could not be placed in any of these categories were excluded from the analysis (n = 27).

Referring to the theoretical considerations presented and discussed in section 7.2: sectoral skill demands and apprentice preferences, two of the sectors within the groupings neatly correspond to either high-skill demands (i.e. 'Law, private insurance, and banking') or lower-skill demands (i.e. 'Commerce and services'). Furthermore, studies preceding this one suggest that 'Public administration' has the lowest stated hiring criteria for low achievers (Protsch 2017; Wilson 2021), which makes it a suitable reference category vis-à-vis the other sector groups.

Difficulty in recruiting. We know from the annual 'Apprenticeship barometer' that many Swiss apprenticeship-providing firms leave positions vacant: a vast majority (67%) because they claim to have not found suitable applicants (SERI 2017: 23). In the quantitative survey, the respondents were asked to indicate to what extent it has been difficult to find an adequate candidate for the commercial employee apprenticeship vacancies during the past twelve months. The response categories ranged from 'very difficult' to 'very easy' on a five-point scale. Subsequently, the answers were recoded so that the 'very easy' and 'easy' categories were collapsed into 'easy', 'neither' was kept as its own category, and 'difficult' and 'very difficult' were collapsed into 'difficult'.

7.3.4 Statistical procedure

This study seeks to explain the variation in the dependent variable 'egalitarian values' of the in-firm vocational trainers, representing the firms and organizations where they are employed. Against the backdrop of the hypotheses presented in the theory section, several explanatory (independent) variables were tested. The potential impact of the explanatory variables on the dependent variable was tested with a binary logistic regression analysis (Kohler and Kreuter 2005). The variance–co-variance matrix of the estimators was used for obtaining robust variance estimates of the model (Kohler and Kreuter 2005). The sample was limited to those respondents who had indicated that they are in fact vocational trainers and who have real influence over the hiring decision when new apprentices are recruited.

7.3.5 Qualitative survey and interviews

To follow up the quantitative survey, a qualitative survey was launched and sent to the respondents in the first survey and aimed to learn more about the in-firm vocational trainers' reasoning and preferences concerning apprentice hiring (see Table 7.3A in the appendix). The author, with collaborators, asked the respondents to elaborate in their own words what they look for in an apprentice candidate and on a CV, how they value grades, aptitude test results, and educational track as indicators of a candidate's abilities and why. Furthermore, they were asked to indicate their perception of different risk factors for dropping out of an apprenticeship (foreign language spoken at home, unstable family situation, etc.), to see if this perceived risk was mirrored in their stated hiring preferences.

With the two surveys and eight interviews at hand, the responses of each participant in the qualitative follow-up study were merged with their responses in the initial quantitative survey to learn more about the 'typical' reasoning in the different sectors. The main interest was in the respondents' views on egalitarianism, who they perceive as the ideal and non-ideal candidate and to the challenges in recruiting.

The responses to the different questions were categorized to detect similarities or differences in reasoning across sectors, and special attention was paid to the responses from the expected most and least egalitarian sectors ('Public administration', 'Law firms, Private insurance, and banks'). In the qualitative results section, the interviewees are coded as Int(number) and the respondents to the qualitative survey are coded as Resp (number).

7.4 Results

In this section the results of, first, the quantitative and, second, the qualitative analyses are presented. The quantitative results are organized after Hypothesis 1 and 2 discussed in section 7.2.

7.4.1 Quantitative study

We start by looking at the factors that influence an egalitarian attitude towards low-qualified youth in the Swiss VET system.

Hypothesis 1 suggests that the visibility of a training firm has an impact on their vocational trainers' inclination to have an egalitarian view on firms' roles in the Swiss VET system. The logistic regression analysis in Table 7.1 shows that the more widely known and visible firms indeed are more prone to have an egalitarian view on low-qualified candidates: the coefficients for 'Swiss-wide recognized' firms is significant on a 10-per-cent level, and positive (Table 7.1). The 'Regionally recognized' and 'Internationally recognized' categories are not significant, but the coefficient is in the same direction as the 'Swiss-wide recognized'. Hypothesis 1, claiming that the level of visibility of a firm is positively associated with an egalitarian view on low-qualified youth in VET, thus has some support.

Hypothesis 2 concerned the impact of the sector type on the in-firm vocational trainers' inclination to have an egalitarian view on low-qualified youth in VET. As the reference category for the sector groups is the 'Public administration' (PA) group. We know from previous research that this segment of the employers was comparatively more egalitarian-oriented compared with private-sector firms (Wilson 2021) and is therefore most suitable as the reference category.

The logistic regression analysis shows that, compared to 'Public administration', the sector group consisting of 'Law firms, private insurance, and banks' (LPIB) is the least likely to be egalitarian among all the sector groups (see Table 7.1). For the LPIB group the coefficient suggests a negative relationship that is significant at the 5-per-cent level. Among the different sector groups, this category was the most skill-demanding in the theory section. Since only the LPIB proved to be less egalitarian-oriented compared to the others, H2 can be corroborated.

The results in Table 7.1, furthermore, show that a high level of perceived difficulty in recruiting an adequate candidate in the last twelve months is associated with decreasing egalitarian attitudes towards the low-qualified apprentices. For the variable 'Perceived difficulty to recruit' the 'Difficult' coefficient is statistically significantly and suggests that recruiters who have trouble hiring adequate apprentices tend to be non-egalitarian. Whether the in-firm vocational trainer primarily trains apprentices in the extended version of the commercial training programme does not impact the dependent variable (see Table 7.1).

To summarize, there appears to be a link between 'employer's visibility' and egalitarian-oriented values on the other, and between the LPIB sector and a non-egalitarian value-orientation on the one hand. The latter link is explored further by means of the qualitative study presented in the following section.

Table 7.1 Factors influencing apprentice recruiters' egalitarian values

Independent variables	Coefficient	Standard error
Sector groups (ref. Public administration)		
Tourism, hotel and restaurant, media, and events	−0.328	(0.420)
Construction, crafts, industry, chemistry, and engineering	−0.243	(0.299)
Education, charity, healthcare, service, and administration	−0.021	(0.313)
Law firms, private insurance, banks	−0.774*	(0.371)
Commerce and service	−0.353	(0.312)
Fiduciary and real estate	−0.067	(0.337)
Number of employees (ref: 1–9)		
10–49	0.040	(0.236)
50–249	0.286	(0.287)
More than 250	−0.390	(0.325)
Difficulty to recruit (ref: Easy)		
Neither easy nor difficult	0.183	(0.215)
Difficult	−0.514*	(0.227)
Employer's level of visibility (ref: Locally recognized)		
Regionally recognized	0.072	(0.211)
Swiss-wide recognized	0.528∞	(0.317)
Internationally recognized	0.625	(0.409)
Importance of apprentice's capacity to integrate (ref. Less important)		
Important	−0.302	(0.380)
Importance of apprentice's capacity of independent work (ref. Less important)		
Important	0.357	(0.233)
Number of years respondent has been involved in recruitment of apprentices	*0.008*	*(0.015)*
Respondent's nationality (ref. Non-Swiss)		
Yes	−0.447	(0.291)
Respondent's age in years	0.010	(0.010)
Respondent's gender (ref. Female)		
Male	0.079	(0.201)
Respondent is vocational trainer at extended commercial programme (ref. No)		
Yes	−0.207	(0.236)
Constant	0.796	(0.738)
N	620	
AIC	813.855	
BIC	911.309	
Ll	−384.928	

Note: Standard errors in parentheses ∞ p<0.1, * p<0.05, ** p<0.01, *** p<0.001.

7.4.2 Qualitative study

7.4.2.1 Overall tendencies among respondents

This section draws on the analysis of the 181 respondents' answers to our qualitative survey and the eight interviews conducted around the time of the two surveys. The objective with the qualitative follow-up study in this chapter is to get a clearer idea of the underlying motives for apprentice preferences among different sector groups.

The main finding is that there are two general lines of argumentation from the respondents. One argument highlights grades and other academic achievements as tools, assesses whether a candidate will be able to complete the apprenticeship, and, in the end, pass the exam. The other argument underscores information about grades, educational track, and aptitude test results as a tool for selecting the most academically qualified candidate for a position (Table 7.2).

Table 7.2 Main answer categories derived from responses to qualitative survey

Answer categories	Frequency	Share relative to total number of answer categories (%)
School achievements used as guarantee for completion of commercial employee training*	63	35
School achievements used as tools for selecting the most academically qualified candidate for commercial training*	60	33
Inconclusive or ambiguous answers*	58	32
Total	181	100
Other strengths equally important when hiring**	42	23
Importance of other strengths not specifically stated	139	77
Total	181	100
Speaking a foreign language at home is a risk factor for dropping out**	34	19
Speaking a foreign language at home is not a risk factor for dropping out	119	66
Did not answer	28	15
Total	181	100
Survey participants	208	
Missing answers	27	
Total number of complete responses	181	

Note: * These categories are mutually exclusive, only one answer category per respondent is possible.
** This category is not mutually exclusive to the other categories.

Table 7.3 Summary of response frequency to qualitative survey questions, by sector groups

Sector groups	School achieve-ments used as guarantee for completion of commercial employee training	School achieve-ments used as tools for selecting the most academically qualified candidate for commercial training	Inconclusive or ambiguous answers	Total
Public administration	29	8	12	49
Tourism, hotel and restaurant, media, and events	4	3	3	10
Construction, crafts, industry, chemistry, and engineering	3	8	10	21
Education, charity, healthcare, service, and administration	14	6	12	32
Law firms, private insurance, banks	2	12	1	15
Commerce and service	10	4	10	24
Fiduciary and real estate	2	8	4	14
Total				165

The former line of argument occurs amongst respondents across the sector groups, including PA (see Table 7.3). Many respondents in various sector groups highlight the importance of a good command of the French language—often, if not most of the time, reflected in a good French grade average and a well-written CV and personal letter—to be able to follow the commercial training programme. However, in public administration, grades, educational track, and aptitude test results are first and foremost seen as indicators or guarantees for the apprentice's successful participation in the programme rather than used as a tool for selecting the most academically qualified apprentice (Table 7.3).

On the other hand, the respondents who highlight the candidates' school results are dominant in the LPIB group (also in the 'Fiduciary and real estate' group) compared to the other sector groups—especially PA (see Table 7.3). According to their responses in the qualitative survey, their view of apprenticeships in their respective branches appears to be that only top-performing candidates are good enough to qualify for their competitive and high-profile lines of business. For these vocational trainers, it is less a matter of whether the apprentice will pass their final exams, and more whether the apprentices can live up to the high standards established by the firms themselves.

Turning our attention to the perceived risk factors for dropping out, which the respondents were asked to grade on a scale from very low risk to very high risk (1–5), we see that a share of the respondents (19%) considers a foreign language at home as a high-risk factor (Table 7.2). Although the respondents with this view are in minority, it is possible that this perceived risk associated with foreign home language and the high demands on competencies in French put candidates with a migrant background at a disadvantage, compared to their Swiss peers. However, there do not appear to be any sectoral differences in responses regarding perceived risk of dropping out (see Table 7.5A in the appendix).

7.4.2.2 Examining the 'typical' cases of non-egalitarian and egalitarian employers

The 'typical' cases were singled out from the least egalitarian sector (LPIB): those who report a non-egalitarian view on firms in the VET system and difficulties in recruiting, and the typical cases from the most egalitarian sector (PA): those who report an egalitarian view in firms in the VET system (see Table 7.1). With this grouping, we can look closer at the specific arguments used in these two extremes, drawing on the qualitative survey and the interviews with the vocational trainers.

The reports from these sources confirm the observation in the overall qualitative part of the study: everyone pays attention to school achievements, but for different reasons. Apprentice recruiters in the LPIB group look to school performance indicators primarily to be able to pick the candidate with highest cognitive capacity (Int6, Resp45, Resp95, Resp97), and apprentice recruiters from the PA group mostly out of concern for the apprentice's ability to follow through with the training (Int2, Int5, Resp81, Resp16, Resp42). One bank trainer interviewed answered the following to the question about who the ideal candidate would be:

> They have to be very good in school, have worked during the school leaves, are motivated, have knowledge about banks. In Utopia, they have all these strengths, like a sheep with five legs![1] (Int6)

---

[1] All quotes were translated from French by the author.

Another law firm respondent emphasized the importance of scholarly excellence in their apprentices, especially reflected by the French grades:

> Good French grades are a prerequisite for succeeding in this branch, they are my priority . . . For me, bad grades are prohibitive. (Resp92)

On the other hand, a PA employee responded the following to the same question:

> [I am] . . . more interested in personal competences rather than technical ones—the apprentices will learn the techniques in their apprenticeship. So, it is, rather, soft skills such as integration into the group, capability of accepting their place in the hierarchy, that's important. . . Between social competence and grades, there is no linkage. [But their] . . . hobbies are interesting to see whether they demonstrate a capacity to integrate themselves into the group or have an open mind . . . I need people with a broader view to work with unemployed people. (Int5)

Overall, many apprentice recruiters considered a candidates' school performance and test results, because in the end everyone wants to see their apprentice successfully complete the training. However, there are those who take it upon themselves to hire someone with the right motivation and spirit—despite poor school achievements—and offer them enough help and support to nevertheless follow the training (Int2, Int5). For example, one vocational trainer in public administration interviewed explained the efforts they made to hire less qualified apprentices:

> I anticipate difficulties with the youth, but I want to give the ones with difficulties a chance since we [employers in public administration] have the possibility of investing more in these people. (Int5)

Another PA employee reasoned in a similar way when asked what elements other than school results are useful for selecting an apprentice:

> The interviews are indispensable for this purpose. We go by 'feeling' a lot. If the candidate is motivated and enthusiastic, we would prefer them over someone with excellent grades on paper but from whom we don't get the right 'feeling'. (Resp23)

In sum, grades are relevant in all sectors, but the tendency that other qualities of the apprentice than his or her school achievements will be given significant weight seems stronger in PA rather than in LPIB.

7.5 Discussion and conclusion

This study sought to answer the question: what factors drive the egalitarian and indeed the non-egalitarian attitudes towards low-qualified apprentices in VET among apprentice recruiters? The results from the analyses of the quantitative and qualitative survey data suggest that different employer characteristics indeed affect the egalitarian attitudes towards low-qualified youth in the VET system. Whereas public administration employers are the most egalitarian-oriented, employers in law and public notary, private insurance and banking sectors are the least egalitarian compared to the employers in all the other sectors in commercial training studied.

Among the employers, the ones recognized across Switzerland are more likely to be egalitarian compared with others. This finding aligns with previous studies of firm behaviour in apprentice recruitment, averring that larger, more visible firms are prone to discriminate less due to more formalized recruitment procedures compared with smaller firms (Kis 2016; Kuczera 2017). These are also inclined to be more egalitarian and inclusive towards low-qualified candidates due to the pressure to maintain a positive public image (Holzer 1998; Vogel 2010; Imdorf and Leeman 2012; Protsch 2017; Imdorf 2017).

In sum, both H1 and H2 are corroborated in the quantitative part, while the reasons behind these patterns of egalitarianism or non-egalitarianism were followed up with a qualitative study.

Drawing on the qualitative study, the findings suggest that the law firms, private insurance firms, and the banks have higher expectations of, and more demanding criteria for, apprentice candidates. Although employers in public administration acknowledge the importance of satisfactory school achievements, they use grades mainly as predictors for future completion of the vocational programme in commercial training. Even in view of the commonality that all the firms in the study share—the provision of in-firm vocational training in the commercial field—they differ markedly in the way they adapt their hiring criteria to fit the particularity of the branch that the firm is located in.

In this regard, it is unsurprising that law firm apprentice recruiters highlight the importance of excellent French grades, and banks and private insurers the need for candidates with the good mathematical capabilities which are needed in their field. Although, apprentice recruiters who are active in these sectors were not more prone to perceive applicants with home languages other than French as being more likely to drop out than their colleagues in public administration. Nevertheless, the exercise to review the specificities of the training firms in the different sectors consolidated knowledge about apprentice recruitment.

The tendency of public administration vocational trainers to be more egalitarian and law firms, private insurance firms, and bank vocational trainers to be less so, other things held equal, is salient and aligns well with the literature presented in the theory section, proposing that employers are prone to homophilic hiring (Castilla et al. 2013; Daehlen 2017). We cannot, however, know for sure whether there is a measure of self-selection at work in this regard. If public administration offers an inclusive and egalitarian work environment, it will perhaps attract candidates (including in-firm vocational trainers) who feel at home in this setting, and vice versa for the less egalitarian sectors.

Although this study has yielded some new insights, it is not without caveats. Certainly, a study of one vocational programme in one canton in one country has a somewhat limited generalizability. For the sake of generalizing the results beyond the borders of Switzerland, this study has likely provided a favourable case of egalitarianism and inclusion when it comes to apprenticeship-providing employers. For example, we know from comparisons between Switzerland and Germany that academically weak students fare better in the Swiss system than in the German counterpart (Buchholz et al. 2012). It is therefore not certain that low-qualified youths, for instance, would have an equally good hiring outlook in other countries' public administration offices as they do in Switzerland.

With this study, we have nevertheless moved a little closer to understanding what influences inclusive apprentice hiring, but there are still puzzles to solve. One such puzzle is the significant visibility factor *and* the connection between the law, private insurance, and bank group and non-egalitarian values. A share of the firms in these sectors are well recognized—both nationally and internationally, especially among the banks and private insurers. To be highly visible can therefore not be considered a sufficient condition for egalitarian values amongst the recruiters, but other scope conditions are likely necessary to pinpoint the true cause for such values.

Furthermore, future research should investigate organizational culture and conventions from the point of view of value-shaping or value-changing in relation to apprentice hiring and delve deeper into the issue of whether egalitarian attitudes also lead to inclusive hiring in real life. Studies focusing on other collective skill formation systems than Switzerland are welcome to broaden the perspective on egalitarianism in apprentice recruitment.

The prognosis for future labour market participants, considering the shift to a knowledge economy, suggests that the lion's share of work in production and industry will either have moved offshore or become obsolete or automatized (Autor 2010; Avis 2018). The service sector however, to which commercial training adheres, is predicted to remain (Buera and Kaboski 2012). Although, it is nevertheless a sector where automatization is prevalent and expected to grow, which might render part of the workforce redundant (Seitzl 2021).

Despite this, the growing service sector is likely to remain an important employer for low achievers, those with a migration background as well as those apprentice candidates who would previously have found apprenticeship and later employment in less demanding occupations (Stalder 2011). It is of high importance to create an understanding of, a dialogue between, and expectations on employers in these sectors to broaden their perspectives even further when it comes to apprentice hiring (see Aerne, in this volume). Such a development would not only benefit the low-qualified candidates but also bolster—and perhaps in the long term secure—the labour supply for future commercial employers.

References

Adkins, C. L., C. J. Russell, and J. D. Werbel. 1994. 'Judgements of Fit in the Selection Process: The Role of Work Value Congruence'. *Personnel Psychology* 47 (3): 605–23.

Auer, D., G. Bonoli, F. Fossati, and F. Liechti. 2019. 'The Matching Hierarchies Model: Evidence from a Survey Experiment on Employers' Hiring Intent Regarding Immigrant Applicants'. *International Migration Review* 53 (1): 90–121.

Autor, D. H. 2010. *The Polarization of Job Opportunities in the U.S. Labor Market. Implications for Employment and Earnings.* Washington, DC: Center for American Progress.

Avis, J. 2018. 'Socio-technical Imaginary of the Fourth Industrial Revolution and its Implications for Vocational Education and Training: A Literature Review'. *Journal of Vocational Education and Training* 70 (3): 337–63.

Bonoli, L. 2012. 'La Naissance de la formation professionnelle en Suisse: entre compétences techniques et éducation morale'. *Education permanente* 192: 209–21.

Bonoli, L. 2016. 'Aux origines de la fonction sociale de la formation professionnelle suisse'. *Formation emploi* 133 (Jan–Mar): 17–34.

Buchholz, S., C. Imdorf, S. Hupka-Brunner, and H.-P. Blossfeld. 2012. 'Sind leistungsschwache Jugendliche tatsächlich nicht ausbildungsfähig? Eine Längsschnittanalyse zur beruflichen Qualifizierung von Jugendlichen mit geringen kognitiven Kompetenzen im Nachbarland Schweiz'. *Kölner Zeitschrift für Soziologie und Sozialpsychologie 64* (4): 701–27.

Buera, F. J., and J. P. Kaboski. 2012. 'The Rise of the Service Economy'. *American Economic Review 102* (6): 2540–69.

Busemeyer, M., and C. Trampusch. 2012. *The Comparative Political Economy of Collective Skill Systems*. Oxford: Oxford University Press.

Castilla, E. J., G. J. Lan, and B. A. Rissing. 2013. 'Social Networks and Employment: Mechanisms (Part 1)'. *Sociology Compass 7* (12): 1013–26.

Daehlen, M. 2017. 'Transition from School-based Training in VET'. *Education and Training 59* (1): 47–60.

Davoli, M., and H. Entorf. 2018. *The PISA Shock, Socioeconomic Inequality, and School Reforms in Germany*. IZA Policy Paper No. 140, Policy Paper Series (August).

Deissinger, T., and P. Gonon. 2016. 'Stakeholders in the German and Swiss Vocational Educational and Training System: Their Role in Innovating Apprenticeships against the Background of Academisation'. *Education and Training 58* (6): 568–77.

Deissinger, T., and S. Hellwig. 2005. 'Apprenticeships in Germany: Modernising the Dual System'. *Education and Training 47* (4/5): 312–24.

Dietrich, H. 2012. *Youth Unemployment in Europe: Theoretical Considerations and Empirical Findings*. Berlin: Friedrich Ebert Stiftung.

Dieckhoff, M. 2008. 'Skills and Occupational Attainment: A Comparative Study of Germany, Denmark and the UK'. *Work, Employment and Society 22* (1): 89–108.

Di Stasio, V. 2014. 'Education as a Signal of Trainability: Results from a Vignette Study with Italian Employers'. *European Sociological Review 30* (6): 796–809.

Emmenegger, P., and L. Seitzl. 2019. 'Collective Action, Business Cleavages and the Politics of Control: Segmentalism in the Swiss Skill Formation System'. *British Journal of Industrial Relations 57* (3): 576–98.

Fossati, F., A. Wilson, and G. Bonoli. 2020a. 'What Signals Do Employers Use When Hiring? Evidence from a Survey Experiment in the Apprenticeship Market'. *European Sociological Review 36* (5): 760–79.

Fossati, F., F. Liechti, and A. Wilson. 2020b. 'Participation in Labour Market Programmes: A Positive or Negative Signal of Employability?' *Acta Sociologica 64* (1): 70–85.

Gaugler, E., W. Weber, G. Gille, H. Kachel, and A. Martin. 1978. *Ausländer in deutschen Industriebetrieben. Ergebnisse einer empirischen Untersuchung*. Königstein: Athenäum Verlag.

Hellan, H., and L. A. Støren. 2006. 'Vocational Education and the Allocation of Apprenticeships: Equal Chances for Applicants Regardless of Immigrant Background.' *European Sociological Review 22* (3): 339–51.

Holzer, H. J. 1998. 'Why Do Small Establishments Hire Fewer Blacks than Large Ones?' *The Journal of Human Resources 33* (4): 896–914.

Hope, D., and A. Martelli. 2019. 'The Transition to the Knowledge Economy, Labor Market Institutions, and Income Inequality in Advanced Democracies.' *World Politics 71* (2): 236–88.

Hupka, S., and B. E. Stalder. 2004. 'Jeunes migrantes et migrants à la charnière du secondaire I et du secondaire II'. In *Le genre en vue. Les Filles et les jeunes femmes face à la formation: Pistes et tendances*, edited by S. Hupka and B. E. Stalder, pp. 87–102. Zürich: Buchs.

Hupka-Brunner, S., S. Sacchi, and B. E. Stalder. 2010. 'Social Origin and Access to Upper Secondary Education in Switzerland: A Comparison of Company-based Apprenticeship and Exclusively School-based Programmes'. *Swiss Journal of Sociology 36* (1): 11–31.

Imdorf, C. 2013. 'When Training Companies Recruit According to Gender: The Recruitment of Apprentices in the Car Repair Sector in Switzerland'. *Revue française de pédagogie recherches en education 183* (2): 59–70.

Imdorf, C. 2017. 'Understanding Discrimination in Hiring Apprentices: How Training Companies Use Ethnicity to Avoid Organisational Trouble'. *Journal of Vocational Education and Training 69* (3): 405–23.

Imdorf, C., and R. J. Leemann. 2012. 'New Models of Apprenticeship and Equal Employment Opportunity: Do Training Networks Enhance Fair Hiring Practices?' *Journal of Vocational Education and Training 64* (1): 57–74.

Jacob, M., and H. Solga. 2015. 'Germany's Vocational Education and Training System in Transformation: Changes in the Participation of Low- and High-achieving Youth over Time'. *European Sociological Review 31* (2): 161–71.

Jørgensen, C. H. 2014. *The Current State of the Challenges for VET in Denmark.* Research report published 2014 by Nord-VET—The Future of Vocational Education in the Nordic Countries. Department of Psychology and Educational Studies, Roskilde University, Denmark.

Juul, I., and C. H. Jørgensen. 2011. 'Challenges for the Dual System and Occupational Self-governance in Denmark'. *Journal of Vocational Education and Training 63* (3): 289–303.

Kis, V. 2016. *Work-based Learning for Youth at Risk: Getting Employers on Board.* OECD Education Working Papers No. 150. Paris: OECD.

Kohler, U., and F. Kreuter. 2005. *Data Analysis Using STATA*, 3rd edition. Milton Park, UK: Taylor and Francis.

Kovacheva, S., and A. Pohl. 2007. 'Disadvantage in Youth Transitions: Constellations and Policy Dilemmas'. In *Social Inclusion for Young People: Breaking down the Barriers*, edited by Helen Colley, Philipp Boetzelen, Bryony Hoskins and Teodora Parveva, pp. 31–42. Strasbourg: Council of Europe.

Kriesi, I., M. Buchmann, and A. Jaberg. 2012. 'Educational Success and Adolescents' Well-Being in Switzerland'. *Swiss Journal of Sociology 38* (2): 245–65.

Kuczera, M. 2017. *Incentives for Apprenticeship*. OECD Education Working Paper No. 152. Paris: OECD Publishing.

Liechti, F. 2020. 'Connecting Employers and Workers: Can Recommendations from the Public Employment Service Act as a Substitute for Social Contacts?' *Work, Employment and Society 34* (4): 587–604.

Liechti, F., F. Fossati, G. Bonoli, and D. Auer. 2017. 'The Signalling Value of Labour Market Programmes'. *European Sociological Review 33* (2): 257–74.

Mohrenweiser, J. 2012. 'Which Firms Train Disadvantaged Youths?' *Empirical Research in Vocational Education and Training 4* (2): 115–30.

Müller, W., and M. Gangl. 2003. *Transitions from Education to Work in Europe: The Integration of Youth into EU Labour Markets*. Oxford: Oxford University Press.

Murphy, E., and D. Oesch. 2018. 'Is Employment Polarisation Inevitable? Occupational Change in Ireland and Switzerland, 1970–2010', *Work, Employment and Society 32* (6): 1099–117.

Nelson, M. 2012. 'Continued Collectivism'. In *The Political Economy of Collective Skill Formation*, edited by M. R. Busemeyer, and C. Trampusch, pp. 179–202. Oxford: Oxford University Press.

OFS—Office Fédéral de la Statistique. 2018. Statistique de la formation professionnelle initiale. Available at: https://www.bfs.admin.ch/bfs/fr/home/statistiques/education-science/diplomes/degre-secondaire-II/professionnelle-initiale.assetdetail.5206903.html [accessed 21 September 2021].

Pilz, M. 2007. 'Two Countries—One System of Vocational Education? A Comparison of the Apprenticeship Reform in the Commercial Sector in Switzerland and Germany'. *Compare: A Journal of Comparative and International Education 37* (1): 69–87.

Powell, W. W., and K. Snellman 2004. 'The Knowledge Economy'. *Annual Review of Sociology 30*: 199–220.

Protsch, P. 2017. 'Getting a Foot in the Door: How Organisational Characteristics Shape Recruitment Decisions in the Dual Apprenticeship System'. *Journal of Education and Work 30* (6): 585–98.

Protsch, P., and M. Dieckhoff. 2011. 'What Matters in the Transition from School to Vocational Training in Germany'. *European Societies 13* (1): 69–91.

Protsch, P., and H. Solga. 2015. 'How Employers Use Signals of Cognitive and Noncognitive Skills at Labour Market Entry: Insights from Field Experiments'. *European Sociological Review 31* (5): 521–32.

Rivera, L. A. 2011. 'Ivies, Extracurriculars, and Exclusion: Elite Employers' Use of Educational Credentials'. *Research in Social Stratification and Mobility* 29 (1): 71–90.

Rivera, L. A. 2015. 'Go with your Gut: Emotion and Evaluation in Job Interviews'. *American Journal of Sociology 120* (5): 1339–89.

Ryan, P. 2012. 'Apprenticeship: Between Theory and Practice, School and Workplace'. In *The Future of Vocational Education and Training in a Changing World*, edited by M. Pilz, pp. 402–32. Hannover: Springer VS.

Scherr, A., C. Janz, and S. Müller. 2015. *Diskriminierung in der beruflichen Bildung. Wie migrantische Jugendliche bei der Lehrstellenvergabe benachteiligt werden.* Wiesbaden: Springer VS.

Schneider, J., R. Yemane, and M. Weinmann. 2014. *Diskriminierung am Ausbildungsmarkt. Ausmaß, Ursachen und Handlungsperspektiven.* Berlin: Sachverständigenrat deutscher Stiftungen für Integration und Migration SVR GmbH.

Seitzl, L. 2021. 'The end of cooperation? Collective skill formation systems in the knowledge economy'. Doctoral thesis, Universität St. Gallen.

Seitzl, L., and P. Emmenegger. 2019. 'How Agents Change Institutions: Coalitional Dynamics and the Reform of Commercial Training in Switzerland'. *Business and Politics 21* (2): 145–71.

SERI—State Secretariat for Education, Research and Innovation. 2017. *Barmomètre des apprentissage/août 2017.* Bern: SERI.

SERI—State Secretariat for Education, Research and Innovation. 2019. *Baromètre des transitions 2e vague/août 2019.* Bern: SERI.

SKBF CSRE—Swiss Coordination Centre for Research in Education. 2018. *Swiss Education Report: 2018.* Aarau: SKBF CSRE.

Solga, H., and B. Kohlrausch. 2012. 'How Low-achieving German Youth Beat the Odds and Gain Access to Vocational Training—Insights from Within-group Variation'. *European Sociological Review 29* (5): 1068–82.

Solga, H., P. Protsch, C. Ebner, and C. Brzinsky-Fay. 2014. *The German Vocational Education and Training System: Its Institutional Configuration, Strengths, and Challenges.* WZB Discussion Paper No. SP I 2014-502. Berlin: Wissenschaftszentrum Berlin für Sozialforschung (WZB).

Stalder, B. E. 2011. 'Le niveau d'exigences intellectuelles des formations professionnelles initiales en Suisse. Classement des années 1999–2005.' Bâle: Université de Bâle/TREE.

Vogel, D. 2010. 'The Private Regulation of Global Corporate Conduct: Achievements and Limitations'. *Business and Society 49* (1): 68–87.

Werfhorst, H. G. van der. 2014. 'Changing Societies and Four Tasks of Schooling: Challenges for Strongly Differentiated Educational Systems'. *International Review of Education 60* (1): 123–44.

Wettstein, E, E. Schmid, and P. Gonon. 2017. *Swiss Vocational and Professional Education and Training (VPET)*. Bern: hep Verlag.

Wilson, A. 2021. 'A Silver Lining for Disadvantaged Youth on the Apprenticeship Market: An Experimental Study of Employers' Hiring Preferences'. *Journal of Vocational Education and Training 73* (1): 124–47.

Wolter S. C., S. Mühlemann, and J. Schweri. 2006. 'Why Some Firms Train Apprentices and Many Others Do Not'. *German Economic Review 7* (3): 249–64.

Wolter, S .C., and P. Ryan. 2011. 'Apprenticeship'. In *Handbook of the Economics of Education*, edited by E. A. Hanushek, S. Machin, and L. Woessmann, pp. 521–76. Amsterdam: North Holland.

Zuckerman, E. W. 1999. 'The Categorical Imperative: Securities Analysts and the Illegitimacy Discount'. *American Journal of Sociology 104* (5): 1398–438.

APPENDIX

Table 7.1A Coding procedure for the 'employer visibility' variable

The 'Employer visibility' variable was coded case-by-case by the author, where each individual employer was assigned a value according to how well established and visible the author deemed them to be to aspiring apprentices. Based on their perceived recognizability and visibility, we may assume that employers differ in the extent to which apprentice candidates know about them and thus would consider submitting their applications to them.

The categories range from 'Locally recognized' to 'Regionally recognized', from 'Swiss-wide recognized' to 'Internationally recognized'. The information about the different employers was retrieved from their webpages. Those employers who did not have a webpage and no other information about the employer was available online, were assigned to the 'Locally recognized' category.

For the 'Locally recognized' category, the employers may only be established on one location only and have ten or fewer employees. For the 'Regionally recognized', the employers may be established in more than two locations but only within the same canton and have more than ten employees. For the 'Swiss-wide recognized' category, the employer is established in more than one canton, has information available in at least French and German languages on their webpage. Finally, in the 'Internationally recognized' category, employers are placed that fulfil the criteria for being placed in the 'Swiss-wide recognized' category but that also are established in one or more countries other than Switzerland.

Employers in the 'Public administration' sector are coded according to their regional competences: communal offices are assigned to the 'Locally recognized' category and cantonal offices are assigned to the 'Regionally recognized' category.

Employers whose webpages revealed ambiguous or lacking information about their establishment were dropped from the analysis.

Table 7.2A Sector groups based on similar business activity and sought apprentice profile

Sector groups	Freq.	%
Public administration	199	21.99
Tourism, hotel and restaurant, media, and events	47	5.19
Construction, crafts, industry, chemistry, and engineering	141	15.58
Education, charity, healthcare, service, and administration	136	15.03
Law and public notary, private insurance, and banks	102	11.27
Commerce and services	151	16.69
Fiduciary and real estate	102	11.27
Other	27	2.98
Total	905	100

Table 7.3A Interviewee details

Interviewee code	Interview mode	Date of interview	Gender	Professional role	Organization characteristics
Int1	Face-to-face	25 May 2016	Female	Apprentice coordinator	PA
Int2	Face-to-face	16 June 2016	Female	Vocational trainer	PA
Int3	Face-to-face	27 September 2016	Female	Career counsellor	Education
Int4	Telephone	22 May 2017	Female	Vocational trainer	Tourism
Int5	Telephone	31 May 2017	Male	Vocational trainer	PA
Int6	Telephone	01 June 2017	Male	Vocational trainer	Bank
Int7	Telephone	01 June 2017	Male	Vocational trainer	PA
Int8	Face-to-face	08 June 2017	Female	Vocational trainer	Commerce

Table 7.4A Details over cited respondents to qualitative survey cited in chapter

Gender	Code	Foreign home language a risk factor for dropping out	Egalitarian	Sector group	School achievements used as guarantee for completion of the apprenticeship	School achievements used for selecting the most academically qualified candidate
Female	Resp16	X	X	PA		
Female	Resp23		X	PA	X	
Female	Resp42		X	PA	X	
Female	Resp45			LPIB		X
Male	Resp81		X	PA	X	
Female	Resp92			LPIB		X
Female	Resp95	X		LPIB		X
Female	Resp97			LPIB		X

Table 7.5A Complementary summary of responses to qualitative survey, by sector groups

Sector groups	Foreign home language a risk factor for dropping out	Foreign home language *not* a risk factor for dropping out	Did not answer	Total	Egalitarian	Non-egalitarian	Total
Public administration	10	35	5	50	32	18	50
Tourism, hotel and restaurant, media, and events	1	7	2	10	3	7	10
Construction, crafts, industry, chemistry, and engineering	4	13	4	21	10	11	21
Education, charity, healthcare, service, and administration	3	22	7	32	18	14	32
Law firms, private insurance, banks	5	8	2	15	3	12	15
Commerce and service	1	17	5	23	15	8	23
Fiduciary and real estate	6	8	0	14	7	7	14
Total				165			165

8

Pride and Prejudice? The Influence of Occupational Prestige on an Integration Programme for Refugees in Switzerland

Annatina Aerne

8.1 Introduction

The literature on collective skill formation systems has highlighted their difficult balance between inclusion and efficiency (Bonoli and Emmenegger 2021; Thelen 2014). A system concerned with efficiency selects the best at the expense of excluding academically less-talented youth. An inclusive training system in contrast is less demanding and aims at integrating young people into the labour market. The literature departs from the assumption that employers (and their associations) tend to wish for a more selective system and a more competitive workforce, whereas state institutions prefer a more integrative skill formation system. Many contributions analyse under what conditions state authorities may convince employers to accept more inclusive training (Bonoli and Emmenegger 2021; Bonoli and Wilson 2019; Durazzi 2017).

But what if employers as well as state authorities vary with respect to their preferences regarding the degree of inclusiveness of a skill formation system? This chapter argues that not all employers oppose inclusiveness, and some state actors prefer the skill formation system to be selective. Taking into consideration prestige concerns allows us to better understand and differentiate vocational education and training (VET) actors' preferences regarding inclusiveness. Depending on the degree of concern about prestige, as well as their position in the prestige hierarchy, public and private VET actors may follow different strategies in maintaining the prestige of the VET system, with marked effects on inclusiveness.

Annatina Aerne, *Pride and Prejudice? The Influence of Occupational Prestige on an Integration Programme for Refugees in Switzerland*. In: *Collective Skill Formation in the Knowledge Economy*. Edited by Giuliano Bonoli and Patrick Emmenegger, Oxford University Press. © Oxford University Press (2022). DOI: 10.1093/oso/9780192866257.003.0008

Theoretically, two strategies in maintaining or increasing the prestige of VET are mentioned in the literature: limiting access or investing in high-quality training. The former clearly does not enhance inclusiveness, whereas the latter does. In analysing public and private VET actors' prestige concerns in the implementation of a training programme for refugees, this chapter shows that VET actors' support for or opposition to an inclusive training system is shaped by their concern for prestige. The chapter thus usefully complements the literature on the trade-offs between efficiency and inclusiveness in VET.

Empirically, this chapter compares the actions of professional training organizations (PTOs)[1] and state institutions in the implementation of integration pre-apprenticeships (Integrationsvorlehre, INVOL) to the strategies to preserve occupational prestige described in the literature. Integration pre-apprenticeships are a collective skill formation programme meant to provide access to vocational education to refugees in Switzerland. The one-year programme combines training in a workplace with language courses and classes in general knowledge. It aims at preparing refugees to join a regular vocational education track after this one year. The programme started as a pilot in 2018.

The programme and context present a case where a prestige loss is most likely to be observed. The above-mentioned programme aims to facilitate access to vocational education for refugees in Switzerland. Switzerland takes great pride in its skill formation system and its occupations. Facilitating access may make these occupations less selective, and as will be discussed, less prestigious. The loss of prestige may result from inclusiveness efforts and be exacerbated by granting access to minority groups who are considered to be at the base of societal hierarchies (Hagendoorn 1995). Migrants are expected to take up low-skilled jobs at the base of the occupational hierarchy (Auer et al. 2019). Accordingly, they usually experience considerable downward mobility and take on the jobs that are not very well paid and rather undesirable in the receiving countries, regardless of their previous position (Moreh 2014: 1759; Piore 1979). Methodologically, the chapter draws on the analysis of twenty semi-structured interviews conducted in 2018 and 2019, before and after the programme had been implemented. The representatives of cantonal authorities and at the federal level were interviewed, as well as national PTOs who implemented the programme.

---

[1] PTOs is an English translation of the German Organisationen der Arbeit (ODA), or the French Organisations du monde du travail (OrTra). PTOs have a central role in the Swiss vocational education and training (VET) system. They determine and revise the content of the curricula, the examination at the end, and organize industry-wide training. Often, they are industry associations, that also assume the task of organizing vocational education in their domain.

In the following, the chapter first discusses the theory on occupational prestige, and deduces three hypotheses. The next part introduces the Swiss vocational education system and its central actors and describes how the INVOL programme fits into this landscape. In a subsequent part, the chapter traces how three main actors—the federal level of VET governance, the cantonal offices, and the PTOs—have agreed or refused to implement the programme. The last section concludes.

8.2 Theory: institutionalist perspective on occupational prestige

In the following, I briefly outline what prestige is, and what strategies protect and build prestige. Prestige is a relative concept, meaning that it is defined in relation to others: one's standing in society is based on the relations one has to others (Bourdieu 1984). Moreover, prestige describes the hierarchical aspect of these relations. Commonly, prestige refers to the fact that in society some defer to others (Freeland and Hoey 2018). According to Goffman (1956: 477), deference refers to that component of activity which functions as a symbolic means by which appreciation is regularly conveyed to a recipient. It may come in two forms. First, deference may take the form of avoidance, e.g. when a subordinate does not enquire after relatives of a superior, while not seeking to be associated with lower-standing counterparts either. In this case, actors try not to interact across hierarchies. Second, deference may be presentational and include salutations, invitations, compliments, and minor services (Goffman 1956: 486). In this case, actors interact across hierarchies, but the lower-standing compensates the more prestigious party by extending a small favour to the more prestigious party.

This deferential behaviour is often based on group boundaries. Groups may first be different, rather than hierarchical. With a different access to resources, knowledge, or power, certain groups command more deference than others. Group adherence may thus become prestigious—commanding deference. One of the categories that command such deference are occupations. Two strands of literature analyse occupational prestige from different perspectives.

8.2.1 Functionalist perspective on occupational prestige

A first strand of literature on occupational prestige dates back to the 1960s. Treiman (1977) describes how a division of labour into different tasks eventually gives rise to a hierarchy of occupations. The differentiation of tasks leads to differences in power, as not all occupations need the same level of skills, require the same level of authority, or access to property (Treiman 1977: 16). These power differentiations consequently are also the basis of economic privilege in society, due to two mechanisms: remuneration and access to resources (Treiman 1977: 16f). The different remuneration of occupations allows certain people to reach an economically more privileged position in society. Moreover, the control over scarce resources in different occupations allows certain groups to allocate themselves a larger share. This affects their economic position and consequently, status in society. Ridgeway et al. (2009) in an experimental study analysed how different remuneration in random groups led to a hierarchization accepted and acted out by adherents of both high-status and low-status groups after only two encounters. This functional logic of occupational prestige thus conceptualizes an occupation's prestige in relation to other occupations.

An understanding of occupational hierarchies based on division of labour suggests that these hierarchies are largely stable over time, across different cultural contexts, and also independent of one's position in this hierarchy. And indeed, empirical evidence to a large extent confirms this (Hodge et al. 1964: 289; Inkeles and Rossi 1956: 332; Nakao and Treas 1994: 15; Treiman 1977: 59, 79ff; Kraus et al. 1978).

Nonetheless, there are variations across countries, which are difficult to explain based on this functional logic of occupational prestige. In fact, Treiman, at the very end of his book marvels at the difference between cab drivers in New York City and London. In London, taxi drivers have to take a difficult test. They consequently also take great pride in their occupation. In contrast, taxi drivers in New York City, don't need to pass a difficult test. Cab drivers in the Big Apple as a consequence are much less proud of their job and dissatisfied with their work, although their wage is about the same as for their London counterparts (Treiman 1977: 233). Functional differentiation may thus not explain everything about occupational prestige hierarchies.

8.2.2 Institutionalist perspective in occupational prestige

The institutionalist literature is the second strand of literature this chapter draws on. It understands occupations as a key societal category actively created and maintained by certain actors (Muzio et al. 2013: 702). Importantly, this institutionalist literature provides insight into two particular strategies applied by actors to preserve their occupation: controlling and limiting access to professions/occupations[2] and ensuring high-quality training and skill levels in the profession/occupation. This more institutional perspective thus conceptualizes occupational prestige around the selection of candidates into that occupation, rather than in relation to other occupations as in the functional perspective on occupations. Occupational prestige is still understood as a relative concept, but not in relation to other occupations, but in relation to the candidates selected into the occupation.

A first strategy through which occupations create prestige is controlling and limiting access to the occupational field (Illich 1977). The relationship between an occupation's accessibility (occupational size) and its occupational prestige is an inverted u-shape. An initial increase in occupational size (and accessibility) increases prestige, but beyond a certain threshold, greater accessibility decreases occupational prestige (Zhou 2005: 108). VET actors thus may try to limit access to their occupation in order to preserve their prestige. The institutionalist literature has analysed through which mechanisms occupations limit access to their occupational field. In the case of American doctors, Abbott describes licensing as an important strategy through which doctors control their domain of work (Abbott 1991: 362). Professionals may also introduce rules and standards that delimit the occupational field (Suddaby and Viale 2011). One example discussed in this regard is the case of accountants who have managed to transnationally define standards that legitimize them as the exclusive interpreters of new rules (Suddaby and Viale 2011: 432).[3]

The second strategy through which occupations maintain their prestige is by incentivizing specialization and motivating high-quality work within

---

[2] Referring to this institutionalist literature when discussing the vocational education system in Switzerland demands clarifying what is meant by an occupation in Switzerland and by the literature. The institutionalist literature for a large part focuses on professions, such as medical doctors or accountants (Lawrence et al. 2009: 8; Leicht and Fennell 2008: 2). Professions designate white-collar occupations, usually enjoying higher levels of prestige (Goode 1957). In contrast, this chapter is concerned with the full range of occupations that are commonly studied through a VET track in Switzerland. These occupations are organized similar to professions, even though they comprise the whole range of occupations. According to Muzio et al. (2011: 806), professions are occupations who control both the products of producers, and the formation of the producers. This certainly applies to the certified and licensed vocational occupations in Switzerland.

[3] This somewhat artificial selectivity resembles the idea of the signalling value of education diploma and certificates (Arrow 1973; Spence 1973). Educational credentials not only indicate that individuals have acquired a certain skill, but serve to signal hard-to-observe qualities, such as productivity (Clark and Martorell 2014; Liechti et al. 2017; Tyler et al. 2000). The two explanations, signalling and prestige, differ insofar as the rationales behind these explanations are on different levels: signalling assumes individual employers to be rational and to care about the productivity of employees. The prestige rationale, however, is rational at a more aggregate level: being selective serves to increase an occupation's prestige, which may make it easier to attract the next generation of talent.

their field (Honingh et al. 2012). In Abbott's analysis on the formation of occupations, training plays a central role, because 'trained skill is necessary for practice and helps differentiate the officially competent from the unofficially competent as well as from the officially incompetent' (Abbott 1991: 363). The creation of schools and formal training are thus important steps to build an occupation (Abbott 1991: 363). Professional associations thereby may demand even higher standards of training than the overall society expects from the professionals, so as to increase the prestige of the occupation (Goode 1957: 195).

The institutionalist literature also provides insight into which actors are chiefly concerned with maintaining and creating occupations (Muzio et al. 2011). Commonly, the associations are seen to maintain and create occupations. But as Muzio et al., following Burrage et al. (1990), observe, three other actor groups are also involved in maintaining and creating an occupation: (1) training institutions, such as universities; (2) clients of the occupations; and (3) most importantly, the state, who is responsible for licensing certain actions (Muzio et al. 2011: 811).

This chapter follows an institutional logic of occupational prestige in that it assumes that actors concerned with the management of occupations try to maximize their occupational prestige. Occupational prestige is thus not simply inherent in a certain occupation. For the analysis of VET actors' strategies in the implementation of the INVOL programme, it is possible to deduce three theoretically motivated expectations:

1. Prestige is protected by limiting access to the occupation, i.e. through formal licensing.
2. Prestige is protected by enforcing high training standards and high levels of skills and quality of work in the respective occupation.
3. Occupational prestige is an issue for various actors concerned with occupations (not only professional training organizations, but also state actors involved in the management of occupations).

Thus, prestige may, on the one hand, stimulate cooperation (i.e. when actors invest in high-quality training), or limit cooperation (i.e. when actors limit access to their occupation) (Aerne 2020). Limiting access reduces inclusiveness, whereas high training standards leading to high skill levels might not be as detrimental to inclusiveness. Following VET actors closely allows us to understand that their strategies may be motivated by pride for their occupation, as well as reluctance to accept newcomers (prejudice).

8.3 Context, case selection, and methods

8.3.1 Context

Switzerland features a collectivist skill formation system where skills are taught both at school and in the workplace. The system teaches portable, certified occupational skills that are nationally recognized. Vocational education is a widely accepted alternative to more academic paths. This is reflected in the high percentage of youth who begin an apprenticeship after secondary school, about 60 per cent of Swiss youth. Around 230 certified and licensed vocational occupations exist. These vocational occupation tracks enjoy high levels of prestige, even when compared to academic tracks (Bolli et al. 2018).

VET is a federal responsibility, but various actors are involved in its governance. The State Secretariat of Education, Research and Innovation (SERI) is ultimately responsible for the VET system. However, in contrast to other collective skill formation systems, the Swiss system does not rely on formal corporatist structures, such as a camber system, but on a number of fora in which professional training organizations (PTOs) coordinate with the state (Aerne and Emmenegger 2022). Professional training organizations (PTOs) occupy an important gatekeeping function in the Swiss skill formation system, as they determine the curricula to be taught and examine the candidates at the end of the programmes. PTOs thus effectively determine who gets to pursue an occupation, and what activities belong to their occupational field. Cantonal VET offices oversee the implementation of VET at the local level.

Important regional differences persist with respect to who teaches vocational education (Gonon 2002: 91). In the German- and Italian-speaking part, vocational education is predominantly dual, whereas in the French-speaking area, vocational skills are more often taught in technical colleges. The difference in importance of VET is also reflected in the share of training rates. In the German-speaking part around 22.48 per cent of the students join an academic baccalaureate school, while these percentage rates are higher for the French-speaking (35.72%) and Italian-speaking part (29.30%) (*Bildungsindikatoren. Abschlussquote auf der Sekundarstufe II—Daten des Indikators* 2020).

8.3.2 Case

To this highly prestigious vocational education system, a new programme was added in 2018. This additional programme channels refugees into vocational education, and eventually into the labour market. The programme responded to the wave of refugees reaching Europe, peaking in 2015. In the presence of this challenge, the Swiss Federal Ministry for Migration (SEM) launched two new programmes, one of them being the integration pre-apprenticeships (Integrationsvorlehre, INVOL) (Schweizerische Eidgenossenschaft: Der Bundesrat, 2015). This one-year programme aims to prepare refugees for a regular vocational education programme, either a short-track programme (Eidgenössisches Berufsattest, EBA), or a regular VET track (Eidgenössisches Fähigkeitszeugnis, EFZ). It is targeted at those recognized as refugees or provisionally admitted persons (*anerkannte Flüchtlinge/vorläufig Aufgenommene*). SEM envisaged the programme to be open to all age groups, but many of the cantons select younger people into this particular programme.

The INVOL programme was approved by the federal government as a pilot for four years and initially received CHF 54 million. Upon the approval in December 2015, SEM needed to set up a vocational education programme, which was neither within their usual responsibilities nor within their core competence. SERI, who is responsible for vocational education in Switzerland, opposed the idea of a new, additional programme (representative of SERI, Bern, 6 February 2019).

Various other actors were needed to implement the programme as shown in Figure 8.1 (Aerne and Bonoli 2021). Cantonal offices of vocational education were responsible for the implementation of the programme. SEM required that the programmes must include a practical part with at least eight weeks of training in a firm. Consequently, the PTOs were needed for the implementation and together with the cantons they developed the INVOL curricula. They were additionally often involved in contacting firms for training places. At the cantonal level, participants were selected by the cantonal immigration authorities, while the local implementation was overseen by cantonal vocational education offices. Training is provided in professional schools and by private or public employers (dual vocational education system). As SEM had little experience in organizing vocational education, it was advised by the Federal University for Vocational Education (Eidgenössische Hochschule für Berufsbildung, EHB).

In the following, I trace how VET actors (right side of Figure 8.1) positioned themselves regarding the introduction of the programme.

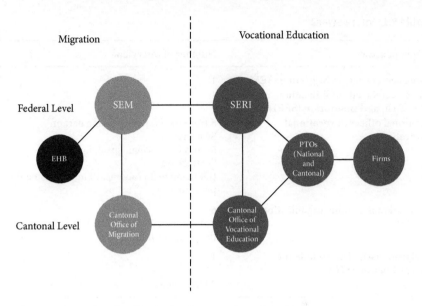

Fig. 8.1 Actors involved in the implementation of INVOL
Source: Own data.

8.3.3 Methods

This chapter draws on twenty interviews conducted with several VET actors involved in the initiation and implementation of the programme. Both the State Secretariat of Migration (SEM) and the ministry responsible for VET, the State Secretariat Education, Research and Innovation (SERI) were interviewed, as well as the federal research institute, the Eidgenössische Hochschule für Berufsbildung (EHB) that supported the implementation of the programme (see table 8.1 below). The selection of interviewees from cantonal vocational education offices was done to maximize the diversity of cantons included: smaller and larger cantons from different language regions, with high and low rates of youth training were included. All interviews were subsequently transcribed and coded by hand. The interview data was triangulated with official documents (see appendix).

The interviews allowed me to trace the implementation of the programme, and understand which actors implemented the programme and how.

Understanding actors' motives is not an easy endeavour. Prestige concerns are empirically difficult to separate from concerns about productivity. Both motives predict that the expected behaviour of employers' associations is

Table 8.1 Interviewees

Types of actors	Number of interviews
State Secretariate of Migration (SEM)	1
State Secretariate of Education, Research, and Innovation (SERI)	1
Cantonal offices of vocational education	5 from the French-speaking part of Switzerland 6 from the German-speaking part of Switzerland (Of the total 26 cantons, 18 implemented the programme)
Professional training organizations (PTO)	6 (Of the total 153 Swiss PTOs, 12 implemented the programme)
Eidgenössische Hochschule für Berufsbildung (EHB)	1
Total	20 interviews

Source: Own data.

to enforce strict selection criteria for entering an occupation. This chapter addresses this difficulty by exploiting occupational variation. The level of prestige, and hence, the degree to which actors are concerned about protecting prestige differs across occupations. Accordingly, the degree to which actors are concerned about protecting their prestige should vary: PTOs responsible for highly prestigious occupations should care more about prestige than PTOs responsible for less prestigious occupations. Productivity concerns, however, should not differ systematically across occupations. If we observe variance in occupational associations' behaviour in the implementation of the INVOL programme, it seems likely that employers and their associations are also concerned with prestige.

8.4 Case study: the implementation of the integration pre-apprenticeship

The INVOL programme needed the support of different public and private actors in order to be implemented, which was not easy to achieve (Aerne and Bonoli 2021). Both public and private actors varied in their support for the programme, conforming to the idea that their central concern was a concern for prestige.

8.4.1 Public actors

On the public side, two different kinds of actors were involved in the implementation of INVOL: SERI as well as the cantonal offices of vocational education and training. Different degrees of support for INVOL can be found among these actors. SERI, and most of the German-speaking cantonal VET offices did not favour the programme, whereas the French-speaking cantons supported the programme more readily. Public actors apparently do not always favour more inclusiveness. Rather, different levels of concern for the prestige of the VET system seems to explain their different positions.

SERI initially opposed the programme, because it was concerned about the prestige of the VET system as a whole. This opposition is quite remarkable, given the considerable political pressure to better integrate refugees into the workforce. When opposition became untenable, SERI reverted to making sure that the programme would not lead to a diploma, facilitating access to any of the recognized occupations. The changes SERI suggested were such that INVOL would not provide a parallel, easier path to the existing qualifications. In this sense, it restricted the access for refugees, because they now have to go through regular vocational education programmes, rather than a shortened version. Restricting access is one strategy to maintain prestige of an occupation, and thus SERI's course of action corresponds to the theoretical expectation. Moreover, it shows that not only PTOs, but also state ministries sometimes restrict access to occupations.

SERI opposed the programme, because an additional short-track programme leading to a nationally recognized diploma posed a danger to the existing tracks. If candidates receive an equivalent diploma through a shorter programme, it devalues the qualifications earned in traditional three-to-four-year programmes. The representative of SERI explained the risk in the following words:

> The risk was a parallel programme to the regular vocational education tracks. A parallel programme, aimed at a specific group, that in the end should somehow be equivalent. (Representative of SERI, Bern, 6 February 2019)

SERI hence favoured integration taking place through existing programmes, because the additional programme was perceived as endangering the present qualifications (representative of SEM, Bern, 11 December 2018, representative of SERI, Bern, 6 February 2019). SERI opposed the creation of an additional pathway for a specific group to the same diploma, because this additional pathway seemed to be less demanding. This corresponds to the expectations regarding VET actors' strategies of limiting access to preserve the prestige of occupations. SEM in contrast, needed to create a clearly visible programme that would respond to the political pressure 'to do something' about the refugee crisis (representative of SERI, Bern, 6 February 2010).

In September 2016, a compromise was reached between SEM, SERI, the vocational education commission of the reunion of cantonal education directors (SBBK), as well as different PTOs (representative of SEM, Bern, 11 December 2018). An additional programme was to be created, but without any formally recognized diploma at the end of the year. This amendment was an important success for SERI. Not issuing a national diploma ensured that no parallel (and less demanding) pathway into an occupation was created. The inclusion of a practical part of at least eight weeks remained, as that had been non-negotiable to SEM (representative SEM, Bern, 11 December 2018). However, cantonal programmes were now also accepted, even though SEM had initially favoured national implementations (representative SEM, Bern, 11 December 2018). Cantons were also asked to complement the funding from SEM (CHF 13,000 per candidate/year). Moreover, SERI had achieved the condition that candidates needed to fulfil certain language requirements before they could join a pre-apprenticeship (representative of SERI, 6 February 2019).

SERI also limited its support in the implementation of the programme. As vocational education is in the core of the competences of SERI, it advised SEM and explained the existing offers to it. However, it neither mediated between the cantonal vocational education offices and SEM, nor the PTOs and SEM. The direct contact which followed between SEM and PTOs and cantonal offices was perceived to provide a valuable learning experience for SEM (representative of SERI, Bern, 6 February 2019). However, it also made the implementation of the programme more difficult.

German-speaking VET offices were reluctant to implement the programme, also because of considerations for the prestige of VET tracks (representative SEM, Bern, 11 December 2018, representative SERI, Bern, 6 February 2019). To understand the concerns of cantonal offices of vocational education in the German-speaking area in implementing the programme, it is helpful to look at a canton that decided not to implement it. The canton of Thurgau (German-speaking) preferred to invest in general education offers for refugees and restricted access to vocational education tracks. In 2015, the canton of Thurgau had just set up a three-year integration programme and was not particularly enthusiastic about implementing another programme which was not easy to combine with their integration measures (cantonal office of vocational education and training, Frauenfeld, 13 November 2018). In this three-stage programme, refugees have to pass a test after each year, and if they do, they can advance to the next level. In each year, the share of training provided at a workplace is increased. In the first year, refugees spend five days at school; the second year has four days of schooling and one day of internship; while in the last year, refugees join the workplace four days a week. The practical parts, however, do not prepare the students for a specific occupation (representative of Thurgau, Frauenfeld, 13 November 2018).

Moreover, the cantonal office of vocational education and training explained that they advise practical trainers and training enterprises to keep the bar high for candidates to join a regular track in vocational education and

> not to take on candidates that were not sufficiently strong in either German or maths under any circumstances. They should really be sent to integration classes one through three beforehand. (Cantonal office of vocational education and training, Frauenfeld, 13 November 2018)

Refugees are thus prepared quite extensively before they are eventually admitted into vocational education after three years of school and three examinations. While the programme is an opportunity for refugees to receive schooling, it is also an effective measure for keeping vocational education selective. Instead of making regular VET programmes more accessible, the canton of Thurgau decided to provide (costly) schooling to refugees. So, while at first sight, Thurgau limited the access to VET for refugees, at the same time, it also invested in schooling refugees. Both of these strategies correspond to the theorized strategies of preserving prestige: limiting and controlling access and ensuring high standards in training.

VET authorities in the French-speaking part more readily implemented the programme. This corresponds to the initial theoretical expectations that vocational education enjoys not as much prestige in French-speaking cantons as in German-speaking cantons. In general, French-speaking cantons were more willing to implement the programme. In fact, all French-speaking cantons implemented the programme, whereas the eight non-implementing cantons are all located in the German-speaking area. One possible explanation for this pattern is that in French-speaking cantons vocational education is less prevalent, and also less prestigious (Bolli et al. 2018). This can also be seen comparing the baccalaureate quota (Maturitätsquote) across cantons. As already mentioned, French-speaking cantons (Geneva, Vaud, Valais, Fribourg, Jura, Neuchâtel) have a higher share of baccalaureate than German-speaking cantons.

This implementation pattern is even more surprising, given that implementation was probably easier to achieve in German-speaking cantons. German-speaking cantons have generally higher training rates, and more dual vocational education positions. One would expect that cantons that have a strong tradition in dual VET would be better equipped to implement a collective skill formation programme. National PTOs were reluctant to implement the programme in the French-speaking part since they expected an insufficient number of members would be willing to provide training places (VISCOM, Bern, 10 August 2018). Correspondingly, most implementations in the French-speaking part take place in cooperation with cantonal PTOs, rather than the national ones. Even though it was assumed to be more difficult for French-speaking cantons to implement the programme, they were more willing to do so.

Thus, public actors differed with respect to their support for INVOL. Presumably VET actors concerned about prestige—SERI and the German-speaking VET offices—were more reluctant to implement the programme. In order to protect the prestige of the VET system, they opposed INVOL and thereby limited occupational access. This directly affects the inclusiveness of the VET system.

8.4.2 Private actors

There are also remarkable differences across PTOs' implementation of the programme. The PTOs that implemented the programme most readily were (low-prestige) occupations that recruit academically less-inclined school leavers (logistics, construction, catering/hotel industry). These PTOs did not fear a loss of prestige in admitting refugees into their occupations and teaching them occupational content. In contrast, more high-prestige occupations were more reluctant to implement the programme. PTOs responsible for high-prestige occupations implementing the programme followed other rationale, such as corporate image, or keeping their gatekeeping function. Accordingly, these PTOs responsible for high-prestige occupations were also more reluctant to provide actual content to their curricula, thereby limiting access to their occupational field.

The occupational fields in which PTOs implemented the programme are remarkably diverse: bakers, construction-related industries, retail trade, catering/hotel industry, cleaning, rail construction, logistics, print media, meat industry, mechanics and automation, building technology, and agriculture. In the following the occupations are separated into three groups, based on the level of prestige and their hypothesized motive for implementing the programme. The categorization is supported by certain characteristics of the implementation, e.g. the amount of content provided in their curricula and their efforts organizing training spots for refugees.

In certain (presumably low-prestige) occupations, PTOs were very active in designing curricula and recruiting companies: construction sector, gastronomy/hotel services, cleaning, and agriculture. In these occupations, the INVOL curricula are also comparatively rich in content, thus refugees learn a lot of occupational tasks. The PTO for logistics printed extra booklets and learning material; they also include a course on forklifting, taught in their national training centre. Similarly, the PTO for construction, *Polybau*, prepared a detailed curriculum, including a course in their training centre. They also provide the pre-apprentices with appropriate shoes and work clothes so they could be employed from day one without a lot of friction in the companies (representative of Polybau, Uzwil, 13 March 2018). They also recruited companies to provide training.

These occupations absorb Swiss youth who had a rather difficult time in school (representative of Polybau, Uzwil, 13 March 2018). They are less selective than other occupations and recruit academically weaker candidates. Occupational associations are well aware of the differences in prestige among the various occupations, as the representative of the professional training organization for construction explained:

> Who integrates difficult young people into the workplace? Where do the difficult adolescents go? They go into construction. Those who are not talented in school do not go into commercial school or become laboratory chemists. [. . .] The academically weaker students go into construction, most of the time. And academically weaker students are those that are a bit difficult. We have a large share of young people who are difficult to educate, and we socialize them. All of these difficult young people who pass the apprenticeship have been socialized by the construction sector. [. . .] The construction sector to a large part is responsible for the successful socialization and integration of difficult youngsters and migrants. This is neither recognized nor supported. [. . .] Does the commercial sector participate in the integration pre-apprenticeship?—certainly not!

In a sense, these occupations do not see their prestige threatened by recruiting refugees as much as other occupations, because they are aware of being at the lower end of the prestige hierarchy. They therefore readily facilitated access for refugees to their occupations, creating curricula with relevant occupational content, and extra courses at their training centres. As these occupations rely on academically less-inclined candidates, restricting access is not a viable option for their PTOs anyway. Instead, they focus on providing high-quality training in order to build and maintain their occupational prestige.

The second group of occupations also put a lot of effort into their implementation of the programme: printing technology, retail trade, and rail construction. These are presumably more selective (and prestigious) occupations, as they do not usually recruit the academically less-inclined. The efforts of the PTOs responsible for these occupations seem to have been motivated by concerns for their corporate image.

The interviews with representatives from these PTOs suggest that either the association or the member companies cared about being perceived as socially responsible. The PTO for printing, VISCOM, also has a function as a trade association and is actively involved in lobbying the political process (VISCOM, Bern, 10 August 2018). At the time of the implementation of the programme, VISCOM also opposed new public procurement rules that facilitated federal-level authorities printing their publications and reports abroad. It is not unlikely that they were hoping to gain political goodwill also for other issues by implementing the programme (representative of SERI, Bern, 6 February 2019).

The participation of login, the PTO for rail construction, was primarily driven by the fact that the national rail company (Schweizerische Bundesbahnen, SBB) represented by this PTO are public (representative of login, Olten, 3 July 2018). SBB is the state-owned public transportation company and had been ordered directly from the federal council to implement the programme (representative of login, Olten, 3 July 2018). Accordingly, login, the PTO responsible for the occupations taught in the workplaces of SBB, had been in direct contact with SEM regarding implementation (representative of SEM, Bern, 11 December 2018).

An interesting case in this regard is also the implementation in the field of retail trade. In this occupation, the two largest retailers in Switzerland, Migros and Coop, decided to implement the programme by themselves, independently of their PTO (representative of SEM, Bern, 11 December 2018). As both of these large retailers advertised their involvement in their weekly newspapers to their customers, it may well be that they also saw this as an opportunity to portray themselves as responsible employers.

The third group of PTOs who implemented the programme are responsible for high-prestige occupations. They implemented the programme because they were afraid of losing their gatekeeping power. The PTO for construction technology (Suissetec), and mechanics and automation (Swissmem) implemented the programme responding to specific offers of another actor to develop a curriculum in their occupational field (representative of Swissmem, Winterthur, 29 January 2019). This corresponds to the theoretical expectations, since controlling access is central to managing the prestige of an occupation. In the example of mechanics and automation, the PTO for rail companies (login) initiated the development of a programme (representative of login, Olten, 3 July 2018, representative of Swissmem, Winterthur, 29 January 2019, representative of Suissetec, Bern, 6 February 2019). Suissetec was approached by SEM in 2016 directly, but only decided to implement the programme when the canton of Zurich initiated a programme on its own (representative of Suissetec, Bern, 6 February 2019). These PTOs mainly implemented the INVOL programme after threats of losing their gate-keeping power to control access to the occupation.

These PTOs implemented a programme when others threatened to provide a programme in their domain. Their effort in developing these curricula was limited. In interviews, these PTOs also explicitly mentioned that an overlap with the content learned in the INVOL with the content provided in a regular apprenticeship during the first year should be avoided (representative of login, Olten, 3 July 2018, representative of Swissmem, Winterthur, 29 January 2019, representative of SERI, Bern, 6 February 2019). This corresponds to the theoretical expectations in that it constitutes a form of limiting access to the occupational field. Upon completion of the INVOL programme refugees have not learned a lot of occupational content that would help them be successful in the regular vocational education track. Meaning these programmes do not facilitate access to their occupation as much as would be possible.

The INVOL competence profile for mechanics and automation, for instance, expects refugees to learn to put a workpiece into a machine, that they start the machine, that they then take the workpiece out, clean it, measure whether it fits the specifications and put it where it is stored (representative of Swissmem, Winterthur, 29 January 2019). This does not seem to be a lot of content to dominate in one year of training, even if one is not fully proficient in the local language. Or, as the representative of Swissmem explained:

> The purpose of integration pre-apprenticeships is not to teach any professional, occupational content. [. . .] Content-wise they do not have to learn anything, but they have to work, so that they have all these side-effects, such as language, culture, punctuality, and so on. (Representative of Swissmem, Winterthur, 29 January 2019)

Table 8.2 Hypothesized motives of PTOs to participate in the programme

Occupations implementing the program	Occupational prestige	Hypothesized motive to implement INVOL	PTO recruits' training places	Industry training at training centre
Logistics (ASVL)	Lower	Potential demand for unskilled labour	Yes	Yes
Catering/hotel industry	Lower	Potential demand for unskilled labour	Yes	Yes
Cleaning (login)	Lower	Potential demand for unskilled labour	Yes	No
Agriculture	Lower	Potential demand for unskilled labour	Yes	Yes
Bakers	Lower	Potential demand for unskilled labour	Yes	Yes
Construction-related industries (Polybau)	Lower	Potential demand for unskilled labour	Yes	Yes
Meat industry	Lower	Potential demand for unskilled labour	Yes	No
Retail trade (Migros and Coop)	Higher	Corporate image	Yes	No
Rail construction (login)	Higher	Corporate image	Yes	No
Print media (VISCOM)	Higher	Corporate image	Yes	No
Building technology (Suissetec)	Higher	Maintain gatekeeping function	No	Yes
Mechanics and automation (Swissmem)	Higher	Maintain gatekeeping function Skill shortage	No	No

Source: Own data.

Table 8.2 summarizes the discussion so far. Depending on their occupational prestige, occupational associations follow different motives when implementing INVOL. Moreover, their commitment differs (recruitment of training places, provision of industry training at their training centre).

Private VET actors are thus not always in favour of promoting selectivity. Particularly PTOs responsible for low-prestige occupations invested in high-quality training for refugees, contributing to inclusiveness. PTOs responsible for highly prestigious occupations however tried to restrict access, limiting the inclusiveness of the VET system.

8.5 Discussion and conclusion

Finding a balance between the social inclusion of academically less-inclined candidates versus training the most competitive workforce is a key challenge in collective skill formation systems. This chapter shows that concerns for occupational prestige influence how willing private and public actors are at promoting inclusiveness in collective skill formation systems. It thus sheds light on the dynamics behind this balance. When concerned about the prestige of VET, key stakeholders either limit access or ensure high quality of training. While the former is detrimental to inclusiveness, the latter may also benefit less competitive candidates.

This case study shows that private as well as public actors vary with respect to how concerned they are with the prestige of the VET system. They also vary with respect to the strategy they pursue when protecting this prestige. Public actors—including the federal authority, SERI, as well as cantonal VET offices—opposed INVOL and limited access to refugees when they were concerned with prestige. SERI ensured that INVOL would not lead to a nationally recognized certificate, thereby limiting access to the labour market in the respective occupation without the regular qualification. Moreover, German-speaking cantons were not as willing to implement the programme, presumably because vocational education is perceived as more prestigious relative to more academic tracks when compared with the French-speaking cantons.

Private actors limited access or invested in training depending on their standing in the prestige hierarchy. PTOs responsible for high-prestige occupations hesitated to provide occupational content in INVOL, because they were concerned that it would make it easier for refugees to subsequently follow the regular tracks. This can also be seen as an informal hurdle of limiting access into an occupation. Less prestigious occupations more readily implemented INVOL and ensured high standards in training and consequently, high quality of work in their occupations. PTOs in the logistics sector, but also in the construction sector made a substantial effort in preparing additional teaching materials and designed rich curricula, providing a lot of occupation-specific content. Since these occupations recruit academically weaker candidates anyway, the only way these occupations can maintain their prestige is to ensure a high level of training.

Consequently, this case study shows that prestige considerations are an important concern for VET actors, and that they directly affect the balance between efficiency and inclusiveness. Interestingly, concerns for prestige may work both ways: it may contribute to a highly selective system, limiting inclusiveness, or it may ensure high-quality training for all. Further research is needed to understand better when VET actors protect occupational prestige by limiting access, and when they protect occupational prestige by providing high-quality training.

References

Abbott, A. 1991. 'The Order of Professionalization'. *Work and Occupations 18* (4): 355–84.

Aerne, A. 2020. 'Prestige in Social Dilemmas: A Network Analytic Approach to Cooperation among Bogotá's Art Organizations'. *Social Networks 61*: 196–209.

Aerne, A., and G. Bonoli. 2021. 'Integration through Vocational Training: Promoting Refugees' Access to Apprenticeships in a Collective Skill Formation System'. *Journal of Vocational Education and Training*. Published online 1 October 2020.

Aerne, A., and P. Emmenegger. 2022. 'Neo-corporatism and Collective Skill Formation: The Policy Network of Swiss Professional Training Organizations'. In *Governance Revisited: Challenges and Opportunities for VET*, edited by R. Bürgi and P. Gonon, pp. 159–86. Bern: Peter Lang.

Arrow, K. J. 1973. 'Higher Education as a Filter'. *Journal of Public Economics 2* (3): 193–216.

Auer, D., G. Bonoli, F. Fossati, and F. Liechti. 2019. 'The Matching Hierarchies Model: Evidence from a Survey Experiment on Employers' Hiring Intent Regarding Immigrant Applicants'. *International Migration Review 53* (1): 90–121.

Bildungsindikatoren.Abschlussquote auf der Sekundarstufe II—Daten des Indikators. 2020. Retrieved from: https://www.bfs.admin.ch/bfs/de/home/statistiken/bildung-wissenschaft/bildungsindikatoren/themen/bildungserfolg/maturitaetsquote.assetdetail.14715815.html.

Bolli, T., L. Rageth, and U. Renold. 2018. *The Social Status of Vocational Education and Training in Switzerland*. In *KOF Studies*, edited by KOF Swiss Economic Institute. Zurich: KOF Swiss Economic Institute.

Bonoli, G., and P. Emmenegger. 2021. 'The Limits of Decentralized Cooperation: Promoting Inclusiveness in Collective Skill Formation Systems'. *Journal of European Public Policy 28* (2): 229–47.

Bonoli, G., and A. Wilson. 2019. 'Bringing Firms on Board: Inclusiveness of the Dual Apprenticeship Systems in Germany, Switzerland and Denmark'. *International Journal of Social Welfare 28* (4): 369–79.

Bourdieu, P. 1984. *Distinction: A Social Critique of the Judgement of Taste*. London: Routledge.

Burrage, M., K. Jarauch, and H. Siegrist. 1990. 'An Actor-based Framework for the Study of Professions'. In *Professions in Theory and History*, edited by M. Burrage and R. Torstdendahl, pp. 203–25. London: Sage.

Clark, D., and P. Martorell. 2014. 'The Signaling Value of a High School Diploma'. *Journal of Political Economy 122* (2): 282–318.

Durazzi, N. 2017. 'Inclusive Unions in a Dualized Labour Market? The Challenge of Organizing Labour Market Policy and Social Protection for Labour Market Outsiders'. *Social Policy and Administration 51* (2): 265–85.

Freeland, R. E., and J. Hoey. 2018. 'The Structure of Deference: Modeling Occupational Status Using Affect Control Theory'. *American Sociological Review 83* (2): 243–377.

Goffman, E. 1956. 'The Nature of Deference and Demeanor'. *American Anthropologist 58*: 473–502.

Gonon, P. 2002. 'The Dynamics of Vocational Training Innovation in Switzerland'. In *Towards a History of Vocational Education and Training (VET) in Europe in a Comparative Perspective*, edited by Cedefop, pp. 88–99. Luxembourg: Cedefop.

Goode, W. J. 1957. 'Community within a Community: The Professions'. *American Sociological Review 22* (2): 194–200.

Hagendoorn, L. 1995. 'Intergroup Biases in Multiple Group Systems: The Perception of Ethnic Hierarchies'. *European Review of Social Psychology 6* (1): 199–228.

Hodge, R. W., P. M. Siegel, and P. H. Rossi 1964. 'Occupational Prestige in the United States, 1925–63'. *American Journal of Sociology 70* (3): 286–302.

Honingh, M., W. Trommel, and T. Brandsen. 2012. 'Thijs Jansen, Gabriël van den Brink, Jos Kole: Professional Pride: A Powerful Force'. *Voluntas 23*: 834–6.

Illich, I. 1977. 'Disabling Professions: Notes for a Lecture'. *Contemporary Crisis 1*: 259–370.

Inkeles, A., and P. H. Rossi. 1956. 'National Comparisons of Occupational Prestige'. *American Journal of Sociology 61* (3): 329–39

Kraus, V., E. O. Schild, and R. W. Hodge. 1978. 'Occupational Prestige in the Collective Conscience'. *Social Forces 56* (3): 900–18.

Lawrence, T. B., R. Suddaby, and B. Leca. 2009. 'Introduction: Theorizing and Studying Institutional Work'. In *Institutional Work: Actors and Agency in Institutional Studies of Organizations*, edited by T. B. Lawrence, R. Suddaby, and B. Leca, pp. 1–28. Cambridge: Cambridge University Press.

Leicht, K. T., and M. L. Fennell. 2008. 'Institutionalism and the Professions'. In *The SAGE Handbook of Organizational Institutionalism*, edited by R. Greenwood, C. Oliver, R. Suddaby, and K. Sahlin, pp. 431–48. London: SAGE.

Liechti, F., F. Fossati, G. Bonoli, and D. Auer. 2017. 'The Signalling Value of Labour Market Programmes'. *European Sociological Review 33* (2): 257–74.

Moreh, C. 2014. 'Prestige and Status in the Migration Process: The Case of Social Differentiation in a Romanian "Community" in Spain'. *Journal of Ethnic and Migration Studies 40* (11): 1758–78.

Muzio, D., D. M. Brock, and R. Suddaby. 2013. 'Professions and Institutional Change: Towards an Institutionalist Sociology of Professions'. *Management Studies 50* (5): 699–721.

Muzio, D., I. Kirkpatrick, and M. Kipping. 2011. 'Professions, Organizations and the State: Applying the Sociology of the Professions to the Case of Management Consultancy'. *Current Sociology 59* (6): 805–24.

Nakao, K., and J. Treas. 1994. 'Updating Occupational Prestige and Socioeconomic Scores: How the New Measures Measure up'. *Sociological Methodology 24*: 1–72.

Piore, M. J. 1979. *Birds of Passage: Migrant Labor and Industrial Societies*. Cambridge: Cambridge University Press.

Ridgeway, Cecilia L., An E. Li, Kristan Erickson, Kristen Backor, and Justine E. Tinkler. 2009. 'How Easily Does a Social Difference Become a Status Distinction? Gender Matters', *American Sociological Review 74*: 44–62.

Schweizerische Eidgenossenschaft: Der Bundesrat. 2015. *Begleitmassnahmen Artikel 121a BV: Verstärkung der Integrationsmassnahmen für Flüchtlinge und vorläufig Aufgenommene*. Bern: Schweizerische Eidgenossenschaft: Der Bundesrat.

Spence, M. 1973. 'Job Market Signaling'. *The Quarterly Journal of Economics 87* (3): 355–74.

Suddaby, R., and T. Viale. 2011. 'Professionals and Field-level Change: Institutional Work and the Professional Project'. *Current Sociology 59* (4): 423–42.

Thelen, K. 2014. *Varieties of Liberalization and the New Politics of Social Solidarity*. Cambridge: Cambridge University Press.

Treiman, D. J. 1977. *Occupational Prestige in Comparative Perspective*. New York: Academic Press.

Tyler, J. H., R. J. Murnane, and J. B. Willett. 2000. 'Estimating the Labor Market Signaling Value of the GED'. *The Quarterly Journal of Economics 115* (2): 431–68.

Zhou, X. 2005. 'The Institutional Logic of Occupational Prestige Ranking: Reconceptualization and Reanalyses'. *American Journal of Sociology 111* (1): 90–140.

List of analysed government documents

Eidgenössisches Departement für Wirtschaft, Bildung und Forschung. 2017. *Zusammenarbeit Arbeitslosenversicherung und Sozialhilfe. Berichte der Arbeitsgruppen Arbeitsmarktfähigkeit, Finanzierungsmodell und Rahmenvereinbarung.* Bern: Eidgenössisches Departement für Wirtschaft, Bildung und Forschung (WBF), Staatssekretariat für Wirtschaft (SECO), Konferenz Kantonaler Volkswirtschaftsdirektoren (VDK CDEP), Verband Schweizerischer Arbeitsmarktbehörden (VSAA), Konferenz der kantonalen Sozialdirektorinnen und Sozialdirektoren (SODK), Schweizerische Konferenz für Sozialhilfe (SkOS), Schweizerischer Gemeindeverband, Städteinitiative Sozialpolitik.

Landert, C., and D. Eberli. 2015. *Bestandsaufnahme der Zwischenlösungen an der Nahtstelle 1.* Zürich.

Regierungsrat des Kantons Basel-Stadt. 2017. *Anzug Sarah Wyss und Konsorten betreffend Fachkräftemangel beheben durch Nachholbildung von Zugezogenen.* Basel.

Eidgenössisches Departement für Wirtschaft, Bildung und Forschung. 2014. *Berufsabschluss und Berufswechsel für Erwachsene. Bestehende Angebote und Empfehlungen für die Weiterentwicklung.* Bern: Eidgenössisches Departement für Wirtschaft, Bildung und Forschung.

Schweizerische Eidgenossenschaft: Der Bundesrat. 2015. *Begleitmassnahmen Artikel 121a BV: Verstärkung der Integrationsmassnahmen für Flüchtlinge und vorläufig Aufgenommene.* Bern: Schweizerische Eidgenossenschaft: Der Bundesrat.

SEM—Staatssekretariat für Migration. 2016. *Eckpunkte Pilotprogramm 'Integrationsvorlehre'.* Bern: Eidgenössisches Justiz- und Polizeidepartement EJPD.

SEM—Staatssekretariat für Migration. 2017. *Modell Kantonsübergreifende Zusammenabeit im Pilotprogramm 'Integrationsvorlehre (INVOL)'.* Bern: Staatssekretariat für Migration.

SEM—Staatssekretariat für Migration. 2018. *Anhang 4 zum Rundschreiben vom März 2017 zum Pilotprogramm Integrationsvorlehre: Übersicht aktuelle Zusammenarbeit mit nationalen OdA.* Bern: Staatssekretariat für Migrationn.

List of analysed newspaper articles

Felber, P. 2017. 'Die Zeit drängt, sonst ist das Geld weg'. *Basellandschaftliche Zeitung.*

Schneider, H. 2019. 'Vorlehre wird als Chance betrachtet'. *Frutigländer* (5 February)

Schöchli, H. 2019. 'Stärker motiviert als Schweizer Lehrlinge'. *Neue Zürcher Zeitung* (26 February).

9

The Credibility of Vocational Qualifications as a Barrier to Increasing the Flexibility of Collective Skill Formation Systems

An Analysis of the Slow Expansion of Recognition of Prior Learning (RPL) in Switzerland

Markus Maurer

9.1 Introduction

Rapidly changing labour markets and technological transformations have put pressure on education and training systems the world over to adapt. One of the current policy challenges is to make these systems more flexible and open to lifelong learning, i.e. to ensure that individuals can (re-)enter education and training systems at any point in their lives to acquire those competencies or qualifications that the labour market currently needs (Guo 2014; Lee and Jan 2018).

A key element of lifelong learning strategies is the validation or, as it is more commonly referred to (at least in the Anglo-Saxon research literature), 'recognition' of prior learning (RPL), particularly in vocational education and training (VET), where it is considered a key instrument for granting access to vocational qualifications to those who have acquired competencies through experience in a particular occupational field but lack the requisite formal credentials (Bohlinger 2017). Some may have acquired a vocational qualification in a different country before, which they can no longer make use of, whilst others (for instance recent migrants) may lack any formal vocational qualification. In recent decades, RPL has become popular in skill formation systems worldwide (Council of the European Union 2012;

Markus Maurer, *The Credibility of Vocational Qualifications as a Barrier to Increasing the Flexibility of Collective Skill Formation Systems*. In: *Collective Skill Formation in the Knowledge Economy*. Edited by Giuliano Bonoli and Patrick Emmenegger, Oxford University Press. © Oxford University Press (2022). DOI: 10.1093/oso/9780192866257.003.0009

Cedefop 2015; ILO 2018). However, it has reportedly evolved much more slowly than many of its proponents had hoped (Harris et al. 2011; Cooper et al. 2017).

Claims to promote RPL have also been made within collective skill formation systems through dual apprenticeship training. In fact, it can be argued that RPL is particularly important to these systems because, firstly, their programmes and qualifications are so specific that re-qualification is necessary for the considerable number of individuals who change their original occupational field (Maurer 2013; Wolnik and Holtrup 2017), and, secondly, these systems are linked to occupational labour markets, in which access to employment in specific positions is often dependent on occupational qualifications (see e.g. Marsden 1999; Trampusch 2020). Yet, most collective skill formation systems have been quite cautious in actively promoting RPL or have stuck to comparatively restrictive forms of it.

Puzzlingly, however, policymakers in Switzerland—a country that otherwise features a prototype collective skill formation system (Trampusch 2010; Gonon and Maurer 2012; Emmenegger and Seitzl 2019)—have strongly advocated RPL and adopted a comparatively liberal form of it, namely the so-called validation of non-formal and informal learning (VNIL), which allows candidates to access a VET qualification without having to undergo the traditional VET final examination (Maurer et al. 2016). Yet, even in Switzerland, RPL is expanding much more slowly than many would have expected (Schmid 2019).

Against this backdrop, this chapter aims to examine the case of Switzerland in order to better understand institutional change in the field of RPL. Within the group of countries that have developed collective skill formation systems, Switzerland is an outlier, given the fact that, at least in terms of formal policy, it has promoted a more liberal approach to RPL (Seawright 2016). This chapter addresses two main questions. First: under what circumstances does RPL appear in collective skill formation systems? Second: what can the process of establishing and implementing RPL in Switzerland tell us about the conflicts and challenges that we can expect in the course of introducing RPL into other collective skill formation systems?

The chapter is based primarily on analysis of both policy and legal documents as well as curricula and further implementation documents at the federal and the sub-national levels. It furthermore analyses the questions placed by members of parliament vis-à-vis the federal council on matters of RPL from the year 2010 (when VNIL was formally introduced) to 2019; contributions by representatives of key actors in Swiss VET to a colloquium organized at the Zurich University of Teacher Education in the years 2014–2017; and one complementary qualitative interview with a representative of the State Secretariat of Education, Research and Innovation (SERI).

The chapter first describes different forms of RPL, from the liberal to the restrictive, and looks at how these forms are employed in both statist and collective skill formation systems. It then proceeds with a theoretical framework for understanding the evolution of RPL, reviewing the educational literature and then advancing a political economic perspective that pays particular attention to the interests of different categories of actors in relation to RPL. Here the main argument is presented—that the development of RPL depends largely on the stance of key actors with respect to the credibility of VET qualifications. This argument is then elaborated in more detail through the analysis of the Swiss case.

9.2 Liberal versus restrictive forms of RPL—and their role in different skill formation systems

As Bohlinger states, '[Recognition] refers to the idea of (publicly) accepting, accrediting and somehow valuing learning results and/or previously received formal qualifications and certificates' (2017: 589). With the help of RPL it is possible to avoid the scenario of knowledge and skills being acquired several times over, 'without formal alignment between the different learning processes'. RPL is employed at different levels of education and training systems and takes various forms (see Maurer 2019).

9.2.1 Different forms of RPL

RPL schemes can be internal or external to skill formation systems; it can be an element of formal VET systems (internal measure), or an initiative to help individuals gain access to formal VET or non-formal qualifications (external measures) (Bonoli and Emmenegger, in this volume).

Of particular interest are forms of RPL that are designed as internal measures, because they directly alter access to formal VET qualifications. In this context, it is important to distinguish between more liberal and more restrictive approaches to RPL.

At the *liberal* end, we find the development of so-called *alternative qualifications* procedures—procedures that allow individuals who meet certain conditions (e.g. number of years of relevant work experience) to acquire a qualification without having to undergo the regular qualifications procedure. Instead of, for instance, having to pass the theoretical and practical exams that adolescents or young adults normally would do at the end of a VET programme, candidates are provided with the opportunity of having their relevant work experience or qualifications validated in a different way, e.g. through a portfolio and an assessment that has been specifically designed for such candidates. Accordingly, such candidates are not normally required to attend the classes that would otherwise be critical for passing the regular exams (or at least not all of them). In the educational literature, such liberal approaches have traditionally been viewed as RPL in the *true* sense, focused on recognizing (with the use of various instruments) competencies acquired in informal or non-formal ways (e.g. Andersson et al. 2004: 60; Knight 2006; Fejes and Andersson 2009). In most cases, such liberal forms of RPL can be considered internal skill formation measures.

At the restrictive end are the approaches that insist on candidates having to undergo an existing qualifications procedure, e.g. the regular practical and theoretical exams. A very common form of this approach is that of allowing candidates to directly access the qualifications procedure, e.g. a final exam, so that they do not have to undergo the fully fledged training programme that normally would be a pre-condition to register for the final exam. Still, given that these exams generally require candidates to be able to present knowledge and skills in a clearly defined format, many candidates still end up joining the regular classes, which raises questions about the potential of this approach to ease access to qualifications. Another, even more restrictive, form of RPL is that of admitting only those individuals to the qualifications procedure who can prove that they have acquired the relevant competencies, thus exempting them only from parts of the training, while making them undergo other parts of the training (Annen 2012; Bohlinger 2017).

In the *middle* of the spectrum are forms that allow candidates to be exempted from parts of the existing qualifications procedure, e.g. from exams for specific modules of an education and training programme (Annen 2012; Bohlinger 2017). This, however, requires programmes to be modularized to a certain extent (as we will see with the cases of Denmark and Sweden later). The exemption can be based on an individual portfolio as well, while the remaining parts of the qualification's procedure are undertaken in the traditional manner.

9.2.2 A comparative view: liberal versus more restrictive forms of RPL in different skill formation systems

While the forms of RPL outlined above are not mutually exclusive and are sometimes used in parallel, most countries typically opt for one or the other, and can also attach more or less political importance to the promotion of RPL. In the following, a brief overview of the use of RPL in some European countries will be presented, with a focus on statist and collective skill formation systems. While the collective skill formation systems are at the core of this chapter (and this volume), statist skill formation systems are of interest because they tend to promote RPL more actively.

9.2.2.1 Statist skill formation systems

France and Sweden are countries with statist skill formation systems, where public authorities' strong interest in the promotion of RPL is very visible. Their education and training systems have, for a long time, been developed in accordance with social policy ('equity') objectives.

France can certainly be considered an early starter in the field. RPL in this country has evolved to be an internal VET measure that follows a very liberal approach, with Validation des acquis de l'expérience (VAE) being an important means to enhance equitable access to VET qualifications (Cedefop 1997; Breton 2017). Not only was VAE defined as an individual right, but VAE ensured access to virtually any officially listed vocationally or professionally oriented qualification (including at the level of higher education). Access to qualifications through VAE occurs not by taking regular exams, but rather by presenting a written portfolio with a subsequent assessment (including interviews) (Mathou 2019).

Sweden is one of the other European countries that has strongly promoted RPL. In contrast to France, however, Sweden has, for many years, developed RPL schemes as external measures that lead to non-formal qualifications (e.g. issued by the labour market authority), mainly with the objective of improving labour market access for socio-economically marginalized migrants (Olsson and Ragnarsson 1998; Andersson et al. 2004; Heikkilä 2014). More recently, RPL schemes have also been crafted as internal measures that follow an intermediary approach: these include the assessment of portfolios and ordinary exams that in most cases lead to partial qualifications and cover the VET part of the gymnasium programmes (Maurer 2021). This approach is facilitated by the fact that the curriculum of the Swedish gymnasium is fully modularized and does not require students to undergo a final exam (Lundahl et al. 2010). Most notably, most of the successful RPL candidates do not achieve the full upper-secondary VET qualification but try to enter the labour market with only the partial qualification (Valideringsdelegationen 2019).

9.2.2.2 Collective skill formation systems

Within the group of collective skill formation systems, the traditional final exam, covering both theory and practice, is one of the critical, constitutive elements, as its contents are selected in close cooperation with labour market actors. Attempts to do away with the final exam and to craft alternative pathways to vocational qualifications are therefore less common than in statist skill formation systems. Nevertheless, in most collective skill formation systems, these traditional final exams have been open to candidates who had never undergone a formal VET programme, but had acquired their competencies informally, i.e. on the job, or through education and training programmes not formally recognized by the respective authorities. It can be argued that in collective skill formation systems RPL tends to be designed as an internal measure and in a comparatively restrictive way.

In *Germany*, for instance, candidates wanting to undergo the final exam (Externenprüfung) are required to have gathered work experience in the relevant occupation or occupational field for a length of time that exceeds the regular duration of the respective VET programme by 50 per cent. In order to pass the theoretical part of the exam, most candidates attend preparatory classes (Annen and Schreiber 2011; Bohlinger 2017; Gutschow 2020).

In *Austria*, individuals with relevant work experience can take the regular final exam without being compelled to attend the regular classes, even though many of them nevertheless take some preparatory courses to pass the theoretical part of the exam. In contrast to Germany, there also exists a scheme that allows candidates of foreign origin to be exempted from parts of the final exam, if they have completed formal VET programmes in their countries of origin that are officially recognized as comparable to the Austrian programmes (Pfeffer and Skrivanek 2013; Pfeffer and Skrivanek 2018).

In *Switzerland*, by the time they take the exam, candidates must have accumulated work experience of at least five years, only two to three years of which must be occupation specific. In addition to this scheme, there is the (VNIL) scheme, mentioned above (Maurer et al. 2016), which represents, in principle, a more liberal approach to RPL, and which will be at the core of this chapter's analysis.

Though company-based training plays a significant role in *Denmark*'s upper-secondary VET, the qualifications procedure is substantially different from the procedures in Germany, Austria, and Switzerland. Instead of a final exam covering both practical and theoretical elements, VET programmes are more modularized (Pilz et al. 2018), making it possible to single out specific VET modules and make them accessible in the context of adult education. Certificates for specific modules can then also be accessed through more liberal forms of RPL, e.g. portfolio-based (Field et al. 2012; Andersen 2016). Similar to the Swedish case, however, such certificates are then not comparable with the fully fledged upper-secondary VET qualifications.

Finally, the *Netherlands* follows a dual approach. As an external RPL measure, individuals with some work-experience (be it in the country or abroad) can have their competencies recognized, but only towards attaining non-formal qualifications (*ervaringscertificaat* or *vakbekwaamheidsbewijs*) that are not officially recognized within the education system. As an internal RPL measure, candidates with relevant work experience can also undergo different forms of validation towards partial qualifications associated with recognized upper-secondary VET programmes, but they would also have to take most VET programmes in the regular mode (Duvekot 2018).

9.3 The evolution of RPL from a theoretical perspective

The evolution of RPL schemes in different skill formation systems has hardly been systematically analysed. Therefore, in the following, I first present an overview of why and how such arrangements have evolved according to the RPL literature. This is followed by my own analysis of the evolution of RPL in terms of a more institutionalist perspective, taking important insights from the comparative education literature.

9.3.1 Explanations from the educational RPL literature

An overview of the literature on RPL suggests that the drive to promote the recognition of prior learning clearly comes from policymaking at the national and multilateral levels, where RPL is promoted in pursuit of a number of social and economic objectives, including improving equitable access to qualifications, integrating migrants into labour markets, and harnessing existing skills (e.g. Guo 2014; Singh 2015). Some authors have also argued that the promotion of RPL is an element of a neoliberal education policy agenda that ultimately serves the purpose of lowering public expenses to education and training (Allais 2014; Andersson et al. 2004; Bagnall 2000). In any case, there is no evidence in the literature that employers would necessarily be in favour of RPL and lobby for it at national level. Rather, such pressure seems to emanate from interest groups with a focus on equity issues, representing individuals with limited access to the labour market (e.g. Jansen 2002).

Whilst few scholars have examined the factors causing RPL's worldwide growth, a number have examined the question of why it has not advanced as quickly as many of its proponents would have hoped. One important strand of this research points to difficulties in the implementation process that result when key actors see existing quality standards (and the benefits resulting from them) being threatened. In particular, it points to the conflicting objectives of *equity* and *quality* and argues that, while equity is a core value at the level of policymaking, stakeholders at the level of implementation often do not share these policy goals; they profit from unequal power relations and therefore insist on adhering to traditional measures of quality (Pitman and Vidovich 2012; Cooper and Harris 2013; Ismail 2014; Aarkrog and Wahlgren 2015; Andersen 2016). Other contributions argue that the slow implementation of RPL policies in many countries is not a result of a lack of political will, unequal power relations, or non-supportive pedagogical agency, but rather of 'deeper, epistemological constraints' (Cooper and Harris 2013: 448). Thus competencies gained from life and work experience are of a quality that is very different from competencies and knowledge gained in more formal learning environments, such as schools or universities, and can therefore not be easily proven/validated in ways that provide access to formal qualifications.

9.3.2 RPL from a political economic perspective

Some of the existing educational literature on RPL clearly points to diverging interests between actors and can therefore contribute to a political economic perspective on skill formation. Of particular relevance is the finding outlined earlier that tensions in the field of RPL often centre around the conflicting objectives of *equity* and *quality*, to which different actors attach different weight. From a political economy perspective (Bonoli and Emmenegger, in this volume), looking at the dynamics in skill formation in view of the conflicting objectives of equity and efficiency, the phenomenon that is labelled *quality* in the educational literature needs to be seen as contributing to the efficiency function of skill formation systems.

This connection between the quality of education and training and the concept of efficiency is quite obvious when looking at the literature. *Employers*, who are usually at the centre of political economy analyses of skill formation's efficiency function (e.g. Bonoli and Emmenegger, in this volume; Carstensen and Ibsen 2021), benefit from educational quality at different levels. For example because apprentices and graduates contribute to value addition (*productive function*), but also because qualifications allow employers to assume that potential employees have acquired certain skills during the course of training (*signalling function*) or have certain characteristics independent of the training (e.g. a high work ethic, intellectual ability) that are important for work (*screening function*) (Bedard 2001; Brown and Sessions 2004). As we can easily see, skill formation's contribution to efficiency is less about the *quality* of training per se, but more about the *credibility* of the resultant qualifications. The credibility of VET qualifications is thus a core element of the efficiency function of skill formation.

Of course, it is not only the employers who benefit from the credibility of qualifications, but also those who have acquired them and are thereby able to access employment. These individuals, also referred to as *insiders* in the political economy literature (Rueda 2005), can assume that their qualifications provide them with a comparatively privileged position in the labour market, for example, by giving them exclusive access to jobs that require such qualifications or by enabling them to negotiate higher wages. They are thus in a position of advantage relative to those who do not possess these qualifications (*outsiders*). It is obvious that employers and insiders or the organizations representing them would in most cases do their best to preserve the credibility of qualifications that serve the efficiency function on both sides. From the point of view of the outsiders (and the organizations representing them), this credibility is not as important as improving access to qualifications—thus increasing equity.

At the same time, of course, credibility is only one element contributing to the efficiency function of skill formation. Further elements are the fact that skill formation allows companies, first, to access a sufficient number of employees with the relevant qualifications and, second, in the case of dual VET systems, to employ VET learners as apprentices and thus lower labour costs. These different elements—or sub-functions—of the efficiency function of skill formation can also be in conflict with each other, as this chapter will illustrate.

9.3.3 Actors and actors' interests
Against this backdrop, we now outline how key actors in skill formation might view RPL. The focus here is on RPL schemes that are designed as internal measures—both liberal and restrictive.

Public authorities might promote RPL as an internal measure because they would expect it to increase equitable access to employment (equity function) but also because they see it as helping to reduce skills shortages in critical sectors of the labour market (efficiency function). However, they might also be critical of more liberal forms of RPL because they want barriers to VET qualifications to remain high and retain their credibility—a critical element of the efficiency function of skill formation. As an alternative, they would then tend to promote RPL as an external measure—one that does not risk undermining the credibility of existing VET qualifications.

Employers and their representatives—mainly interested in the efficiency function of VET—can be expected to be mostly critical of RPL (particularly if it is designed as an internal measure and in a liberal form). This is fully in line with the comparative literature, in which few incidences of employers strongly promoting RPL are recorded. In employers' eyes, RPL (or liberal forms of it) might undermine the credibility of existing qualifications. Still, some employers might be willing to promote RPL under particular circumstances, for instance where there is a shortage of qualified job applicants, or if increasing access to VET qualifications might provide opportunities for lowering wages. This suggests that there might be conflicts between employers over the relative importance of different elements of the efficiency function.

Employees with VET qualifications (insiders) and the organizations representing them can expect to be mostly critical of RPL, again particularly if such schemes are crafted as internal measures and in a liberal form. There are two main reasons for this: firstly, lower access barriers to qualifications increase competition in the labour market, undermining insiders' privileged position. Secondly, insiders are likely to suffer from the diminishing credibility of VET qualifications, especially if employers decide to eventually recruit employees with other types of qualification (e.g. from tertiary education).

In contrast, individuals who are in precarious positions in the labour market and lack relevant VET qualifications (outsiders) as well as the organizations (mainly trade unions) representing them can be expected to be mostly in favour of RPL as an internal measure, as it could enhance outsiders' position in the labour market. At the same time, the unions representing their interests can be expected to understand the importance of maintaining the credibility of VET qualifications—and of preventing a decline in their value.

9.3.4 Theorizing RPL in collective skill formation systems

As we have seen above, RPL has not been strongly promoted in collective skill formation systems, particularly as compared to statist skill formation systems. Yet, in collective skill formation systems there is a preference for internal and quite restrictive forms of RPL. Why—from a theoretical perspective—might this be the case?

Firstly, all key actors in collective skill formation systems are committed to retaining the high credibility of collectively governed vocational qualifications, in line with promoting 'vocational education as a fully viable and credible alternative to academic (higher) education' (Busemeyer and Trampusch 2019: 156). This implies that if vocational competencies shall be recognized, this recognition tends not to be an external measure leading to non-formal qualifications, as these would not be collectively governed by the key actors and would potentially undermine existing (formal) VET qualifications. This stands in contrast to the Swedish approach, where authorities as well as employers' organizations designed RPL approaches to be external measures that lead to non-formal qualifications (see section 9.2.2.1, 'Statist skill formation systems'). The collective effort to maintain high credibility of VET qualifications furthermore leads to a critical stance towards liberal forms of RPL, especially among employers, insiders, and their representatives, who can be assumed not to profit from liberal forms of RPL (see section 9.3.2, 'RPL from a political economic perspective').

Secondly, many companies in collective skill formation systems benefit economically from apprenticeship training (see e.g. Dionisius et al. 2009), making them critical of alternative pathways to qualifications that might remove options of employing young learners. RPL thus stands in potential conflict with a second element of the efficiency function in collective skill formation systems.

Nevertheless, RPL has been introduced in collective skill formation systems, and, in Switzerland, even in a comparatively liberal form. There may be various reasons for such transformative institutional change, but the analysis of actors' interests earlier suggests that the following might be particularly important: first, public authorities—the stakeholders who tend to promote RPL the most—manage to introduce RPL because of political pressure on the skill formation system as a whole, usually to boost equity in education and training systems. Second, there might also be support for RPL from employers in sectors in which apprenticeship training does not cover recruitment needs, and in which the traditional qualifications procedures are less solidly established. In such cases, an element of the efficiency function—the potential supply of employees with VET qualifications—would act as a driver of RPL. The following analysis of the Swiss case will allow us to test such assumptions.

9.4 The evolution of RPL in Swiss vocational education and training

9.4.1 The two main forms of RPL in Swiss VET

As early as 1930, a scheme was introduced in Switzerland to allow adults with work experience in a specific occupation to be directly admitted to the final VET examination (Maurer et al. 2016). This scheme—an internal VET measure—still exists today for all occupations at upper-secondary-level VET. It provides individuals with at least five years' work experience (of which two to three years must be occupation specific), with the opportunity of being exempted from having to undertake formal apprenticeship training.

Over seventy years after the inception of that scheme, the revised VET Act of 2004 enabled an additional RPL scheme to be devised—the VNIL procedure (BBT 2010b). Again, it was crafted as an internal VET measure, and it targeted individuals with at least five years' work experience. Two key features make it a more liberal form of RPL: first, candidates are no longer required to undergo the regular final exam. Rather, the assessment is based on a portfolio composed by the candidates, which is the most important basis for experts when deciding whether or not the required competencies can be validated. Second, creation of portfolios and validation by experts are based on so-called qualifications profiles, which are tabulated overviews of competencies required for a specific occupation, each of which can be assessed as 'passed' or 'not passed'. Thus, a modular approach was designed for the first time in Swiss VET at upper-secondary level.

9.4.2 The reasons underlying the emergence of a more liberal approach to RPL

The introduction of this new RPL scheme was brought about by a coalition of actors who, traditionally, had not been influential in Swiss VET: a key role was played by innovative cantons, particularly Geneva. From the 1990s onwards, a number of initiatives were taken here to recognize prior learning, at first by simply issuing statements on the competencies individuals had acquired (an approach inspired by similar developments in neighbouring France); then, by providing access to qualifications that were recognized only at the cantonal level, and finally, by pushing the federal authorities to allow such candidates to also achieve the federal-level VET qualifications (Morand-Aymon 2004; Fleischmann 2005). These and similar initiatives in Geneva were and are elements of a 'comparatively state-centred, social-policy approach to VET' (Maurer 2019: 8) which strongly links vocational education to adult education and aims to promote social integration and equity, much more than is the case at the federal level and in other cantons (Imdorf et al. 2016). This is also in line with the fact that Geneva, like some other French-speaking cantons, has considerably lower rates of enrolment in the dual apprenticeship system, and the prestige of VET is lower in the French-speaking part of Switzerland (Berner and Bonoli 2018; BFS 2019).

In the 1990s, a further important role was played by representatives of adult education, located within both cantonal administrations and educational providers. They argued that fixed VET programmes were not adequate to meet the needs of the rapidly changing labour market, and that it was therefore important to increase the flexibility of the VET system, e.g. by entirely modularizing it (e.g. Widmer et al. 1999). Their efforts were supported by women's organizations which were in turn supported by both centre-right and leftist members of the federal-level parliament. These feminist interest groups pressed for reforms which would facilitate women's access to the labour market, and lobbied for RPL (see e.g. Calonder Gerster 1993). Such efforts were subsequently also made by some innovative members of the federal VET administration, who started to compose a first draft of a revised VET act (Schweizerischer Bundesrat 2000).

When, in 2002, the Swiss parliament passed a revised VET Act, many ambitious reform proposals were compromised. Still, the revised Act included a number of new regulations, in particular the possibility of introducing 'alternative qualifications procedures' (Art. 33), which opened the door to VNIL.

9.4.3 Restrictive approach to implementation and slow expansion of VNIL

After the revised VET Act came into effect in 2004, the federal authorities launched a project to make VNIL the key 'alternative qualification procedure', with guidelines prescribing how VNIL should be implemented at the level of cantons (BBT 2010b). Whereas normally in Swiss VET at upper-secondary level, such regulations would be designed in an occupation-specific way (with employers' associations centrally involved in this process), the approach to VNIL was different. Given the pioneering role of cantons in the French-speaking part of Switzerland, and their preference for continuing their own chosen approaches, the procedures were to be crafted by the cantons themselves, based on the federal guidelines (BBT 2010a).

Most importantly, these guidelines defined the phases of VNIL procedures and emphasized the central role of the portfolio (see section 9.4.1, 'The two main forms of RPL in Swiss VET'). Clearly, they mirrored the federal authorities' as well as the other main VET actors' concern that VNIL could, if not tightly regulated and controlled, lower access barriers to VET qualifications, and thus negatively influence their credibility. In particular, VNIL was not designed for individuals with lower levels of general education. For instance, it was obvious that the composition of the portfolio would require a high degree of writing skill and reflection capacity, potentially going beyond what was required of regular VET learners. Furthermore, it was specified that access to a VET qualification through VNIL would also require the validation of competencies in 'language, communication, and society' (LCS), a compulsory element of every VET programme, with the aim of ensuring a minimum level of general education among all VET learners (BBT 2010c). For some occupations which emphasize manual skills and highly specific vocational knowledge (e.g. in crafts), the requirements in terms of writing skills and reflection capacity are actually higher for VNIL than for the regular final exam (Maurer et al. 2016). In many cases, it takes candidates more than a year to compile their portfolio, upon submission of which they then wait for another couple of months to see the results. A large proportion of candidates take 'complementary training', which adds yet more months (Maurer et al. 2016).

Given the high barriers, the expansion of VNIL in formal VET since its introduction has been slow in Switzerland: in 2017, not even 7 per cent of all adults (over 25) who achieved a VET qualification had their competencies recognized through VNIL (SBFI 2019: 16). Everyone else went through the regular qualification procedure, including the final exam, some of them accessing it directly, others after having passed a regular or a shortened apprenticeship training.

A further important reason for slow growth is the role of decentralized governance in VET, which results in uneven provision of VNIL across Switzerland. As a matter of fact, the share of VNIL candidates is higher in cantons which were highly supportive of it (e.g. in Geneva). Overall, in 2019, only nine out of twenty-six cantons were offering VNIL—with seven of these nine cantons being either fully or partly francophone—and following, like Geneva (see section 9.4.2, 'The reasons underlying the emergence of a more liberal approach to RPL'), a VET policy approach that gives stronger weight to the objective of equity (Aerne, in this volume; Maurer 2019). Furthermore, in 2019, VNIL was available for only twelve (out of approximately 230) occupations in VET at upper-secondary level (though arguably for the most popular ones), with some cantons only offering VNIL for a single occupation (SDBB 2021). The two occupations with the largest share of VNIL candidates are health-care and social-care workers (Wettstein 2016). Two factors were key in the expansion of VNIL in these occupations: first, both of them were quite new and had developed precisely in those years when VNIL was under discussion. Thus, relevant professional organizations were more open towards alternative forms of qualification procedure. Second, both occupations attracted a high proportion of women who had already achieved a VET qualification and wanted to change career (Schmid et al. 2017: 33). Many of them therefore had good reading and writing skills and were well prepared to write portfolios.

9.4.4 Conflicts in the implementation process

The implementation of VNIL in Switzerland was linked to a number of conflicts, the analysis of which provides important insights into the dimensions that are at stake.

A first set of conflicts occurred at the political level, in the form of regular critiques by members of the federal parliament addressed at the federal authorities.[1] Most of these pressed for greater expansion of VNIL by making it available in a higher number of occupations and cantons. Whereas leftist members of parliament tended to argue that VNIL should be promoted to facilitate the integration of refugees or the re-integration of the unemployed into the labour market, centre-right parliamentarians were more inclined to ask authorities to accelerate RPL to mitigate skills shortages in a number of economic sectors and occupations (including health care). The federal-level VET authorities countered that the existing legal framework (the competencies defined in the qualification profiles) did not allow for more flexibility, and that the key roles in the implementation process were anyway played by the cantons and the professional organizations, with limited opportunity for the federal-level authorities to directly promote VNIL.

A second set of conflicts emerged between the federal administration and the cantons as well as the professional organizations. One of the most critical debates centred around the diverging approaches of cantons to the implementation of the federal VNIL guidelines. In particular, the approach of the canton of Geneva, promoting VNIL to enhance social equity, was viewed critically by a number of (mostly German-speaking) cantons as well as by representatives of the federal administration, who feared that it lowered

---

[1] This section is based on an analysis of the parliamentary interventions on the issue of RPL between 2010 and 2019, namely, five interpellations (numbers 13.3432, 13.3724, 15.3037, 16.3091, 17.4118), eight parliamentary motions (numbers 13.3278, 13.3471, 13.3517, 14.3162, 15.3136, 15.3575, 15.3700, 17.3813) and one postulate (11.4026), see Das Schweizer Parlament (2021).

access barriers to VET qualifications (Salort 2015). Other cantons promoted RPL more strongly in view of companies' needs for qualified employees, which again, for some observers, conflicted with the aim of maintaining the credibility of VET qualifications. As an example, the canton of Zug, politically dominated by the centre-right, started to accept employers' certificates as proof of competence in the portfolios (Troxler 2013; Schuler 2017). Other cantons, such as the canton of Zurich, did not allow this for long, on the grounds that employers would too easily issue such proofs of competence to employees whom they hoped would quickly attain their qualification (e.g. in health care) (Kehl et al. 2013; Troxler 2013). Cantonal authorities—such as the VET office in Zurich, which, similarly to the federal administration, insisted on high access barriers—were thus criticized on the grounds of both efficiency *and* equity concerns.

A further critical debate centred around the diverging approaches of the different occupations. Here, professional organizations (mostly representing employers) argued that the federal-level VNIL guidelines should be implemented in a flexible way, but with the overall aim of maintaining the credibility of the qualifications. Some of these associations, for instance the ones representing cooks or logisticians, introduced a practical assessment, while the health-care association started to ask most candidates to undergo a course in medical technology—with all arguing that it was virtually impossible to evaluate the relevant competencies based on a portfolio and an oral assessment only. In all these cases, the federal administration claimed that such practices were not in line with the VNIL regulations.[2] This suggests that it was not only the authorities which were acting to maintain the credibility of the VET qualifications.

9.4.5 The restrictive redesign of the Swiss approach to RPL

Even though the discussions at the level of the federal parliament did not result in any changes to the VET Act, they made clear that the federal VET administration was expected to promote RPL more vigorously. Whilst RPL has usually been promoted to facilitate access of migrants to the labour market (particularly in statist skill formation systems, such as in Sweden), the pressure in Switzerland grew, paradoxically, out of a popular referendum aiming to *reduce* immigration to Switzerland. When the referendum

---

[2] Information based on an interview with a representative of the State Secretariat of Education, Research and Innovation (SERI), conducted on 7 October 2019.

result was accepted in early 2014, many employers feared difficulties in the recruitment of adequately qualified employees. Policymakers therefore saw the promotion of RPL as a means to support existing participants in the Swiss labour market who lacked up-to-date skills and qualifications by providing them with better opportunities to access a vocational qualification more in line with current economic needs. VET for adults thus became one of the priority areas of Swiss education and training policy (SBFI 2014), supported by all relevant actors in VET policymaking, including cantons, employers' associations, and labour unions. The discussions that followed resulted not in increased efforts to expand the comparatively liberal VNIL approach, but instead in aligning the RPL regulations with the interests of the dominant actors in Swiss VET. This rendered the Swiss approach to RPL more restrictive again—refocusing on the final exam as the point of departure for modularization and reinforcing the role of professional organizations in VNIL.

In fact, the federal authorities had initially planned to simply revise the VNIL guidelines. But the revision they proposed (SBFI 2016) met with considerable opposition from both cantons and professional organizations, many of which were of the view that VNIL had had its chance, and that its slow expansion was a clear indication that this approach was not in line with the structure of VET in Switzerland. The VNIL guidelines were therefore replaced by two documents: a handbook on VET for adults and a set of guidelines for RPL. While the handbook put into perspective the existing VNIL procedures (dedicating one of 32 pages to this topic) and gave considerable weight to the option of splitting up final exams into several parts (SBFI 2017), the RPL guidelines provided details of how, even within the existing legal framework and beyond VNIL, prior learning could be recognized much more systematically, e.g. by exempting candidates from specific parts of the final exam (SBFI 2018a). This suggests that the modular approach to RPL—and thus to VET—has at least become acceptable to key stakeholders in the Swiss skill formation system.

With regards to the governance of VNIL, the cantons were no longer allowed to design VNIL procedures along the lines of federal guidelines. Instead, VNIL procedures would have to be defined in occupation-specific ways by the relevant professional organizations, based on a template issued by SERI (SBFI 2018b). This change in the governance of VNIL reflects a turn towards a common standard in Swiss VET, of governing access to VET qualifications mainly through occupation-specific regulations defined by professional organizations.

9.5 Interpretation and conclusions

This analysis of the Swiss case confirms that the promotion of RPL, and in particular of liberal approaches to it, faces considerable challenges in collective skill formation systems. The chapter argues that this results from the fact that key actors involved in the governance of these skill formation systems—most of the employers and their representatives as well as the VET authorities—are concerned that RPL could undermine a key element of the efficiency function: the credibility of VET qualifications. It also shows that, even in such systems, some employers may be willing to promote RPL because they see it as a means to contribute to another element of the efficiency function of skill formation: better access to employees with relevant VET qualifications. Yet, as the Swiss case shows, key actors seem to agree that maintaining the long-term credibility of VET qualifications is more important than improving short-term access to qualified labour in specific sectors. Furthermore, it confirms the assumption that actors advancing the social equity case for RPL (e.g. trade unions representing the interests of 'outsiders') have little leverage, as they have comparatively little weight in RPL systems' governance structures. This stands in contrast to statist skill formation systems, such as in Sweden, where the dominant actors (notably the public authorities) are freer to advance RPL in view of social equity objectives (Olsson and Ragnarsson 1998; Andersson et al. 2004; Heikkilä 2014).

The Swiss case also suggests that, even in collective skill formation systems, liberal forms of RPL can evolve (albeit under very specific circumstances) and that decentralized governance can be a potential source of transformative change in this regard. In the genesis of regulations around Swiss VNIL, an extraordinarily important role was played by innovative cantons, notably Geneva, which itself takes a quasi-statist approach to skill formation and attaches great importance to the role of VET in mitigating social inequalities. Furthermore, VNIL in Switzerland would have expanded even less, had the health- and social-care sectors not promoted it, due to their unmet demand for employees with relevant VET qualifications. Tellingly, neither of these sectors are covered by VET laws in many other collective skill formation systems (e.g. Germany). Decentralized governance is, however, also a potential source of conflict in collective skill formation systems, as actors at the sub-national levels prioritize equity and efficiency objectives in different ways.

The most recent reforms in Switzerland also suggest that, in the field of RPL, a middle course might be more likely to gain support from key actors.

This approach splits the regular final exam into parts, from some of which candidates can be exempted if they can demonstrate—in comparatively simple ways—that they have already acquired the relevant competencies. Such a model also exists in Austria (though it is not widely used) and is in line with modular VET approaches. Still, the comprehensive modularization of VET as a whole is unlikely to occur in most collective skill formation systems—even though many observers argue that the transformation of economies and the growing importance of mass migration require exactly this (Pilz et al. 2018; Seufert 2018). In view of the comparatively high social status of VET qualifications in collective systems, it is also quite unlikely that RPL will be liberalized to provide better access for refugees to VET qualifications and the labour market. More likely, in this regard, is the development of external measures, such as preparatory courses for VET (Aerne, in this volume), or internal measures that provide additional support to disadvantaged learners or the host companies training them (see also Bonoli and Emmenegger, in this volume).

References

Aarkrog, V., and B. Wahlgren. 2015. 'Assessment of Prior Learning in Adult Vocational Education and Training'. *International Journal for Research in Vocational Education and Training 2* (1): 41–58.

Allais, S. 2014. *Selling out Education: National Qualifications Frameworks and the Neglect of Knowledge.* Rotterdam/Boston/Taipei: Sense Publishers.

Andersen, M. 2016. 'Tools of Assessment in Recognition of Prior Learning (RPL) within Vocational Education in Denmark'. *PLA Inside Out: An International Journal on Theory, Research and Practice in Prior Learning Assessment 5*: 1–15.

Andersson, P., A. Fejes, and S.-E. Ahn. 2004. 'Recognition of Prior Vocational Learning in Sweden'. *Studies in the Education of Adults 36* (1): 57–71.

Annen, S. 2012. *Anerkennung von Kompetenzen: Kriterienorientierte Analyse ausgewählter Verfahren in Europa.* Bielefeld: Bertelsmann.

Annen, S., and D. Schreiber. 2011. 'Anerkennung informellen Lernens in Deutschland und Frankreich—ein Vergleich zwischen Externenprüfung und VAE'. In *Prüfungen und Zertifizierungen in der beruflichen Bildung*, edited by E. Severing and R. Weiss, pp. 135–55. Bielefeld: Bertelsmann.

Bagnall, R. G. 2000. 'Lifelong Learning and the Limitations of Economic Determinism'. *International Journal of Lifelong Education 19* (1): 20–35.

BBT—Bundesamt für Berufsbildung und Technologie. 2010a. *Hinweise zur Anerkennung von kantonalen Validierungsverfahren im Bereich berufliche Grundbildung*

(Zusatzdokument zu 'Validierung von Bildungsleistungen: Leitfaden für die berufliche Grundbildung'). Bern: Bundesamt für Berufsbildung und Technologie.

BBT—Bundesamt für Berufsbildung und Technologie. 2010b. *Validierung von Bildungsleistungen: Leitfaden für die berufliche Grundbildung.* Bern: Bundesamt für Berufsbildung und Technologie.

BBT—Bundesamt für Berufsbildung und Technologie. 2010c. *Validierungsinstrumente für die Allgemeinbildung (Zusatzdokument zu 'Validierung von Bildungsleistungen: Leitfaden für die berufliche Grundbildung').* Bern: Bundesamt für Berufsbildung und Technologie.

Bedard, K. 2001. 'Human Capital versus Signalling Models: University Access and High School Dropouts'. *Journal of Political Economy 109* (4): 749–75.

Berner, E., and L. Bonoli. 2018. 'La formation professionnelle suisse entre Confédération et cantons: Eléments d'une histoire complexe'. In *Les enjeux de la formation professionnelle. Le 'modèle' suisse sous la loupe,* edited by L. Bonoli, J.-L. Berger, and N. Lamara, pp. 53–78. Zürich: Seismo.

BFS—Bundesamt für Statistik. 2019. *Lehrstellenquote nach Kanton der Arbeitstätten, 2017.* Neuchâtel: Bundesamt für Statistik.

Bohlinger, S. 2017. 'Comparing Recognition of Prior Learning (RPL) across Countries'. In *Competence-based Vocational and Professional Education: Bridging the Worlds of Work and Education,* edited by M. Mulder, pp. 589–606. Cham: Springer.

Breton, H. 2017. 'La reconnaissance et la validation des acquis de l'expérience en France: le paradigme de l'expérientiel à l'épreuve des certifications'. *Lifelong Lifewide Learning 13* (30): 62–74.

Brown, S., and J. G. Sessions. 2004. 'Signalling and Screening'. In *International Handbook on the Economics of Education,* edited by G. Johnes and J. Johnes, pp. 58–100. Cheltenham: Elgar.

Busemeyer, M. R., and C. Trampusch. 2019. 'The Politics of Vocational Training: Theories, Typologies, and Public Policies'. In *The Wiley Handbook of Vocational Education and Training,* edited by L. Unwin, pp. 137–64. Chichester: John Wiley.

Calonder Gerster, A. 1993. *Aus Sackgassen in Laufbahnen: Thesen für ein frauenfreundliches Bildungssystem.* Lucerne: Donna Mobile.

Carstensen, M. B., and C. L. Ibsen. 2021. 'Three Dimensions of Institutional Contention: Efficiency, Equality and Governance in Danish Vocational Education and Training Reform'. *Socio-Economic Review 19* (3): 1037–63.

Cedefop. 1997. *Identification, validation et accréditation de l'apprentissage antérieur et informel - France.* Thessaloniki: Cedefop.

Cedefop. 2015. *European Guidelines for Validating Non-formal and Informal Learning.* Luxembourg: Publications Office of the European Union.

Cooper, L., and J. Harris. 2013. 'Recognition of Prior Learning: Exploring the "Knowledge Question". *International Journal of Lifelong Education 32* (4): 447–63.

Cooper, L., A. Ralphs, and J. Harris. 2017. 'Recognition of Prior Learning: The Tensions between its Inclusive Intentions and Constraints on its Implementation'. *Studies in Continuing Education 39* (2): 197–213.

Council of the European Union. 2012. *Council Recommendation of 20 December 2012 on the Validation of Non-formal and Informal Learning.* Brussels: Council of the European Union.

Das Schweizer Parlament. 2021. 'Curia Vista Geschäftsdatenbank'. Online: https://www.parlament.ch/de/search-affairs-advanced [accessed 30 September 2021].

Dionisius, R., S. Muehlemann, H. Pfeifer, G. Walden, F. Wenzelmann, and S. C. Wolter. 2009. 'Costs and Benefits of Apprenticeship Training: A Comparison of Germany and Switzerland'. *Applied Economics Quarterly 55* (1): 7–37.

Duvekot, R. 2018. *European Inventory on Validation of Non-formal and Informal Learning 2018 Update. Country Report: The Netherlands.* Luxembourg: Cedefop.

Emmenegger, P., and L. Seitzl. 2019. 'Collective Action, Business Cleavages and the Politics of Control: Segmentalism in the Swiss Skill Formation System'. *British Journal of Industrial Relations 57* (3): 576–98.

Fejes, A., and P. Andersson. 2009. 'Recognising Prior Learning: Understanding the Relations among Experience, Learning and Recognition from a Constructivist Perspective'. *Vocations and Learning 2* (1): 37–55.

Field, S., J.-L. Álvarez-Galván, F. Hénard, V. Kis, M. Kuczera, and P. Musset. 2012. *A Skills beyond School Review of Denmark.* Paris: OECD.

Fleischmann, D. 2005. 'Wir können mehr, als wir wissen: Zürcher Zentrum für Kompetenzbilanz ab Januar 2006 auf Vollbetrieb'. *bbaktuell 154*: 1–2.

Gonon, P., and M. Maurer. 2012. 'Educational Policy Actors as Stakeholders in the Development of the Collective Skill System: The Case of Switzerland'. In *The Comparative Political Economy of Collective Skill Formation*, edited by M. R. Busemeyer and C. Trampusch, pp. 126–49. Oxford: Oxford University Press.

Guo, S. 2014. 'Revisioning Education for All in the Age of Migration: Global Challenges and Opportunities for Lifelong Learning'. *International Review of Education 60* (4): 481–97.

Gutschow, K. 2020. 'Validierung und Anerkennung informell erworbener Kompetenzen'. In *Handbuch Berufsbildung*, edited by R. Arnold, A. Lipsmeier, and M. Rohs, pp. 455–70. Wiesbaden: Springer.

Harris, J., M. Breier, and C. Wihak (eds). 2011. *Researching the Recognition of Prior Learning: International Perspectives.* Leicester: NIACE.

Heikkilä, E. 2014. European Inventory on Validation of Non-formal and Informal Learning 2014. Country Report: Sweden. Thessaloniki: Cedefop.

ILO—International Labour Office. 2018. *Recognition of Prior Learning (RPL): Learning Package*. Geneva: International Labour Office.

Imdorf, C., E. Berner, and P. Gonon. 2016. 'Duale versus vollzeitschulische Berufsausbildung in der Schweiz: Zwei Institutionalisierungsmuster der beruflichen Bildung aus rechtfertigungstheoretischer und kantonal vergleichender Perspektive'. In *Die Organisation von Bildung. Soziologische Analysen zu Schule, Berufsbildung, Hochschule und Weiterbildung*, edited by R. J. Leemann, C. Imdorf, J. J. W. Powell, and M. Sertl, pp. 186–207. Weinheim: Beltz Juventa.

Ismail, S. 2014. *Future Directions for the Recognition of Prior Learning (RPL)—How to Incorporate Knowledge from Below into the Academy? Paper presented to SAERA conference. Durban, 13–15 August*. Durban: SAERA.

Jansen, J. D. 2002. 'Political Symbolism as Policy Craft: Explaining Non-reform in South African Education after Apartheid'. *Journal of Education Policy 71* (2): 199–215.

Kehl, F., F. Wigger, and J.-P. Wolf. 2013. *Schlussbericht Evaluation Validierungsverfahren Kanton Zürich*. Zürich: KEK-CDC Consultants.

Knight, B. 2006. *Assessment for Recognition of Prior Learning in Technical and Vocational Education and Training in Australia: Where to from Here*. Adelaide: NCVER.

Lee, M., and S. K. Jan. 2018. 'Lifelong Learning Policy Discourses of International Organisations since 2000: A Kaleidoscope or Merely Fragments?' In *The Palgrave International Handbook on Adult and Lifelong Education and Learning*, edited by M. Milana, S. Webb, J. Holford, R. Waller, and P. Jarvis, pp. 375–96. London: Palgrave Macmillan.

Lundahl, L., I. E. Arreman, U. Lundström, and L. Rönnberg. 2010. 'Setting Things Right? Swedish Upper Secondary School Reform in a 40-Year Perspective'. *European Journal of Education 45* (1): 46–59.

Marsden, D. 1999. *A Theory of Employment Systems: Micro-foundations of Societal Diversity*. Oxford: Oxford University Press.

Mathou, C. 2019. *European Inventory on Validation of Non-formal and Informal Learning 2018 Update: France*. Luxembourg: Cedefop.

Maurer, M. 2013. 'Herausforderungen für das schweizerische Berufsbildungssystem—ein Ausblick'. In *Herausforderungen für die Berufsbildung in der Schweiz: Bestandesaufnahme und Perspektiven*, edited by M. Maurer and P. Gonon, pp. 243–50. Bern: hep Verlag.

Maurer, M. 2019. 'The Challenges of Expanding Recognition of Prior Learning (RPL) in a Collectively Organised Skill Formation System: The Case of Switzerland'. *Journal of Education and Work 32* (8): 665–77.

Maurer, M. 2021. 'The Limits of Reforming Access to Vocational Qualifications: The Slow Expansion of Recognition of Prior Learning (RPL) in Sweden and Switzerland'. *Journal of Vocational Education and Training*. Published online 8 April 2021.

Maurer, M., E. Wettstein, and H. Neuhaus. 2016. *Berufsabschluss für Erwachsene in der Schweiz: Bestandesaufnahme und Blick nach vorn*. Bern: hep Verlag.

Morand-Aymon, B. 2004. *Les effets de la reconnaissance et de la validation des acquis, de la formation et de la qualification sur les publics 'non qualifiés'. Rapport d'enquête; Synthèse*. Geneva: Faculté de Psychologie et des Sciences de l'Éducation.

Olsson, B., and E. Ragnarsson. 1998. *Validering av utländsk yrkeskompetens (SOU 1998:165)*. Stockholm: Regeringskansliet/Utbildningsdepartementet.

Pfeffer, T., and I. Skrivanek. 2013. 'Institutionelle Verfahren zur Anerkennung ausländischer Qualifikationen und zur Validierung nicht formal oder informell erworbener Kompetenzen in Österreich'. *Zeitschrift für Bildungsforschung 3* (1): 63–78.

Pfeffer, T., and I. Skrivanek. 2018. 'Why Is the Recognition of Credentials Not Just a Matter of Good Will? Five Theories and the Austrian Case'. *European Journal of Cultural and Political Sociology 5* (4): 389–422.

Pilz, M., J. Li, R. Canning, and S. Minty. 2018. 'Modularisation Approaches in Initial Vocational Education: Evidence for Policy Convergence in Europe?' *Journal of Vocational Education and Training 70* (1): 1–26.

Pitman, T., and L. Vidovich. 2012. 'Recognition of Prior Learning (RPL) Policy in Australian Higher Education: The Dynamics of Position-taking'. *Journal of Education Policy 27* (6): 761–74.

Rueda, D. 2005. 'Insider-outsider Politics in Industrialized Democracies: The Challenge to Social Democratic Parties'. *American Political Science Review 99* (1): 61–74.

Salort, C. 2015. *Modularisierung in der Berufsbildung für Erwachsene am Beispiel Genf. Präsentation an der PH Zürich vom 19. Mai*. Zürich: PH Zürich.

SBFI—Staatssekretariat für Bildung, Forschung und Innovation. 2014. *Spitzentreffen der Berufsbildung 2014: Gemeinsame Erklärung der Verbundpartner*. Bern: Staatssekretariat für Bildung, Forschung und Innovation.

SBFI—Staatssekretariat für Bildung, Forschung und Innovation. 2016. *Validierung von Bildungsleistungen: Leitfaden für die berufliche Grundbildung. Entwurf für die Anhörung*. Bern: Staatssekretariat für Bildung, Forschung und Innovation.

SBFI—Staatssekretariat für Bildung, Forschung und Innovation. 2017. *Handbuch Berufliche Grundbildung für Erwachsene*. Bern: Staatssekretariat für Bildung, Forschung und Innovation.

SBFI—Staatssekretariat für Bildung, Forschung und Innovation. 2018a. *Leitfaden Anrechnung von Bildungsleistungen in der beruflichen Grundbildung*. Bern: Staatssekretariat für Bildung, Forschung und Innovation.

SBFI—Staatssekretariat für Bildung, Forschung und Innovation. 2018b. *Leitvorlage Regelung des Qualifikationsverfahrens mit Validierung von Bildungsleistungen vom 1. April 2018*. Bern: Staatssekretariat für Bildung, Forschung und Innovation.

SBFI—Staatssekretariat für Bildung, Forschung und Innovation. 2019. *Berufsbildung in der Schweiz: Fakten und Zahlen 2019*. Bern: Staatssekretariat für Bildung, Forschung und Innovation.

Schmid, M. 2019. 'Validierung am Scheideweg? Eine Einschätzung'. *SGAB Newsletter* (3).

Schmid, M., S. Schmidlin, and D. S. Hischier. 2017. *Berufsabschluss für Erwachsene: Sicht von betroffenen Erwachsenen (Schlussbericht)*. Bern: Staatssekretariat für Bildung, Forschung und Innovation.

Schuler, B. 2017. *Berufsbildung für Erwachsene: Entwicklung und neue Ansätze. Präsentation an der PH Zürich vom 12. September 2017*. Zug: Amt für Berufsbildung.

Schweizerischer Bundesrat. 2000. *Botschaft zu einem neuen Bundesgesetz über die Berufsbildung (Berufsbildungsgesetz, BBG)*. Bern: Bundesamten für Bauten und Logistik.

SDBB. 2021. 'Validierungsverfahren in den Kantonen. Online: https://www.berufsberatung.ch/dyn/show/26870 [accessed 30 September 2021].

Seawright, J. 2016. 'The Case for Selecting Cases That Are Deviant Or Extreme on the Independent Variable'. *Sociological Methods & Research* 45 (3): 493–525.

Seufert, S. 2018. *Flexibilisierung der Berufsbildung im Kontext fortschreitender Digitalisierung: Bericht im Auftrag des Staatssekretariats für Bildung, Forschung und Innovation SBFI im Rahmen des Projekts 'Berufsbildung 2030—Vision und Strategische Leitlinien'*. Bern: Staatssekretariat für Bildung, Forschung und Innovation SBFI.

Singh, M. 2015. *Global Perspectives on Recognising Non-formal and informal learning: Why recognition matters*. Wiesbaden: Springer.

Trampusch, C. 2010. 'The Politics of Institutional Change: Transformative and Self-Preserving Change in the Vocational Education and Training System in Switzerland'. *Comparative Politics* 42 (2): 187–206.

Trampusch, C. 2020. 'Social Partners' Policy Reactions to Migration in Occupational Labour Markets: The Case of the Swiss Construction Industry'. *European Journal of Industrial Relations* 26 (2): 157–72.

Troxler, I. 2013. 'Büffeln, was man schon weiss'. *Neue Zürcher Zeitung*, 30 January, p. 17.

Valideringsdelegationen. 2019. *Validering—för kompetensförsörjning och livslångt lärande. Slutbetänkande av Valideringsdelegationen.* Stockholm: Statens Offentliga Utredningar.

Wettstein, E. 2016. *Berufsabschluss für Erwachsene: Statistik der Abschlüsse.* Zürich: Berufsbildungsprojekte Dr. Emil Wettstein GmbH.

Widmer, J., J.-P. Gindroz, R. Jost, E. Kemm, and R. Marty. 1999. *Berufliche Weiterbildung im Baukastensystem. Schlussbericht über die Pilotphase 1996 bis 1998.* Bern: Bundesamt für Berufsbildung und Technologie.

Wolnik, K., and A. Holtrup. 2017. *Berufswechsel-Chancen und Risiken: Ausmaß, Motive, Gestaltungserfordernisse.* Bremen: Universität Bremen.

10

Employer Influence in Vocational Education and Training

Germany and Sweden Compared

Marius R. Busemeyer and Kathleen Thelen

10.1 Introduction

Maintaining and adapting skill formation systems in advanced economies is a dynamic process that requires continuous commitment from policymakers and labour market actors to update existing institutions. In this regard, the advent of the new knowledge economy poses significant new challenges to traditional vocational education and training (VET) systems in Europe. Firms are confronted simultaneously with two problems: the need to augment traditional occupational skills with the more general education workers increasingly need in order to keep pace with rapid technological change while at the same time counteracting the drift on the part of youth away from vocational training towards more academic tracks.[1]

This chapter examines recent developments in Germany and Sweden, two countries which have traditionally embraced different approaches to the provision of vocationally oriented education and training. Germany is a classic example of the 'collectivist' system focused on in this volume. The country's 'dual' system of VET emphasizes firm-based training at the secondary level and relies on high levels of employer involvement and employer coordination. Sweden, by contrast, is a prime example of the alternative statist system identified by Bonoli and Emmenegger (in this volume: Table 1.1). The country historically rejected the collectivist model of an employer-dominated

[1] We are indebted to Olivia Bergman, Lara Prasad, and Léonie Trick for excellent research assistance. We thank Patrick Emmenegger, Giuliano Bonoli, Niccolo Durazzi, Lukas Graf, Matthias Pilz, and Christine Trampusch as well the participants in the workshop in St. Gallen in 2019 for excellent comments and feedback.

Marius R. Busemeyer and Kathleen Thelen, *Employer Influence in Vocational Education and Training*. In: *Collective Skill Formation in the Knowledge Economy*. Edited by Giuliano Bonoli and Patrick Emmenegger, Oxford University Press. © Oxford University Press (2022). DOI: 10.1093/oso/9780192866257.003.0010

VET system and embraced instead an alternative state-run system of school-based VET.

These differences in starting points mean that employers in Germany and Sweden confront mirror-image challenges in the current period. Germany's firm-based VET system is heavily oriented towards the acquisition of practical vocational skills, leaving advanced firms in particular with deficits in the more general theoretical skills that are increasingly prominent in the new knowledge economy. Sweden's school-based system, conversely, has traditionally been stronger in the provision of general education at the upper-secondary level, leaving manufacturing firms, especially, short of the more practical skills these firms value and on which they continue to rely.

Comparing these 'contrasting contexts', we identify a shared trend towards the growing involvement of employers in public educational institutions—in Germany at the level of higher education as a way of augmenting the country's heavily practical VET with more theoretical content, and in Sweden at the upper-secondary level to inject a practical component into school-based training in order to strengthen the connection to local firms. In Germany, the key innovations have involved the expansion of so-called dual study programmes at the intersection of traditional VET and higher education. These arrangements allow large firms in particular to make use of the public educational infrastructure at the post-secondary level to augment their own firm-based training. The parallel development in Sweden is occurring at the upper-secondary level, where manufacturing employers have become active in offering additional firm-based training through public–private partnerships with local schools. These initiatives are aimed at enhancing the attractiveness of VET and strengthening the practical component in the country's school-based system.

Our comparative-historical account should be considered as an example of contrasting contexts in the sense of Skocpol and Somers (1980), i.e. we aim 'to bring out the unique features of each particular case [. . .] and to show how these unique features affect the working-out of putatively general social processes' (Skocpol and Somers 1980: 178). The underlying general process is the growing role of business in the knowledge economy, which manifests itself in different institutional outcomes in the two countries. In Germany's collectivist system, the trends we observe reflect pressures towards 'decollectivization' within the VET system identified by Bonoli and Emmenegger (in this volume)—an attenuation of employer coordination through innovations (especially by large firms) to address their skill needs outside the traditional collectivist framework. In Sweden's statist, school-based system, the trends we observe involve a partial 'privatization'[2] within the traditional state-dominated system, via the addition of firm-sponsored training alongside the general public component. In both cases, changes are occurring less through outright reform of traditional educational institutions and more through the addition of new arrangements in and around existing institutions, i.e. a process of institutional layering (Streeck and Thelen 2005).

In both countries, employers are the driving force of recent policy changes, as they confront changing skill needs because of the rise of the knowledge economy and a related drift of youth into more academic tracks. The most successful changes have proceeded through bottom-up experimentation, with leading firms pioneering new arrangements, which then diffuse more broadly with additional support from state actors. In the case of Germany, such layering served to circumvent influential veto players (in the cases of the traditional VET system, unions, because employers prefer greater firm-specific content, and within the traditional higher-education sector, universities, because firms seek more 'practical' academic education). In the case of Sweden, these changes did not sideline unions, which play a role on the supervisory boards of these new programmes. Despite their historic opposition to firm involvement in post-secondary education, unions do not oppose these developments because the programmes augment rather than supplant the existing general educational curriculum, and because they are seen as a way to ease the school-to-work transition for young adults in a country long plagued by high youth unemployment.

The remainder of this chapter is organized as follows. We begin by laying out the logic of the comparison and the empirical puzzle around which the analysis is organized. We then turn to each of the two case studies, outlining the process through which employer involvement in VET has grown, focusing on the specific examples of dual study programmes in Germany and the so-called technical colleges (Teknikcolleges) in Sweden. In the concluding section, we revisit the comparison to highlight both the parallels and the differences between these two trajectories of change.

10.2 Employer influence in VET: Germany and Sweden compared

It is commonplace in the literature on vocational training to draw a sharp contrast between the German and Swedish systems (Busemeyer 2009, 2015;

---

[2] 'Privatization' in this context is highly partial because these new programmes are layered on top of the regular public programmes, but as elaborated below, the additional content of training is heavily influenced by local employers (in collaboration with municipal authorities).

Thelen 2014). Germany preserved a strong system of firm-sponsored vocational education at the upper-secondary level, and the country's widely admired apprenticeship system relies very heavily on the private sector to train a significant share of the country's youth. Precisely this model of employer-dominated training is what Swedish social democrats rejected in the 1960s, presiding instead over a move towards universalism and a wholly school-based model of vocational education under the supervision and control of the central government (Dobbins and Busemeyer 2015).

The German and the Swedish systems are typically seen as exhibiting distinctive strengths and weaknesses. The former has been praised for the way in which its high-quality VET has provided opportunities for working-class youth to gain access to stable and relatively well-paid jobs, particularly in manufacturing. Strong private-sector involvement in secondary education makes for a comparatively smooth school-to-work transition (Gangl 2003; Wolbers 2007; see also Busemeyer 2015: Chapter 4), which is one reason why the country's youth unemployment rates typically run well below the OECD average. At the same time, however, the German system has been criticized for stratifying educational opportunities (and with that, subsequent employment prospects) along class lines, as students are sorted early on into either a vocational or an academic track (Pfeffer 2008). Germany's comparatively low rate of university attendance—still below many other rich democracies—speaks simultaneously to the continued attractions of the VET system and to the relatively high barriers to entry for those students who did not enter the academic track at the upper-secondary level (Baethge and Wolter 2015; Powell and Solga 2011).

The strengths and weaknesses of the Swedish system are in many ways the mirror image of those in Germany. Here, reforms in the 1960s largely eliminated early tracking by introducing comprehensive compulsory schooling governed by a centralized and standardized national curriculum for all children until the age of sixteen. Upper-secondary education was initially organized into separate tracks—a three-year university-preparatory track and a two-year vocational track, but subsequent reforms in effect from 1991 to 2011 extended all vocational programmes to three years and opened a path to university to all (Halldén 2008: 253–54).[3] The Swedish emphasis on uniform educational opportunities is often credited for internationally low levels of educational inequality, and the porous line between academic and vocational tracks has produced much higher levels of tertiary education—a potential plus in the 'knowledge economy'. Yet, Sweden's school-based training has

---

[3] In 2011 the government reintroduced an apprenticeship track that does not lead automatically to a university entrance credential, although the rate of take-up by youth has been lacklustre.

also been criticized, above all, for the lack of a tight connection between the content of training and the needs of firms, making for an overall more difficult school-to-work transition (Busemeyer 2015: Chapter 4). Thus, youth unemployment has been a persistent problem in the Swedish labour market even in the best of times (Crouch et al. 1999).

By comparing the two cases, we aim at identifying common development trajectories that can be observed *across* these different cases, thereby indicating broader development trends for other cases as well. We follow the comparative strategy of 'contrasting contexts' (Skocpol and Somers 1980: 178), which brings out the unique features of a particular case and highlights how these features reflect and contribute to a common trend across cases. A shared feature in both countries is a growing concern to address the dual challenges of technological change and academic drift through new partnerships between public institutions and private interests, and an effort to adapt education institutions to the needs of employers, often under the banner of enhancing 'employability'.

These processes, however, unfold differently in the two divergent contexts. In Germany, where VET has been heavily firm-based and employer dominated, a number of incremental, yet significant changes combine traditional dual apprenticeship training with studies at institutions of higher education in response to specific employer needs (see Thelen and Busemeyer 2012; Busemeyer 2012 for a more detailed discussion of these issues). In Sweden, by contrast, manufacturing employers in particular have sought to shore up vocational education at the upper-secondary level through public–private partnerships which augment school-based training at the upper-secondary level with more firm-based experience.

These developments signal significant departures from the established politics of VET in both countries—in Sweden introducing a firm-sponsored component into a system that historically sought to minimize employer influence over the education of the country's youth, and in Germany, an expansion of employer influence into the realm of tertiary education for which there is no historical precedent. In both cases, the initial momentum for these changes were bottom-up demands from employers rather than large-scale policy reforms from 'the top'. However, state actors and policymakers in both countries have welcomed the increased involvement of business actors, which they view as important in promoting the labour market integration of young persons and in enhancing the competitiveness of industry. Unions have either quietly acquiesced (Germany) or been enlisted to participate (Sweden) in these developments.

In the following sections, we trace policy developments in both Germany and Sweden, demonstrating an overall trend towards new forms of employer influence in shaping the content of VET. Complementing Thelen and Busemeyer (2012), we focus on the emergence of so-called dual study programmes at the intersection between VET and higher education in Germany, and we analyse the introduction of new vocationally oriented supplementary programmes, Teknikcolleges, at the upper-secondary level in Sweden (see also Carstensen and Ibsen, in this volume). In Germany, the key institutional innovators are large industrial employers in the export sector who have taken advantage of opportunities afforded by regulatory gaps at the intersection of VET and higher education to partner with universities of applied sciences (Fachhochschulen) and other higher-education institutions to offer new, highly attractive, educational opportunities that augment the strong practical training they already provide with the enhanced theoretical content on which they increasingly rely (Durazzi and Benassi 2020; Graf 2018). In Sweden, government reforms of the 1980s and 1990s decentralized some aspects of education policy, thus opening a new window of opportunity for manufacturing interests to work with local education authorities and unions to launch public–private partnerships at the upper-secondary level designed to counteract academic drift by bolstering the attractiveness of vocational training while also addressing the specific skill needs of local employers.

10.3 Germany: dual study programmes at the intersection of the labour market and higher education

The German training system has long been seen as one of the core pillars on which the strength of the German export economy rests. Despite signs of increasing academic drift, this system continues to enjoy high popularity and strong support from all of the major organized actors in politics and in the political economy. Nevertheless, technological changes associated with the move to advanced manufacturing and the diverging interests of the VET system's stakeholders have begun to pose some new and more difficult challenges.

The German system rests on a national eco-structure that includes multiple veto points and a wide range of interests. These include, among others, the handicraft and industry chambers that oversee and certify firm-based training, the tripartite oversight bodies that oversee the system and revise and update the training profiles offered, and the state-level vocational schools that provide the school-based component of training. The system as currently constituted continues to function rather well for a large number of firms who participate, even though there is a long-term declining trend in the participation rate of firms (Thelen and Busemeyer 2012). However, it is increasingly challenged by divergent firm needs and, relatedly, the heterogenous profiles of apprentices, which puts the system under pressure from two sides. On the one hand, firms in the craft sector are increasingly worried about finding qualified candidates to fill their training slots, and apprentices are complaining about decreasing quality standards in low-level service occupations, e.g. in the restaurant and hotel sectors. On the other hand, large firms in the export-oriented sectors of the economy are feeling the pressures of academic drift acutely as talented youth who would be prime candidates for the more advanced types of apprenticeship training opt for university studies rather than VET. Unions, meanwhile, are mostly concerned with declining training quality in some sectors of the economy as well as persistent problems for low-skilled youth to get access to firm-based training.

In the face of these competing demands on the system and the difficulties of outright reform, employers, in particular in the export-oriented sectors of the economy, have sought to address the specific challenges they face while avoiding institutional veto players through a process of institutional layering. Specifically, they have taken advantage of the regulatory 'grey zone' between the VET system and university studies to develop new hybrid arrangements at the intersection of higher education and traditional firm-based vocational training (see esp. Graf 2013, 2018; as well as Durazzi and Benassi 2020). The term 'dual study' encompasses a variety of institutional arrangements, depending on the statutory regulation of higher education in the different Länder (Graf 2013: 95–7; Minks et al. 2011). In this article, however, we focus on the two most prevalent models, which together account for a large majority (70%) of all participants (Meyer-Guckel et al. 2015: 10). The first type encompasses programmes in which participants receive both a degree from a higher-education institution and a recognized vocational degree (*ausbildungsintegrierend*).[4] In the second type, extended practical phases are integrated into the study programme (*praxisintegrierend*), but participants only receive a degree from a higher-education institution.

10.3.1 Origins of the dual study model

Today's dual study programmes represent an expansion of programmes pioneered by prominent manufacturing companies decades ago. Such programmes were originally piloted in Baden-Württemberg in the late 1970s

---

[4] About a third of study programmes commonly referred to as 'dual study programmes' fit this model (Minks et al. 2011: IV).

when leading companies were concerned that the newly established universities of applied sciences (*Fachhochschulen*) would not pay sufficient attention to practical and firm-specific skill needs, and potentially reduce interest among youth for more traditional firm-sponsored training (Graf 2018: 193).[5] Daimler Benz, Bosch, and Standard Elektrik Lorenz co-sponsored the first 'vocational academy' (*Berufsakademie*) as an alternative to the classic university model to offer post-secondary education that was less academic in nature and included more practical training. Some Länder have followed the example of Baden-Württemberg and established vocational academies themselves (e.g. Rhineland-Palatinate and Saxony). In other states, for example, Bavaria and North Rhine-Westphalia, dual study programmes involve collaboration between local firms and existing universities of applied sciences or—more exceptionally—regular universities.[6] Overall, the majority (64% in 2018) of dual study programmes are located at public or private universities of applied sciences (Wegweiser Duales Studium 2018: 8), only 23 per cent at vocational academies, 7 per cent at regular universities and 6 per cent at the '*duale Hochschule*' in Baden-Württemberg, which is the successor to the earlier vocational academies established in this particular *Land*.

Dual study programmes have expanded significantly and especially rapidly in recent years.[7] In 1996, forty-four dual study programmes were counted across Germany (Kupfer et al. 2014: 5). Table 10.1 documents an impressive expansion of dual study programmes across different dimensions over the last ten years. In 2004, an online database of available dual study programmes ('AusbildungPlus') counted 512 dual study programmes (i.e. a more than ten-fold increase since 1996). This number increased further to a stunning 1,592 dual study programmes being registered in 2016. In these programmes, higher-education institutions cooperate with more than 47,000 employers (up from 18,000 in 2004), although some firms may be counted several times if they participate in more than one dual study programme. The number of students also increased strongly from about 40,000 in 2004 to more than 100,000 in 2016.

---

[5] This was in a context in which changes to the education system resulting from the student movement were aimed at 'democratizing' education in Germany by softening the strict system of secondary school tracking.

[6] States with Berufsakademien mostly implement the second (*praxisintegrierend*) model and the states with FHS collaborations mostly implement the first (*ausbildungsintegrierend*) model and result in degrees recognized across the country.

[7] An online database ('AusbildungPlus') documents the number of dual study programmes and the participants therein (https://www.bibb.de/de/ausbildungplus_index.php). However, this data is still incomplete because the announcements and notifications in this database are voluntary. Only very recently, more efforts have been undertaken to collect the statistical data on dual study programmes in a more systematic fashion (BIBB 2017: 5; Wegweiser Duales Studium 2018). This is why the most recent figures are only partially comparable to previous years.

Table 10.1 Expansion of dual study programmes, 2004–2016

Year	Number of dual study programmes	Number of cooperating firms	Number of students
2004	512	18,168	40,982
2005	545	18,911	42,467
2006	608	22,003	43,536
2007	666	24,246	43,220
2008	687	24,572	43,991
2009	712	26,121	48,796
2010	776	27,900	50,764
2011	929	40,874	61,195
2011*	879	40,555	59,628
2012*	910	45,630	64,093
2013*	1,014	39,622	64,358
2014*	1,505	41,466	94,723
2015*	1,553	42,951	95,240
2016*	1,592	47,458	100,739

Source: BIBB 2017, 9.
Note: * indicates that these values only refer to study programmes for initial education and training (study programmes for further education might be included in previous years).

Relative to the overall size of the higher-education sector, dual study programmes still occupy a rather small segment (about 4% of all beginning students, cf. Meyer-Guckel et al. 2015: 16). However, the expansion of dual study programmes can be regarded as 'disproportionately relevant because they are increasingly diverting the most capable and motivated youths from [the] traditional system' of both apprenticeship training and classical higher-education studies (Graf 2018: 190). Studies have found that the educational background of students in dual study programmes is very similar to the background of students in regular higher-education programmes (Hähn 2015: 31; see also Gensch 2014: 2; for the case of Bavaria as well as Graf 2013: 115–16). In fact, a study of the vocational academies in Baden-Württemberg revealed that students in dual study programmes have completed the higher-education qualifying exam (Abitur) with grades that are as good or even slightly better compared to students in traditional university programmes (Graf 2013: 115–16). Despite their practical character, dual study programmes clearly are *not* second-best options for weak performers in schools, nor do they aim at integrating students from lower socio-economic backgrounds. (Indeed, competition for these slots is intense, with an average of 33 applications for each training position; see Kupfer 2013: 27) Instead, they have become important tools for firms to recruit the best students as early as possible in their educational careers (Graf 2018: 190).

In terms of subject matter and regional distribution, the dual study programmes are closely aligned with the needs of German industry, in particular large manufacturing and export-oriented companies (Durazzi and Benassi 2020). In 2018, 39 per cent of dual study programmes offered training in engineering, 48 per cent in business studies, finance, management, and economics, followed by IT (13%) as well as health (9%), public administration (6%), media, social services, and tourism (jointly 9%) (Wegweiser Duales Studium 2018: 11). The vast majority of dual study programmes are located at institutions at the centre of the German export economy, in Bavaria (20% of study programmes), North Rhine-Westphalia (26%) and Baden-Württemberg (21%) (Wegweiser Duales Studium 2018: 15). Durazzi and Benassi (2020) found a high correlation between the presence of large manufacturing firms in a given Land and the development of dual study programmes in that *Land*. Thus, both in terms of study subjects as well as regional distribution, dual study programmes correspond well with the needs of German industry.

10.3.2 Driving forces of change and employer influence in dual study programmes

Why have dual study programmes expanded so rapidly? What are the driving forces behind their growth? As argued above, we posit that the ultimate driving force of the expansion of dual study programmes are employers and their changing skill needs. However, the significant expansion in recent years is also due to changing educational behaviour of young people, i.e. students, and the complementary interests of higher-education institutions.

Starting with employers and their interests, dual study programmes are very attractive from the perspective of Germany's largest and most technically sophisticated export firms. For firms that rely increasingly on sophisticated technology and high-end theoretical skills, dual study programmes provide the kind of theoretical training associated with university education but also allow for a much stronger integration of practical and firm-specific content. In surveys, 97 per cent of employers who participate in such programmes give as their prime motivation the match between the study programme and the needs of work practice (Hähn 2015: 35; Kupfer 2013: 26). A second advantage for employers is that they themselves can select the students for dual study programmes, whereas in traditional university programmes, students are selected by the higher-education institutions, if at all (Durazzi and Benassi 2020: 10; Graf 2018). Since the selection criteria of universities and employers are not necessarily the same, employers have much more leeway in dual study programmes to screen for potential future workers. Indeed, firms invest heavily in screening the applicants to these programmes, e.g. testing applicants for several days in assessment centres (Kupfer et al. 2014: 31).

Moreover, unlike traditional university curricula, dual study programmes offer employers more influence over the design of the theoretical part of the study programme because when choosing their particular cooperation partner, employers can 'shop around' until they find a higher-education institution that is willing and able to offer a study programme that fits their needs (Becker 2006: 6, 36; Durazzi and Benassi 2020; Graf 2013: 100).[8] In some cases, this shopping-around results in employers choosing to partner with higher-education institutions located in a different region from their own (Graf 2018: 197). This represents an important difference to traditional dual apprenticeship training, where firms are obliged to work with the local vocational schools. The design of the study programme essentially depends on cooperation between individual employers (or groups of employers) and higher-education institutions. Studies have confirmed that the process of developing new dual study programmes is basically a 'bottom-up' process, with employers approaching higher-education institutions rather than study programmes being planned 'from above' by academics or governmental bureaucrats (Graf 2013: 99; Graf 2018; Hähn 2015: 40; Kupfer et al. 2014: 15, 25).

In short, compared to traditional university study programmes, employers have much more leeway in promoting practical and firm-specific skill needs. Moreover, compared to vocational training programmes in the dual system, individual employers do not have to cooperate and negotiate with employers' associations or trade unions. In the traditional corporatist process of devising and revising training profiles in dual apprenticeship training, employers with specific skill needs have to mobilize support within their respective employers' or trade association. For almost any significant change, the Federal Institute for Vocational Education and Training (the BIBB) would need to be brought in as well, which then sets in motion the complex, corporatist process of designing new training curricula (cf. Busemeyer 2009 for an overview). In this process, the demands of individual employers are confronted with the demands from other political stakeholders, in particular trade unions, as well as other employers' associations and government bureaucrats. Instituting a dual study programme is much simpler, since the

---

[8] Kupfer (2013: 27) reports that 67 per cent of participating firms mention this factor explicitly as a motivation to participate in dual study programmes.

individual employer only has to identify a higher-education institution that is willing to enter a cooperation agreement. Moreover, and again different from VET politics, trade unions are largely absent in the process of devising dual study programmes since there is no statutory role for them in the higher-education sector (Baethge 2015; Graf 2018). At the same time, even though employers have traditionally had little influence in higher-education governance as well, dual study programmes open up new avenues for employers to influence the content of education in that sector (Durazzi and Benassi 2020). Also sidelined are Länder governments, because while the school-based component of the traditional dual apprenticeship training takes place in vocational schools under Länder control, the content of the theoretical part of dual study programmes is set by the higher-education institution in more or less explicit collaboration with employers.

Dual study programmes are also much less regulated in other matters compared to traditional apprenticeship training (Becker 2006: 27). For instance, the Federal Law on Vocational Education and Training (Berufsbildungsgesetz—BBiG) explicitly prohibits employers from binding apprentices to the training firm after graduating from apprenticeship. Thus, firms have no legal instrument to recoup their sometimes-significant training investments should apprentices decide to leave the firm after the completion of training. The situation is different in the case of dual study programmes. Employers can (and do) enter contracts with student-apprentices that require graduates to stay with the training firm for a specific period of time or pay back the student subsidies. Forty-five per cent of firms participating in dual study programmes state that they indeed have contracts with binding clauses (*Bindungsklauseln*) included (Kupfer 2013).[9] This is effectively an insurance policy for firms against the risk of poaching.

Even though some of these regulations are disadvantageous for students, dual study programmes are still highly popular among young people for several reasons. First of all, dual-study student-apprentices usually receive some kind of compensation/wage. The exact nature (and level) of this allowance depends on the particular contract they conclude with their respective employers. Whatever the rate, however, dual-study students differ from their 'regular' university student counterparts because they receive financial support from employers. Furthermore, the chances for graduates of dual study programmes to be offered a job in their training firm are very high. Employers apply sophisticated test procedures to select students in the

---

[9] According to another recent study of the students in dual study programmes in Bavaria, 36 per cent of these students are required by contract to stay with the training firm for at least three years (Gensch 2014: 4).

first place and then use dual study programmes as screening devices for future high-skilled workers (Meyer-Guckel et al. 2015: 30). According to a survey among firms participating in dual study programmes conducted in 2012, 89 per cent of graduates from dual study programmes continue to be employed with their training firm (Kupfer 2013: 28). Finally, compared to a traditional vocational training programme, dual study programmes offer a more prestigious qualification, because they include elements of tertiary education.[10]

From the perspective of higher-education institutions and policymakers, dual study programmes are attractive because of their popularity with students, parents, and employers alike (Graf 2013: 110). For individual higher-education institutions, cooperating with well-known regional employers increases the prestige as well as the marketing value of these programmes, in particular if it can be shown that completing them leads to stable and well-paid employment (Kupfer et al. 2014: 16). Furthermore, establishing dual study programmes entails significant pecuniary benefits as well, because the cooperating firms might further contribute by financing personnel or providing equipment (Becker 2006: 31).

The rise of dual study programmes poses a challenge for trade unions, however. On the one hand, they welcome the fact that higher-education institutions are developing more practical and vocationally oriented study programmes. On the other hand, unions have little or no control over the content of dual study programmes (Graf 2013: 100). To the extent that the graduates of dual study programmes substitute for graduates of traditional apprenticeship training (for which there is some, though not conclusive evidence, see Baethge 2015; Baethge and Wolter 2015; Becker 2006: 44; Graf 2013: 111; Hähn 2015: 32; Krone 2015: 260), this could signal a significant shift in the balance of power if dual study programmes continue to expand as they have in the past years. Furthermore, wages and employment conditions for students in dual study programmes (in particular of the *praxisintegrierte* variety) are much less regulated compared to the traditional apprenticeship system. It might also be much more difficult to recruit student-apprentices for union work compared to regular apprentices.

In sum, the rise of dual study programmes is an impressive example of educational reform through initiatives promoted mostly by large employers in

---

[10] Dual study programmes do *not* necessarily open up new access routes to academic higher education for individuals with a vocational training background because a requirement for participating is a university entrance qualification—i.e. dual study participants would also anyway be eligible to enrol in regular university programmes.

the export sector who have acted as institutional entrepreneurs in the introduction and expansion of dual study programmes (Durazzi and Benassi 2020; Graf 2018: 194; Krone 2015: 248). Large firms both have the capacities (in terms of fiscal and personnel resources) and the need to develop this type of hybrid qualification. From the point of view of these employers, the skills provided within traditional vocational training are no longer sufficient, and traditional university studies are too theoretical. A recent survey confirms the dominance of large firms in dual study programmes: more than two-thirds of participating firms employ more than 250 employees (40% even more than 1,000 employees) (Kupfer et al. 2014: 24; see also Graf 2013: 108–9; Hähn 2015: 34). Therefore, the expansion of dual study programmes is part and parcel of the ongoing trend towards segmentalism in German skill formation (Durazzi and Benassi 2020; Graf 2018) as the centre of gravity in the skill formation process moves from small and medium-sized firms to larger firms. At the same time, if one adopts a broader perspective on the relationship between vocational and academic education that goes beyond the traditional apprenticeship system, the expansion of dual study programmes strengthens the vocational aspects of the German skill system as a whole, even though this comes at the price of more segmentalism.

10.4 Sweden: decentralization, marketization, and employer influence in public education

The problems facing Swedish industry are in some ways the opposite of those confronting German employers, though the solutions bear a strong family resemblance. As noted earlier, one of the longstanding deficits of Sweden's school-based system is that there is a looser connection to the labour market and with that, an overall rockier school-to-work transition for Swedish youth. Swedish employers have complained of a mismatch between the training system and their actual skill needs, and the failure of the system to connect strongly to the labour market (and thus jobs after graduation) likely also serves as a disincentive for students to choose vocational training, especially in a context in which the alternative academic track has for decades been open to all. However, if the problems are distinct, the trend is broadly familiar and, as in Germany, it involves partnerships between firms and public institutions, through in this case at the upper-secondary level in cooperation with municipal education authorities who are interested in promoting local economic growth and reducing youth unemployment.

As in Germany, the most important current initiatives have developed in a bottom-up fashion and through the initiatives of employers in manufacturing. Thus, one important innovation in Sweden has been the introduction, in some schools, of additional vocational training alongside the traditional (general) upper-secondary curriculum. These so-called *Teknikcolleges* are set up as partnerships between schools and local manufacturing firms and designed not to displace but to augment traditional school-based upper-secondary education by adding opportunities for acquiring additional practical firm-based experience.[11] The participation of Swedish unions may seem paradoxical, and it certainly departs from their traditional aversion to firm-based secondary training. However, these programmes supplement (rather than substitute for) the existing general secondary education curriculum, and unions share with employers an interest in reducing academic drift (which for them has been associated with declining membership) and with local authorities an interest in mitigating the country's chronically high levels of youth unemployment.

Experimentation in this area goes back to major school reforms undertaken by the centre-right government in the early 1990s. These reforms included two broad—analytically separate but empirically closely related—changes: the decentralization of authority for education from the central to the municipal level, and the privatization and associated increased competition in the education market by allowing for the entry of independent ('free') private schools (Blanchenay et al. 2014: 11). The reforms of this period aimed to enhance local autonomy and introduce greater flexibility to adapt education programmes to local needs. Overall, these reforms 'created a system in which national goals would be set by the central administration, while decisions and responsibilities on how to reach those goals would be left with municipalities' (Blanchenay et al. 2014: 8). School decentralization opened a window of opportunity for increased cooperation in many municipalities between upper-secondary schools (whether public or privately operated) and local employers. City governments are keen to strengthen the link between schools and the labour market, both to address youth unemployment and to promote economic growth. Local employers, for their part, are more than happy to cooperate in adapting school curricula to address their specific skill needs.

[11] The Teknikcollege programme on which we focus in this chapter is specifically by and for industry (which pioneered the model, and which is most widespread and successful such initiative). A similar initiative was launched for nursing and health care (Vård och omsorgscollege) based on cooperation between the Swedish Association of Local Authorities and Regions (SKL) and the Swedish Association of Health Professionals (Vårdförbundet). By contrast, a similar initiative in the service sector (Service College) failed (interview with representative of ALMEGA, the employers' association for services, January 2019).

10.4.1 Origins of the model: industriskolor

Just as Germany's dual study programmes build on older models pioneered by leading German firms, so too does the Swedish Teknikcollege model build on models pioneered by a few of Sweden's largest and most storied companies—Volvo, SKF, ABB, Scania, among others. These companies in fact directly operate their own upper-secondary schools—so-called enterprise schools (*industriskolor*). Some of these enterprise schools date back to the pre-WWII period, while others were founded after the reforms of the 1990s.[12] Two of the oldest are SKF Technical Gymnasium in Gothenburg, founded by the precision bearing manufacturer SKF in 1937, and Mälardalens Technical Gymnasium (MTG) in Södertälje (just outside Stockholm), founded in 1941 by Scania AB (a major producer of automobiles and commercial vehicles).[13]

These long-standing enterprise schools have been joined by new initiatives, typically joint ventures between prominent local companies and municipal governments. Examples include: Göranssonska skolan (Sandvikens tekniska gymnasium), founded in 2002 and jointly owned by the corporation Sandvik (91% ownership) and Sandvikens municipality (9%); Göteborgs tekniska gymnasium, founded in 1999 and co-owned by Volvo (51%) and the city of Gothenburg (49%); and Peabskolan, a group of five schools in different locations across Sweden, founded and run by Peab (construction and civil engineering) in 2006 (Persson 2014).[14]

This model of direct firm sponsorship of upper-secondary schools remains a rarity. Their more important function has been as a model for other, more modest initiatives, discussed later. Nonetheless, the foundings and refoundings of the late 1990s and early 2000s suggest enhanced interest, particularly on the part of municipal governments in the wake of the decentralization reforms discussed earlier. While there is no official register or even 'count',

[12] The following account of Sweden's enterprise schools draws heavily on Kristine Persson (2014), which is to our knowledge the only extended empirical study of Sweden's industry schools, based on interviews in five such schools.
[13] Since 2012 MTG has been run jointly by Scania and the pharma giant AstraZeneca, in cooperation with Telge, a corporate group operated by the Södertälje municipality (see http://www.malardalenstekniska.se/). Volvo also started an industrial school, in Skövde, in 1952. The resilience of these schools through the social democratic reforms of the 1960s is probably worthy of a study unto itself. The short version, however, is that these schools persevered thanks to the power and influence of the entrepreneurs who stood behind them and through ongoing adaptation to changes in the regulatory environment ('they just adapted what they were doing to conform to whatever new national rules were in place', according to Thomas Persson, former superintendent of Stockholm's public school system, interview January 2016).
[14] See also the government report (SOU 2015: 97, 205) which has a brief section on Företagsskolor and industrigymnasier.

experts estimate that there are between five and twelve such schools across the country, and they all list the same handful of companies, which reads like a who's who of Swedish industry—Volvo (Gothenburg Technical College), SKF, ABB, Sandvik, Scania, Peab. Even where the schools pre-date the school reforms of the early 1990s, some of these companies have used the opportunity of privatization to outsource the administration of the school by partnering with education firms or to forge more explicit partnerships with municipal governments, while however often maintaining the firm's 'brand'. No national statistics are maintained to capture the number of students these schools enrol, but Kristine Persson (2014) provides some figures on enrolments for the five schools she studied, where enrolments at the time of her study ranged from twenty to fifty students per year.[15]

All such schools were and remain local initiatives, whose terms are worked out between the companies and the municipalities in which they operate (and with whom they are often in partnership).[16] Whether they operate as part of the public school system or as independent or 'free schools', these technical gymnasiums are still required under the law to cover the same national curriculum as any other Swedish upper-secondary school—including the core curriculum of English, Swedish, history, mathematics, etc. As part of the official upper-secondary system, these schools also all get the same public funding as any other schools, though as we will see below, the companies often then contribute rather significant resources beyond this.

However, the industry schools augment the nationally required minima with additional training presumably geared to the specific needs of the firm or industry. Thus, for example, while all upper-secondary students in Sweden are required to spend a minimum of approximately twenty-five hours in classes,[17] industry schools often require students to attend school for forty hours per week, with the extra hours spent in additional courses— whether more technical or more theoretical—or in gathering practical experience in the firm (interviews January 2016). The practical component of the training in these schools thus goes well beyond the nationally mandated minimum (VET programmes at the upper-secondary level must offer a minimum of 15 weeks of work placement in firms over 3 years). At *Mälardalen Technical*

---

[15] Persson reports that GS enrolled 188 students in the spring of 2014 (across 3 years), MTG had 140 (again across 3 years). Scania enrolled about forty-eight students per year, SKF about sixty-five per year. GTC has about 350 students enrolled 'at any given time' and Peab (across 5 schools) educates 450–500 students.

[16] At least one such school—Volvogymnasiet in Skövde—used to partner with the local public upper-secondary school, but is now an independent school (*friskola*) (Persson 2014).

[17] It varies a bit depending on the particular programme in which they are enrolled—VET students having somewhat longer class times than academic programmes.

Gymnasium for example, students spend a minimum of twenty-six weeks in practical training. Since most of the firms sponsoring such schools are among the most technically sophisticated, many offer additional theoretical training alongside the practical components. At least one of them (Göteborgsregionens Tekniska Gymnasium) also offers advanced (post-secondary) training (Persson 2014).

A key difference to Germany is that the students are not apprentices within the firm (therefore also not paid) but rather upper-secondary students as at any other school. However, cooperating firms often offer opportunities for paid summer jobs and, in the case of Mälardalen, the possibility of receiving SEK1,000 in 'study bonuses' paid by the companies (http://www.malardalenstekniska.se/). Moreover, students are almost guaranteed six months employment after graduation in one of the participating companies. The quality of the training at all such industry schools is widely seen as extremely high (as a senior advisor at the Ministry of Education and Research put it, 'a dream education') and these programmes are highly selective. And as in Germany, companies find that the investment is well worth it for the way this system allows them to recruit especially promising upper-secondary students and train them for a career in the company (Persson 2014: 15).[18]

10.4.2 The diffusion of the model: Teknikcollege

Just as the German dual study model incubated in Baden-Württemberg was emulated by states and enterprises throughout that country, in Sweden, too, the core impetus behind the industrial school inspired further moves in this area. Thus, a more pervasive—albeit 'lighter'—version of some of the basic idea behind the industry schools is the 'technical college' (Teknikcollege—TC) initiative. Whereas *industriskolor* described in the previous section are an initiative of a few large companies, the Teknikcollege concept grows out of a national-level agreement between unions and employer associations in the engineering industry in the late 1990s.[19] A key reason that unions

[18] These leading Swedish companies are also involved in other initiatives designed to promote interest in the occupations they need. For example, Volvo launched the 'Second Step' project in five Gothenburg schools (including their 'own' Gothenburg Technical College). The project involves engineers employed at Volvo to collaborate with teachers from five upper-secondary schools in the city. Over the course of the year, the engineers themselves spend twenty hours teaching in the classroom and invest another forty hours in planning lessons with the teachers. The project takes place 'within the framework of the normal school curriculum' but it is designed to enhance interest among youth 'by providing real-life problems and challenges for the course, and by informing [students] about the breadth and scope of the engineering profession' (Volvo press release).

[19] On the genesis and growth of the Teknikcollege in Swedish engineering, see especially Persson and Hermelin (2018). The parties to the agreement, whose representatives sit in the national steering

do not oppose these programmes is that they *supplement* rather than supplant the common upper-secondary curriculum. These add-ons are seen as a way to provide youth with vocational skills and smooth the school-to-work transition in a country long plagued by high levels of youth unemployment.

Any upper-secondary school whose industry programmes are brought into conformity with eight criteria defined by the national steering committee is eligible to be certified as a Teknikcollege.[20] Most of the criteria are expressions of general principles and goals. Thus, for example, the criteria stress that the training should seek close integration of training to local business needs, that the training be conducted in a 'creative, stimulating learning environment', that the training should follow a coherent educational plan, and that the training facilities be outfitted with the appropriate equipment.

Some of the more specific elements of the Teknikcollege model represent an effort to emulate some of the features of the industrial schools just discussed. As usual, the schools must conform to the national curriculum. However, similar to industrial schools (and different from 'regular' public schools), students are expected to spend forty hours per week at the school (i.e. going significantly beyond the mandatory 20–25 hours). And as with the industry schools, the additional time can be spent in supplementary courses (e.g. more theoretical training on the university track within the upper-secondary schools),[21] or it could be spent acquiring more practical experience (though this would be less than at the industry schools which are on or near company premises). Beyond this, the extra time is simply filled with homework, since part of the idea is to acclimatize students to a regular working day.

The timing of the Teknikcollege initiatives (planning began in the late 1990s) suggests that the school reform in the early 1990s played a role in preparing the ground for this initiative, particularly regarding the aspect of administrative decentralization. A majority of TC's are public institutions,[22] but municipalities offering these tracks are often quite eager to have this certification as a way to demonstrate close connections to local business (to facilitate the mandatory fifteen-week work placements, to enhance

---

committee—Industrirådet—include the unions IF Metall, Unionen, and Sveriges Ingenjörer, along with the employers' associations Teknikföretagen, Industri Arbetsgivarna, Trä & Möbel företagen, Livsmedelsföretagen, Industri och Kemigruppen, and Facket för Skogs-, Trä- och Grafisk Bransch.

[20] The criteria are available at www.teknikcollege.se/certifiering.

[21] A full regular programme is 2,500 credits but these TCs have to offer 2,800 (though they cannot demand that pupils take this, in practice they do). And whereas the regular school-based VET track requires students to spend fifteen weeks in a firm context (5 weeks per year over 3 years), some TCs provide additional practical training.

[22] According to information published by the advisory council for TCs in 2013, there are '*138 godkända enskilda utbildningsanordnare*' (138 approved 'individual' educational providers), while 180 TCs involved municipalities. A government source with 2014 data counts 143 certified educational providers and 180 municipalities (SOU 2015: 97, 187).

later job prospects for students, and possibly to receive some extra funding or equipment from affiliated firms). Decentralization offers the possibility for municipal-level school officials to work with local industry to shape the course offerings (within parameters set by the core curriculum) to maximize overlap with local skill needs. Thus, beyond the core upper-secondary curriculum, the particular mix of specializations offered at a school are jointly decided by local school administrators in collaboration with local business partners.[23]

Unlike in the case of Germany's dual study programme, Swedish unions do have a role in the Teknikcollege system, as one of the sponsoring parties and through their participation in the national steering committee that oversees the programme and decides which schools qualify to be certified as Teknikcolleges. The national steering committee is composed of representatives of all the unions (blue and white collar) in manufacturing, as well as a wide variety of employers' associations in industry (see again footnote 20). Below the national level, twenty-four regional steering committees then exercise closer oversight over the programmes in their jurisdictions. These regional committees appoint regional project managers—sometimes a representative from one of the companies, sometimes from the school or a regional school authority—who are responsible for monitoring the schools in their jurisdiction, and evaluating the teachers and the equipment to ensure that the training fulfils the criteria for the programme. These project managers receive some training by the Teknikcollege and are paid a stipend—which according to experts, amounts to about 10 per cent of their income. They are encouraged to network among themselves to exchange information and share best practices.

Importantly, however, these oversight committees only certify the schools (determining whether they meet the criteria required to bear the Teknikcollege designation), but not the students. Thus, in contrast to the German dual system, there is no system for standardizing or certifying the skills or the training that students receive at the TC. The content of training is worked out locally between the schools and local companies, and the specializations offered are a function of what companies in the region want and need in terms of skills. The primacy of employer interests is reflected in the Teknikcollege

---

[23] The industrial technology programme (the VET track for industry) includes a number of foundational subjects: English, history, physical education and health, mathematics, natural sciences, religion, social studies, and Swedish or Swedish as a second language. Beyond this, students choose one of four different programme-specific subject areas: industrial technological processes, people in industry, production knowledge, and production equipment. Within these broad designations, students specialize further in specific programme specializations that vary from school to school—it is here where firms work with schools to encourage the school to offer particular specializations (see Skolverket 13 August 2012).

certification criteria themselves, which make clear that the participating firms should dominate the organization and management of individual TCs to ensure that the training is well aligned to the needs of local business (www. teknikcollege.se/certifiering).

2016 marked the tenth anniversary since the first Teknikcollege was certified, and since then a significant share of the upper-secondary schools that offer the industrial programmes carry the Teknikcollege label. Currently over three thousand companies offer Teknikcollege programmes in cooperation with 150 educational institutions across Sweden (www.teknikcollege. se). Government sources suggest that approximately sixteen thousand students are enrolled in these programmes (Teknikcollege i siffror 2107/18).[24] While this constitutes a small percentage of any individual cohort, these programmes cover a significant share of those upper-secondary students who are specifically interested in going into industry (and have therefore chosen either the Industrial Technology programme (VET track) or the Technology programme (academic track) in school.

The Teknikcollege model is popular with manufacturing firms because it offers employers the opportunity of inserting practical training at the upper-secondary level and can also serve as a valuable recruitment tool. As such, the model better meets the dual objectives noted at the outset—of increasing the practical components of education while also maintaining a curriculum that emphasizes the general theoretical skills they increasingly demand. For unions, the Teknikcollege does not replace but supplements general upper-secondary studies. The pathway to university thus remains open to students, while the TCs provide an option for those who choose it to acquire practical skills and in-firm experience, thus easing the transition into work for those who opt out of continuing their studies at a post-secondary level. Municipal and national education authorities value the programme as a way to reduce youth unemployment by strengthening ties between upper-secondary education and regional labour markets.

10.5 Conclusion

This chapter documents similar trends in two otherwise quite contrasting cases, towards increased employer involvement in education and in shaping some of the content of training in the public and private general educational

---

[24] For reference: there are approximately 100,000 youth in each cohort, of which approximately 98 per cent go to upper secondary. Thus, these figures must be seen in relation to the approximately 294,000 students in the upper-secondary system at any one time (98,000 per year x 3 years).

institutions with which they partner. As is usually the case in advanced industrial democracies, these reforms have not happened in a 'big bang', but in an incremental manner and often in the form of institutional layering as new institutions have been established alongside existing ones. We posit that the driving force behind this trend is the advent of the knowledge economy—associated with both the changing skill needs of employers and the problem of academic drift in these two countries, and in both cases, employers have taken the initiative by making use of existing institutional 'gaps', or windows of opportunity. In so doing, they have gradually expanded their role in the provision of education—in Sweden at the upper-secondary level and in Germany at the intersection of VET and higher education. In Germany, other stakeholders, primarily the state, but increasingly unions and education institutions as well, have mostly followed the lead of business actors. In Sweden, the Teknikcollege programme by design reflects a more collaborative process in which unions are involved at the level of the national steering committee, though as in Germany the content of the training itself reflects first and foremost the needs of the firms.

The fact that similar dynamics can be observed in the otherwise quite different cases of Germany and Sweden holds generalizable implications for other countries as well. Many policymakers are keen on expanding employer involvement in skill formation due to its real and perceived benefits on the labour market integration of youth. The general implication of our analysis is that it provides evidence in support of the central dilemma of collective skill formation identified in Chapter 1 of this volume by Bonoli and Emmenegger (see also Carstensen and Ibsen 2019, in this volume).

On the one hand, many of the reforms outlined in this chapter enhance the 'efficiency' of skill formation in the sense of ensuring a supply of high-skilled workers for increasingly demanding jobs and improving the match of training with employers' needs. Furthermore, students and parents often welcome new types of education, which are closer to the needs of the labour market. Improving the link between education and employment contributes to smooth transitions between these sectors and to lower levels of youth unemployment. In contrast to liberal market economies, such as the United States, students and apprentices in European coordinated market economies still enjoy strong support from the public sector during their studies and may even receive a salary instead of paying tuition fees (Graf and Powell 2017).

On the other hand, the subordination of educational needs to more short-term requirements of the labour market in the name of 'employability' might contribute to a redefinition of the purpose of education with potentially negative consequences for social inclusion in the long run (Carstensen and Ibsen 2019; Durazzi and Benassi 2020; Durazzi and Geyer 2020). Even though the reforms analysed in this chapter have often been supported by stakeholders other than business, employers have become and remain 'pivotal actors' (Busemeyer 2012) in these new arrangements, constituting a high degree of dependence on the part of state actors on the continued commitment of employers (Busemeyer and Thelen 2020). This is a significant difference to the politics of skill formation in the 1970s and 1980s, where policymakers often implemented policies geared at the promotion of educational and social mobility, which often went along with infringements of the leeway of employers in VET (Carstensen and Ibsen (2019) report a similar trajectory of the case of Denmark). Time will tell whether the inclusive potential of a more segmentalist, employer-driven skill formation system is sufficiently high in order to maintain the high level of support for dual training schemes among stakeholders other than business.

References

Baethge, Martin. 2015. 'Die schleichende Erosion im Governance-Modell des deutschen Berufsbildungssystems'. In *Wandel der Governance der Erwerbsarbeit*, edited by Irene Dingeldey, Aandré Holtrup, and Günther Warsewa, pp. 273–99. Wiesbaden: Springer VS.

Baethge, Martin, and Andrä Wolter. 2015. 'The German Skill Formation Model in Transition: From Dual System of VET to Higher Education?' *Journal of Labour Market Research* 48: 97–112.

Becker, Andreas. 2006. *Duale Studiengänge. Eine Übersichtsstudie im Auftrag der IG Metall-Jugend*, Frankfurt am Main: IG Metall Vorstand. Ressort Jugendarbeit und -politik. http://www.dhbw-studium.igm.de/static/qualitaet/file.duale.studiengaenge.pdf [accessed 12 September 2021].

BIBB (Bundesinstitut für Berufsbildung) (ed.). 2017: *AusbildungPlus Duales Studium in Zahlen 2016: Trends und Analysen*. Bonn: Bundesinstitut für Berufsbildung.

Blanchenay, Patrick, Tracey Burns, and Florian Köster. 2014. *Shifting Responsibilities: 20 Years of Education Devolution in Sweden*. OECD Education Working Papers No. 104. Paris: OECD Publishing.

Busemeyer, Marius R. 2009. *Wandel trotz Reformstau: Die Politik der beruflichen Bildung seit 1970*, Frankfurt a. M., New York: Campus.

Busemeyer, Marius R. 2012. 'Business as a Pivotal Actor in the Politics of Training Reform: Insights from the Case of Germany'. *British Journal of Industrial Relations* 50 (4): 690–713.

Busemeyer, Marius R. 2015. *Skills and Inequality: The Political Economy of Education and Training Reforms in Western Welfare States.* Cambridge: Cambridge University Press.

Busemeyer, Marius R., and Kathleen Thelen. 2020. 'Institutional Sources of Business Power'. *World Politics 72* (3): 448–80.

Carstensen, Martin B., and Christian L. Ibsen. 2019. 'Three Dimensions of Institutional Contention: Efficiency, Equality and Governance in Danish Vocational Education and Training Reform'. *Socio-Economic Review*. OnlineFirst. https://doi.org/10.1093/ser/mwz012.

Crouch, Colin, David Finegold, and Mari Sako. 1999. *Are Skills the Answer? The Political Economy of Skill Creation in Advanced Industrial Countries.* Oxford: Oxford University Press.

Dobbins, Michael, and Marius R. Busemeyer. 2015. 'Socio-economic Institutions, Organized Interests and Partisan Politics: The Development of Vocational Education in Denmark and Sweden'. *Socio-Economic Review 13* (2): 259–84.

Durazzi, Niccolo, and Chiara Benassi. 2020. 'Going Up-Skill: Exploring the Transformation of the German Skill Formation System'. *German Politics 29* (3): 319–38.

Durazzi, Niccolo, and Leonard Geyer. 2020. 'Social Inclusion in the Knowledge Economy: Unions' Strategies and Institutional Change in the Austrian and German Training Systems'. *Socio-Economic Review 18* (1): 103–24.

Gangl, Markus. 2003. 'The Structure of Labour Market Entry in Europe: A Typological Analysis'. In *Transitions from Education to Work in Europe: The Integration of Youth into EU Labour Markets,* edited by Walter Müller and Markus Gangl, pp. 107–28. Oxford: Oxford University Press.

Gensch, Kristina. 2014. *Dual Studierende in Bayern-sozioökonomische* Merkmale, *Zufriedenheit, Perspektiven.* Munich: Bayerisches Staatsinstitut für Hochschulforschung und Hochschulplanung. http://www.ihf.bayern.de/uploads/media/IHF_Studien_zur_Hochschulforschung-84.pdf [accessed 12 September 2021].

Graf, Lukas. 2013. *The Hybridization of Vocational Training and Higher Education in Austria, Germany, and Switzerland.* Opladen: Budrich UniPress.

Graf, Lukas. 2018. 'Combined Modes of Gradual Change: The Case of Academic Upgrading and Declining Collectivism in German Skill Formation'. *Socio-Economic Review 16* (1): 185–205.

Graf, Lukas, and Justin J. W. Powell. 2017. 'How Employer Interests and Investments Shape Advanced Skill Formation'. *PS: Political Science and Politics 50* (2): 418–22.

Hähn, Katharina. 2015. 'Das duale Studium—Stand der Forschung'. In *Dual Studieren im Blick. Entstehungsbedingungen, Interessenlagen und Umsetzungserfahrungen in dualen Studiengängen,* edited by Sirikit Krone, pp. 29–50. Wiesbaden: Springer VS.

Halldén, Karin. 2008. 'The Swedish Educational System and Classifying Education Using the ISCED-97'. In *The International Standard of Classification of Education (ISCED-97). An Evaluation of Content and Criterion Validity for 15 European Countries*, edited by Silke L. Schneider, pp. 253–67. Mannheim: Mannheimer Zentrum für Europäische Sozialforschung (MZES).

Krone, Sirikit. 2015. 'Zusammenfassung und Ausblick'. In *Dual Studieren im Blick. Entstehungsbedingungen, Interessenlagen und Umsetzungserfahrungen in dualen Studiengängen*, edited by Sirikit Krone, pp. 247–62. Wiesbaden: Springer VS.

Kupfer, Franziska. 2013. 'Duale Studiengänge aus Sicht der Betriebe—Praxisnahes Erfolgsmodell durch Bestenauslese'. *Berufsbildung in Wissenschaft und Praxis (BWP)*, April. https://www.bwp-zeitschrift.de/de/bwp.php/de/bwp/show/7105.

Kupfer, Franziska, Christa Kolter, and Christiane Köhlmann-Eckel. 2014. *Analyse und Systematisierung dualer Studiengänge an Hochschulen. Abschlussbericht*. Bonn: Bundesinstitut für Berufsbildung.

Meyer-Guckel, Volker, Sigrun Nickel, Vitus Püttmann, and Ann-Katrin Schröder-Kralemann (eds). 2015. *Qualitätsentwicklung im dualen Studium. Ein Handbuch für die Praxis*. Essen: Stifterverband für die Deutsche Wissenschaft.

Minks, Karl-Heinz, Nicolai Netz, and Daniel Völk. 2011. *Berufsbegleitende und duale Studienangebote in Deutschland: Status quo und Perspektiven*. Hannover: Hochschul-Informations-System (HIS).

Persson, Bo, and Brita Hermelin. 2018. 'Mobilising for Change in Vocational Education and Training in Sweden: A Case Study of the "Technical College" Scheme'. *Journal of Vocational Education and Training 70* (3): 476–96.

Persson, Kristine. 2014. *Effekter av abretsplatsförlagt lärande på företag*. Ratio Report No. 14. Stockholm: Ratio Research Institute.

Pfeffer, Fabian T. 2008. 'Persistent Inequality in Educational Attainment and its Institutional Context'. *European Sociological Review 24* (5): 543–65.

Powell, Justin J. W., and Heike Solga. 2011. 'Why Are Higher Education Participation Rates in Germany So Low? Institutional Barriers to Higher Education Expansion'. *Journal of Education and Work 24* (1–2): 49–68.

Skocpol, Theda, and Margaret Somers. 1980. 'The Uses of Comparative History in Macrosocial Inquiry'. *Comparative Studies in Society and History 22* (2): 174–97.

SOU—Statens Offentliga Utredningar. 2015. *Välja yrke*, Stockholm: Statens Offentliga Utredningar.

Streeck, Wolfgang, and Kathleen Thelen. 2005. 'Introduction: Institutional Change in Advanced Political Economies'. In *Beyond Continuity: Institutional Change in Advanced Political Economies*, edited by Wolfgang Streeck and Kathleen Thelen, pp. 1–39. Oxford: Oxford University Press.

Thelen, Kathleen. 2014. *Varieties of Liberalization and the New Politics of Social Solidarity*. Cambridge: Cambridge University Press.

Thelen, Kathleen, and Marius R. Busemeyer. 2012. 'Institutional Change in German Vocational Training: From Collectivism toward Segmentalism'. In *The Political Economy of Collective Skill Formation*, edited by Marius R. Busemeyer and Christine Tampusch, pp. 68–100. Oxford: Oxford University Press.

Wegweiser Duales Studium. 2018. *Duales Studium 2018: Statistiken & Trends*, Cologne: Wegweiser-Duales-Studium.de.

Wolbers, Maarten H. J. 2007. 'Patterns of Labour Market Entry: A Comparative Perspective on School-to-Work Transitions in 11 European Countries'. *Acta Sociologica* 50 (3): 189–210.

11
Employers' Cooperation in the Knowledge Economy

Continuing Vocational Training in Switzerland

Gina Di Maio and Christine Trampusch

11.1 Introduction

When do employers co-provide and co-finance transferable skills? The knowledge economy requires investments and cooperation between employers in training and education more than ever (see Bonoli and Emmenegger, in this volume). In this context, not only is initial educational qualification crucial but especially further training and continuing education throughout the working life plays a significant role in keeping skills up to date. Continuing vocational training (CVT) is an important means to deepen and update occupational skills while expanding managerial competences.

However, most studies on collective action in training focus on initial vocational training (IVT), thereby often overlooking the politics and the institutional context of CVT even though there may be substantial differences between CVT and IVT (Bowman 2005: 572–4; Cognard 2011, 2015; Crouch et al. 1999: 21; Johansen 2002). Furthermore, research on CVT tends to be biased towards firm-based training or national training policies (on which see Trampusch and Eichenberger 2012), overlooking sectoral policies. Thus, the questions of what gets employers to cooperate in the provision of transferable, vocational, and certified skills through CVT and which patterns of employers' cooperation evolve on the sectoral level still need further examination.

Our study focuses on sectoral differences of employers' cooperation through associations in CVT in Switzerland to address this question.[1] Within

[1] We would like to thank our twenty-six interview partners for sharing their insights and knowledge about the functioning of the Swiss continuing vocational training (CVT) system with us. Also, we would

Gina Di Maio and Christine Trampusch, *Employers' Cooperation in the Knowledge Economy*. In: *Collective Skill Formation in the Knowledge Economy*. Edited by Giuliano Bonoli and Patrick Emmenegger, Oxford University Press.
© Oxford University Press (2022). DOI: 10.1093/oso/9780192866257.003.0011

the big pool of CVT, we focus on a specific type of CVT: post-secondary, tertiary, vocational training that leads to standardized and nationally recognized certificates. In Switzerland, this training is referred to as Higher Vocational Training (HVT, *Höhere Berufsbildung (HBB)*) and it makes up 44 per cent of all tertiary certificates awarded at the level of a bachelor's degree (SKBF 2018: 272). HVT is deeply rooted in the Swiss vocational training system and about every fourth employee who completed initial vocational training holds an HVT degree (BFS 2009: 4).

We chose to study Switzerland because 'in terms of economic governance' the Swiss political economy 'relies extensively on collective or associational self-regulation in various economic and social spheres' (Mach and Trampusch 2011: 16), accompanied by a weak central state and weak and fragmented unions (Mach and Trampusch 2011: 16; see also Eichenberger and Mach 2011; Kriesi and Farago 1989; Trampusch 2020). However, in contrast to German chambers, the role of Swiss business in training is not 'licensed' by compulsory membership of their associations. Therefore, Switzerland allows the gaining of deeper insights into the underlying reasons for employers' cooperation. Furthermore, the Swiss collective skill formation system is characterized by employers' dominance at the industry level (Rohrer and Trampusch 2011: 148), thereby allowing us to conduct an in-depth study of sectoral differences. Finally, HVT is mainly based on theory instruction by private and public providers and equips employees with an occupation and work experience with a tertiary upgrade of their vocational certificate. HVT increases employees' professional knowledge while providing entrepreneurship and leadership skills (Fazekas and Field 2013: 27). Thus, these skills are transferable between firms and thus there is a danger of poaching and the free-rider problem. This raises the question as to why employers are willing to cooperate in order to collectively provide and finance HVT.

We focus on four sectors—the construction sector, the metal and mechanical engineering (MEM) sector, the banking sector, and the pharmaceutical-chemical sector—which differ in the intensity of employer cooperation in the provision and financing of training. Our study not only describes different *intensities* of sectoral employers' cooperation but also explains how the combination of different factors can foster or hinder cooperation.

Our analysis contributes to the literature about employers' collective action in vocational and further training (Bowman 2005; Cognard 2011,

like to thank our GOVPET team which includes the helpful comments and feedback of Carmen Baumeler and Philipp Gonon for inspiring discussions on the Swiss vocational education and training (VET) system. We gratefully acknowledge the helpful feedback of the participants of the book workshop 'Skill Formation in the Knowledge Economy' which took place in November 2019 in St. Gallen, Switzerland.

2015; Culpepper 2007; Trampusch and Eichenberger 2012) and to studies of business associations (Kriesi and Farago 1989; Schmitter and Streeck 1999; Streeck 1989). It identifies a configuration of conditions that help to explain the different levels of collective action in the provision and financing of portable vocational skills through CVT. More specifically, we find that employers' associations cooperate in order to provide and finance skills when: (1) they rely on internal labour markets for recruitment, (2) there are institutional spill-over effects between employers' cooperation in initial and continuous vocational training, (3) large firms are committed to collective training, (4) there is a tradition of collective labour agreements (CLAs), (5) employers' associations' logic of organization building includes training policies as an important means to attract members, and (6) they do not prefer universities (of applied sciences) as an alternative and substitutive track to enhance the general skills of their employees.

The period under investigation runs from the mid-1990s until 2017. Data were collected from primary documents and secondary literature. In addition, we conducted twenty-six expert interviews. For all four sectors, we covered representative firms, key HVT providers, employees' as well as employers' associations, trade and occupational associations.[2] Our study distils hypotheses on potential causal factors determining employers' collective action in HVT from the above-mentioned strands of literature and tests for their plausibility by a four-sector comparison.

This chapter is structured as follows. The second section presents the main characteristics of the Swiss HVT system. We also explain our concept of employers' cooperation. In section 3, we map our theoretical framework and discuss the method. Section 4 displays our empirical findings by comparing our four case histories. The last section draws conclusions.

11.2 The Swiss HVT system and conceptualizing employers' cooperation

HVT aims to prepare students for vocational leadership positions (*fachspezifische Kaderpositionen*). The training is based mainly on theory instruction with classes taking place one or two days a week. Participants work 70–90 per cent in a related area but this is not counted as part of the training. HVT is a crucial factor in keeping the VET system attractive for good students

---

[2] At the request of our interviewees, we treat all information in strict confidence. Therefore, the list of the interviews which contains information about the affiliated institution and position of the interviewee is kept anonymous. In the main text we indicate only the respective sector.

because it is an important means of climbing the career ladder (INT10). In Switzerland, about two-thirds of a cohort opts for dual vocational training after compulsory schooling (SBFI 2017). In 2016, more than 26,300 HVT diplomas[3] were awarded in Switzerland (BFS 2017b).

HVT has a long tradition in Switzerland, but two major reforms have restructured it. First, with the introduction of universities of applied sciences (UoAs) in the 1990s more than half of the HVT tracks were turned into bachelor's and master's degrees (Baumeler et al. 2014: 21; Graf 2013). At the same time, the Federal Vocational Baccalaureate (FVB; *Berufsmaturität*) was introduced. The vocational baccalaureate can be obtained in parallel or after dual apprenticeship training and enables the graduate to enter a bachelor's degree programme at a university of applied sciences. Even though HVT is by law equal to higher education, it is thus challenged. The introduction of the vocational baccalaureate established a path for holders of a vocational certificate to enter UoAs. Thus, it opens an attractive alternative to HVT because graduates of UoAs receive an internationally recognized bachelor's degree and tuition fees are quite low in comparison to HVT (Graf 2013; INT16).

The second major reform came with the new VET law of 2004 (see Bürgi et al., in this volume). The law defines HVT as the 'tertiary B' level in the Swiss educational system which lifts it to the same level as universities and UoAs ('tertiary A' sector). Furthermore, the 2004 reform enhanced the possibility of establishing binding sector-specific training funds. The government can turn sector-specific voluntary funds into 'binding' funds, which means that all employers of a certain sector are obliged to contribute. This strengthening of collective training funds was strongly supported by the Swiss Union of Small Businesses and Trade (SGV 2004; Trampusch 2010b; INT2) which plays a major role in the Swiss VET system and is dominated by the small and medium-sized firms of the *Gewerbe* (crafts) (INT2). These sector-specific funds complement a complex system of cantonal funds and those anchored in the CLAs, some of which were established in the 1960s and 1970s (Fluder 1991: 339, 355; Wicki 1991: 449, 451).

Baumeler et al. (2014: 32) offer a detailed overview of the complex Swiss HVT system. They highlight that HVT is characterized by great regional differences, with 80 per cent of it occurring in the German-speaking part. Companies, especially small and medium-sized enterprises (SMEs) and those operating at the nexus of theoretical development and its practical application, seem to benefit from HVT. As with IVT, the content and examinations

---

[3] Swiss HVT offers three different diplomas: (1) the Federal PET Diploma (*eidgenössischer Fachausweis*), (2) the Advanced Federal PET Diploma (*Eidgenössisches Diplom*), (3) professional college's diplomas (*Höhere Fachschulen* (HF)).

are organized along occupational lines which means that the associations develop the training content. However, as there is no regulation on how to provide and finance higher VET, there is great variation in the investment by employers in collective training activities. No study systematically maps and explains this.

In our study, we are interested in what makes employers cooperate in order to collectively provide and finance HVT. Cooperation is the 'pursuit of a common interest' (Bowman 1982: 575). When it comes to the provision and financing of portable skills there is a danger of free-rider firms poaching the skilled labour force. Consequently, firms may be less willing to encourage candidates to upgrade their skills (Culpepper 2003; Marsden 1999). This also may reduce employers' willingness to invest in collective training activities. Employers' associations are seen as a way to overcome this problem (Streeck 1989). Employers' associations bundle competences and act on behalf of their members. They can be regarded as institutionalized cooperation among employers and may solve collective action problems by providing selective incentives (Crouch et al. 1999: 18, 28; Johansen 1999: 103). For this reason, we take into account the activities of the key employers' associations in the four sectors to describe the different *intensities* of employers' cooperation. Our theory section lists probable factors affecting employers' associations' willingness and capacities to provide and finance HVT courses. We concentrate on these two key tasks of the governance of training because we observe different patterns of employers' cooperation in the implementation of these tasks. Thus, our dependent variable is represented by the involvement of the employers' associations in the provision and financing of higher vocational training.

11.3 Employers and HVT: Theory and method

Although disentangling specific and general skills is not easy (Busemeyer 2009a, 2009b; Culpepper and Finegold 1999: 3; e.g. Streeck 2012), it is most often argued that one major factor affecting employers' investment decisions is skill specificity. Following Becker's classic human capital account, one major finding is that the more the skills are marketable and portable among firms (which means that these skills increase productivity in the non-training firm as well), the less likely it becomes that firms will invest in such training (Becker 1962). As the Swiss HVT schemes aim at providing employees (who in most cases already have a job) with transferable skills which are certified, it is reasonable to assume that potential employers' investments in institutions providing this type of training are particularly prone to the collective good dilemma.

The literature on collective skill formation systems highlights that persuading individual firms to cooperate in providing and financing transferable skills requires cost-effective incentives or sanctions (Streeck 1989; Crouch et al. 1999; Culpepper and Finegold 1999; Johansen 2002; Bowman 2005; Busemeyer and Trampusch 2012). However, in particular with regard to CVT, explaining variations in employers' cooperation at the industry level has been neglected so far. In order to understand employers' collective action in Swiss HVT properly, our study brings together the literature on employers' collective action in IVT and CVT (Bowman 2005; Crouch et al. 1999; Johansen 2002; Trampusch and Eichenberger 2012) with studies of employers' associations (Kriesi and Farago 1989; Streeck 1989; Traxler 2010). The first strand of literature highlights the impact of institutions linked to labour markets on employers' associations' willingness and capacity to provide and finance training (Marsden 1999). The second one shows that employers' associations may use employers' cooperation in HVT as a selective incentive to increase their own membership and use collective CVT as an instrument for their internal interest.

11.3.1 Employers' collective action in initial and CVT

Previous studies on employers' collective action in IVT have identified the following five conditions prompting employers to invest in transferable skills: the *skill requirements of production regimes* (e.g. high-quality goods and services); the *certification* of skills; *state intervention and public policies* sponsoring employers' activities (e.g. state subsidies, tax reductions); the impossibility of hiring the required general skills on the external labour market in combination with the *existence of internal labour markets* (e.g. as firms believe that employment security and good working conditions help to retain workers (Soskice 1994: 32)); and, finally, the *tradition of CLAs* leading to wage compression and to collectively negotiated measures sponsoring training (Bowman 2005; Busemeyer and Trampusch 2012; Culpepper 2007; Soskice 1994; Streeck et al. 1987; Thelen 2004).

Even though studies of IVT identified these factors as crucial, we expect them to be also influential in encouraging employers to invest in CVT. However, we should also acknowledge that the politics as well as the institutional context of CVT may substantially differ from that of IVT (Bowman 2005: 572–4; Cognard 2011; Crouch et al. 1999: 21). Firstly, we may expect that the heterogeneity of employers' preferences for investing in transferable skills is even greater in CVT than in IVT (Trampusch and Eichenberger 2012). In contrast to large firms, SMEs are against any measures which enhance the general skill profile of their employees (Culpepper 2007: 616) because they are less able to bear the generally higher costs as well as the administrative load of CVT (Cognard 2011: 31). Large firms can usually rely on internal labour markets (Soskice 1994: 31–2) and are more likely to have production strategies which require general skills and can therefore maintain and protect their managerial prerogative (Bowman 2005: 579). Collective action in CVT may depend much more *on large firms' commitment* than for IVT. Secondly, the *institutional set-up of IVT may create spill-over effects* on employers' investments in CVT (Aventur et al. 1999: 2) because the institutional infrastructure which supports employers' cooperation in IVT may also enhance employers' collective action in further training. Such spill-over effects can be affected by the educational or cultural background of managers, HR authorities, and the headquarters' corporate identity (Ballauf 2011: 15; Beck et al. 2009: 1374; Muehlemann 2014). A third specificity of CVT to be acknowledged is that those forms of CVT which provide transferable and certified skills are also subject to *intensified competition with higher education programmes*. Employers may view the tertiary academic schemes of universities (of applied sciences) as alternative tracks to enhance the general skills of their employees but the competition with higher education institutions may likewise prompt employers to bring academic options together with the vocational principle in order to maintain the dual training system as an instrument in career advancement (Gonon 2013). In Switzerland this competitive relationship between HVT and the university track has further intensified with the introduction of the vocational baccalaureate (Graf 2013; INT16).

11.3.2 Employers' associations

Employers' associations organize collective interests and contribute to collective goods in the labour market and the industrial relation system (e.g. Coleman and Jacek 1989; Eichenberger and Ginalski 2017: 620; Streeck 1990, 27). In the literature on employers' associations, we find only a little empirical research on industry-level differences in employers' associations training activities (exceptions are: Johansen 1999; Streeck et al. 1987). However, Schmitter and Streeck (1999) develop a theoretical framework for analysing variation in the structure and tasks of business associations. These authors suggest that two bundles of factors (Schmitter and Streeck 1999: 21), namely the logic of membership (which refers to their members' interests) and the logic of influence (which refers to how employers' associations interact with the state and unions) affect employers' associations' collective economic and political activities. Schmitter and Streeck (1999: 14–15) also highlight the major influence of business associability, thus the heterogeneity in business interests and how this heterogeneity is reflected in employers' associations' organizing capacities. This leads us to assume that employers' associations use CVT as an organizational device and selective incentive to recruit members and to mediate internal interest heterogeneity. In other words, we assume that industry-level differences in employers' cooperation in the provision and financing of CVT is strongly linked to the *logic of organization building* in which the 'management of diversity' (Schmitter and Streeck 1999: 15) plays a crucial role. Recently, the studies by Brandl and Lehr (2019), Johansen (1999, 2002), and Cognard (2011, 2015) have confirmed these considerations.

To sum up, the following conditions might influence employers' associations' cooperation in CVT: (1) *skill requirements*, (2) *certification* of skills, (3) *state intervention and public policies*, (4) *existence of internal labour markets*, (5) *tradition of CLAs*, (6) *large firms' commitment*, (7) *competition with higher education schemes*, (8) *spill-over effects of collectively organized IVT*, (9) employers' associations' *logic of organization building* (HVT is used as a means to recruit members). Thus, previous studies give us a net of nine conditions influencing employers' collective action in IVT and CVT. In our comparison across sectors, we seek to identify which specific configuration of conditions have made employers' associations' willingness to provide and finance HVT courses more likely and which of the above-mentioned conditions can be excluded by our comparison.

11.3.3 Method

Our study aims to better understand the driving forces behind employers' cooperation in collective skill formation systems. We understand 'sectors' as parts of the economy that are characterized by 'firms producing a similar range of products for the same product market using similar inputs of raw materials, technology, and labour' (Streeck 1990: 16). We look at four sectors that provide a larger share of employment in Switzerland (BFS 2017a): (1) the construction, (2) the metal and mechanical engineering (MEM), (3) the pharmaceutical-chemical (PC), (4) and the banking sector. Our case selection is based on our dependent variable: the degree of employers' cooperation. We selected two sectors with high and two with low involvement of the employers' association in the provision and financing in HVT. The construction and the MEM sector are characterized by high employers' collective action in HVT. In contrast, the PC and banking sectors are characterized by low collective action. Methodologically, our study combines Mill's methods of agreement and difference. We apply the method of agreement: we compare the construction sector with the MEM and the banking with the PC sector. Subsequently, we apply the method of difference by comparing these two groups. In our analysis we respect the historical integrity and pathways of our four cases. This allows us to identify combinations of conditions (configuration) fostering/hindering employers' collective action in HVT but also means that we do not apply Mill's method in a strict deterministic manner.

11.4 Employers' cooperation in HVT in Switzerland

In the following, we present our four cases: the construction sector, the metal and machinery sector, the pharmaceutical-chemical sector, and the banking sector. Each case is presented in the following way. We first describe the extent to which funding and the provision of HVT is organized collectively (our dependent variable). Then, we elaborate on the case-specific conditions fostering (or hindering) employers' associations' cooperation.

11.4.1 Construction sector

11.4.1.1 High level of employer cooperation

The provision and financing of HVT in the construction sector[4] is characterized by a high level of employer cooperation facilitated by the employers' association *Schweizerischer Baumeisterverband* (SBV). The association stands at the centre of the sector's training policies and negotiates the CLAs (SBV 2017a; Swissmem 2007; Trampusch 2020). The SBV was founded in 1897 and represents the occupational, employers', and product market-related interests of the construction sector (SBV 2017b).

In the construction sector, the training centre called *Campus Sursee* is the most important HVT provider, known as the central place for elite training (*Kaderschmiede*) (Schilliger 2014; INTs 8, 12) and for developing new

---

[4] We focus on the main construction industry (Bauhauptgewerbe), which excludes peripheral industries (Baunebengewerbe).

technologies (INTs 10, 12). This school was founded in 1972 by the SBV. Even though the school is an independent foundation now, the SBV and the construction industry are strongly involved in funding and steering it (INTs 1, 6). Campus Sursee is subsidized by a large number of cheap loans from the SBV for constructing and renovating the buildings (Diana 2012; INT6; SBV 2005: 3; Zofinger Tagblatt 2006). The cooperative HG Commerciale (HGC), a construction material provider with a market share of 50 per cent (Richenberger 1997), also has close connections with the SBV and Campus Sursee. It donates materials as well as investing part of its profits in Sursee, which strengthens the ties between the school and the employers (Diana 2012; INT6). For the IVT and HVT training at Sursee the Swiss construction machinery industry provides its newest machines, which are leased to the school (INTs 6, 10). The SBV is responsible for the four most important HVT programmes in the construction sector. Unions are also partly involved but effectively they have little or no say (INTs 4, 5). Within the SBV, specialized commissions (with occupational experts) define the content and procedures of the HVT examinations (INT 4).

Funding is also collectively organized in the construction sector. The collective training fund Parifonds was founded in 1970 (Wicki 1991: 451). It is the most striking element of collective action in the construction sector. The fund is anchored in the CLAs and all employers and employees of the construction sector are obliged to pay into it (SVK 2016). In return, the fund covers tuition fees, travels costs, and compensation for the reduced wage during the training (Parifonds Bau 2017b). In 2016, the Parifonds Bau collected 40.6 million CHF out of which 26.9 million CHF are dedicated to financing educational tasks (Parifonds Bau 2017a). Therefore, the fund indirectly finances the HVT school (INTs 1, 6, 8, 12, 13). The SBV runs a second collective fund, the employer-based Berufsbildungsfonds Bau (BBF Bau) which finances the SBV's activities in IVT and HVT. It was declared a binding sectoral fund in 2009 (Schweizerischer Bundesrat 2009).

11.4.1.2 Conditions fostering cooperation

The construction sector consists of a broad variety of firms of different sizes. Several bigger ones dominate certain regions (INT 8), so that this sector is partially cartelized (INTs 10, 26). The interviewees emphasized that all companies in the construction sector fulfil very similar tasks (INTs 1, 6, 8) and therefore need similar skills (INT 8). Due to the shortage of middle managers (*Kader*) in the external labour market, the *internal labour market* is of major importance. There are some very specific requirements for leadership positions on a construction site. These include practical experience (INTs 1, 12), knowledge of the 'language of the engineers' (INT 12) in combination with being familiar with the vocational construction culture in Switzerland (INT 3). It is difficult to fill these positions with people coming from higher education or from abroad (INTs 1, 3, 12). Of the employees in middle management in a construction firm, about 95 per cent have completed an apprenticeship (INT 8). They highly value vocational training, including HVT (INTs 8, 12, 13), thus we assume that *spill-over effects of IVT* foster employers' cooperation in CVT. According to our interviewees, *large firms* also feel that they benefit greatly from the collective funding scheme (INTs 1, 8, 12, 13). They view the Parifonds as 'very important' (INT 12) and as the 'supporting element' (INT 13) because they would not be able to finance and provide the training themselves (INTs 6, 13). Thus, for employers, the *tradition of CLAs* in the sector is beneficial for their engagement in CVT. We find a long tradition of the institutionalization of collective financing of vocational training through the collective fund Parifonds Bau which is anchored in the CLAs (SVK 2016). We also find evidence that the employers' association uses HVT as a *means to organization building*. The SBV views its engagement in training as an important way to increase its membership. The central importance of IVT and HVT makes employers join the association in order to influence the training content and reap the benefits; if companies train, 'at the least they will then become members of the SBV' (INT 8). The costs of nonmembership are rather high (INT 3). The employers' associations use positive sanctions to encourage support for their association and therefore collective action in training. The SBV bundles together the provision and financing for IVT as well as HVT. For example, Campus Sursee started off as a school for IVT but soon integrated leadership courses (Campus Sursee 2012: 3).

11.4.2 MEM sector

11.4.2.1 High level of employer cooperation

The business association in the MEM sector is called Swissmem. Similar to the SBV, Swissmem is strongly engaged in training policies and negotiates the CLAs. Swissmem emerged in 1999 when the MEM employers' association (Arbeitgeberverband der Schweizer Maschinenindustrie (ASM) founded in 1905) and the MEM trade association (Verein Schweizerischer Maschinen-Industrieller (VSM) founded in 1883) merged (Swissmem 2017).

In the MEM sector, Swissmem is the key player in HVT with more than twenty employees working on IVT/HVT (INTs 4, 26). Swissmem is involved in financing and running two important HVT schools: the sfb

(Bildungszentrum für Technologie und Management) and the Swissmem Academy. The sfb was founded in 1970 by the employers' association for mechanical engineering in cooperation with the unions and is anchored in the CLAs. Swissmem Academy is the provider of managerial HVT training and is run exclusively by Swissmem. The MEM sector is more diversified than the construction sector and a greater variety of providers offer HVT (INT 4). One example of another important provider is the professional college ABB, founded by the big firm ABB in 1971.

Similar to the construction sector, in the MEM sector, different collective VET funds finance the 'structure behind the examinations' (INT 4) in HVT. Since 1969 the Weiterbildungsfonds of the machinery, electro, and metal industry has been anchored in the CLAs. It is co-funded by employers' and employees' contributions (Fluder 1991: 333). Among others, this fund finances the HVT school sfb and the organization of HVT examinations. Swissmechanics, the employers' association of the SME in the MEM sector, runs the collectively funded Swissmechanics Berufsbildungsfonds. In addition to paying for IVT, this fund finances 'the quality development of the [HVT training] modules' (Swissmechanic 2005).

11.4.2.2 Conditions fostering cooperation

The heterogeneity of the MEM sector leads to a great diversity of skill needs, including vocational as well as academic ones (INTs 4, 7, 24). Engineers, trained at universities and UoAs, are especially needed in the research and development departments (INT 4). Even though firms tend to outsource production processes abroad, a great part of the MEM sector is still active in manufacturing. Therefore, manual skills are required and are provided through vocational training (INT 4). Also, the outsourcing trend increases the need for higher vocational skills as the remaining tasks become more complex (INT 24). The interviewees representing large MEM firms emphasized that HVT is essential for the implementation of new techniques developed by engineers (INTs 7, 24). *Large employers* in particular run development departments which is why they need HVT skills for the transfer from the theoretical to the practical level (INT 24). Due to the great heterogeneity in the MEM sector and its product market, which is represented in firm's specialization (INT 24) and export-orientation (INT 26) (heterogeneity of markets), large firms seem to view each other less as competitors. This increases their willingness to invest in collective training measures (INT 26).

Global external labour markets are important for MEM firms when it comes to the recruitment of academically trained engineers. But for filling the 'intermediate levels' ('*Zwischenbau*') (INT 24) between development and practical implementation MEM firms seem to rely on *internal labour markets*. HVT is an important means for updating skills, however other tertiary education programmes are gaining in importance. Some of our MEM interviewees noted that with internationalization comes a more international management who might not be as familiar with vocational skills. This reduces their willingness to invest in HVT (INTs 7, 24).

Similar to construction, in the MEM sector, HVT is fostered by the *logic of organization building, spill-over effects of IVT*, and *the tradition of CLAs*. The employers' association represents employers' interests in HVT policies. Thus, Swissmem creates positive incentives for firms to become members (INT 4). Firms benefit from the membership because they can communicate their training preferences and influence HVT (INTs 24, 25, 26). In the MEM sector, the institutional ties between IVT and HVT are strong. Swissmem bundles employers' competences and represents employers' interests in the governance of IVT as well as HVT. It also represents the employers' interests in the CLA negotiations. As in the construction sector, the CLA establishes the collective financing and provision of HVT with specific reference to the sfb school (Swissmem 2013: 55). The metal industry even has its own CLA, which establishes a separate collective fund.

Applying the method of agreement in our comparison of the two sectors with strong employers' associations' engagement in the provision and financing of HVT, let us conclude that in the construction and the MEM sector the *internal labour market, spill-over effects of IVT, large firms' commitment, the tradition of CLAs, and the logic of organization building* foster employers' cooperation in HVT. We do not find evidence that in these two sectors employers view the tertiary academic schemes of universities (of applied sciences) as a substitute for enhancing the general skills of their employees. In contrast, our interviewees confirmed that they use HVT to update and upgrade the skills of those employees which have completed their IVT schemes in the past. Thus, the *competition with tertiary academic schemes of universities (of applied sciences)* does not harm employers' associations' engagement in HVT.

11.4.3 Pharmaceutical-chemical sector

11.4.3.1 Low level of employer cooperation

In the pharmaceutical-chemical sector, we find little collective action in providing or financing HVT. For example, the sector lacks any collective training funds. Also, the employers' association which supports the CLAs (Employers' Association of Pharmaceutical, Chemical and Service Enterprises in Basel) is a specialized association which consists of only fifteen employers (GAV 2012). It is not involved in IVT and HVT provision and financing (INTs 15, 26) and was described as a 'very weak organization' that does not even run its own website (INT 26). Instead, the trade association scienceindustries gets involved in training policies. For example, it develops the curricula in IVT (SKB 2014). However, in practice the training activities are governed by the inter-firm training network aprentas. This is due to the tradition in the pharmaceutical-chemical sector to organize vocational training at firm level. However, when the big Ciba-Geigy AG was split up in 1996, three of the biggest pharmaceutical firms founded aprentas in 2000. They wanted to secure the provision of IVT (INT 14). Later, the firms asked aprentas to offer HVT too (INT 15). Today, aprentras is supported by two of the founding firms and seventy-eight member firms (aprentas 2017). Aprentas is located close to Basel because the Swiss pharmaceutical-chemical sector (the founding firms) is concentrated in the region of Basel. However, employers in other regions are reluctant to participate in aprentas, due to the spatial distance (INT 21). Interestingly, aprentas not only provides the training but also represents employers in developing training policies (INTs 15, 26).

Also, the collective funding is limited to the decentralized support of aprentas. Aprentas is essentially a collective funding mechanism because the two carrying firms (*Trägerfirmen*) provide substantial financial assistance (INT 14). Also, the member firms pay membership fees. This means that aprentas bundles together the financial resources of its members. However, this cooperation applies only to training firms. There are no collective training funds in the PC sector. In other words, in the PC sector, the collective provision and financing of HVT is limited to an inter-firm network without the involvement of the employers' association.

11.4.3.2 Conditions hindering cooperation

The PC sector is dominated by a few very large employers who are concentrated in the region around Basel. While the smaller companies are rather specialized, the large companies invest in research and development but were traditionally also involved in manufacturing (INT 17). However, manufacturing is increasingly outsourced abroad which—in contrast to the MEM sector—reduces the need for manual skills, obviating the need for vocational training (INTs 14, 15, 17). The big companies can satisfy their rising skill demands with highly skilled labour from a global as well as the internal labour market (INT 14). As companies prefer to recruit those with the highest qualifications (INT 14), international MA and PhD graduates compete with HVT graduates. In addition, for the updating of skills in the internal labour market, HVT does not seem to be the most important tool for the big companies. Especially in training for leadership positions, big firms rely on internal training rather than on HVT (INT 14). Large firms have the resources to maintain an extensive internal training system (INTs 14, 17) and they are not interested in the exchange of expertise (which would be facilitated by collective training activities) because they face intense competition in the market (INT 14). About 90 per cent of the students at aprentas come from SMEs (INT 15). Large employers support their apprentices in completing the vocational baccalaureate in order to enter a bachelor programme at a university of applied sciences (INT 17). About 60 per cent of the apprentices pursue this path (INT 15).

Furthermore, vocational training does not play an important role for the employers' associations (INT 26). They do not mix their organizational interests with training policies (INT 26). Even though the trade association gets involved, it delegated the provision to aprentas. Scienceindustries even referred us to aprentas when we asked for an interview (email from the Scienceindustries secretariat 10 May 2017). The association does not use HVT as a way to attract members.

In contrast to the previous two cases, the pharmaceutical-chemical sector lacks a tradition of collective action in training. Traditionally, initial vocational training in the pharmaceutical-chemical sector was organized by firms. Aprentas, the inter-firm training network, established a kind of segmented skill system and extended its training activities to HVT. Additionally, the sector does not rely on encompassing sector-wide CLAs. Furthermore, the interviewees explained that in the pharmaceutical-chemical sector, the often international (non-Swiss) management is not familiar with vocational training programmes and therefore prefers to support academic training with which it is familiar (INTs 15, 17).

11.4.4 Banking sector

11.4.4.1 Low level of employer cooperation

The employers' association of the banking sector, the *Employers' Association of Banks in Switzerland* (*Arbeitgeber Banken*), was founded in 2009 with the support of the trade association *Swissbanking* (Arbeitgeber Banken 2015). Arbeitgeber Banken replaced a loose network of regional banking associations which was dominated by the banking association of Zurich (Arbeitgeber Banken 2015). The trade association Swissbanking was founded in 1912 (Vogler 2017). Even though Swissbanking is the trade association, and therefore concerned with the product market (INT 26), it deals with vocational training policies and runs its own division for training (INTs 18, 26; Swissbanking 2010). In the banking sector, HVT was popular until the 1990s (INTs 18, 20) but this changed with the introduction of the UoAs. In response, in the early 2000s, Swissbanking decided to support the provision of HVT through a professional college which would focus on professional skills in banking (INT 18). Swissbanking was reluctant to run the college itself and looked for an external provider. The profit-oriented enterprise Kalaidos Bildungsgruppe AG opened the professional college Höhere Fachschule Banking+Finance (HFBF) in 2006. Swissbanking controls the steering committee of the college (INT 18) but does not invest further resources. The college receives 25 per cent of its funding from the cantons and needs to cover the rest of the costs from tuition fees (INT 16). The college focuses on training in the field of retail banking. International private banks do not send their employees to the college because they focus on different fields of banking, such as international asset management (INTs 19, 20). Because HVT is provided by a profit-oriented private provider, we consider collective action among banks (via Swissbanking) as very weak.

The financing of tuition fees is left completely to individual agreements between employer and employees. In our interviews, the relatively high wages were named as a reason for the absence of collective mechanisms (INTs 19, 20). However, most firms pay the tuition fees for their employees and in return the employee is obliged to stay with the firm, which amounts to a 'company-based loan' (INTs 14, 17, 20). The banking sector lacks any mechanism for collective funding.

11.4.4.2 Conditions hindering cooperation

The banking sector, even more so than the pharmaceutical-chemical sector, shifts its skill preferences towards academic training (INTs 17, 18). The large employers that focus on international customers require skills which are updated with very specific internal training (INT 19). These large banks can draw on their internal labour markets as well as on the global labour markets that offer labour with higher education certificates (INT 16). Moreover, banks seem to prefer their internal training systems because they compete for highly skilled and experienced labour. They perceive the competitiveness of the product market to be very intense and they fear poaching through collectively organized courses (INT 19). Especially large banks are able to establish their own internal training systems including very specialized courses and bilateral cooperation with universities, where needed (INT 18). Furthermore, one interviewee pointed out that the professional college focuses on retail banking which makes it less attractive for banks focusing on asset management (INT 19). Additionally, large banks support the vocational baccalaureate. The share of apprentices completing a vocational baccalaureate rose from less than 50 per cent in the 1990s to more than 65 per cent nowadays (INTs 16, 18). This shift becomes visible in the declining number of students enrolled in the professional college (INT16; AKAD HFBF 2016). In response, the training at the professional college is now embedded into the structure of the Kalaidos University of Applied Sciences (AKAD HFBF AG 2016). In other words, large banks are reluctant to participate in collective training activities.

In the banking sector, it was the trade association Swissbanking that tried to get involved in HVT in the 1990s. However, this approach failed because its members increasingly concentrated on higher and specialized training through academic training. One of our interviewees confirmed that this development challenges the role of the trade association (INT 18).

In the banking sector, IVT was traditionally organized by the Swiss Association of Commercial Employees (KV Schweiz) (Trampusch 2010a). The banks' employers' association had limited influence on IVT. Moreover, the tradition of commercial IVT training is characterized as 'all sector training' ('*Allbranchen Ausbildung*', INT 2) because it cuts across various sectors so that occupational identity overlaps less with the sectors, as in the construction and MEM sectors (INTs 2, 10). 'All sector training' also runs counter to the logic of organizing employers' interests at the sector level, which may also explain why employers' associations do not centralize collective action in training (INT 26). In 2003, the reform of commercial training shifted competences from the KV to the sectors, but in banking it was not the employers' association but the trade association that got involved. As a reaction to the 2003 reform, 'the largest Swiss banks in cooperation with Swissbanking' (CYP 2017) founded the training network CYP. In contrast to aprentas, which only handles inter-firm cooperation, Swissbanking is involved in the steering of CYP. However, Swissbanking is only one member among the founding banks, which is why CYP has a strong sectional character. Furthermore, CYP does not provide standardized HVT. Spill-over effects are further limited because, as a trade association, Swissbanking is not involved in the bargaining of the CLAs. A selection of fifty banks (VAB 2016) supports a specialized association for the purpose of negotiating the CLAs. Some employers choose to have company-based labour agreements. Furthermore, the CLAs do not address the collective provision or financing of VET. On the contrary, the CLAs underline the responsibility of individual employers and employees (VAB 2016: 6).

In the interviews, it became clear that the banks' international and/or academically trained managers and HR authorities lack knowledge about HVT due to their academic educational cultural background. This reduces their willingness to invest in it (INTs 16, 18).

Applying the method of agreement in our comparison of the pharmaceutical-chemical sector with the banking sector we conclude that in these two sectors' external labour markets are of similar importance to internal ones. In both sectors, there are no spill-over impacts of IVT on CVT and large firms are less committed. The tradition of CLAs is limited and the associations do not use HVT as a device and selective incentive for organization building. Moreover, employers prefer the recruitment of graduates from universities (of applied sciences) and in the competition with these tertiary schemes HVT has lost ground.

Furthermore, we conclude that the *skill requirements of product markets, the certification of HVT skills*, and *state support* cannot explain employers' cooperation. These conditions are equal in our two groups of cases, meaning that they cannot explain the difference. In all four sectors, training and certificates in HVT are available (SBFI 2017). The educational statistics show that in all four sectors employees make use of HVT and that the numbers of HVT certificates are rising (BFS 2020). Furthermore, the interviewees all pointed out that they serve markets for high-quality goods and services (INTs 1, 4, 15, 18). In addition, we did not find cross-sectoral differences in state support for HVT. Thus, from the nine conditions discussed above, three conditions can be eliminated.

This leaves us with the following six conditions fostering employers' associations willingness to provide and finance HVT courses: (1) the *internal labour market*, (2) *institutional spill-over effects of IVT*, (3) *large firms' commitment*, (4) *the tradition of CLAs*, and (5) employers' associations' *logic of organization building*; moreover, (6) employers' view on the *tertiary academic schemes of universities (of applied sciences)* is important: if they do not prefer these schemes as an alternative and substitutive track to enhance the general skills of their employees, they invest in the provision and financing of HVT. We have identified these conditions by applying the method of agreement within the two groups of cases and the method of difference across the two groups.

11.5 Conclusion

Our study has started to disentangle the complex variety of conditions that influence employers' decision to invest in collective skill provision. Our findings contribute to better understanding the diversity of ways concerning how and why CVT is organized in collective systems. With regard to rising skill demands, the importance of further education is growing. Understanding why different employers' associations invest in collective training is thus of great relevance. We emphasized that collective action in training cannot be explained solely by one factor. A combination of different interrelated conditions has to be considered in order to understand why employers' associations provide skills that benefit even non-training firms. Collective action does not (only) depend on employers' goodwill, but other factors, such as the supply of needed skills by external labour markets, play an important role. With regard to the knowledge economy, this means that changes in one dimension do not automatically lead to the collapse of collective skill governance. Against this backdrop, it can be concluded that collective skill formation is more robust to changes than some studies might suggest.

References

AKAD HFBF AG. 2016. 'Information zur Weiterentwicklung der Höheren Fachschule Bank + Finanz HFBF'. Thomas Suter (Präsident des Verwaltungsrats AKAD HFBF AG). aprentas. 2017. 'Mitgliedfirmen'. Accessed 13 October 2017. http://www.aprentas.ch/aprentas/mitgliedfirmen.cfm.

Arbeitgeber Banken. 2015. 'Historie'. Accessed 28 December 2017. http://arbeitgeber -banken.ch/de/verband/organisation.

Aventur, Francois, Christian Campo, and Martine Möbus. 1999. 'Factors in the Spread of Continuing Training in the European Community'. *Training and Employment* 35: 3–6.

Ballauf, Helga. 2011. *Karriere mit beruflicher Fortbildung*. Bundesministerium für Bildung und Forschung (BMBF). Bonn, Berlin: Referat Ordnung und Qualitätssicherung der beruflichen Bildung.

Baumeler, Carmen, Katja Dannecker, and Ines Trede. 2014. *Höhere Berufsbildung in der Schweiz*. SWIR: EHB.

Beck, Nikolaus, Rüdiger Kabst, and Peter Walgenbach. 2009. 'The Cultural Dependence of Vocational Training'. *Journal of International Business Studies* 40 (8): 1374–95.

Becker, Gary S. 1962. 'Investment in Human Capital: A Theoretical Analysis'. *Journal of Political Economy 70* (5): 9–49.

BFS. 2009. *Personen mit einem Abschluss der höheren Berufsbildung auf dem Arbeitsmarkt*. Neuchâtel: Bundesamt für Statstik.

BFS. 2017a. 'Beschäftigte nach Vollzeitäquivalente und Wirtschaftsabteilungen'. Bundesamt für Statistik. Accessed 14 December 2017. https://www.bfs.admin.ch/bfs/de/home/statistiken/industrie-dienstleistungen/unternehmen-beschaeftigte/beschaeftigungsstatistik/beschaeftigte.assetdetail.3865848.html.

BFS. 2017b. 'Tertiärstufe—Höhere Berufsbildung'. Accessed 19 November 2017. https://www.bfs.admin.ch/bfs/de/home/statistiken/bildung-wissenschaft/bildungsabschluesse/tertiaerstufe-hoehere-berufsbildung.html.

BFS. 2020. 'Ausgewählte Bildungsabschlüsse, Entwicklung'. Bundesamt für Statistik, Accessed 6 October 2020. https://www.bfs.admin.ch/bfs/de/home/statistiken/bildung-wissenschaft/bildungsabschluesse/sekundastufe-II/berufliche-grundbildung.assetdetail.2950613.html.

Bowman, John R. 1982. 'The Logic of Capitalist Collective Action'. *Rationality and Society 21* (4/5): 571–604.

Bowman, John R. 2005. 'Employers and the Politics of Skill Formation in a Coordinated Market Economy: Collective Action and Class Conflict in Norway'. *Politics and Society 33* (4): 567–94.

Brandl, Bernd, and Alex Lehr. 2019. 'The Strange Non-death of Employer and Business Associations: An Analysis of their Representativeness and Activities in Western European Countries'. *Economic and Industrial Democracy 40* (4): 1–22.

Busemeyer, Marius R. 2009a. 'Asset Specificity, Institutional Complementarities and the Variety of Skill Regimes in Coordinated Market Economies'. *Socio-Economic Review 7*: 375–406.

Busemeyer, Marius R. 2009b. *Wandel trotz Reformstau: Die Politik der beruflichen Bildung seit 1970*. Frankfurt am Main: Campus.

Busemeyer, Marius R., and Christine Trampusch. 2012. 'The Comparative Political Economy of Collective Skill Formation'. In *The Political Economy of Collective Skill Formation*, edited by Marius R. Busemeyer and Christine Trampusch, pp. 3–38. Oxford: Oxford University Press.

Campus Sursee. 2012. *40 Jahre Campus Sursee Bildungszentrum Bau Vom Grundstein zum breitesten Bildungsangeboit der Schweizer Baubranche*. Sursee: Campus Sursee Bildungszentrum Bau.

Cognard, Etienne. 2011. 'Varieties of Capitalism and Financial Cooperation between Employers: The Initial and Continuous Vocational Training in Comparison'. *European Journal of Industrial Relations Journal 17* (1): 25–40.

Cognard, Etienne. 2015. 'Path Dependency, Cross-Class Coalitions, and the Slow Road of the French Further Training System away from Solidarism'. Annual Conference of the European Sociological Association, Prague, 25–28 August.

Coleman, William, and Henry Jacek. 1989. Regionalism, Business Interests and Public Policy. Sage Series in Neo-Corporatism, edited by Philippe C. Schmitter and Alan Cawson. London: SAGE.

Crouch, Colin, Mari Sako, and David Finegold. 1999. 'The Dispiriting Search for the Learning Society'. In *Are Skills the Answer?: The Political Economy of Skill Creation in Advanced Industrial Countries*, edited by Colin Crouch, Mari Sako, and David Finegold, pp. 1–31. Oxford: Oxford University Press.

Culpepper, Pepper D. 2003. *Creating Cooperation: How States Develop Human Capital in Europe*. Ithaca: Cornell University Press.

Culpepper, Pepper D. 2007. 'Small States and Skill Specificity: Austria, Switzerland, and Interemployer Cleavages in Coordinated Capitalism'. *Comparative Political Studies 40* (6): 611–637.

Culpepper, Pepper D., and David Finegold (eds). 1999. *The German Skills Machine: Sustaining Comparative Advantage in a Global Economy*. New York: Berghahn Books.

CYP. 2017. 'CYP Partner'. Accessed 20 March 2017. https://cyp.ch/ueber-uns/partner.

Diana, Massimo. 2012. 'Das "Schiff" Campus Sursee bricht zu neuen Horizonten auf'. Fachmagazin Baukader (December): p. 15. Accessed 20 March 2017.

Eichenberger, Pierre, and Stephanie Ginalski. 2017. '"Si vis pacem, para bellum"— The Construction of Business Cooperation in the Swiss Machinery Industry'. *Socio-Economic Review 15* (3): 615–35.

Eichenberger, Pierre, and André Mach. 2011. 'Organized Capital and Coordinated Market Economy: Swiss Business Interest Associations between Socio-economic Regulation and Political Influence'. In *Switzerland in Europe: Continuity and Change in the Swiss Political Economy*, edited by Christine Trampusch and André Mach, pp. 63–81. London: Routledge.

Fazekas, Mihaly, and Simon Field. 2013. *A Skills beyond School Review of Switzerland*. Paris: OECD.

Fluder, Robert. 1991. 'Arbeitnehmerorganisationen in der Maschinenindustrie'. In *Gewerkschaften und Angestelltenverbände in der schweizerischen Privatwirtschaft*, edited by Robert Fluder, Heinz Ruf, Walter Schöni, and Martin Wicki, pp. 201–386. Zürich: Seismo.

GAV. 2012. 'Gesamtarbeitsvertrag für Basler Pharma- Chemie- und Dienstleistungsunternehmen'. Accessed 6 October 2017. www.gav-service.ch/FileSpooler.axd?fileId=8819.

Gonon, Philipp. 2013. 'Federal Vocational Baccalaureate: The Swiss Way of "Hybridity"'. In *Hybrid Qualifications: Structures and Problems in the Context of European VET Policy*, edited by Thomas Deissinger, Josef Aff, Alison Fuller, and Christian Helms Jørgensen, pp. 181–96. Bern: Peter Lang.

Graf, Lukas. 2013. *The Hybridization of Vocational Training and Higher Education in Austria, Germany and Switzerland*. Opladen: Budrich UniPress.

Johansen, Lars-Henrik. 1999. 'Transferable training and the collective action problem for employers: an analysis of further education and training in four Norwegian industries'. PhD thesis, LSE (Fafo Report 335).

Johansen, Lars-Henrik. 2002. 'Transferable Training as a Collective Good'. *European Sociological Review 18* (3): 301–14.

Kriesi, Hanspeter, and Peter Farago. 1989. 'The Regional Differentiation of Business Interest Associations in Switzerland'. In *Regionalism, Business Interests and Public Policy*, edited by Wiliam Coleman and Henry Jacek, pp. 153–71. London: SAGE.

Mach, André, and Christine Trampusch. 2011. 'The Swiss Political Economy in Comparative Perspective'. In *Switzerland in Europe: Continuity and Change in the Swiss Political Economy*, edited by Christine Trampusch and André Mach, pp. 11–23. London: Routledge.

Marsden, David. 1999. *A Theory of Employment Systems: Micro-Foundations of Societal Diversity*. Oxford: Oxford University Press.

Muehlemann, Samuel. 2014. 'Training Participation of Internationalized Firms: Establishment-level Evidence for Switzerland'. *Empirical Research in Vocational Education and Training 6* (5): 1–11.

Parifonds Bau. 2017a. '2016/ Geschäftbericht Parifonds Bau'. Accessed 17 January 2017. https://www.consimo.ch/_cms/lib/f_dbstream.php?tn=tab_file&fd=file&mt=application/pdf&id=1195&hxfile&f=AK66_ELAR-#6128007-v16-2016_Parifonds_Bau_Gesch%C3%A4ftsbericht_de.pdf.

Parifonds Bau. 2017b. 'Beitrags- und Leistungsreglement'. Accessed 17 January 2017. https://www.consimo.ch/_cms/lib/f_dbstream.php?tn=tab_file&fd=file&mt=application/pdf&id=1173&hxfile&f=063682_Parifonds_Leistungsreglement_IH_d_neu.pdf.

Richenberger, Hans. 1997. 'Die Schweiz ist noch lange nicht gebaut'. Neue Zürcher Zeitung, 12 March 1997.

Rohrer, Linda, and Christine Trampusch. 2011. 'Continuity and Change in the Swiss Vocational Training System'. In *Switzerland in Europe: Continuity and Change in the Swiss Political Economy*, edited by Christine Trampusch and André Mach, pp. 144–61. New York: Routledge.

SBFI. 2017. 'Berufsverzeichnis Höhere Berufsbildung'. Accessed 23 November 2017. http://www.bvz.admin.ch/bvz/hbb/index.html?lang=de.

SBV—Schweizerischer Baumeisterverband. 2005. 'Jahresbericht'. Accessed 6 October 2017. www.baumeister.ch/de/component/edocman/1043-jahresbericht-2005-d-pdf/download.

SBV—Schweizerischer Baumeisterverband. 2017a. 'Wir als Verband Leitbild und Ziele'. Schweizerischer Baumeisterverband. Accessed 6 October 2017 www.baumeister.ch/de/component/edocman/2778-leitbild-sbv-deutsch/download.

SBV— Schweizerischer Baumeisterverband. 2017b. 'Wir über uns'. Accessed 6 October 2017. http://www.baumeister.ch/de/der-sbv.

Schilliger, Pirmin. 2014. 'Bauwirtschaft; Baumeister gehen schwimmen'. *HandelsZeitung*, 4.9.2014.

Schmitter, Philippe C., and W. Streeck. 1999. 'The Organization of Business Interests. Studying the Associative Action of Business in Advanced Industrial Societies'. In *MPIfG Discussion Paper 99/1*. Köln: Max-Planck-Institut für Gesellschaftsforschung (MPIfG).

Schweizerischer Bundesrat. 2009. 'Bundesratsbeschluss über die Allgemeinverbindlicherklärung des Berufsbildungsfonds Bau'. Accessed 6 October 2017. https://www.fedlex.admin.ch/eli/fga/2009/1502/de.

SGV. 2004. *Finanzrelevante Aus- und Weiterbildungsaktivitäten der schweizerischen Berufsverbände*. MIMEO.

SKB. 2014. 'Bildungsplan Chemie- und Pharmatechnologin / Chemie- und Pharmatechnologe mit eidgenössischem Fähigkeitszeugnis (EFZ)'. Accessed 6 October 2017. http://www.cp-technologe.ch/wp-content/uploads/2016/07/Bipla_37005_d.pdf

SKBF. 2018. *Bildungsbericht Schweiz 2018*. Schweizerische Koordinationsstelle für Bildungsforschung. Aarau.

Soskice, David. 1994. 'Reconciling Markets and Institutions: The German Apprenticeship System'. In *Training and the Private Sector*, edited by Lisa M. Lynch, pp. 25–60. University of Chicago Press.

Streeck, Wolfgang 1989. 'Skills and the Limits od Neo-Liberalism: The Enterprise of the Future as a Place of Learning'. *Work, Employment & Society 3* (1): 89–107.

Streeck, Wolfgang 1990. 'Interest Heterogeneity and Organizing Capacity: Two Class Logics of Collective Action'. *Estudio/Working Paper* 1990 (2): 1–44.

Streeck, Wolfgang 2012. 'Skills and Politics: General and Specific'. In *The Political Economy of Collective Skill Formation*, edited by Marius R. Busemeyer, and Christine Trampusch, pp. 317–352. Oxford: Oxford University Press.

Streeck, Wolfgang, Josef Hilbert, Karl-Heinz van Kevelaer, Frederieke Maier, and Hajo Weber. 1987. *Die Rolle der Sozialpartner in der Berufsausbildung und beruflichen Weiterbildung: Bundesrepublik Deutschland*. Berlin: CEDEFOP.

SVK. 2016. 'Landesmantelvertrag für das schweizerische Bauhauptgewerbe'. Schweizerische Paritätische Vollzugskommission Bauhauptgewerbe, Accessed 21

November 2017. http://www.gav-service.ch/Contract.aspx?stellaNumber=100001 &versionName=8.

Swissbanking. 2010. 'Statuten Schweizerische Bankiervereinigung (SwissBanking)'. Accessed 17 January 2018. www.swissbanking.org/de/bankiervereinigung/ueber-uns/statuten_sbvg_2010.pdf.

Swissmechanic. 2005. 'Reglemente zum Berufsbildungsfonds'. Accessed 22 November 2017. www.swissmechanic.ch/documents/Reglemente_zum_BBF.pdf.

Swissmem. 2007. 'Statuten Swissmem'. Accessed 6 October 2017. https://www.swissmem.ch/fileadmin/_migrated/content_uploads/swissmem_statuten_07.pdf.

Swissmem. 2013. 'Gesamtarbeitsvertrag der Maschinen-, Elektro- und Metall-Industrie'. Accessed 6 October 2017. https://www.swissmem.ch/fileadmin/user_upload/Sozialpartner/pdf/GAV_01.07.2013_-_30.06.2018_D.pdf.

Swissmem. 2017. 'Geschichtlicher Hintergrund'. Accessed 11 October 2017. https://www.swissmem.ch/de/organisation-mitglieder/verband/geschichtlicher-hintergrund.html.

Zofinger Tagblatt. 2006. 'Erneuerung AZ Sursee'. Zofinger Tagblatt, 20 March 2006.

Thelen, Kathleen. 2004. *How Institutions Evolve: The Political Economy of Skills in Germany, Britain, the United States, and Japan.* New York: Cambridge University Press.

Trampusch, Christine. 2010a. 'Employers, the State and the Politics of Institutional Change: Vocational Education and Training in Austria, Germany and Switzerland'. *European Journal of Political Research* 49 (4): 545–73.

Trampusch, Christine. 2010b. 'Transformative and Self-preserving Change in the Vocational Education and Training System in Switzerland'. *Comparative Politics* 41 (2): 187–206.

Trampusch, Christine. 2020. 'Social Partners' Policy Reactions to Migration in Occupational Labour Markets: The Case of the Swiss Construction Industry'. *European Journal of Industrial Relations* 26(2): 157–172. doi: https://doi.org/10.1177/0959680119840574.

Trampusch, Christine, and Pierre Eichenberger. 2012. 'Skills and Industrial Relations in Coordinated Market Economies—Continuing Vocational Training in Denmark, the Netherlands, Austria and Switzerland'. *British Journal of Industrial Relations* 50 (4): 644–66.

Traxler, Franz. 2010. 'The Long-term Development of Organised Business and its Implications for Corporatism: A Cross-national Comparison of Membership, Activities and Governing Capacities of Business Interest Associations, 1980–2003'. *European Journal of Political Research* 49 (2): 151–73.

VAB. 2016. 'Vereinbarung über die Anstellungsbedingungen der Bankangestellten (VAB)'. Accessed 6 October 2017. www.sbpv.ch/fileadmin/user_upload/Geschuetzter_Bereich/VAB/VAB_2016.pdf.

Vogler, Robert U. 2017. 'Geschichte'. Accessed 12 November 2017. http://www.swissbanking.org/de/bankiervereinigung/ueber-uns/geschichte.

Wicki, Martin. 1991. 'Gewerkschaften im Baugewerbe'. In *Gewerkschaften und Angestelltenverbände in der schweizerischen Privatwirtschaft*, edited by Robert Fluder et al., pp. 387–457. Zürich: Seismo.

Table 11.1A Overview of expert interviews 2016/2017 on higher vocational education in Switzerland

Code	Actor Group	Date
INT1	Employers' and trade association of the construction sector	29 November 2016
INT2	Cross-sector employers' and trade association SMEs	09 December 2016
INT3	Cross-sector employee association	12 December 2016
INT4	Employers' and trade association of the MEM sector	13 December 2016
INT5	Cross-sector employee association	13 December 2016
INT6	HVT provider in the construction sector	15 December 2016
INT7	HVT provider in the MEM sector	02 February 2017
INT8	Construction firm	06 March 2017
INT9	Cross-sector employee association	15 March 2017
INT10	Former politician	15 March 2017
INT11	Cross-sector employee association	16 March 2017
INT12	Construction firm	20 March 2017
INT13	Construction firm	21 March 2017
INT14	Pharmaceutical and chemical firm	28 March 2017
INT15	HVT provider pharmaceutical-chemical sector	28 March 2017
INT16	HVT provider banking sector	31 March 2017
INT17	Pharmaceutical and chemical firm	04 April 2017
INT18	Trade association banking sector	07 April 2017
INT19	Bank	19 April 2017
INT20	Bank	20 April 2017
INT21	Occupational association pharmaceutical-chemical sector	10 May 2017
INT22	HVT provider MEM sector	15 June 2017
INT23	Cross-sector employee association	26 June 2017
INT24	MEM firm	10 October 2017
INT25	MEM firm	26 October 2017
INT26	Cross-sector employers' association	24 November 2017

12

Enhancing Permeability through Cooperation

The Case of Vocational and Academic Worlds of Learning in the Knowledge Economy

Nadine Bernhard and Lukas Graf

12.1 Introduction

Like other advanced economies, Germany is currently undergoing a partial transformation from an industrial economy into a knowledge economy.[1] The latter is characterized by an increase in the numbers of both higher-qualified service jobs and knowledge-intensive manual jobs (Protsch and Solga 2015). As Thelen (2019) points out, in collective skill formation systems, this transformation can unfold in very different ways. Germany, for example, concentrates on the adaptation of its traditionally strong industry-based sectors. What most countries have in common, however, is that there is an increase in the demand for more academically oriented qualifications. Job profiles have changed and are becoming increasingly complex. Progressively, cognitive competencies are becoming more important (Baethge and Wolter 2015; Bonoli and Emmenegger, in this volume; Mayer and Solga 2008). These are traditionally competencies associated with an educational pathway in higher general education (HGE).[2]

Technological change, which in Germany is often addressed under the headings digitization, internet of things, or Industry 4.0, further reinforces and accelerates these changes. Forecast research shows that in the next

[1] We would like to thank Giuliano Bonoli, Patrick Emmenegger, Marius Busemeyer, Ulf Banscherus, Justin Powell, Florian Waldow, Heike Solga, and Yvonne Blos, as well as the participants of the book workshop in St. Gallen and the research seminar of the Centre for Comparative and International Education at Humboldt-Universität zu Berlin for their very insightful comments.

[2] HGE refers to academically oriented educational pathways mainly at the upper-secondary level. The prime example of this in Germany is the *Gymnasium*.

Nadine Bernhard and Lukas Graf, *Enhancing Permeability through Cooperation*. In: *Collective Skill Formation in the Knowledge Economy*. Edited by Giuliano Bonoli and Patrick Emmenegger, Oxford University Press. © Oxford University Press (2022). DOI: 10.1093/oso/9780192866257.003.0012

decades, a large proportion of jobs will substantially change in their activity profiles due to technological innovations (Arntz et al. 2016; Euler and Severing 2019) resulting in an increasing demand for academically trained workers (Bonoli and Emmenegger, in this volume; Frommberger 2019). This poses a major challenge for vocational training, especially in collective skill formation systems like in Germany, in which high-quality manufacturing has always relied heavily on firm-based vocational education and training (VET) (Thelen 2019). On the one hand, this involves adapting VET to the rapidly changing environment and, on the other, to continue making VET attractive for young, talented people.

In recent years, the challenge of attracting apprentices has been further exacerbated by a change in individual educational-choice behaviour in Germany. As more and more students choose to enter secondary general educational pathways to obtain an *Abitur* (the general higher-education entrance qualification), the proportion of those who begin a vocational training education versus the ones who embark on the academic track has decreased significantly. Since 2011, the majority of school leavers have completed their school careers with a higher-education entrance qualification, predominantly with an *Abitur* (Autorengruppe Bildungsberichterstattung 2018). That is, in 2011, for the first time, university enrolments have narrowly outnumbered enrolments in apprenticeships (Baethge and Wolter 2015). Enrolment in higher education (HE) has grown strongly in recent years, from 20 per cent in the 1980s to 45 per cent in 2016. (Autorengruppe Bildungsberichterstattung 2018: Table F2-2A).

In sum, the historical dominance of VET – and the dual system that combines learning in the workplace and in the school – is being challenged in Germany. Against the background of structural and technological change, institutional permeability between VET and HGE represents one key pathway to reach a higher overall qualification level that can meet the current demand for skills. At the same time, enhanced permeability is an opportunity to demonstrate the attractiveness and the equivalence of VET in relation to HE in view of the challenge employers face in attracting bright and talented students. While we acknowledge the complex relationship between permeability between VET and HGE and the knowledge society and the different consequences it might have on the VET system (Busemeyer and Trampusch 2012),[3] we argue that institutional permeability is a very important aspect that

---

[3] A historical discourse analysis by Bernhard (2017) shows that enhancing institutional permeability to increase attractiveness of VET is a traditional point of view of VET actors in Germany. However, the fear of an 'academic drift' (Busemeyer and Trampusch 2012) and a loss of trained personnel due to permeability exists, too.

can help cope with the current upskilling challenges collective skill formation systems face.

What exactly can be understood by the concept of permeability and how is permeability made possible through cooperation? In this chapter, we focus on institutional permeability and not social or spatial mobility. The concept of institutional permeability refers to regulative, normative, and cultural institutional structures (Scott 2008) that break up institutional divisions and enable more flexible educational pathways. The question of institutional permeability is essential especially in stratified education systems like the German one that do not connect relevant educational sectors like VET and the HGE well and, thus, are likely to impede equal access to educational and employment opportunities (Bernhard 2017). We analyse actors and institutional structures and how they foster permeability between VET and HGE. It is important to note that the realization of inclusiveness in the form of social mobility builds on such institutional permeability in the education system. Our chapter thus speaks to the emerging literature that links governance concepts with questions of social inclusiveness in education and training (e.g. Powell et al. 2012; Gonon 2013; Thelen 2014; Bonoli and Wilson 2019; Carstensen and Ibsen 2021; Di Maio et al. 2019; Durazzi and Geyer 2020; Bonoli and Emmenegger 2021).

While the challenge to enhance institutional permeability between VET[4] and HGE is increasingly felt by all stakeholders in Germany (Bernhard 2017), the actual building of programmes that promote such permeability is highly demanding as it often requires the cooperation of actors who have been largely isolated from each other and often have diverging interests. This holds true in particular in the case of educational projects integrating both worlds of learning. While various initiatives to increase permeability have been launched in recent years (e.g. Bernhard 2017; Banscherus et al. 2016), little is known about how actors cooperate in the establishment and implementation of these permeability-enhancing projects. To address this research gap, we develop a conceptualization combining institutional permeability and types of cooperation in collective skill formation systems. We systematically link four key permeability dimensions (Bernhard 2017) with the three major types of cooperation that have been identified for systems of collective skill formation: information exchange, coordination, and collaboration (Emmenegger et al. 2019). The combination of these two conceptualizations enables us to explore the intensity of cooperation between key actors from

---

[4] When VET is mentioned in this chapter we mainly refer to dual VET (i.e., apprenticeship training).

VET and HGE—which contributes to our understanding of how actors in collective skill formation systems adapt to the demands of the knowledge economy.

Our case is Germany, which represents one of the world's major collective skill formation systems, but which is arguably the least successful collective skill formation system in terms of creating a systematic approach to enhancing such permeability (Baethge and Wolter 2015; Graf 2013). However, within Germany, we explore programmes that indeed provide a high degree of permeability between vocational and academic worlds. More specifically, we focus on programmes in which dual VET is systematically combined with the *Abitur*. Our institutional analysis is based mainly on document analysis and expert interviews.

We find that despite different interests, the educational actors in the two separate educational sectors of VET and HGE realized that enhancing permeability with the help of such double qualification programmes can help them to reach their respective goals. This compatibility enables cooperation. In the initiation phase of such programmes, actors of VET and HGE strongly collaborated. However, once the programme is established, constant collaboration is no longer necessary for ensuring institutional permeability. In the case of problems in the day-to-day operation of the programme, actors try to solve these first through information exchange and, if this is not sufficient, through coordination. Over time, this enhances mutual understanding between the actors despite their original position on two different sides of the institutional divide between VET and HGE and their dissimilar interests. Nonetheless, sometimes an incompatibility of interests arises and makes cooperation difficult. We show that increasing permeability is by no means a trivial task and that a fine-grained understanding of both permeability and cooperation can help uncover how actors take a differentiated approach to handling adjustments of collective skill formation to the knowledge economy.

In the next section, we explore what exactly can be understood by the concept of permeability and how permeability is made possible through cooperation, which provides the ground for our analysis of the case of dual qualification programmes. We then outline the institutional division between VET and HGE in Germany before analysing the dual qualification programmes in question and the respective level of cooperation involved in each of the four dimensions of institutional permeability. We conclude by discussing the dynamic relationship between institutional permeability and cooperation in collective skill formation.

12.2 Conceptual framework: four dimensions of institutional permeability and their governance through cooperation

In this section, we develop a framework that allows us to capture the cooperation types involved in building institutional permeability between VET and HGE.

12.2.1 The four dimensions of institutional permeability

Institutional permeability should not be understood too narrowly, i.e. as just the possibility of transitioning from one educational sector or level to another. Analytically, the concept of institutional permeability can be further differentiated along four dimensions (Bernhard 2017): (1) access, (2) recognition and validation, (3) organizational interlinkages, and (4) institutional support structures to meet the diverse needs of learners.

Access to educational programmes and sectors can be unconstrained, without predetermined conditions. Alternatively, access may depend on entitlements based on certificates, like the HE entrance certificate. Finally, the relevant educational organization and participating actors may decide on alternative access possibilities based on, for instance, admission tests or interviews.

Recognition and validation of prior learning, as a second dimension, is based on the notion that different learning pathways can lead to equivalent competencies. Here it has to be examined whether and to what extent previously acquired knowledge and skills match those of the target educational course and thus can replace components of the educational programme.

The third dimension of institutional permeability comprises the organizational interlinkage of the educational sectors of VET and of HGE at the organizational and programme level. A distinction can be made here between the consecutive linking of (parts of) educational programmes from different educational sectors (institutionalized transitions) and the linking of different educational sectors within one programme or organization (i.e. linkage through organizational integration) (Bernhard 2017) by offering double qualifications and integrating, for instance, curricula, didactics, methodology, and learning venues (cf. Young et al. 1997). Permeability via integration thus involves breaking down the existing institutional boundaries (Baethge 2006) by institutionalizing the logic, norms, and/or regulations typical of both VET and HGE in one programme. In this chapter, we mainly refer to this second and stronger from of organizational interlinkage, namely *organizational integration*. A common example for the integration of VET and HE are the dual study programmes in Germany (Graf 2013).

The fourth dimension emphasizes that permeability implies not only securing access or opportunities for recognition and validation, but also supporting diverse learners to enable them to successfully complete the course (Bernhard 2017; Wolter et al. 2014). Hence, it comprises institutional structures aimed at *meeting the heterogeneous needs* of learners. Support structures can take the form of information and counselling services, securing funding for the learners, offering flexibilized learning structures (e.g. blended learning courses) and adapting curricula and didactic orientations.[5]

In sum, institutional permeability implies far more than granting transition opportunities from one educational area to another. Instead, we argue that our multi-dimensional understanding is helpful in uncovering structural conditions for successful learning and increased inclusiveness especially in the context of collectively organized skill formation systems in the era of the knowledge economy.

12.2.2 Cooperation on institutional permeability

From a governance perspective, shaping successful learning pathways between VET and HGE is clearly a challenge. The actors in the two different organizational fields of HGE and VET, which have been separated for such a long time, do not 'speak the same language' (Baethge 2006). Normally, these actors hardly ever cooperate with each other. For the implementation of a programme located at the nexus of VET and HGE, however, it can be assumed that close cooperation is necessary. At the same time, actors who represent different interests must come together. This includes employers who want to increase the attractiveness of training and seek to train highly skilled workers able to adapt to changing working conditions (Thelen 2014). Trade unions are traditionally interested in ensuring the attractiveness of VET and in maintaining equivalence between VET and HGE, but also that

---

[5] Hemkes (2018) also develops several types of permeability that comprise the first three dimensions of the framework by Bernhard (2017). The fourth dimension used here relating to the different needs of learners is not used in Hemkes's conceptualization. However, we contend that this dimension is important because permeability should not only enable transitioning or breaking up institutional barriers but also enable successful learning (Bernhard 2018). Following Bernhard (2017, 2019) and others (Wolter et al. 2014), in our understanding permeability is not sufficiently achieved when, for instance, VET students are allowed to enter HE but systematically fail their studies more often compared to students with a HGE background because of disadvantageous institutional structures.

students and apprentices are treated fairly (Durazzi and Geyer 2020). In Germany, trade unions have been favouring educational programmes that align VET and general education at the secondary level as long as the education is encompassing and not mainly job or firm specific (Bernhard 2017). Actors in HGE itself, like *Gymnasien* and teachers, often defend the social importance and quality of general education qualifications and especially the *Abitur*. This was also evident in the development of the German Qualification Framework (Bernhard 2017). Universities, who increasingly act as political actors in their own right (Graf 2018), aim to enhance their prestige in a competitive HE sector. To a lesser extent, this also holds for schools at the secondary level that seek to recruit talented students. Finally, state actors typically strive for a functioning, coordinated education system that is attractive to their constituents, firms, and citizens, and in which learners complete their training programme and are successful on the labour market (Di Maio et al. 2020).

Thus, actors are traditionally not only separated, but they often also have different interests. But why do they cooperate, nonetheless? Why and to what extent do the actors overcome the challenge of cooperating to enhance institutional permeability? In this context, we need to better understand what such cooperation looks like. For this, we connect the four permeability dimensions with recent research on the type and intensity of cooperation in collective skill formation. Crucially, we contend that the four dimensions of permeability can be linked to different degrees of cooperation between the actors in the respective organizational fields.

To analyse cooperation, we follow Emmenegger et al. (2019: 32–3) in referring to *information exchange, coordination*, and *collaboration* as the three core types of cooperation in systems of collective skill formation. This conceptualization is inspired by Buschfeld and Euler's (1994) conception of learning sites cooperation in VET. *Information exchange* is the most basic type of cooperation. The governance of apprenticeship training on its own already requires substantial information exchange among various actors, for instance, about available training places. Crucially, the need for information exchange is further elevated in programmes that aim to connect the previously separated actors from VET and HGE. In turn, *coordination* denotes 'situations in which actors mutually adjust their behaviour upon the exchanged information' (Emmenegger et al. 2019: 13). It means creating alignment of actions and inter-connectivity. The next level of cooperation is collaboration (or co-production), which requires joint activity from the involved actors to achieve a common objective, like the joint development of the German Qualification Framework (Hemkes 2018).[6]

The three types of cooperation also reflect different degrees (or levels of intensity) of cooperation: information exchange is the weakest and collaboration the strongest form of cooperation. Concurrently, as we show in our empirical analysis, if interests are not aligned between the participating actors, higher degrees of cooperation are more difficult to achieve.

12.3 Dual vocational training with *Abitur* in Germany: key characteristics, case selection, and methods

The institutional conditions within German educational federalism lead to a significant fragmentation in terms of initiatives to enhance permeability. That is, while the German case displays a number of (often individual) programmes and initiatives to enhance permeability, it suffers from a lack of institutionalized structures at the national level (Banscherus et al. 2016). Against the backdrop of such a highly differentiated landscape, acknowledging the decentralized character of educational governance in Germany becomes obvious. In collective skill formation, this typically refers to variation at the regional, sectoral, and occupational levels (Emmenegger et al. 2019). Instead of aiming to fully capture such variety, we zoom in on policy initiatives at the regional level, which address specific sectors and occupations to enhance permeability between VET and HGE. More specifically, we focus on the case in which dual vocational education and training is systematically combined with the *Abitur*. The respective programmes display a high degree of institutional permeability—despite the historically evolved institutional divide between the worlds of vocational and academic learning. We provide an in-depth study of the double qualification programme in Saxony that is referred to as dual apprenticeship training with *Abitur* (Duale Berufsausbildung mit *Abitur* in Sachsen, DuBAS). Essentially, graduates of this programme acquire both the official VET certificate and the *Abitur*. That is, they are eligible to directly enter the labour market as skilled workers and higher VET but also have the same access to universities as graduates of academic upper-secondary schools (e.g. *Gymnasium*). Currently, most initiatives aiming to increase permeability in Germany concentrate on the

---

[6] Hemkes (2018) is helpful when it comes to connecting the three cooperation types to the topic of permeability but uses a different terminology, which we translate here into our terms.

HE system. One example is dual study programmes, which systematically combine university studies with workplace-based training. In comparison, double qualification programmes combining dual training in firms with the *Abitur* have been extremely rare and are not widely institutionalized education options in Germany. DuBAS thus represents a frontrunner initiative located at the secondary-educational level—combining vocational with academic worlds of learning.

To illustrate the permeability character of this programme, it can be noted that DuBAS differs, for instance, from the vocational baccalaureate in Switzerland or the double qualification offered by the vocational colleges in Austria. The Swiss vocational baccalaureate can be acquired in parallel or subsequently to apprenticeship training. However, it offers direct access only to universities of applied sciences, while its holders have to pass a supplementary examination (known as *passerelle*) if they want to enter standard universities. Vocational colleges in Austria offer a VET certificate and a general HE entrance qualification. Yet, they do not involve a proper apprenticeship training but rather simulated workplace-based learning in school labs, thus reducing the degree of practice orientation and related cooperation challenge. Instead, DuBAS integrates a full apprenticeship with a general HE entrance qualification, which makes is it even more interesting for our analysis.

Double qualification programmes at the secondary level that combine some form of vocational education with some form of upper-secondary general education are by now a key topic in collective skill formation systems (Graf 2013; Deißinger et al. 2013a). Studies on permeability between VET and HE argue for an expansion of opportunities to acquire HE entrance qualifications via vocational education and training, in particular through double qualification programmes (Frank et al. 2015; Frommberger 2019). Crucially, such initiatives can be seen to complement adaptations carried out within the VET system that stay within the traditional logic of the VET system (Protsch 2014). In Germany, programmes that combine dual VET with an *Abitur*—i.e. the certificate that grants general access to all HE programmes—existed in the German Democratic Republic but were largely abandoned after reunification (Graf 2013: 104–6). They have also been discussed in (West) Germany since the 1970s (Deißinger 2013b; Wolter 2019: 26).[7] However, they have not yet been widely institutionalized (Frommberger 2019). Until now, only individual initiatives of this kind have been (re-)introduced. Existing programmes

---

[7] The most influential one, the Kollegstufe in Nordrhein-Westfalen, was a school-based approach of integration of vocational and general education but without direct interaction with the dual VET system (Blankertz and Gruschka 1975).

mainly provide a connection between VET and the entrance qualificaton for universities of applied sciences (*Fachhochschulreife*, FHR) in a consecutive manner (Deißinger et al. 2013b).[8]

The four-year DuBAS programme, launched in 2011 in Saxony, was one of the first projects after reunification to systematically combine dual VET with the *Abitur*. Since the 2017–2018 school year, six German states have been participating in a similar pilot project that was initiated by the chambers of crafts. These initiatives stand in the same tradition as the older DuBAS programme and are reactions to the challenges the German education system is facing in VET, in particular. The current trend of implementing pilot programmes integrating dual VET and *Abitur* shows that the need to enhance permeability is also acknowledged by VET policy actors (ZDH and KMK 2015; IHK Berlin 2018). Due to a shortage of applicants and skilled workers, firms like to get involved in these projects because in these they see an opportunity to recruit and retain talented young people at an early stage. The chambers worked together with the Standing Conference of the Ministers of Education and Cultural Affairs of the *Länder* in Germany (*Kultusministerkonferenz*, KMK) on the new dual qualification programmes and developed several models that are to be tested at the various school locations (Pollmer and Roser 2016). However, these initiatives are too young to be meaningfully analysed at this point in time. We therefore focus on the case of DuBAS. DuBAS is a regional project that now includes four different schools in four different cities in Saxony covering different occupations.[9] It was successfully integrated into the Saxon education system after the end of the trial period in 2018—allowing us to draw more general conclusions regarding the other, more recent initiatives.

As programmes leading to such double qualifications are rare in the German context and currently undergoing rapid change with hardly any research literature available, we opted for an explorative research design and gathered primary literature and interview data. We conducted semi-structured expert interviews (Meuser and Nagel 2005) of sixty to ninety minutes each with representatives of one training organization, with representatives of the Saxony education ministry, and with representatives in charge of the scientific evaluation of the DuBAS programme.[10]

---

[8] In 2013, there were more than 1,800 offers nationwide to acquire an FHR as an additional qualification to a vocational qualification, with 9,226 trainees starting this additional qualification (BIBB 2014).

[9] IT specialist or IT system electronics technician, industrial mechanic, tool mechanic, machining mechanic, and industrial clerk.

[10] Interview S1: Dresden, 23 February 2016; Interview S2: Dresden, 23 February 2016; Interview S3: Dresden, 23 February 2016.

In our analysis of the interview data, we applied the tools of theory-guided qualitative content analysis (Gläser and Laudel 2009), combining qualitative content analysis with inductive category formation. Among the overarching categories are the dimensions of institutional permeability and the connected questions of governance and the corresponding barriers or facilitating factors. To complement the interviews, we reviewed existing reports and documents on the DuBAS project, as well as documents and the websites of the participating actors and educational providers. In addition, we checked existing databases that provide relevant information on the VET–HGE nexus (e.g. the ausbildungplus.de database of the Federal Institute of Vocational Education and Training).

12.4 Case study: integrating vocational and academic worlds of learning

In this section, we first analyse in more detail the traditional division between vocational and academic education in Germany. Then, we introduce the Dual Vocational Training with *Abitur* in Saxony (DuBAS) in the context of institutional permeability. Next, we trace the historical evolution of this programme. In the main part, we apply our conceptual framework to the empirical case.

12.4.1 Institutional division between HE and VET in Germany

The German education system is characterized by a historically evolved, institutionalized division between VET and general education (including HE), resulting in two distinct 'institutional orders' (Baethge and Wolter 2015). The differences between these institutional orders can be identified along several lines: first, in their respective governance structures (corporatist actors on the VET side and mainly state actors on the academic side); second, in how they are financed (private and public vs. largely public financing); third, in the status the learners hold during their studies (paid apprentices vs. students/pupils); and lastly, regarding the learning venues (workplace and school vs. only school) (Baethge 2006; Baethge and Wolter 2015).

The renowned German VET system has grown mostly separately from HGE, leading to limited direct pathways in particular for the vocationally qualified individuals to HE. Access to HE in Germany is usually secured via general education. Here, two major types of HE entrance qualifications can be differentiated: the general higher entrance qualification, also referred to as *Abitur*, which allows entrance to all HE institutions, and the FHR that only allows access to universities of applied sciences (Fachhochschulen).

The 'general institutional logic of segregated learning' (Powell and Solga 2011: 54) in Germany, which begins with dividing students at an early age (between 9 and 11) into different tracks, has served to maintain and strengthen the strong divide between HGE and VET, as each track typically leads to one or the other educational career. The tracks that end after lower-secondary schooling traditionally lead to VET. The academic high school track—often realized in the *Gymnasium* or the *Berufsgymnsasium* (vocational *Gymnasium*), where the students receive the *Abitur* or FHR respectively—leads primarily into HE. Accessing the HE system via the VET track has been difficult. VET graduates usually re-enter the general education system and pass their *Abitur* or FHR. Other possibilities, like entrance tests or study trials, are dependent on the existing regulations of the HE laws of the sixteen German states and tend to differ significantly at state and local levels (Ulbricht 2016).

The early tracking in schooltypes after primary education and later in VET and HGE leads to social segregation (Shavit and Müller 2000) and is mirrored in the high social selectivity in access to the HE system (Reimer and Pollak 2010). Thus, from a social inequality perspective, the question of permeability is particularly crucial in education systems that can be described as highly tracked as the German one (Kerckhoff 2001).[11] Without adequate forms of permeability, systems that build on early tracking can 'lock in' individuals into specific educational paths, preventing flexible transitions into other paths. This is particularly problematic in the context of the rising knowledge economy which pushes individuals as well as employers to continuously upgrade their skills portfolio (Powell and Solga 2011).

In recent years, several institutional changes to further institutional permeability between VET and HE have taken place mainly at the post-secondary level (Bernhard 2017; Banscherus et al. 2016). A paradigmatic change happened when access into HE was liberalized in 2009 by the KMK and for the first time higher VET qualifications entitled individuals to enter HE without *Abitur* or other further examinations (KMK 2009). Graduates of initial

---

[11] Not surprisingly, there is a wage premium for academically qualified individuals in Germany. However, it is, on average, lower than in systems without strong tracking structures and a well-established VET system (Powell and Solga 2011). In relative terms, income inequality is less structured by the divide between academic and non-academic jobs in Germany compared to many other countries. Nonetheless, the societal status of the academic pathway is higher than that of the vocational one, as recent survey results have shown again (Bergerhoff et al. 2017).

VET can now enter HE study programmes that are connected to their VET discipline if they have acquired at least three years of professional experience after VET graduation. However, they usually must pass an entry exam or can only enter in trial studies in which they have to perform well in order to be able to keep on studying. It should be noted that in 2016 only around 2.5 per cent of all students in Germany accessed HE without *Abitur* or FHR (Statista 2019). Programmes that support permeability from HE to VET for those who drop out of HE are also beginning to be established. Furthermore, since 2002, 50 per cent of a study programme can be validated via the recognition of prior non-academic learning (see Maurer, in this volume). However, no standardized procedures of recognition exist (Hanft and Müskens 2019). In the following, we focus on the case of institutional permeability related to dual qualification programmes.

12.4.2 Introducing dual vocational training with *Abitur* in Saxony in the context of institutional permeability

DuBAS is a four-year double-qualifying educational programme linking dual vocational training (involving learning in the workplace and the vocational school) with the *Berufsgymnsasium* in Saxony. By integrating both pathways, DuBAS is two years shorter than the consecutive completion of both programmes. In the course of their studies, the students/apprentices repeatedly switch between the learning environment of the firm and school. They learn in blocks, which usually last several weeks, in one of the two environments. They take part in the intermediate and skilled worker examinations as well as the central *Abitur* examinations (Musch 2016; SMK Sachsen 2013).

DuBAS opens up access both to occupations for which a certified VET programme is required as well as to HE—i.e. it offers permeability in both directions. DuBAS is especially interesting to investigate from the perspective of institutional permeability as the integration of VET and the *Abitur* in a single educational programme removes institutional separation at an early stage. Double qualification programmes can be differentiated in consecutive programmes and integrated programmes. DuBAS is an example of an integrated programme, which requires bringing the actors of upper-secondary general education and VET closer together and is, hence, challenging in terms of its governance. It enhances institutional permeability not only between VET and HE but also at secondary level between VET and upper-secondary general education.

Since DuBAS begins at the upper-secondary level and has as its target group students at the lower-secondary schools rather than at the *Gymnasien*, this model is particularly interesting in view of equality of educational opportunity. Research has shown that in Germany an admission to a *Gymnasium* and thus the acquisition of the *Abitur* is strongly dependent on the socio-economic status of the parents (Hillmert and Jacob 2010; Schindler 2015). This selection hurdle could be lower in DuBAS.[12] Moreover, this programme appeals to individuals who require a stable income early on (by preference or by circumstance).

By recruiting students from less prestigious lower-secondary schools and not from *Gymnasium*, the DuBAS programme is an attractive option for students with a lower socio-economic status (SES) and can enhance social mobility. However, here the target group for institutional mobility is not the most vulnerable youth who may fail to get access to decent education or training opportunities. Rather, DuBAS is a way to address those young people who would have a good chance of securing a regular stand-alone apprenticeship but who feel the pressure of upskilling in the knowledge economy. In this way DuBAS can offer upward social mobility for talented students while bringing them into—and potentially keeping them in—the dual VET system. It is for these people who were tracked into the vocational road outside the general *Gymnasien* but are both vocationally interested and academically talented that a programme like DuBAS offers a promising pathway into a dynamically evolving labour market. If the alternative for these young people is to opt for a purely academic education, this would be disadvantageous for VET as it would lose touch with an important pool of talent.[13] At the same time, the combined skills sets that students acquire in a programme like DuBAS are suitable for the knowledge economy (especially in a country like Germany with its bias towards advanced manufacturing) if such programmes successfully integrates both worlds (vocational and academic).

12.4.3 The historical origins of the DuBAS programme

In 2011, the DuBAS project started at two vocational school centres in Leipzig and Dresden for two IT[14] and three metalworking professions.[15] Meanwhile, it is also possible to enter an apprenticeship as an industrial clerk, a vocation

---

[12] Until now, research data on the students' SES enrolled in the DuBAS programmes is nonexistent. However, the interviewees indicated that the participants primarily come from supportive parental homes with an affinity for practical professional activities. That is, they do not regard *Gymnasien* as the only possible route to professional success (Interview S3).

[13] In the DuBAS programme there is always the possibility to change to the academic track at the *Berufsgymnasium* or on to the vocational track and staying with the firm for an initial VET degree in case the double qualification programme turns out to no longer fit the student's wishes and performance. This construction offers a safety net so that students do not have to drop out and firms also do not (completely) lose their investment in the VET-oriented students (Professur für Didaktik des beruflichen Lernens der TU Dresden 2010).

[14] IT specialist or IT system electronics technician.

[15] Industrial mechanic, tool mechanic, and machining mechanic.

with greater demand among female students (Interview S3). The starting point of the programme was the demand for skilled workers, especially by small and medium-sized enterprises (SMEs) in Saxony, in particular in the science, technology, engineering, and mathematics (STEM) sector (Professur für Didaktik des beruflichen Lernens der TU Dresden 2010). For this reason, the chambers, on behalf of SMEs, were important partners in the DuBAS project from the very beginning (Interviews S2, S3). The main interests of the employers and chambers to institutionalize the programme is therefore to attract motivated future employees to their firms at an early stage and plan their careers together. SMEs in particular have difficulty in retaining well-trained specialists, e.g. from universities. With the increasing importance of school certificates qualifying for HE and the trend towards dual study programmes, DuBAS aims to increase the attractiveness of initial VET, and, in particular, of some less popular but important and cognitively demanding training occupations (Interview S3, Musch and Hortsch 2016). In the process of the establishment of DuBAS, the chambers helped select the sectors and occupations and in finding the firms for the pilot. They also cooperated with the different stakeholders in defining the learning block structure and thus also on the distribution of time spent in school and in firms.

The DuBAS programme, initially being a school trial, was conceived in cooperation with vocational educational scientists from Technical University Dresden (TU Dresden) and the Saxon Ministry of Education (Staatsministerium für Kultus) who had just previously reformed the *Berufsgymnasium* in Saxony. The State Ministry of Education was interested in developing a new programme that fitted into the educational architecture of Saxony. The new training course was intended as a possible step towards the vocational academy (*Berufsakademie*) in Saxony which at that time requested the *Abitur* as an access requirement.[16] At the same time, the popular technical universities of applied sciences preferred students with an *Abitur*, too. Thus, if the new educational programme was to be competitive, it had to be possible to acquire the *Abitur* and not just the FHR (Interview S2).

The DuBAS project was, hence, established through strong cooperation between several actors: in particular, the chambers as mediator for the SMEs, the State Ministry of Education, the selected *Berufsgymnasien*, and local vocational education scientists. There were different reasons and interests among the actors to initiate such a common educational programme.

---

[16] The Saxon vocational academy offers dual study programmes that are practice-integrated and end with a bachelor's degree and not with a double qualification (dual apprenticeship and bachelor).

However, these were compatible to the extent that a joint DuBAS programme, on the one hand, maintains the importance of HGE and, on the other hand, makes VET attractive and helps to address the demand for upskilling and the shortage of skilled workers. Eventually, from the perspective of the federal state it creates an attractive, functioning educational programme that also helps to render Saxony attractive as a business location and fits into its educational landscape. However, to make the programme work, it is still necessary to overcome cooperation problems.

12.4.4 The four institutional permeability dimensions in DuBAS and its governance

We next use the multi-dimensional permeability heuristic to investigate DuBAS to determine which dimensions of permeability are promoted and how. Combining it with the types of cooperation, we can analyse how institutional permeability between VET and HGE is organized in the DuBAS programme. Our focus is on institutional permeability at the upper-secondary level as the programme is institutionalized on this level. Yet, since DuBAS per se also enhances permeability to the post-secondary level due to the offered double qualification, we also briefly review to what extent and how permeability to the post-secondary level is enhanced through the cooperation of the actors.

12.4.4.1 Access to education

Access to a DuBAS course is granted to those students who also meet the admission requirements for a *Berufsgymnasium* (Musch 2016). Thus, here the respective regulation of the general education system is decisive. However, at the beginning of the second year, students must have found a firm to train them. The firms decide who is to be trained and stay within the programme. It is therefore a two-step procedure in which the governance regulations of both the school and the vocational training side are applied regarding access to DuBAS. That is, actors from both VET and HGE secured their influence over the selection of the students to ensure the quality of the programme. In the implementation of the access dimension, corporate actors and school actors do not cooperate very strongly with each other. However, in some cases, firms ask the schools about possible promising apprentice candidates (*information exchange*) and the schools sometimes coordinate with the chambers to assist students with their search for an apprenticeship place (*coordination*).

12.4.4.2 Recognition and validation

Questions of recognition and validation had to be clarified during the joint conception of the DuBAS programme. Here a close *coordination* of the participating actors was necessary, given that the two programmes with a duration of three years each needed to be shortened into a programme of four years. However, there were no concrete attempts to validate professional practices and competencies learned in the firms regarding the school-based learning at the *Berufsgymnasium*. In fact, accreditation was limited to the school-based part of dual VET with regards to the requirements of the *Berufsgymnsasium*. For the actors representing general education (*Berufsgymnasien* and the Ministry) it was particularly important that there should be no major deviations from the exact timetable of the *Abitur*, which is determined by the KMK (Interview S1, S3). The fear was that the certificate would not be recognized nationally as a real *Abitur*. However, the chambers emphasized that the criteria of the final exams of the VET diploma also need to be met without any concessions. The resulting strict regulation of the number of hours is also a reason why other models, such as the vocational baccalaureate in Switzerland and Austria, are not regarded as equivalent to the German *Abitur* or *Fachhochschulreife* by parts of the KMK, and partially why the Swiss and Austrian models are also not used to advertise DuBAS (Interview S3). Today, in the day-to-day operations of DuBAS, issues around validation rarely occur.

12.4.4.3 Organizational integration

The DuBAS programme systematically combines the learning contents and venues of vocational training with those of the upper-secondary general education of the *Berufsgymnasium* into one programme and makes it possible to obtain a double qualification. Thus, the competences acquired at school are enriched and applied through recurrent practical experiences in firms. This mutual reflection of practice and theory was assessed by the students as particularly positive and represents a strong indicator for the potential success of these integrated educational pathways, in contrast to consecutive ones (Interview S1, S3).

Crucially, *collaboration* by the involved actors was necessary to create this programme. When actors decided to build an integrated double qualifying programme, they had to *collaborate* intensely on what the programme should look like: they decided on the occupational sectors, the curricula, the time schedule (length of block structures), and the financial aspects (apprentices get paid from the second to the fourth year).

When looking at the day-to-day practice and the implementation of the curriculum, continuous *coordination* between the teachers involved in the vocational school and *Berufsgymnasium* (in all subjects) as well as the in-firm trainers is crucial (SMK Sachsen 2013, Interview S1). For instance, schoolteachers turn to the firms to *inform* them about a perceived lack of practical knowledge of the trainees, while the firms point out the lack of theoretical or basic knowledge. One reaction to such *feedback processes* was the adaptation of corresponding learning units in the schools (Interview S1). The two spheres of learning in the firms and in the school stay mostly sepa-rate but actors are involved in *mutual feedback processes* regarding students' development and the working structure of the programme. Nonetheless, the students do the main boundary work in combining what they have learnt in each venue.

A further example of *coordination* is that the blocks of time spent in firms and at school were adapted in one school after the firms criticized the exist-ing structure. The interests of the firms, in particular the SMEs, are that students stay for a longer period of time in the firms so that they can be a productive workforce and are able to learn about the whole work process. The school-side, however, feared that the quality of the education would suffer and that the students could fail more easily because too long a time away from school makes it difficult for the students to start where they left off. Eventu-ally, a compromise could be found through intensive *coordination* (Interview S1, S3).

12.4.4.4 Dealing with heterogeneous needs

When analysing support structures dealing with the heterogeneous needs of the learners and the related actors' cooperation, we found that the DuBAS programmes offer various counselling, information, and support services which are intended to help participants to succeed. Since this is a relatively new educational programme, information and counselling services that draw attention to DuBAS are important. This is done in a *coordinated* way. All the relevant actors in both VET and general education are involved in these activities (Interview S1).

The DuBAS programme can be regarded as rather demanding since the time burden on students is high. In addition to this, the constant re-orientation from school to professional requirements is described as very challenging (Interview S3). To cushion these burdens, support structures in the form of trust teachers were set up in the course of the training itself to help with problems at school or in the firms. This structure is mainly situated in the school but is thought to assist individual students in relation to the whole programme. In this context, *information exchange* between firms and school takes place and sometimes *coordinated* action too.

Finally, continuous, systematic meetings between firms and schools are held to draw attention to problems and difficulties within the educational programmes (Interview S1, S3). Here *information* is not only *exchanged*, but possible measures to ameliorate the educational situation for the actors and students involved are discussed and then implemented. For this, *coordination* between the actors is necessary.

12.4.4.5 DuBAS and permeability to the post-secondary educational level

After the successful completion of the DuBAS programme, the double qualification dual VET with *Abitur* opens up possibilities to access both higher VET as well as HE institutions. Institutional permeability regarding access is thus secured. Since the double qualification legally entitles the students to enter both higher VET and HE, cooperation after graduation is not necessary for the respective actors. Currently, no concrete cooperation is taking place with actors of post-secondary educational organizations either regarding validation of competencies, support structures, or in the form of institutionalized linkages to specific organizations. Cooperation in DuBAS thus mainly takes place between actors at the secondary level. Hence, in the DuBAS programme itself, specific counselling on the various educational opportunities with this certificate in HE or higher VET remains limited, i.e. no explicit support structures to facilitate transitions after graduation are in place. Only the obligatory vocational counselling takes place. As became clear in the interviews, opinions amongst the actor-types differ strongly in these matters. For instance, while schoolteachers ask why it would be necessary to work hard to obtain the *Abitur* if a transition to HE is not intended, the firms do not see HE as the necessary next step but more as an option for the future (Interview S1, S2). Many schoolteachers see studying as the natural next step after graduating with the *Abitur*, while for firms DuBAS is mainly a way to keep talented youth in the VET system. The scientific monitoring of the DuBAS project has shown that more than half of those surveyed plan to take up studies immediately after graduation (Musch 2016), a fact that is partly dissatisfying for the firms trying to retain their students. However, the employers hope that DuBAS graduates are more likely to consider coming back after studying (Interview S2). With this in mind, the participating *Berufsgymnasien* tend to act with caution and avoid displeasing firms or chambers by proactively promoting HE pathways. Thus, while no collaboration between the DuBAS stakeholders takes place concerning educational pathways after graduation, the schools still act with their corporative DuBAS partners in mind. Hence, actors at the post-secondary level still act in a *coordinated way* in order to secure the viability of the DuBAS programme.

12.4.4.6 Key findings and summary

The DuBAS programme enhances institutional permeability between VET and HGE in all four dimensions, in particular regarding organizational integration at the upper-secondary level and access to higher VET and HE. In addition, the high demands of the programme for the individual learners are considered by way of institutionalizing support structures. Nevertheless, it is the students who must do the main boundary work of combining the two worlds of learning in practice.

Table 12.1 illustrates the types of cooperation paired with the permeability dimensions for the time of the initiation of DuBAS as well as the time of implementation, i.e. its day-to-day operation. We find that during the

Table 12.1 Key examples for permeability between vocational and academic worlds of learning—a multi-dimension analysis of the DuBAS case

Cooperation		Dimensions of permeability			
Intensity	Type	Access	Recognition and validation	Organizational integration	Support for heterogeneity
Low	Information exchange	Exchange to find apprentices/ apprenticeships	Exchange on crediting decisions regarding the programme curriculum (during initiation)	Exchange on curriculum and learning structure	Exchange regarding counselling and trust teachers
Medium	Coordination	Schools coordinate with chambers to assist students with their search for apprenticeship places	Curriculum adaptation of the school part to reduce the overall length of the programme (during initiation)	Implementation and adaptation of the curriculum and learning structures; institutionalized transitions for dropouts	Advertisement of the programme; institutionalized coordination between schools and firms (e.g. counselling services)
High	Collaboration			Setting up of the overall programme	

initiation phase, the actors of VET and HGE needed to strongly collaborate to set up this programme. To overcome the long-standing institutional division between vocational and academic worlds, the most demanding form of cooperation was necessary. Here the focus was on integrating the different qualifications, venues, timetables, modes of finance, and curricula into one programme (*organizational integration*). In particular, questions around curricula and what could be validated presuppose intense negotiations (*recognition and validation*). However, the strict requirements for the *Abitur* prevented stronger curricular collaboration and integration beyond the vocational school part.

Constant collaboration to ensure institutional permeability seems not to be essential once the programme is established. For instance, access is regulated in a consecutive way leaving the control in the hands of both the stakeholders of VET and HGE. However, we find that if problems or difficulties in the programme occur—e.g. regarding the search and recruitment of apprentices (*access*), the proper measurement of learning blocks (*organizational integration*), or the competence development and learning processes of the students (*support for the learners*)—the actors come together and try to solve the problems first through information exchange and—if that is not sufficient—through coordination. The problem-solving takes place with the help of institutionalized cooperation forms like regular meetings or spontaneously when difficulties arise. But since learning venues stay relatively independent from each other, these are rarely collaborative activities. Rather, by using information exchange and coordination, most of the problems are then tackled in the respective venues.

The main actors involved changed between the initiation phases and day-to-day practice. During the establishment of the programme, the chambers, on behalf of the firms, the Ministry of Education, the schools, and the scientific experts were the main actors involved. After DuBAS was set up, the cooperation was more localized between the firms, the respective schools, and sometimes the chambers since the reasons for the cooperation were situated less on the governance level of the overall DuBAS programme in Saxony but were linked more to specific local and sometimes individual problems in the schools and firms.

12.5 Outlook

As collective skill formation systems adapt to the knowledge economy, the question of institutional permeability between vocational and academic worlds of learning has become increasingly salient. While the challenge to enhance institutional permeability is felt by all stakeholders, the actual building of programmes that promote such permeability is highly demanding as it often requires the cooperation of these actors from two different fields and their respective—and at least partially conflicting—interests. This is even more true in the case of educational projects integrating both worlds of learning into one programme, as in the case of double qualification programmes like DuBAS. Yet, these initiatives provide several advantages. They can create institutional permeability, can enhance the attractiveness of initial VET, can help firms to recruit skilled workers at an early age, and can increase equality of educational opportunity since they are tailored to be within reach for students from less prestigious lower-secondary schools as well.

We asked in which ways the DuBAS programme provides institutional permeability and how and why the actors of VET and HGE cooperate to enable the programme. For this purpose, we developed a conceptual framework that allowed us to capture the cooperation types involved in building institutional permeability between VET and HGE. We find that DuBAS, which promotes a polyvalent skill set well suited for the demands of the knowledge economy, enhances institutional permeability between VET and HGE in all four dimensions: DuBAS provides access to higher VET and HE. The programme itself promotes organizational linkages by integrating dual VET and the *Abitur*. During this process also questions of what can be recognized and validated to integrate the curricula and decrease the programme length were answered. Finally, it is acknowledged that the integration of VET and HGE is also challenging for the students who must shoulder the main burden of the boundary work. Therefore, the stakeholders institutionalized support structures that help students to successfully graduate.

We find that programmes such as DuBAS present all the stakeholders involved with numerous challenges but also opportunities. On the one hand, the integration of VET and HGE is very demanding for everyone involved. On the other hand, it can be asserted that the added value of this form of training lies precisely in overcoming potential conflicts based on the different interests of the various actors. In this context, relying on less demanding forms of cooperation can be an option where compromise is difficult to reach. Collaboration (the most demanding level of cooperation) took place in the phase of initiation. The program was then set up in a way that its further implementation is mainly based on information exchange and coordination. Our case study thus suggests that in the initiation phase of such a permeability programme, actors of VET and HGE need to collaborate strongly. However, constant collaboration to ensure institutional permeability is not a necessary condition once the programme is established. That is, once governance challenges arise in the implementation, actors can come together and try to solve the problems first through information exchange and, if this is not sufficient, through coordination. Over time, information exchange and coordination can enhance mutual understanding of the actors involved from the two sides of the institutional divide between VET and HGE and thus help to overcome taken-for-granted assumptions on the respective sectors, which is arguably a key condition for the successful institutionalization of permeability-enhancing programmes in the long run.

Another important feature of DuBAS is its orientation to the needs of the local economy. Further research could consider in more detail the regional composition of employers regarding such permeability measures. Especially SMEs can be strong partners in the development of dual qualification programmes. While it is mainly large firms that benefit from rapidly expanding dual study programmes (Graf 2018), SMEs are often left on their own in their struggle to cope with the shortage of skilled workers. Programmes such as DuBAS offer the advantage that they allow SMEs to recruit talented young people, while also being attractive to larger firms. Thus, it seems politically possible to form coalitions among SMEs and larger enterprises around such programmes—together with other stakeholders at the respective regional, sectoral, and occupational levels. However, it should be borne in mind that—given the complex decentralized governance configuration of collective skill formation—increasing permeability is not a trivial task. This implies that a fine-grained understanding of both permeability and cooperation is needed to capture how actors work to adjust collective skill formation to the knowledge economy.

References

Arntz, M., T. Gregory, and U. Zierahn. 2016. *The Risk of Automation for Jobs in OECD Countries*. OECD Social, Employment and Migration Working Paper No. 189. Paris: OECD.

Autorengruppe Bildungsberichterstattung. 2018. *Bildung in Deutschland 2018*. Bielefeld: wbv.

Baethge, M. 2006. 'Das deutsche Bildungs-Schisma'. *SOFI-Mitteilungen 34*: 13–27.

Baethge, M., and A. Wolter. 2015. 'The German Skill Formation Model in Transition'. *Journal for Labour Market Research 48* (2): 97–112.

Banscherus, U., N. Bernhard, and L. Graf. 2016. *Durchlässigkeit als mehrdimensionale Aufgabe. Bedingungen für flexible Bildungsübergänge.* Berlin: Friedrich-Ebert-Stiftung.

Bergerhoff, J. N., B. Hemkes, P. K. Seegers, and K.-M. Wiesner. 2017. *Attraktivität der beruflichen Bildung bei Studierenden.* Bonn: BIBB.

Bernhard, N. 2017. *Durch Europäisierung zu mehr Durchlässigkeit? Veränderungsdynamiken des Verhältnisses von Berufs- und Hochschulbildung in Deutschland und Frankreich.* Leverkusen: Budrich UniPress.

Bernhard, N. 2018. 'Gesteigerte Durchlässigkeit bei gleichzeitigen Schließungsprozessen: Veränderungsdynamiken zwischen Berufs- und Hochschulbildung in Frankreich'. *Zeitschrift für Soziologie der Erziehung und Sozialisation 38* (3): 267–83.

Bernhard, N. 2019. 'Répondre aux besoins des diplômés de l'enseignement professionnel allemand: vers une perméabilité institutionnelle?' *Formation emploi 146*: 129–47.

BIBB. 2014. *AusbildungPlus in Zahlen. Trends und Analysen 2013.* Bonn: BIBB.

Blankertz, H., and A. Gruschka. 1975. 'Kollegstufe Nordrhein-Westfalen als Testfall demokratischer Bildungsreform'. *Paedagogica Europaea 10* (2): 147–58.

Bonoli, G., and P. Emmenegger. 2021. 'The Limits of Decentralized Cooperation: Promoting Inclusiveness in Collective Skill Formation Systems?' *Journal of European Public Policy 28* (2): 229–47.

Bonoli, G., and A. Wilson. 2019. 'Bringing Firms on Board. Inclusiveness of the Dual Apprenticeship Systems in Germany, Switzerland and Denmark'. *International Journal of Social Welfare 28* (4): 369–79.

Buschfeld, D., and D. Euler. 1994. 'Überlegungen zur Kooperation der Lernorte'. *BWP 23* (2): 9–13.

Busemeyer, M. R., and C. Trampusch. 2012. 'The Comparative Political Economy of Collective Skill Formation'. In *The Political Economy of Collective Skill Formation*, edited by M. R. Busemeyer and C. Trampusch, pp. 3–38. Oxford: Oxford University Press.

Carstensen, M. B., and C. L. Ibsen. 2021. 'Three Dimensions of Institutional Contention'. *Socio-Economic Review 19* (3): 1037–63.

Deißinger, T., J. Aff, A. Fuller, and C. H. Jørgensen (eds). 2013a. *Hybrid Qualifications.* Bern: Peter Lang.

Deißinger, T., R. Wem, R. Heine, and M. Ott. 2013b. 'Progression from VET into Higher Education via Hybrid Qualifications in Germany'. In *Hybrid Qualifications,* edited by T. Deißinger, J. Aff, A. Fuller, and C. Helms Jørgensen, pp. 111–45. Bern: Peter Lang.

Di Maio, G., L. Graf, and A. Wilson 2019. 'Torn between Economic Efficiency and Social Equality? Short-track Apprenticeships in Denmark, Germany, and Switzerland'. *European Educational Research Journal 18* (6): 699–723.

Di Maio, G., L. Graf, and A. Wilson 2020. 'Embedded Flexibilization and Polite Employer Domination: The Case of Short-track Apprenticeships in Switzerland'. *Empirical Research in Vocational Education and Training 12* (2): 1–21. https://doi. org/10.1186/s40461-020-00088-7.

Durazzi, N., and L. Geyer. 2020. 'Social Inclusion in the Knowledge Economy'. *Socio-Economic Review 18* (1): 103–24.

Emmenegger, P., L. Graf, and C. Trampusch. 2019. 'The Governance of Decentralised Cooperation in Collective Training Systems: A Review and Conceptualisation'. *Journal of Vocational Education and Training 71* (1): 21–45.

Euler, D., and E. Severing. 2019. *Berufsbildung für eine digitale Arbeitswelt*. Gütersloh: BertelsmannStiftung.

Frank, I., M. Heister, and G. Walden. 2015. *Berufsbildung und Hochschulbildung. Durchlässigkeit und Verzahnung als bildungspolitische Herausforderungen*. Bonn: BIBB.

Frommberger, D. 2019. *Wege zwischen beruflicher und hochschulischer Bildung*. Gütersloh: BertelsmannStiftung.

Gläser, J., and G. Laudel. 2009. *Experteninterviews und qualitative Inhaltsanalyse als Instrumente rekonstruierender Untersuchungen*. Wiesbaden: VS.

Gonon, P. 2013. 'Federal Vocational Baccalaureate: The Swiss Way of "Hybridity."' In *Hybrid Qualifications*, edited by T. Deißinger, J. Aff, A. Fuller, and C. Helms Jørgensen, pp. 181–96. Bern: Peter Lang.

Graf, L. 2013. *The Hybridization of Vocational Training and Higher Education in Austria, Germany, and Switzerland*. Leverkusen: Budrich UniPress.

Graf, L. 2018. 'Combined Modes of Gradual Change: The Case of Academic Upgrading and Declining Collectivism in German Skill Formation'. *Socio-Economic Review 16* (1): 185–205.

Hanft, A., and W. Müskens. 2019. 'Anerkennung und Anrechnung beruflicher Qualifikationen und Kompetenzen im Hochschulbereich'. In *Durchlässigkeit zwischen beruflicher und hochschulischer Bildung*, edited by B. Hemkes, K. Wilbers, and M. Heister, pp. 184–98. Leverkusen: Barbara Budrich.

Hemkes, B. 2018. 'Zwischen Studium und Beruf: Formate und Handlungskoordinationen im Kontext von Durchlässigkeit'. *BWP 34*: 1–23.

Hillmert, S., and M. Jacob. 2010. 'Selections and Social Selectivity on the Academic Track'. *Research in Social Stratification and Mobility 28* (1): 59–76. doi: 10.1016/j.rssm.2009.12.006.

IHK Berlin. 2018. 'Berlin führt das Duale Abitur/Berufsabitur ein'. https://www. ihk-berlin.de/presse/presseinfo/Archiv-Pressemitteilungen/pressemitteilungen-2018/pressemitteilungen-04-06/Neuer_Inhalt2018-06-27-duales-abitur/4114938 [accessed 1 November 2019].

Kerckhoff, A. C. 2001. 'Education and Social Stratification Processes in Comparative Perspective'. *Sociology of Education 74*: 3–18.

KMK—Kultusministerkonferenz. 2009. 'Hochschulzugang für beruflich qualifizierte Bewerber ohne schulische Hochschulzugangsberechtigung, Beschluss der Kultusministerkonferenz vom 06. 03.2009'. http://www.kmk.org/fileadmin/veroeffentlichungen_beschluesse/2009/2009_03_06-Hochschulzugang-erful-qualifizierte-Bewerber.pdf [accessed 1 November 2019].

Mayer, K. U., and H. Solga (eds). 2008. *Skill Formation*. New York: Cambridge University Press.

Meuser, M., and U. Nagel. 2005. 'ExpertInneninterviews'. In *Das Experteninterview*, edited by A. Bogner, B. Littig, and W. Menz, pp. 71–94. Wiesbaden: VS.

Musch, R. 2016. 'Berufsausbildung mit Abitur'. *BWP 46* (1): 44–7.

Musch, R., and H. Hortsch. 2016. 'DuBAS—Duale Berufsausbildung mit *Abitur* Sachsen. Ergebnisse der begleitenden Evaluation'. https://tu-dresden.de/gsw/ew/ibbd/bp/ressourcen/dateien/Abschlussbericht_DuBAS. pdf?lang=5Bu%27%5D&set_language=de [accessed 8 July 2020].

Pollmer, M., and G. Roser. 2016. 'Duale Ausbildung und *Abitur*'. *BWP 45* (6): 52–3.

Powell, J. J. W., N. Bernhard, and L. Graf. 2012. 'The Emerging European Model in Skill Formation: Comparing Higher Education and Vocational Training in the Bologna and Copenhagen Processes'. *Sociology of Education 85* (3): 240–58.

Powell, J. J. W., and H. Solga. 2011. 'Why Are Participation Rates in Higher Education in Germany So Low?' *Journal of Education and Work 24* (1–2): 49–68.

Professur für Didaktik des beruflichen Lernens der TU Dresden. 2010: 'Schulversuch Duale Berufsausbildung mit *Abitur* Sachsen'. http://docplayer.org/6329321-Schulversuch-duale-berufsausbildung-mit-abitur-sachsen-dubas-konzeption. html [accessed 18 December 2021].

Protsch, P. 2014. *Segmentierte Ausbildungsmärkte*. Opladen: Budrich UniPress.

Protsch, P., and H. Solga. 2015. 'How Employers Use Signals of Cognitive and Noncognitive Skills at Labour Market Entry'. *European Sociological Review 31* (5): 521–32.

Reimer, D., and R. Pollak. 2010. 'Educational Expansion and its Consequences for Vertical and Horizontal Inequalities in Access to Higher Education in West Germany'. *European Sociological Review 26* (4): 415–30.

Schindler, S. 2015. 'Soziale Ungleichheit im Bildungsverlauf?' *Kölner Zeitschrift für Soziologie und Sozialpsychologie 67* (3): 509–37.

Scott, W. R. 2008. *Institutions and Organizations*. Thousand Oaks: Sage Publications.

Shavit, Y., and W. Müller. 2000. 'Vocational Secondary Education, Tracking, and Social Stratification'. In *The Handbook of the Sociology of Education*, edited by M. T. Hallinan, pp. 437–52. New York: Kluwer.

SMK—Sächsisches Staatsministerium für Kultus. 2013: 'Erprobungslehrplan Berufsschule/Berufliches Gymnasium'. http://www.schule.sachsen.de/download/download_sbi/LP_DuBAS_Informationstechnik_2013_Endfassung.pdf [accessed 20 March 2016].

Statista. 2019. 'Immer mehr Studis ohne Abi'. https://de.statista.com/infografik/13424/studierende-in-deutschland-ohne-abitur/ [accessed 31 October 2019].

Thelen, K. 2014. *Varieties of Liberalization and the New Politics of Social Solidarity*. New York: Cambridge University Press.

Thelen, K. 2019. 'Transitions to the Knowledge Economy in Germany, Sweden, and the Netherlands'. *Comparative Politics 51* (2): 295–315.

Ulbricht, L. 2016. *Föderalismus als Innovationslabor?* Baden-Baden: Nomos.

Wolter, A. 2019. 'Abschied vom Bildungsschisma'? In *Studienintegrierende Ausbildung*, edited by D. Euler, V. Meyer-Guckel, and E. Severing, pp. 21–41. Essen: Edition Stifterverband.

Wolter, A., U. Banscherus, C. Kamm, A. Otto, and A. Spexard. 2014. 'Durchlässigkeit zwischen beruflicher und akademischer Bildung als mehrstufiges Konzept'. *Beiträge zur Hochschulforschung 36* (4): 8–39.

Young, M., K. Spours, C. Howieson, and D. Raffe. 1997. 'Unifying Academic and Vocational Learning and the Idea of a Learning Society'. *Journal of Education Policy 12* (6): 527–37.

ZDH and KMK. 2015. 'Gemeinsames Positionspapier. Stärkung der Attraktivität der Berufsbildung'. Berlin: Zentralverband des Deutschen Handwerks (ZDH) and Kultusministerkonferenz (KMK).

13

Declining Collectivism at the Higher and Lower End

The Increasing Role of the Austrian State in Times of Technological Change

Lina Seitzl and Daniel Franz Unterweger

13.1 Introduction

Collective skill formation systems are prime examples of coordinated capitalism given their high levels of coordination between public and private actors (Crouch et al. 1999; Streeck and Yamamura 2001; Thelen 2014; Hall and Soskice 2001). However, the knowledge economy, characterized by 'production and services based on knowledge-intensive activities that contribute to an accelerated pace of technological and scientific advance' (Powell and Snellman 2004), challenge the premises these systems build on. The jobs apprenticeships have traditionally prepared for—mid-level jobs in the industrial sector—disappear (Anderson and Hassel 2013; Wren et al. 2013; OECD 2005). Against it, due to upskilling or skill polarization, higher and more general skills become increasingly important, reinforcing cooperation dilemmas in collective skill formation systems (Culpepper and Thelen 2008). Thus, the question arises how these systems react to the pressure the knowledge economy puts on them.

The literature on the comparative political economy of skill formation systems has outlined the reform trajectories of collective skill formation systems in the face of these pressures. While many countries reform dual vocational education and training (VET) around the specific needs of business in order to trigger continued employer coordination (Thelen and Busemeyer 2012; Emmenegger and Seitzl 2019; Graf 2018), literature has paid less attention on the potential role of the state in responding to structural pressures (see Thelen 2014 for a prominent exception). In this chapter, we analyse employer

Lina Seitzl and Daniel Franz Unterweger, *Declining Collectivism at the Higher and Lower End*. In: *Collective Skill Formation in the Knowledge Economy*. Edited by Giuliano Bonoli and Patrick Emmenegger, Oxford University Press.
© Oxford University Press (2022). DOI: 10.1093/oso/9780192866257.003.0013

reactions to situations in which the state replaces firms in the provision of skills.[1] We argue that, while initially not intended, the expansion of statist training in the face of structural challenges reinforces the decline of the number of training firms because it 'unconstrains' firms, offering an attractive exit opportunity from employer coordination. While we do not focus on the political determinants that lead to an expanded role of statist training, we examine the potential effects this expanded role can have on the nature of collective skill formation systems and coordinated capitalism more broadly.

We analyse such trajectories in the case of Austria, a prototypical collective skill formation system (Busemeyer and Trampusch 2012). Specifically, we look at the higher as well as the lower end of the upper-secondary level skill distribution: the expansion of vocational training to the field of information and communication technologies (ICT) (higher end) and the introduction of public training workshops (lower end). This case selection allows us to shed light on the two areas of the skill distribution particularly affected by the knowledge economy. Trends towards higher skill needs do not only lead to a growth of educational options at the higher end of the skill distribution but also necessitate the integration of those unable to cope with increasing skill demands (e.g. the lower end). Consequently, both sectors can be expected to expand as the growth of the knowledge economy progresses—albeit mediated by economic trends and political contestation.

In both of our cases, the same processes are visible. Drawing on primary and secondary literature, a series of semi-structured expert interviews and newspaper articles, we find that institutional change in Austria's skill formation system is a case of layering, where statist elements are added to collective solutions. Although employers and/or their associations initially opposed these state-led solutions, they have increasingly learned to like them over the course of time because they allow them to save costs while the provision of a well-trained workforce is still ensured. In both cases, employers and their associations developed policy preferences supportive to a further decline of collective training, as they learned to appreciate the benefits that these statist VET schemes offer.

[1] The chapter was presented at the GOVPET Conference 'Collective Skill Formation in the Knowledge Economy' (21–22 November 2019), the SASE Virtual Conference (2–5 July 2020), as well as the 7th Austrian Conference on VET Research (8–8 July 2021). The authors are grateful for the comments received in these settings. Furthermore, we thank the editors and Jörg Markowitsch for helpful comments on earlier versions of this chapter.

13.2 Statism in collective skill formation

Collective skill formation systems are characterized by a high degree of employer coordination in the provision, financing, and administration of VET (Busemeyer and Trampusch 2012). The knowledge economy, characterized by increasing demand for higher and more general skills, challenges this high level of coordination (see also Bonoli and Emmenegger, Chapter 1). On the one hand, many accounts argue that jobs at the higher and lower end of the skill distribution become increasingly important, and the service sector grows (Cedefop 2018; Goos and Manning 2007; Goos et al. 2009). This increases not only the skill provision at the higher end but also raises the question of whether newly created jobs at the lower end still necessitate costly collective training. On the other hand, Oesch and Rodríguez Menés (2011) and Helmrich et al. (2016) are critical of the polarization thesis and find that labour markets are comprehensively 'upgraded' towards higher skill levels in some economies. Still, the jobs apprenticeships have traditionally prepared for—mid-level jobs in the industrial sector—disappear, increasing the importance of integrating academically weaker and socially disadvantaged groups into the labour market. In sum, the collective nature of dual training systems is under pressure, as the declining number of training firms in collective skill formation systems shows (Culpepper and Thelen 2008; Thelen 2014, 2009; Thelen and Busemeyer 2012). The question arises how collective skill formation systems react to this pressure on the higher and lower end of the skill distribution.

The comparative political economy literature has increasingly identified dualizing reform trajectories of coordinated market economies (Palier and Thelen 2010; Emmenegger et al. 2012; Rueda 2005). Dualization is characterized by increasing divisions between labour market insiders, employed in core sectors shaped by continued employer coordination and covered by generous institutional arrangements concerning welfare and labour market policies, and uncovered outsiders at the periphery. The processes that lead to a dualization of skill formation systems have been described in the research on institutional change in the collective training systems of Germany and Switzerland. A process of 'segmentalism' is argued to be an answer to the massive decline in the number of training firms (Thelen and Busemeyer 2012). In order to stop this decline and keep employer coordination in place, collective skill formation systems increasingly cater to the demands of (large) firms which prefer firm-specific training content over more general skills, leading to the division of the VET system into ever-smaller segments (Busemeyer 2012; Thelen and Busemeyer 2012; Busemeyer and Iversen 2012). Thereby, instances of segmentalism can be found at the higher (Graf 2018;

Emmenegger and Seitzl 2019) as well as the lower end of the skill distribution (Busemeyer 2012; Thelen and Busemeyer 2012).

In the face of structural pressures, the state can also play an increasing role. Streeck (1997a) has shown that social institutions, 'based in formal law or in a common culture', can trigger collective action by constraining employer behaviour. As the benefits of participating in dual VET cannot be safely and permanently appropriated by an individual firm, their cost-benefit calculations are subject to substantial uncertainty. Consequently, employers favour short-term economic benefits over long-term investments in training. However, the presence of constraints like high wages, egalitarian wage-setting, employment security (Streeck 2004; Sorge and Streeck 2018), and an environment where the '[c]ontinuous monitoring of one's short-term balance of economic advantage is not a social norm' can incentivize firms to train (Streeck 1997b). More specifically, such institutions are 'transforming the preferences of actors [. . .], teaching them what they really want' (Streeck 1997a)—namely collective skill formation. Recently, for example Martin and Thelen (2007) and Unterweger (2020) have shown how the state, responding to structural trends, can still implement new constraints on employer behaviour and cajole employers into collective action.

Acknowledging the potential key role of the state in responding to structural pressures, we are focusing on a different type of state involvement. Similar to Thelen (2014), albeit less interested in the inclusiveness dimension, we focus on instances where the state replaces employer coordination instead of fostering collective action among firms. More specifically, we aim to shed light on the potential processes of employer withdrawal when the state steps in. What happens to collective skill formation if the state takes over tasks previously fulfilled by employers?

We acknowledge that the state can respond to the pressures of the knowledge economy by expanding its role at the higher and lower end of the skill distribution in order to make up for declining employer coordination. But most importantly, we argue that such expansion of the state's role may reinforce the decline of training firms. As an unintended but essential side-effect of responding to an initial decrease in employer coordination due to structural pressures, the state 'unconstrains' employers by providing them with an attractive exit opportunity from employer coordination and costly collective training. Statist training elements, if they are of sufficient quality, allow firms to recruit skilled workers while circumventing the costs of collective training. Consequently, the role of the state becomes more interventionist, but in contrast to state intervention in the form of 'beneficial constraints', it changes its nature from being 'discretion-limiting to discretion-enhancing' (Howell 2016).

This does not necessarily mean that employers will actively support such an expanded role for the state. First, employer associations are not primarily driven by the short-term cost considerations of their member firms but are instead interested in securing long-term influence (Carstensen and Ibsen 2021; Streeck and Schmitter 1985). Collective training enables associations to exercise control because they are substantially involved in the governance of these arrangements. Therefore, they might consider increasing state involvement as a threat and respond with opposition. Second, not all individual firms might welcome statist training initially, due to quality concerns for example.

However, associations and firms might later reconsider and learn to like the respective statist schemes. As emphasized by Streeck (2004), employers are 'learning from experience and thereby redefining, if not their interests, then their preferences' in politically redefined contexts. In our case, this is visible in a process of 'layering', where new elements are added to existing institutions and set 'in motion dynamics through which they, over time, actively crowd out or supplant by default the old system' (Streeck and Thelen 2005) by 'affecting the interests and strategic options available to various groups' (Thelen 2004). In other words, the newly available statist training schemes give business new attractive opportunities to train outside the collective system that did previously not exist, thereby over time shaping their policy-preferences in favour of statist training. This does not only hold for individual firms, but also associations. While the latter might initially oppose an expanded role for the state, it is unlikely that they can also act against the preferences of their member firms in the long term.

Thus, while not necessarily intended by decision-makers during their introduction, statist elements can create new supportive preferences among employers, reinforcing the expansion of statist instruments at the cost of collective training.

13.3 Statist training in Austria's skill formation system

In order to show how employer coordination decreases when the state steps in, we look at the case of Austria. Austria is considered a prototypical collective skill formation system, characterized by a high share of VET and a strong corporatist tradition (Busemeyer and Trampusch 2012; Katzenstein 1984). Similar to other collective skill formation systems, the number of training firms in Austria has been shrinking continuously since the late 1990s. With only a few exemptions, there were always more apprenticeship seekers than open apprenticeship positions (Dornmayr and Nowak 2018). However, in contrast to Germany, this did not lead to an increasing influence of large firms. Instead, statist tendencies in skill formation have been increasing in Austria.

In this chapter, we analyse reform trajectories at the higher and the lower end of the skill distribution, triggered by the 1998 National Action Plan for Employment (NAP).[2] This case selection allows us to shed light on the two areas of the skill distribution particularly affected by the knowledge economy. Trends towards higher skills do not only lead to a growth of educational options at the higher end of the skill distribution but also necessitate the integration of those unable to cope with increasing skills demands (e.g. the lower end). Both areas of the skill distribution can be expected to grow as the growth of the knowledge economy progresses—albeit mediated by economic trends and political contestation.

First, at the lower end of the skill distribution, the NAP initiated the introduction of public training workshops that offer individuals unsuccessful on the apprenticeship market the opportunity to participate in VET (see also Durazzi and Geyer, in this volume). Originally only introduced as a preliminary emergency measure to 'rescue' dual training, workshops have developed into a permanent feature of the Austrian skill formation system. Second, at the higher end of the skill distribution, the federal government expanded VET as part of the NAP to ICT, a field that is characterized by higher and more general skill needs (Eurostat 2019; Wren et al. 2013). Therewith, Austria attempted to follow Germany and Switzerland's success in establishing ICT apprenticeships in the 1990s (Stern et al. 2003; Borch and Weissmann 2000). However, in Austria, the introduction of ICT training in full-time schools crowded out employer participation in dual VET at the higher end of the skills distribution. Both ICT full-time schools and public training workshops, layered on top of the standard collective training system, freed firms from constraints by providing new exit options from standard dual training that resulted in the further decrease of collectivism in the Austrian skill formation system. In both instances, employer associations initially defended the collective system, but as firms themselves learned to like statist training, the policy preferences of the business community were transformed over time.

---

[2] The NAP was supposed to tackle a crisis in Austria's apprenticeship market, which coincided with rising unemployment in the European Union more generally. The EU member states committed themselves to create individual 'National Action Plans for Employment' in accordance with common employment guidelines in exchange for access to EU funding (European Commission 1997). These guidelines were formulated on a very broad level, leaving the member states substantial leeway for implementation.

While we do not focus on the political determinants that resulted in an expanded role for statist training, we show the potential effects such an expanded role can have on employer coordination and consequently, the nature of collective skill formation systems. We trace the processes resulting from the abovementioned statist policies since their respective introduction. Thereby, we rely on secondary literature, primary documents, newspaper articles, as well as a series of semi-structured expert interviews with stake-holders in the Austrian VET system.[3] Interview partners include representatives from the social partners, government ministries, and research institutes (see appendix for more details).

13.4 Declining collectivism at the lower end: public training workshops

In the mid-1990s, Austria's dual VET system experienced a severe crisis as a consequence of demographic changes and structural economic trends away from industrial production towards the service sector (Schneeberger 2009). In 1996, the so-called apprentice gap already accounted for 4,642 places, and continued growing to 5,000 in 1998, thereby creating a persisting state of emergency for a small economy like Austria. While around half of all VET graduates go to full-time VET schools in Austria, these schools could not alleviate the situation on the apprenticeship market, as they target the medium and higher end of the upper-secondary-level skill distribution (Graf et al. 2012). Unsuccessful apprenticeship seekers were rather unlikely 'to have the option for continuing at [VET] school due to their previous [lacking] school achievement' (Lechner et al. 2004).

The NAP in 1998 aimed to tackle these problems through the introduction of a time-limited 'emergency package' (*Jugendausbildungs-Sicherungsgesetz*) consisting of public training workshops. Initially, Austria's main employers' association, the Austrian Economic Chamber (WKÖ), and their Christian Democratic allies strongly opposed the introduction of these workshops in Austria. The chamber feared a loss of the employers' long-term influence in the collective training system as well as competition with firm-based VET, reducing the supply of apprenticeship seekers and putting pressure on apprentices' wages and working conditions (AT3, AT4). This would have been especially detrimental for those firms using apprentices as cheap labour.

---

[3] Where direct quotes from interviews, newspaper articles, or official documents are presented, they were translated from German into English.

In short, the chamber saw training workshops from a more system-wide, long-term perspective, and therefore negatively. Only due to the influence of labour unions (Durazzi and Geyer 2020), the Social Democrats, and a heavy increase in the political salience connected to the ineffectiveness of subsidies proposed by the Austrian Economic Chamber (Unterweger 2019), public training workshops were introduced as part of the NAP for a limited period of two years. However, public training workshops were continuously prolonged and ultimately transformed into a permanent instrument called ÜBA (*Überbetriebliche Berufsausbildung*) and integrated into the Vocational Training Act of 2008 (Bergmann et al. 2011). This was implemented as part of a 'youth guarantee', where every individual received the right to education and training until the age of 18 (Salzmann-Pfleger 2016). For those who successfully completed lower-secondary school and who are registered at the public employment office (AMS) as an apprenticeship seeker, this also translates to a right for an apprenticeship place at a training workshop if no place in a private firm is available.

Workshop-based apprentices are organized on two tracks. Apprentices in the *fully* workshop-based apprenticeship track sign apprenticeship contracts with training workshops for all the years of apprenticeship (ÜBA1), with short-term internships (mostly around 1–3 months per year) in private firms (Bergmann et al. 2011). The internship in private firms plays a far more important role and is longer (mostly with a maximum of up to 6 months) in the *partially* workshop-based apprenticeship track (ÜBA2), where apprentices sign apprenticeship contracts for only one year and are supposed to switch to a standard apprenticeship at their internship provider in the second year of training. While apprentices in partially workshop-based apprenticeship tracks are not supposed to stay for the whole apprenticeship, trainees not hired as an apprentice by their respective firms after their internship can be offered a prolongation of their training contract. Trainees on both tracks receive subsistence grants from the public employment office.

As can be seen in Figure 13.1, public workshop-based apprenticeships have increased significantly in the years since their introduction.[4] Already for the 2001/2002 cohort, public workshop-based training accounted for 4.7 per cent of all apprenticeship starters (Biffl et al. 2008). Despite periodically improving demographic and economic conditions, training workshops remained a significant feature of the Austrian skill formation system. Today, conservative

---

[4] The number of apprentices in workshops is captured by the apprenticeship survey as well as data from the public employment service (AMS). The latter is used for Figure 13.1, which is said to over-report the number of individuals in training workshops, while the former under-reports them. Workshops were not captured by the apprenticeship survey before 2009. See Dornmayr and Nowak (2018) for details.

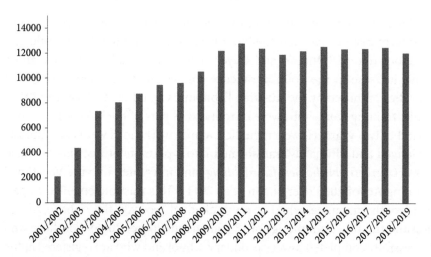

Fig. 13.1 Number of participants in public training workshops according to AMS data, 2001–2019

Data source: AMS (2020).

calculations show that at least 9 per cent of all apprenticeship starters visit these workshops (WKÖ 2019).

The fact that public training workshops have become a permanent sector of the Austrian skill formation system points towards the changing preferences of business. Initially, the Austrian Economic Chamber, as well as the Christian Democrats, strongly opposed the introduction of public training workshops in Austria. However, interviews, including with a representative from the Economic Chamber, confirmed that on the level of individual firms, business has increasingly learned to appreciate training workshops to a certain extent. As one independent expert argued:

> Publicly, nobody hung a lantern on it, but indeed there are companies that are not unhappy [with the workshops]. For example, with outsourcing the first year of apprenticeship into the partially workshop-based apprenticeship. And then you [as a firm] say, OK, I look at the applicants [scheduled to leave the partially workshop-based track] who want to apply for a standard apprenticeship at your firm. Then I have the very nice opportunity to choose. I can take the really good ones. And that is indeed true. But it was politically, from business's side, always denied that such considerations exist. (AT2)

Consequently, the internship in the partially workshop-based track allows firms to pre-select individuals they want to take on as standard apprentices, picking out only stronger individuals from the pool of workshop apprentices.[5] According to Bergmann et al. (2011), 'the acquisition of and becoming acquainted with potential future firm-based apprentices' is by far the primary motive for firms to offer such internships. This pool of workshop-based apprentices is already a pre-selection of apprentices who cannot find an apprenticeship, as special offers exist for the weakest of all candidates (Litschel and Löffler 2015). Over the years, ties between individual public training workshops and firms have been fostered, with firms proactively and systematically hiring the best apprentices out of workshops after their first year of apprenticeship (AT2, AT6). In general, firms appear to be as satisfied with the quality of workshop apprentices as they are with standard apprentices (Bergmann et al. 2011; Salzmann-Pfleger 2016).

In addition, many firms have realized that training workshops pay off financially. In Austria, 33–40 per cent of firms gain net benefits of regular (not workshop-based) apprenticeship training (Lassnigg 2011). But on average, apprenticeship training after subsidies still imposes net costs on Austrian employers in all years of the apprenticeship (Dornmayr et al. 2016). However, Austrian firms gain higher post-training benefits through 'retaining a higher share of apprentices and savings on future hiring costs' than, for example, Swiss firms (Moretti et al. 2019). Consequently, the ÜBA allows companies to avoid the net costs of the first year of apprenticeship, while still profiting from post-training benefits. Furthermore, all firms that hire apprentices out of workshops are subsidized via a lump-sum payment of 1,000 euros per apprentice hired (WKÖ 2018), which further increases the financial attractiveness of workshops from a firm perspective.

Firms have also learned to profit from the short-term internship students complete at partially (and in some cases also fully) workshop-based apprenticeship tracks before they potentially become standard apprentices at a private firm. Firms do not have to sign an apprenticeship contract for these interns, making this internship cheaper and less risky than taking on standard apprentices in the first year (AT4). Furthermore, training content of the internship is de facto mostly unregulated due to a lack of supervision, which allows firms to use interns as cheap, unskilled labour, for example in times of peak orders (AT3, AT6). Indeed, there have been incidents where companies solely relied on interns for such uses without signing any apprenticeship contracts (AT3).

As the shift to the knowledge economy further progresses, workshops might become more widespread. By the late1990s, training participation had

---

[5] In other words, a Matthew effect is visible, where 'the least-disadvantaged individuals among a targeted group are more able to benefit from a social policy scheme than their more disadvantaged counterparts' (Pisoni 2018).

shrunk partly due to a shift away from industrial production to the service sector. If the skill polarization thesis proves to be right, we should see a partial downgrading of skill requirements for some occupations. Consequently, it can be expected that firms will conclude that investments in apprenticeship training generating mid-level skills do not pay off anymore. Rather, they might choose to rely on workshop trainees who necessitate lower investment in training. On the other hand, upgrading of skill requirements for certain occupations also means that there are more apprenticeship seekers who are not seen as fit by companies to enter firm-based apprenticeship training. Workshops also seem to provide some of the new skill needs that firms find underrepresented in standard apprenticeship seekers, as most workshops provide substantial soft-skill coaching in their first year (AT6; Bergmann et al. 2011).

Employers (and their association) never actively campaigned in favour of workshops. It was always the labour side, emphasizing positive inclusiveness effects, that pushed politically for strengthening the workshop-based sector. However, as shown, the fact that public training workshops have become a permanent feature of the Austrian skill formation system is also a result of the preferences of firms, who increasingly learned to like statist training measures. Ultimately, this resulted in the WKÖ consenting to workshop-based training—at least under certain conditions. This is clearly reflected in the association's *current* position on training workshops. Their rhetoric is still not favourable towards workshop-based training, for example highlighting alleged quality and cost problems associated with workshops and articulating their clear preference for standard dual apprenticeships. However, they seem to have accepted its existence to a certain extent and currently do not demand an all-out abolishment of workshops but rather a reduction of fully workshop-based apprenticeships combined with a restructuring of workshops towards the partially workshop-based apprenticeship model (AT2, AT3, AT4).

This is not surprising, as firms profit particularly from partially workshop-based apprentices. There, trainees have longer internships at companies and have to find a standard apprenticeship after their first year in the workshop in order to graduate. This also tackles the WKÖ's fear that fully workshop-based apprenticeships would reduce the supply of standard apprenticeship seekers, pushing up wages and working conditions. Therefore, the WKÖ prefers these partially workshop-based apprenticeships over their fully workshop-based counterpart. In the same vein, in order to prevent such alleged competition between fully workshop-based apprenticeships and private firms for apprenticeship seekers, the WKÖ favours a substantial reduction of the 'subsistence grant' for workshop-based apprentices. According to the WKÖ's position, this would make standard apprenticeships (due to their higher wages) more attractive for students and would especially hurt trainees in the fully workshop-based apprenticeship.

All these demands were also reflected in the business-friendly agenda of various coalition governments between the populist radical right and the Christian Democrats. For example, the first right-wing coalition government abolished the fully workshop-based apprenticeship tracks in 2001 and changed this possibility only to a measure of last resort (Lechner et al. 2004). The fully workshop-based apprenticeships were reintroduced only after a change of government in 2006. Furthermore, coming into effect in 2020, the renewed right-wing coalition (2017–2019) abolished the possibility of individuals signing apprenticeship contracts in fully workshop-based tracks upfront for all years of the apprenticeship, with the main difference between fully (ÜBA1) and partially workshop-based (ÜBA2) tracks now being the longer internship periods at companies in the partially workshop-based track (Rechnungshof Österreich 2021). Finally, the WKÖ, supported by their allies in the right-wing government, also managed to substantially reduce the subsistence grants for workshop-based trainees (Knecht and Bodenstein 2019).

The Chamber of Labour as well as labour unions are critical of such developments. In general, labour favours a reduction of partially workshop-based apprenticeships in favour of fully workshop-based apprenticeships. They recognize the potentially detrimental effect of the partially workshop-based apprenticeship for the training participation of firms due to the financially beneficial outsourcing of the first year of apprenticeship (Trinko 2013). Similarly, they suggest that certain firms abuse the more extended internship of partially workshop-based apprenticeships without hiring their interns afterward as standard apprentices and also favour shorter internships for fully workshop-based apprentices (AT3). In other words, while the specific design of training workshops is the subject of political debates, overall, both sides of the political spectrum increasingly accept the growing role of the state in dual training. Interestingly, in particular, the track favoured by right-wing parties (e.g. the partially workshop-based apprenticeship) seems to have high potential to substitute standard dual training due to firms' interests in outsourcing the first year of apprenticeship to workshops in the partially workshop-based track and/or for hiring cheap workshop interns.[6]

---

[6] While it could be argued that the partially workshop-based apprenticeship is still a collective arrangement after the first year of apprenticeship, overall, the role of the state is substantially increased compared to traditional dual apprenticeships.

Summing up, this section has shown how employers, due to cost-considerations combined with the high quality of statist training, have learned to profit from training workshops. Consequently, public training workshops have contributed at least partially to the ongoing low training participation of companies because they offer firms attractive exit opportunities from employer coordination, consequently removing constraints from firms. While employer associations initially defended the collective system, firms themselves learned to like statist training, over time changing the policy preferences of the business community. The next section addresses the same dynamics at the higher end of the secondary-level skill distribution, namely upper-secondary VET in the field of ICT.

13.5 Declining collectivism at the higher end: training in the ICT sector

The 1998 NAP did not only implement VET emergency measures at the lower end of the skill distribution, but it also pointed out the importance of reforms at its higher end. Most importantly, it emphasized that employment in the ICT sector should be increased and that training should play a decisive role in this: 'In light of structural changes, especially because of the rise of the service sector and the massive use of information technologies, we need to tap into new training fields' (BMAGS et al. 1998).

Therewith, the National Action Plan reflected a broader debate taking place in Austria in the 1990s, which mirrored the fear that Austria might not be able to compete economically in a digitalized and globalized world. This fear was mostly voiced by ICT firms and employer associations. In 1998, the deputy director-general of Beko, a technology service provider and one of the larger IT companies in Austria, Paul Michal, explained, 'About 1,000 to 1,200 ICT graduates leave the universities, universities of applied sciences and VET colleges every year. In Austria, we would need, however, 5,000 graduates' (Die Presse 1998). Similarly, the Federation of Industries, an employer association representing mostly large industrial firms, criticized that Austria was one of the countries least prepared for the new century and that ICT experts especially were missing (APA 1999a). The debate was not restricted to Austria. In the same year, the OECD warned of a global economic crisis because of the lack of skilled labour (Die Presse 1998). As the quote by Michal shows, the discussion on the lack of ICT experts focused mostly on the role of universities, universities of applied sciences, and VET colleges in the training of these experts. However, as will be shown in the following, both full-time school-based VET and dual VET reforms were implemented in order to promote ICT training.

On the one hand, ICT became a topic for dual apprenticeships, where the social partners and the Ministry of Economic Affairs are the dominant stakeholders. Initially, the Austrian Economic Chamber came up with the idea of introducing apprenticeships in the field of ICT. Together with the Institute for Research on Qualifications and Training of the Austrian Economy (ibw), a research institute that is closely interlinked with the Economic Chamber, they developed a draft for the respective VET ordinance (AT4) and quickly found support at the Chamber of Labour (AT3) as well as in the Ministry of Economic Affairs (APA 1999c, Der Standard 1999a). As a consequence, it was emphasized in the NAP that ICT training should take the form of dual apprenticeships: 'The development of new apprenticeship occupations [in ICT] is of high importance' (BMAGS et al. 1998).

The VET ordinances for the new training occupations were developed consensually between the Economic Chamber and the Chamber of Labour in the Federal Advisory Board on Apprenticeships (Bundesberufsausbildungsbeirat, BBAG). The BBAG is an advisory body to the Ministry of Economic Affairs and is responsible for developing drafts of VET ordinances, which are then enacted by the Ministry of Economic Affairs (Emmenegger and Seitzl 2020). In 1998, the Ministry enacted VET ordinances for various apprenticeship occupations in the ICT sector, amongst others in computer science and ICT electronics, and for IT clerks (APA 1999b). When the new apprenticeship occupations were announced to the press, the responsible minister of economic affairs stated that the new ordinances were a reaction to business demand for highly qualified ICT experts while at the same time offering more practically talented youth the possibility of starting a career in ICT (APA 1999b).

Thus, ICT apprenticeships were established in a consensual process that involved the Economic Chamber, the Chamber of Labour, and the Ministry of Economic Affairs. They shared a similar motive when developing dual training in the field of ICT: the three institutions feared that dual training would become less attractive to employers and school graduates if such a prospering training field would take place only at VET colleges and in higher-education institutions. As one interview partner put it: 'If we did not move towards new sectors, dual apprenticeships would lose automatically and only account for 20 per cent instead of 40 per cent of upper-secondary education' (AT4). Both chambers and especially the members of the Federal Advisory Board on Apprenticeships have a great interest in maintaining a stable and attractive apprenticeship system because they can influence it to a much higher degree than full-time school-based VET (Emmenegger and Seitzl 2020). The same is true for the VET experts in the Ministry of Economic Affairs. In contrast, firms did not engage in the establishment of ICT apprenticeships. They were asked by the Economic Chamber for their opinion, 'but we [the WKÖ] received zero feedback. [...] At that time, relatively little came from the industries' (AT4). Therefore, similar to the introduction of the training workshops, the Economic Chamber as an intermediary association did not necessarily follow the preferences articulated by its members. Instead, its behaviour shows that they pursued this goal in order to maintain high levels of autonomy and influence in VET policies (Emmenegger and Seitzl 2019; Schmitter and Streeck 1999; Traxler and Huemer 2007).

These measures to protect dual VET and adapt it to technological change were implemented alongside similar developments in Austria's full-time school-based sector. Most importantly, VET colleges[7] intensified their efforts to train ICT experts (Der Standard 1999b). VET colleges, especially those with a focus on technology (Höhere Technische Lehranstalten, HTL) had taught courses on electronic data processing since the 1980s. In the 1990s, the number of training courses was significantly increased in order to meet the economy's need for ICT experts. In addition, the Ministry of Education established the first VET college for information technology in Vienna in 1999 (AT7). In subsequent years, another ten VET colleges with a focus on ICT were established in Austria. The increased focus on ICT in VET colleges was promoted by the Ministry of Education but also by data scientists from the Technical University Vienna (AT7). The VET colleges are entirely under the control of the Ministry of Education. The social partners have no formal say in their administration and training content definition, although labour market actors might be consulted in the development of the curricula.

To summarize, the VET system in Austria has clearly reacted to the debate in the 1990s about the lack of ICT experts in the economy. On the one hand, new apprenticeship occupations were created in order to train computer scientists and other ICT-related experts within the dual training system. The Economic Chamber collaborated with the Chamber of Labour and the Ministry of Economic Affairs to establish these apprenticeships. On the other hand, the Austrian state expanded statist training opportunities by layering

---

[7] Two types of full-time VET schools exist at the upper-secondary level: vocational schools (Berufsbildende Mittlere Schulen, BMS) that offer intermediate-level skills and vocational colleges (Berufsbildende Höhere Schulen, BHS) that offer high levels of skills and university entrance qualifications. In general, the reputation of BHS is similar to the general education track offered in Gymnasien (Graf et al. 2012).

ICT VET colleges and new schools with an emphasis on ICT training onto the collective training system.

This introduction of full-time school-based ICT training came at the expense of apprenticeship training, as firms continuously learned to acknowledge the benefits of full-time school-based VET. While both apprenticeships and full-time schools have existed in Austria for a long time (Graf et al. 2012) with around half of all VET graduates going to full-time schools (Eurostat 2020), ICT occupations are *predominantly* offered in such full-time schools. Figure 13.2 shows the number of apprentices and training firms in the ICT occupations[8] between 2002 and 2018. While the number of ICT apprentices varies over the years, on average, 1,800 young people were trained in an apprenticeship during this period. The number of training organizations includes firms and public training workshops. It is more stable than the number of apprentices, being slightly below a thousand training organizations between 2002 and 2018. Overall, compared to other training occupations, the number of training organizations (Dornmayr and Nowak 2018: 33) and apprentices (Dornmayr and Nowak 2018: 19) is still rather low. For example, in 2017, more than nine thousand apprentices were trained in the occupational field of tourism, and more than ten thousand apprentices were trained in mechanical engineering (Dornmayr and Nowak 2018: 19).

Collectively organized apprenticeship training in private firms stands in contrast to the more statist solutions of public training workshops and VET colleges. Figure 13.2 also displays the number of apprentices in workshops. It ranges from less than a hundred between 2004 and 2007 to more than four hundred in 2011. But most importantly, the comparison with ICT students at VET colleges shows that ICT apprenticeships in firms play only a minor role in the provision of ICT experts in Austria. Between 2002 and 2018, there were on average 3,500 ICT students at VET colleges. Figure 13.3 displays the share of ICT students in VET colleges and public training workshops compared to ICT apprentices in firms. It thus contrasts the training efforts of firms compared to the statist solutions of workshops and full-time school-based VET.[9] During 2002 and 2018, 70 per cent of ICT VET training took

---

[8] This includes the following occupations: information technology (2002–2006: EDV-Technik; since 2006: Informationstechnologie—Technik), computer science (2002–2006: Informatik; since 2006: Informationstechnologie—Informatik), system technology (2002–2017: EDV-Systemtechnik; since 2018: Informationstechnologie—Systemtechnik), operation technology (Informationstechnologie—Betriebstechnik, new since 2018), ICT commercial employee (EDV-Kauffrau; E-Commerce-Kauffrau, new since 2018), and app developing/coding.

[9] ICT VET at upper-secondary level is also taking place at VET schools (Berufsbildende Mittlere Schulen, BMS) but statistics on students in these schools are not available. Therefore, the share of ICT students in a non-firm environment is even underestimated here.

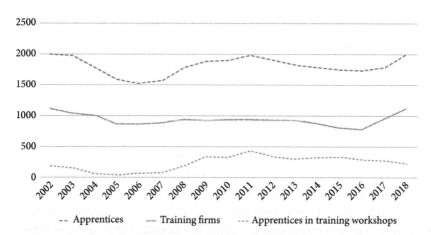

Fig. 13.2 Number of all apprentices, apprentices in public training workshops and training organizations in the ICT occupations, 2002–2018

Data source: WKÖ (2020)Note: The WKÖ also includes mechatronics engineers (introduced in 2015) in the statistics for ICT apprenticeships. While mechatronics engineering is also available in full-time schools, the data on ICT students at VET colleges displayed here only include computer science and data technology but not mechatronics engineering. For reasons of comparison, this occupation is consequently not displayed in the statistics shown here. However, this might slightly underestimate the number of training firms in the years after 2015 because organizations that train in an ICT occupation in addition to mechatronics engineering are not taken into account.

place in VET colleges and public training workshops and only 30 per cent in apprenticeships. The share remains very stable over time.

Thus, in Austria, firms prefer statist to collective VET training in the ICT occupations. The availability of an exit option relaxes the beneficial constraints of dual apprenticeships, and the firms are happy to take this opportunity. There are at least two reasons why training ICT apprentices is less attractive to firms than hiring graduates from VET colleges. On the one hand, firms believe that ICT apprentices do not meet the skill demands of firms: 'They [the firms] think that more talented youths go to VET colleges and less talented youths stay as apprentices' (AT3). Accordingly, firms in the ICT sectors have difficulty in finding apprentices that can meet the firms' expectations: 'We have found out that it does not work with the very young people that come directly from the school. Typically, our apprentices did not succeed at a VET college and are thus older and more experienced' (AT8).

On the other hand, firms have an economic argument not to train apprentices but to hire graduates from VET colleges. According to Moretti et al. (2019), the 'publicly financed school-based VET system [...] puts upward pressure on wages'. Thus, the training of ICT experts in VET colleges even increases pressure on apprenticeship wages by reducing the supply of

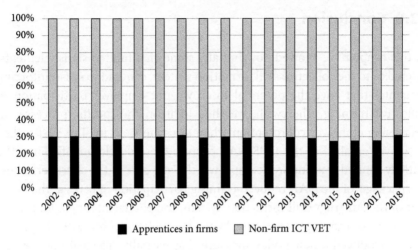

Fig. 13.3 Share of firm-based and non-firm-based VET training in the ICT occupations, 2002–2018

Data source: WKÖ (2020)

apprenticeship seekers. In sum, training an apprentice in Austria creates more costs than benefits to a firm (Moretti et al. 2019). Asked if firms in the ICT sector prefer graduates of VET schools or colleges, representatives of a federal ministry were very open: 'Of course, because they [the firms] do not have to pay for it' (AT7). Costs per student in full-time school-based VET are ten times higher than in part-time schools in dual VET (Graf et al. 2012). Compared to dual VET, this reveals the higher quality of training as well as the 'substantial silent shift of VET costs' from firms to the state in full-time schools (Lassnigg 2011).

Thus, the increased importance of ICT has weakened the collective part of the Austrian VET system. As Lassnigg (2011) argues, 'the more dynamic sectors have turned towards full-time VET colleges and higher education as a primary source of skilled workers'. As the sectors fuelled by digitization grow, the trend towards decreasing collectivism and increasing statism is likely to continue. Similar to our case of public training workshops, employer associations initially defended the collective system, but firms themselves learned to like statist training, and the policy preferences of the business community were transformed over time. The newly available ICT full-time schools freed firms from constraints by providing new exit options from standard dual training, ultimately resulting in a crowding-out of collective apprenticeships. Since the majority of ICT experts with a VET degree come from full-time vocational schools, the question arises of how collective training can be sustained in the knowledge economy.

13.6 Conclusion

In this chapter, we showed how initially somewhat limited statist elements, layered onto the collective skill formation system, can lead to self-reinforcing dynamics that have the potential to crowd out employer participation in collective training. Therewith, we shed light on the specific processes of decreasing employer coordination when the state steps in. The VET policy initiatives entailed in the 1998 NAP capture these developments. First, the initially limited training workshops, which were part of the short-term 'rescue package' of the NAP, reduced training participation of firms at the lower end of the Austrian skill formation system, thereby facilitating a long-term expansion of training workshops. With the public training workshops, the NAP introduced a new policy measure that partially crowded out the collective provision of training. Second, in the case of the ICT occupations, the school-based sector has crowded out employer participation in dual VET at the higher end of secondary-level training. Thus, it limited the adaptability and viability of collective training in the knowledge economy. In other words, collective action in the new NAP occupations is hard to achieve due to the parallel establishment of specific ICT-dedicated VET colleges. In both cases, employers developed new preferences that contributed to a further decline of collective training, as they learned to appreciate the benefits that these statist VET schemes offer. In both instances, employer associations initially defended the collective system, but as firms themselves learned to like statist training, the policy preferences of the business community were transformed over time. This process is taking place at the lower as well as at the higher end of the skill distribution in secondary level VET, parts of the skill distribution seen as essential as the shift to a knowledge economy progresses.

Assuming that the knowledge economy leads to the growth of educational options at the higher end of the skill distribution and increasingly necessitates the integration of those unable to cope with increasing skill demands (e.g. the lower end), these dynamics have the potential to facilitate a reconfiguration in the division of labour between collective actors and the state within Austria's skill formation system. Consequently, it can be expected that the role of statist training will increase in future years in Austria—albeit mediated by economic trends and political contestation. While we do not focus on the political determinants that lead to an expanded role for the state, the potential effects of increasing statist training can be expected to also apply beyond the Austrian case. In other words, collective skill formation systems that expand statist training in order to react to a tightening of apprenticeship markets might reinforce the tendencies of declining employer coordination.

For example, it might be worth examining how much the German transition system (Thelen and Busemeyer 2012)—itself a case of statism in collective skill formation—benefits employers, leading to an increasing reluctance on their side to take up 'standard' apprenticeship seekers straight after school.

While this chapter has focused on decreasing employer coordination in skill formation, we are not claiming that such trends should be seen as something socially or economically undesirable. First, Chuan et al. (2019) as well as Anderson and Hassel (2013) highlight that statist skill formation might be better able to cope with the challenges arising from the knowledge economy because they transmit more general skills that enable employees to adapt to new skill demands. In contrast, in collective skill formation systems, employees might be less equipped to respond flexibly to the demands of the labour market. Second, as Thelen (2014) has shown, an increasing role for the state has the potential to increase the inclusiveness of skill formation systems. This holds for the case of training workshops, which are generally praised for the good labour market chances of their graduates and are therefore widely regarded as contributing to labour market inclusiveness (Bergmann et al. 2011; Durazzi and Geyer 2020; Carstensen et al. 2021). However, in the case of Austria's school-based VET, 'dualisation has been rather inbuilt into the system' (Pernicka and Hefler 2015), given the countries' high stratification between different levels of upper-secondary VET (apprenticeships, schools, and colleges) with only the highest-achieving students being accepted into VET colleges. While going beyond the scope of this chapter, future research might therefore be well advised to dig into the determinants of socially and economically 'successful' state intervention.

References

AMS. 2020. *Anzahl Personen im Programm. Überbetriebliche Lehrausbildung durch das AMS. Inhouse Statistik*. Vienna: AMS.

Anderson, K., and Hassel, A. 2013. 'Pathways of Change in CMEs: Training Regimes in Germany and the Netherlands'. In *The Political Economy of the Service Transition*, edited by A. Wren, pp. 171–94. Oxford: Oxford University Press.

APA. 1999a. 'Industriellenvereinigung: Dringender Handlungsbedarf im Jahr 2000'. 17 March 1999.

APA. 1999b. 'Neue moderne Lehrberufe ermöglichen Jugendlichen neue Chancen'. 7 June 1999.

APA. 1999c. 'Wirtschaft begrüßt Einigung über 20 neue Lehrberufe'. 22 July 1999.

Bergmann, N., F. Lechner, I. Matt, A. Riesenfelder, S. Schelepa, and B. Willsberger. 2011. *Evaluierung der überbetrieblichen Lehrausbildung (ÜBA) in Österreich.* Vienna: L&R Sozialforschung.

Biffl, G., J. Bock-Schappelwein, and U. Huemer. 2008. *An der Schnittstelle zwischen Lehrstellen- und Regelarbeitsmarkt.* Vienna: Österreichisches Institut für Wirtschaftsforschung.

BMAGS, BMUK, and BMW. 1998. *Nationaler Aktionsplan für Beschäftigung Österreich.* Vienna: Bundesregierung.

Borch, H., and H. Weissmann. 2000. 'Erfolgsgeschichte IT-Berufe'. *BWP* 6: 9–12.

Busemeyer, M. R. 2012. 'Business as a Pivotal Actor in the Politics of Training Reform: Insights from the Case of Germany'. *British Journal of Industrial Relations* 50: 690–713.

Busemeyer, M. R., and T. Iversen. 2012. *Collective Skill Systems, Wage Bargaining, and Labor Market Stratification.* Oxford: Oxford University Press.

Busemeyer, M. R., and C. Trampusch. 2012. *The Political Economy of Collective Skill Formation.* Oxford: Oxford University Press.

Carstensen, M. B., P. Emmenegger, and D. F. Unterweger. 2021. 'Statism on Employers' Terms: The Politics of Inclusiveness in Austrian and Danish Vocational Education Institutions'. 27th International Conference of Europeanists.

Carstensen, M. B., and C. L. Ibsen. 2021. 'Three Dimensions of Institutional Contention: Efficiency, Equality and Governance in Danish Vocational Education and Training Reform'. *Socio-Economic Review* 19 (3): 1037–63.

Cedefop. 2018. *Less Brawn, More Brain for Tomorrow's Workers.* Cedefop Briefing Note. Thessaloniki: Cedefop.

Chuan, A., C. L. Ibsen, and K. Thelen. 2019. 'Skills for the Future? A Life-cycle Perspective on Systems of Vocational Education and Training'. CES General Conference, 22–24 June 2019, Madrid.

Crouch, C., D. Finegold, and M. Sako. 1999. *Are Skills the Answer? The Political Economy of Skill Creation in Advanced Industrial Countries.* Oxford: Oxford University Press.

Culpepper, P. D., and K. Thelen. 2008. 'Institutions and Collective Actors in the Provision of Training'. In *Skill Formation: Interdisciplinary and Cross-national Perspectives,* edited by K. U. Mayer and H. Solga, pp. 21–49. New York: Cambridge University Press.

Der Standard. 1999a. 'Bis Sommer 14 neue Lehrberufe'. 8 June 1999.

Der Standard. 1999b. 'EDV-Boom nach der Schrecksekunde'. 18 May 1999.

Die Presse. 1998. 'Informatikermangel zur Jahrtausendwende'. 18 October 1998.

Dornmayr, H., and S. Nowak. 2018. *Lehrlingsausbildung im Überblick 2018.* Vienna: ibw—Institut für Bildungsforschung der Wirtschaft.

Dornmayr, H., P. Schlögl, M. Mayerl, and B. Winkler. 2016. *Hintergrundanalyse zur Wirksamkeit der betrieblichen Lehrstellenförderung gemäß §19c BAG: Synthesenbericht.* Vienna: ibw, öibf.

Durazzi, N., and L. Geyer. 2020. 'Social Inclusion in the Knowledge Economy: Unions' Strategies and Institutional Change in the Austrian and German Training Systems'. *Socio-Economic Review 18* (1): 103–24.

Emmenegger, P., B. Palier, and M. Seeleib-Kaiser. 2012. *The Age of Dualization.* Oxford: Oxford University Press.

Emmenegger, P., and L. Seitzl. 2019. Collective Action, Business Cleavages and the Politics of Control: Segmentalism in the Swiss Skill Formation System. *British Journal of Industrial Relations 57* (3): 576–98.

Emmenegger, P., and L. Seitzl. 2020. 'Social Partner Involvement in Collective Skill Formation Governance: A Comparison of Austria, Denmark, Germany, the Netherlands and Switzerland'. *Transfer: European Review of Labour and Research 26* (1): 27–42.

European Commission. 1997. *The 1998 Employment Guidelines. Council Resolution of 15 December 1997.* Luxembourg: European Communities.

Eurostat. 2019. *Statistics Explained: ICT Specialists in Employment* [Online]. Available: https://ec.europa.eu/eurostat/statistics-explained/index.php/ICT_specialists_in_employment#Number_of_ICT_specialists [accessed 25 May 2020].

Eurostat. 2020. 'Participation in Education and Training 2018 (educ_part)'. Luxembourg.

Goos, M., and A. Manning. 2007. 'Lousy and Lovely Jobs: The Rising Polarization of Work in Britain'. *The Review of Economics and Statistics 89* (1): 118–33.

Goos, M., A. Manning, and A. Salomons. 2009. 'Job Polarization in Europe'. *American Economic Review 99* (2): 58–63.

Graf, L. 2018. 'Combined Modes of Gradual Change: The Case of Academic Upgrading and Declining Collectivism in German Skill Formation'. *Socio-Economic Review 16* (1): 185–205.

Graf, L., L. Lassnigg, and J. W. Powell. 2012. 'Austrian Corporatism and Institutional Change in the Relationship between Apprenticeship Training and School-based VET'. In *The Political Economy of Collective Skill Formation*, edited by M. R. Busemeyer and C. Trampusch, pp. 150–78. Oxford: Oxford University Press.

Hall, P. A., and D. Soskice. 2001. 'An Introduction to Varieties of Capitalism'. In *Varieties of Capitalism: The Institutional Foundations of Comparative Advantage*, edited by P. A. Hall and D. Soskice, pp. 1–68. Oxford: Oxford University Press.

Helmrich, R., M. Tiemann, K. Troltsch, F. Lukowski, C. Neuber-Pohl and A.C. Lewalder. 2016. *Digitalisierung der Arbeitslandschaften. Keine Polarisierung der*

Arbeitswelt, aber beschleunigter Strukturwandel und Arbeitsplatzwechsel. Bonn: BIBB.

Howell, C. 2016. 'Regulating Class in the Neoliberal Era: The Role of the State in the Restructuring of Work and Employment Relations'. *Work, Employment and Society 30* (4): 573–89.

Katzenstein, P. J. 1984. *Capitalism and Change: Austria, Switzerland, and the Politics of Industry.* Ithaca: Cornell University Press.

Knecht, A., and M. Bodenstein. 2019. 'Beschäftigungsförderung Jugendlicher unter der ÖVP-FPÖ-Regierung'. *Sozial Extra 43*: 217–20.

Lassnigg, L. 2011. 'The Duality of VET in Austria: Institutional Competition between School and Apprenticeship'. *Journal of Vocational Education and Training 63* (3): 417–38.

Lechner, F., N. Nemecek, A. Riesenfelder, G. Willsberger, G. Michenthaler, and G. Brandenburg. 2004. *Begleitende Bewertung der NAP-Massnahmen für Jugendliche.* Vienna: L&R Sozialforschung.

Litschel, V., and R. Löffler. 2015. *Meta-Analyse zu rezenten Studien im Bereich 'AMP-Massnahmen für Jugendliche': Betrachtungen mit dem Schwerpunkt 'Berufsausbildung'.* AMS Report No. 109.

Martin, C. J., and K. Thelen. 2007. 'The State and Coordinated Capitalism: Contributions of the Public Sector to Social Solidarity in Postindustrial Societies'. *World Politics 60* (1): 1–36.

Moretti, L., M. Mayerl, S. Muehlemann, P. Schlögl, and S. C. Wolter. 2019. 'So Similar and Yet So Different: A Comparative Analysis of a Firm's Cost and Benefits of Apprenticeship Training in Austria and Switzerland'. *Evidence-Based HRM 7* (2): 229–46.

OECD. 2005. *Growth in Services: Fostering Employment, Productivity, and Innovation.* Paris: OECD Publishing.

Oesch, D., and J. Rodríguez Menés. 2011. 'Upgrading or Polarization? Occupational Change in Britain, Germany, Spain and Switzerland, 1990–2008'. *Socio-Economic Review 9* (3): 503–31.

Palier, B., and K. Thelen. 2010. 'Institutionalizing Dualism: Complementarities and Change in France and Germany'. *Politics and Society 38* (1): 119–48.

Pernicka, S., and G. Hefler. 2015. 'Austrian Corporatism: Erosion or Resilience?' *Austrian Journal of Political Science 44* (3): 39–56.

Pisoni, D. 2018. 'Between Idealism and Pragmatism: Social Policies and Matthew Effect in Vocational Education and Training for Disadvantaged Youths in Switzerland'. *Social Inclusion 6* (3): 289–300.

Powell, W. W., and K. Snellman. 2004. 'The Knowledge Economy'. *Annual Review of Sociology 30*: 199–220.

Rechnungshof Österreich. 2021. *Überbetriebliche Lehrausbildung mit Schwerpunkt Oberösterreich und Wien. Bericht des Rechnungshofes.* Vienna: Rechnungshof Österreich.

Rueda, D. 2005. 'Insider-outsider Politics in Industrialized Democracies: The Challenge to Social Democratic Parties'. *American Political Science Review 99* (1): 61–74.

Salzmann-Pfleger, I. 2016. 'AusBildung bis 18: Chance oder Pflicht? Eine Ausbildungsmassnahme im Vergleich'. *Forschungsperspektiven der Pädagogischen Hochschule Wien 8*: 125–40.

Schmitter, P. C., and W. Streeck. 1999. *The Organization of Business Interests: Studying the Associative Action of Business in Advanced Industrial Societies.* MPIfG Discussion Paper No. 99/1.

Schneeberger, A. 2009. 'Bildungsgarantie bis zum 18./19. Lebensjahr: Entwicklungen und Perspektiven in der Berufsbildung'. In *Nationaler Bildungsbericht Österreich 2009 Band 2: Fokussierte Analysen bildungspolitischer Schwerpunktthemen,* edited W. Spechtl, pp. 55 –72. Graz: Leykam.

Sorge, A., and W. Streeck. 2018. 'Diversified Quality Production Revisited'. *Socio-Economic Review 16* (3): 587–612.

Stern, S., T. von Stokar, and C. Schneider. 2003. *Lehrstellenbeschluss 2: Vertiefungsstudie ICT-Förderung im LSB 2.* Bern: BBT, KWB.

Streeck, W. 1997a. Beneficial Constraints: On the Economic Limits of Rational Voluntarism. In *Contemporary Capitalism. The Embeddedness of Institutions,* edited by J. R. Hollingsworth, and R. Boyer, pp. 197–219. Cambridge: Cambridge University Press.

Streeck, W. 1997b. 'German Capitalism: Does It Exist? Can It Survive?' *New Political Economy 2* (2): 237–56.

Streeck, W. 2004. 'Educating Capitalists: A Rejoinder to Wright and Tsakalotos'. *Socio-Economic Review 2*: 425–38.

Streeck, W., and P. C. Schmitter. 1985. 'Community, Market, State—-and Associations? The Prospective Contribution of Interest Governance to Social Order'. *European Sociological Review 1* (2): 119–38.

Streeck, W., and K. Thelen. 2005. *Introduction: Institutional Change in Advanced Political Economies.* Oxford: Oxford University Press.

Streeck, W., and K. Yamamura. 2001. *The Origins of Nonliberal Capitalism: Germany and Japan in Comparison.* Ithaca: Cornell University Press.

Thelen, K. 2004. *How Institutions Evolve: The Political Economy of Skills in Germany, Britain, the United States, and Japan.* Cambridge: Cambridge University Press.

Thelen, K. 2009. 'Institutional Change in Advanced Political Economies'. *British Journal of Industrial Relations 47* (3): 471–98.

Thelen, K. 2014. *Varieties of Liberalization and the New Politics of Social Solidarity.* New York: Cambridge University Press.

Thelen, K., and M. R. Busemeyer. 2012. 'Institutional Change in German Vocational Training: From Collectivism toward Segmentalism'. In *The Political Economy of Collective Skill Formation*, edited by M. R. Busemeyer and C. Trampusch, pp. 68–91. Oxford: Oxford University Press.

Traxler, F., and G. Huemer. 2007. *Handbook of Business Interest Associations, Firm Size and Governance.* London: Routledge.

Trinko, M. 2013. 'Lehrlingsausbildung und Ausbildungsgarantie in Österreich: So funktioniert's'. *A&W Blog.*

Unterweger, D. F. 2019. 'The Redefined Role of the State in Austria's Dual VET System'. *SASE Conference.* The New School, New York City.

Unterweger, D. F. 2020. 'Unconstrained Capital? Multinational Companies, Structural Power, and Collective Goods Provision in Dual VET'. Socio-Economic Review. Published online 2 October 2020.

WKÖ—Wirtschaftskammer Österreich. 2018. *Lehrlinge übernehmen und Prämie sichern*, Vienna: WKÖ.

WKÖ—Wirtschaftskammer Österreich. 2019. *Lehrlingsstatistik. Lehrlinge im 1. Lehrjahr nach Sparten: 2005–2019.* Vienna: WKÖ.

WKÖ—Wirtschaftskammer Österreich. 2020. WKÖ Inhouse Statistik: Sonderauswertung der WKÖ-Lehrlingsstatistik, verschiedene Jahrgänge. Vienna: WKÖ.

Wren, A., M. Fodor, and S. Theodoropoulou. 2013. 'The Trilemma Revisited: Institutions, Inequality and Employment Creation in an Era of ICT-intensive Service Expansion'. In *The Political Economy of the Service Transition*, edited by A. Wren, pp. 108–46. Oxford: Oxford University Press.

Appendix: List of interview partners

AT1 —Interview with independent expert A.
AT2 —Interview with independent expert B.
AT3 —Interview with representative of Austrian Chamber of Labour.
AT4 —Interview with representative A of Austrian Economic Chamber.
AT5 —Interview with independent expert C.
AT6 —Interview with representative of the Federal Ministry for Social Affairs.
AT7 —Interview with two representative of the Federal Ministry of Education, Science and Research.
AT8 —Interview with representative B of Austrian Economic Chamber.
AT9 —Interview with representative of Federal Ministry of Economic Affairs.

14

How Collective Skill Formation Systems Adapt to a Knowledge Economy

Patrick Emmenegger and Giuliano Bonoli

14.1 Introduction

Collective skill formation systems remain attractive in the knowledge economy. The various chapters show that all the main actors—employers, governments, and the trade unions—remain strongly supportive of the logic behind collective systems, even in countries, like Sweden, where vocational education and training (VET) has traditionally been provided by state schools. However, as has always been the case, these systems are heavily dependent on the capacity of key actors to cooperate, which in turn depends on their ability to find win-win solutions to the challenges collective skill formation systems have to confront. Such solutions can be elusive, but they are clearly a necessary condition for the persistence of successful cooperation in the production of the public goods that are a skilled workforce and the social and economic integration of young people. Win-win solutions are essential parts of the successful stories of reform presented in the chapters, and they are usually absent from the accounts of failure.

The importance of cooperation and the search for win-win solutions are arguably the main common findings of the accounts of reform found in this volume's chapters. More precisely, however, we can identify five main themes that help us understand how collective skill formation systems are adapting to a knowledge economy. *First*, several chapters show that one constant preoccupation of employers is to keep dual training attractive for talented youth and avoid academic drift. This is clearly visible in their support for measures aiming to protect the value of VET degrees, to improve the permeability of the overall education system, and to develop new hybrid forms of training that combine academic and vocational training. *Second*, in some countries, but not all, we observe attempts to upskill collective skill formation systems. Such measures include investments in post-secondary VET or new forms of

Patrick Emmenegger and Giuliano Bonoli, *How Collective Skill Formation Systems Adapt to a Knowledge Economy*.
In: *Collective Skill Formation in the Knowledge Economy*. Edited by Giuliano Bonoli and Patrick Emmenegger,
Oxford University Press. © Oxford University Press (2022). DOI: 10.1093/oso/9780192866257.003.0014

cooperation between firm-based training and higher-education institutions. However, in these attempts to upskill, forms of collective governance become more elusive. Instead, individual firms or the state play more prominent roles. *Third*, and related to the previous point, we observe that employers' attachment to collective skill formation remains strong, but they increasingly experience problems to act collectively, which fuels segmentalist tendencies. *Fourth*, over recent decades, states have developed several measures to make collective skill formation systems more inclusive. These measures differ widely with regard to their degree of intrusiveness and the role employers are expected to play. *Fifth*, state pressure on collective skill formation systems to make them more inclusive often—but not always—creates considerable friction, especially if inclusion measures risk undermining the perceived quality of training. In contrast, employers are more open to inclusion measures that target the middle of the skill distribution and aim to increase social mobility. In the following, we elaborate on these insights.

14.2 Preserving and increasing the attractiveness of the vocational route

One constant preoccupation of employers is to keep or make dual training attractive for talented youth and to combat academic drift (see Bernhard and Graf, in this volume; Nijhuis, in this volume). This is not always easy to achieve because there is a tendency to consider universities as superior to VET in all the countries covered in this book, and possibly beyond as well. This trend may be exacerbated by the shift to a knowledge economy, which is likely to imply a higher premium for higher education. In addition, pressures towards making skill formation systems more inclusive may damage their reputation with the middle-class and talented youth. As a result, from the point of view of employers committed to collective training, the prestige and attractiveness of VET need to be protected and actively promoted. Employers are generally seconded by governments in these efforts, as governments recognize the value of a strong collective skill formation system.

The preservation and the increase of the attractiveness of VET takes various shapes. First, in several instances, actors committed to preserving the attractiveness of VET tend to oppose or limit the inclination by governments to make training accessible to everyone. This observation concerns several actors: above all employers and employer organizations, but also state authorities in charge of VET and on occasions also the trade unions (see Busemeyer and Thelen, in this volume; Carstensen and Ibsen, in this volume). The recent history of collective skill formation systems provides several examples of this trend. For instance, improving the reputation of the VET system was a key objective of the Danish reform of 2015. In previous years, the Danish VET system had been increasingly used by the government as a social policy tool, being a key element of its youth guarantee policy. This choice resulted in the system losing its attractiveness for talented youth, who increasingly turned to the academic route. The 2015 reform introduced grade requirements to access VET, precisely in an attempt to improve the reputation of the system (Carstensen and Ibsen, in this volume). The preservation of a good reputation for VET degrees is probably also a key motivation explaining some actors' reluctance to recognize foreign degrees or work experience as a basis for a vocational diploma (Maurer, in this volume).

Second, a strategy to improve the attractiveness of VET for talented youth is to increase permeability. This type of reform is particularly suitable to win-win solutions as (upward) permeability can also be seen as having a socially inclusive function. Reforms or new programmes meant to increase upward permeability, i.e. the notion that youth who enter VET can continue to tertiary education, is a key feature of many of the studies included in this volume. In Germany, various regions are experimenting with programmes that combine VET with an upper-secondary degree that opens access to tertiary education, such as the DuBAS pilot in the state of Saxony (Bernhard and Graf, in this volume). In the Netherlands, various reforms have attempted to mix groups of youth aiming for different educational trajectories in order to improve the permeability of the system. These reforms have been conducted with the support of employers, who saw in them an opportunity to make the vocational route more attractive for talented youth (Nijhuis, in this volume).

Sweden provides a nice counterfactual. The 2011 VET reform reduced upward permeability. This resulted in a decline in the attractiveness of the vocational route, but the system remains state run with little involvement by employers. Employers, on the other hand, are showing considerably more enthusiasm for the Teknikcollege, a relatively new initiative based on the collaboration between local schools and employers, where the latter have considerable influence. Such collaborations are becoming an attractive route for talented youth (Busemeyer and Thelen, in this volume).

Continued employer interest for VET seems to hinge on two parameters: the degree of influence they have over content and the attractiveness of the system for talented youth. Against this background, academic drift is clearly bad news for employers committed to collective skill formation. Many employers' initiatives can thus also be seen as attempts to limit or revert academic drift, which could be especially threatening as the shift to a knowledge economy increases the intellectual requirements of training in general. From this point of view, dual study programmes are best understood as attempts to keep control over training and preserve the attractiveness of the dual training (Busemeyer and Thelen, in this volume; Graf 2013).

14.3 Attempts to upskill collective skill formation

Beyond attempts to maintain the attractiveness of collective skill formation systems for talented youth, actors might also try to upskill collective skill formation systems. Whereas the transformation of (general) education systems in response to the rise of the knowledge has been the topic of considerable research (e.g. Goldin and Katz 2009; Brown et al. 2012; Schulze-Cleven and Olson 2017), attempts to upskill collective skill formation systems with an eye on economic efficiency have not received a lot of attention yet (exceptions include Trampusch and Eichenberger 2012; Graf 2013, 2018; Durazzi and Benassi 2020). However, VET systems should also be seen as a path which can support the upskilling of individuals, because a large share of any age cohort opts for VET at upper-secondary level.

The contributions to this book offer evidence of such activities. In Germany, Busemeyer and Thelen (in this volume) observe the growing involvement of employers in public educational institutions at the level of higher education as a way of upskilling the country's VET system with more theoretical content. Most notably, dual study programmes allow large firms to make use of the public educational infrastructure at the tertiary level to augment their own firm-based training.

In the case of Switzerland, Di Maio and Trampusch (in this volume) examine under what conditions employers co-finance and collectively provide skills at the post-secondary level. They find that employers cooperate in the provision of transferable skills when they rely on internal markets for recruitment, large firms are committed to collective training, there is a tradition of collective labour agreements, there are institutional spill-over effects between training at upper-secondary and at post-secondary level, and employers' associations' logic of organization building includes training policies as an important means to attract members.

However, two important caveats are in order. First, attempts to upskill skill formation systems might come at the expense of collective governance. A comparison of Austrian, German, and Swiss upskilling strategies is interesting in this regard. Switzerland is focused on keeping VET an attractive option at upper-secondary level and provides numerous pathways for VET graduates to access tertiary education. This occurs through the vocational baccalaureate, which creates a pathway between upper-secondary VET and universities of applied sciences, and through a large 'higher' VET sector at post-secondary level (Hippach-Schneider and Schneider 2018; Emmenegger et al. 2021; Di Maio and Trampusch, in this volume). As a result, collectively governed education and training institutions remain a key part of Switzerland's upskilling strategy.

In contrast, Germany is more focused on expanding general education, at both upper-secondary and tertiary levels, and by adding vocational elements at the tertiary level. For instance, Germany incentivizes aforementioned dual study programmes that combine classes at a tertiary general education institution with firm-based training and favours the recruitment of general education graduates by universities of applied sciences. However, in this way, Germany reduces the role of collectively governed education and training institutions (Graf 2018; Durazzi and Benassi 2020; Emmenegger et al. 2021; Busemeyer and Thelen, in this volume), although it should be added that in Germany, an increasing share of youth with university entrance diplomas (e.g. a baccalaureate) starts apprenticeships, which runs somewhat counter to this overall trend of declining collective governance (Pilz et al. 2020).

Similar developments can be observed in Austria where attempts to upskill the skill formation system have come at the expense of collective governance. As Seitzl and Unterweger (in this volume) show, in response to rising skill demands in a knowledge economy, the Austrian state expanded its role in skill provision, opting to provide information and communication technology (ICT) skills through school-based VET rather than collectively governed dual VET. Moreover, they show that state attempts to compensate for insufficient collective good provision by employers may even reinforce the decline of collective training, as employers increasingly learn to appreciate state-provided training because it allows firms to save costs while the provision of a well-trained workforce is still ensured.

Second, while Austria, Germany, and Switzerland are active in upskilling their skill formation systems, albeit sometimes at the expense of collective governance, the same cannot be said about the other two prototypical collective skill formation systems: Denmark and the Netherlands. In these countries, the focus is on inclusion rather than upskilling. Interestingly, however, this inclusion focus triggered a strong response by Danish employers, which led to reforms excluding the weakest students to attract stronger students and employers—albeit with limited success so far (Carstensen and Ibsen, in this volume). In contrast, Dutch employers do not seem to mind this inclusion focus of recent reform activities. Nijhuis (in this volume) argues that Dutch employers did not view the introduction of a school alternative as a threat to the existence of the apprenticeship system—as many of their foreign counterparts did (Esser 2006)—because of the informal and therefore flexible nature of the apprenticeship system but also because of the low status of both preparatory-secondary vocational education and apprenticeship training in general.

14.4 Maintaining employer influence in an era of de-collectivization

The contributions to this book show that overall, employers remain strongly attached to collective skill formation. The shift to a knowledge economy and the more knowledge-intensive training that this shift inevitably requires, has not, so far at least, reduced the trust employers have in a system created in the early days of industrialization. Although the system needs to be adapted, employers, in general, do not support the alternative of abandoning collective skill formation for state-provided VET. Employers are unlikely to trust the state for the provision of an aptly trained workforce (Culpepper 2003). This is not necessarily something new, but the knowledge economy, with the extra requirement in terms more academic and knowledge-intensity training, has not changed this.

Although challenged, collective skill formation systems have proven in many cases to be surprisingly resilient and adaptive. For instance, the reform of collective skill formation systems has led to new forms of cooperation between the state and intermediary associations with the state adopting a more prominent and a more active role (Bürgi et al., in this volume; Busemeyer et al. 2022). Similarly, initiatives have aimed to make skill formation systems more permeable and to improve the connections between different segments of the overall education and training system (Bernhard and Graf, in this volume). In addition, these reforms gave rise to new forms of collective organization that compensate for the absence of the traditional associational infrastructure normally considered necessary for collective governance (Graf et al. 2021; Strebel et al. 2021).

There is an important caveat, however. From the employers' point of view, the value of collective skill formation systems is a function of their ability to produce an adequately trained workforce. If, by contrast, the quality of the system is considered low, employers seem more willing to tolerate more state involvement. Yet once VET systems gain in quality, employers grow more interested in playing a key role in their governance, including the definition of training content and control over the access to training (Nijhuis, in this volume).

The Austrian case offers an interesting variation of this relationship (Seitzl and Unterweger, in this volume). In the case of ICT training, state-led vocational schools were considered more apt at providing training for such demanding occupations—including by employers themselves. This is rather telling of the perceived quality of the Austrian dual VET system, as neighbouring Switzerland displayed no such concerns and opted for dual training in ICT occupations instead (Seitzl 2020). In contrast, in the case of public training workshops, which were supposed to make the Austrian VET system more inclusive, employers initially resisted increased state involvement. However, although the specifics of the public workshop system remain heavily politicized (Carstensen et al. 2022), employers came to appreciate state involvement, as they began to recognize the possibilities for cost savings and concerns about training quality abated. These developments show that employer opposition to more state involvement is not set in stone.

Importantly, the relationship between the state and employers in VET governance is being recalibrated in a period when employers increasingly struggle to organize. These de-collectivization processes have the potential to fuel segmentalist tendencies (Thelen and Busemeyer 2012; Emmenegger and Seitzl 2019). The increasing dominance of large firms in training and the rise of firm-specific skill needs and training strategies reflect the weakening organizational capacities and collective action of employers. The rise of dual study programmes in Germany are some of the most visible examples of these processes (Busemeyer and Thelen, in this volume). Hence, as collective skill formation systems are being adapted to the demands of a knowledge economy, there is a risk that these systems are growing increasingly segmentalist. However, there is considerable variation between sectors with regard to the employers' willingness to co-finance and collectively provide transferable skills.

Several factors help explain these differences in the degree of the collective provision of training. The contributions to this volume show that small firms and the collective representation of firms are the most likely champions of collective provision of training. Small firms struggle to develop firm-specific training systems and are thus dependent on collective training systems to retain access to adequate skills, whereas intermediary associations of employers have an organizational interest in keeping collective training systems thriving. By implication, the more intermediary associations of employers are dependent on collective training for their organizational survival, the more we can expect them to push for collective solutions (Di Maio and Trampusch, in this volume). As a result, the more powerful small firms and intermediary associations are, the more we can expect segmentalist tendencies to be kept at bay.

These reflections suggest that large firms are the most likely drivers of segmentalism (Thelen and Busemeyer 2012; Emmenegger and Seitzl 2019), but there are important cross-sectoral differences. Most notably, in some sectors, large firms are more strongly committed to collective training because they fill their leadership positions within the firm with VET graduates. If, by contrast, large firms are not committed to collective training, they might push for a more segmentalist training system, because such a system would give large firms more institutional control.

14.5 Making collective skill formation more inclusive

The promotion of inclusiveness is an important function in all collective skill formation systems. This is another development that is not entirely new but has been strengthened by the shift to a knowledge economy and by the concomitant developments in terms of increasing social inequality. As argued in the introduction, collective skill formation systems have to bridge an increasingly large gap between the ability of academically weak youth to acquire general and professional skills on the one hand, and the complex skill requirements associated with the shift to a knowledge economy, on the other. In this section, we consider the tools and interventions that have been used in order to preserve and enhance the inclusiveness of these systems. We can identify at least six different types of tools.

First, collective skill formation systems can rely on external measures. This is traditionally the main strategy used to improve the inclusiveness of such systems. External measures do not directly interfere with the functioning of the skill formation system but aim at better preparing weak candidates so that they can succeed in the standard system (Bonoli and Wilson 2019; Bonoli and Emmenegger 2021; Durazzi and Geyer 2022). These measures can be very diverse, and include, for example, remedial education, transition measures that prepare youth for specific professions, or measures that help them find an apprenticeship position. External measures are thus not new but are being reinforced and adapted in many contexts. For example, in recent years, new programmes for youth with a migration background have been introduced (see Aerne, in this volume).

Second, collective skill formation systems can improve their inclusiveness by offering subsidies to employers who are willing to give a chance to academically weak candidates. In Germany, for example, one of the key inclusiveness measures, *Einstiegsqualifizierung*, is a federal subsidy paid to employers who take on young people who have failed to obtain an apprenticeship in the regular way (BMBF 2016: 90). Employers are not required to offer a standard apprenticeship position, but a less demanding 'pre-apprenticeship' slot. If successful in the one-year pre-apprenticeship, the employer can decide to hire the person as a standard apprentice.

However, the issue of paying firms subsidies to hire academically weak youth can be highly controversial if employers consider it excessively intrusive. The German 'training bonus' provides a clear example of an inclusiveness measure that according to employers went too far. The bonus was a subsidy paid to employers willing to hire youth who had failed to obtain an apprenticeship position through the regular channels as apprentices. The measure was opposed by employers (and by the trade unions), but the government forced its adoption. However, this was hardly a victory for the government. The bonus remained vastly underused, and most of the employers who did use it did not change their hiring behaviour (Geyer and Durazzi, in this volume). In general, the contributions to this volume find that employers tend to resist measures that may change the nature of a collective skill formation system by pushing it too far in the direction of inclusiveness, even when they are under no obligation to participate.

Third, the state can also directly improve the inclusiveness of collective skill formation systems by acting in its capacity of employer trainer. Wilson (in this volume) shows that public-sector recruiters are more likely to give a chance to academically weaker applicants in comparison to private firms. However, research also shows that employers display considerable variation in their willingness to hire disadvantaged youth (see also Wilson 2021).

Fourth, collective skill formation systems can respond to the twin (contradictory) demands of providing higher skills and integrating academically weak students by turning to 'degree segmentation'. Basically, as requirements for standard degrees are increased, new degrees with lower requirements can be created, so that those who fail to obtain a standard degree will nonetheless be able to obtain and certify a given, albeit lower, level of skills (Carstensen and Ibsen, in this volume; Nijhuis, in this volume). This strategy has taken the shape of short-track, less ambitious vocational degrees (often lasting only two years instead of three or four). In recent years, short-track degrees have been introduced in Denmark, Germany, and Switzerland. In some cases (Denmark and Switzerland), the explicit objective of short-track degrees was to improve the integrative function of the VET system (Di Maio et al. 2019).

Fifth, and in relation to the decline in the proportion of employment in the middle of the skill distribution, one option is to increase the skill content of training for the less skilled occupations, so that workers become more productive, can obtain higher wages, and avoid the occupational downgrading observed by Ebner et al. (in this volume). The strategy works only if upskilled workers become more productive. For example, training for waiters could incorporate foreign language courses, so that they can cater for an international (and higher-paying) clientele. More concretely, this strategy is implemented through initiatives aiming to standardize and regularly update training curricula and the permeability of the training system (Bernhard and Graf, in this volume; Bürgi et al., in this volume). Importantly, however, this strategy must be in line with labour market needs in order to produce the desired outcomes (see Martin and Knudsen 2010).

Sixth, collective skill formation systems can also contribute to inclusiveness through their skill certification function. This strategy is particularly relevant in relation to the challenge of migration, as individuals trained in other countries may possess skills that are not easy to document to employers in the receiving country. Undetected skills are a problem for individual workers, who may fail to access suitable employment, but also for the economy as a whole who may lose human capital. That is why most collective skill formation systems have developed various tools that allow the certification of skills acquired outside the formal VET system. These generally go under the rubric of 'recognition of prior learning' (RPL). RPL is a promising way to deal with the inclusion of migrant workers, but it is a place where the dilemma between efficiency and inclusiveness plays out very strongly. VET authorities need to balance the accessibility of RPL (and skill certification) with the requirement to protect the value of vocational degrees (Maurer, in this volume).

14.6 The temptation: using collective skill formation systems as social policy

In the previous section, we discussed the tools that are available to governments to preserve and enhance the inclusiveness of their collective skill formation systems. As already hinted, the adoption of these measures can be more or less controversial and generate tension among the various actors that make up a collective skill formation system. In general, governments are keen on increasing inclusiveness, because those who fail to obtain a vocational qualification are exposed to the risk of long-term exclusion from the labour market and dependency on the welfare state. Governments may thus be tempted to use the vocational training system as a social policy. On the other hand, employers are likely to resist such moves. For them a skill formation system is a tool to provide workers with suitable skills, and not a social policy instrument. This tension, which is often referred to as the tension between efficiency and equality, concerns all the different pro-inclusiveness measures discussed earlier. However, it is likely to play out in different ways depending on the precise details of the measure (Bonoli and Emmenegger 2021).

The measures that are by far most likely to escape the tension between efficiency and equality are external measures. These are in a way 'invisible' to employers. Even though they are explicitly targeted towards making the system more inclusive, they act outside of it. Most of these measures are located within the education system, the welfare state, or in an intermediary system that falls very largely under the control of the state. Employers are not directly involved and are as a result unlikely to object to external measures.

Inclusiveness can also be promoted uncontroversially in the middle of the skill distribution, essentially by improving the permeability between the VET and the academic tracks and investment in post-secondary VET (including hybrids such as dual study programmes). In these cases, the objective of inclusiveness is not to lock students into the VET track but allow those who wish to continue to go on to tertiary education. These types of inclusiveness initiatives, as seen earlier, can be supported by employers because they are thought to contribute to making the vocational track more attractive to talented and ambitious youth. That employers' support for permeability is motivated by the latter rather than by a concern for social mobility is clear in the case of the DuBAS pilot in Saxony (Bernhard and Graf, in this volume). In this case, upward permeability exists, but employers were rather reluctant to the idea of including elements in the programme that would genuinely favour such permeability, for example, career counselling, as if their objective was to attract talented youth to VET with the permeability argument, but then try to keep them on the vocational track.

Pro-inclusiveness measures which target the bottom of the skill distribution and which intervene in the functioning of the collective skill formation system directly are the most likely to generate controversy. This is precisely because they imply taking a position on the efficiency–equality dimension. The studies included in this book show that these measures tend to be negotiated with employers and win-win or at least mutually acceptable solutions need to be found. There are very few examples of governments trying to impose inclusiveness at the bottom of the skill distribution without employers' approval. These attempts generally resulted in failure. One example is the already mentioned training bonus in Germany (Durazzi and Geyer, in this volume). The Danish trajectory, characterized by a strong push towards equality and the subsequent reversal in order to restore the attractiveness of the system, provides another good illustration of this point (Carstensen and Ibsen, in this volume).

More generally, the contributions to this book show that pro-inclusiveness measures will be effective if they are perceived as win-win solutions by firms—regardless of the shape these measures take. Such solutions, however, can be elusive, especially when they are targeted at the bottom of the skill distribution. Employers like selectivity, as they compete against each other for the best candidates. So, what can persuade them to side with governments in expanding access?

There are only a few examples of successful win-win solutions in the recent history of collective skill formation systems. These reforms managed to increase inclusiveness without diminishing employers' ability to select. On the contrary, in some cases they even promoted it. One such example is the Austrian public workshop system. These are publicly financed institutions that provide training alongside the standard collective skill formation system for youth who fail to land an apprenticeship position. In one variant of these public workshops, youth spend the first year only there, and are then supposed to enter the standard training system by finding an apprenticeship position in a firm. Public workshops were initially opposed by Austrian employers. With time, however, employers came to appreciate them. This measure makes the state responsible for the first year of training, which is the costliest since productivity is lowest. In addition, employers can select the best candidates to enter a proper apprenticeship from year two, on the basis of the observed performance at the public workshop. What was initially meant to be a pure social policy measure turned out, perhaps unexpectedly, to be a helpful tool for optimizing the delivery of training and selecting candidates for many firms (Seitzl and Unterweger, this volume; Carstensen et al. 2022).

A second example of a pro-inclusiveness measure with a win-win flavour are the short track degrees introduced in Germany, Switzerland, and Denmark. These are meant for youth who have difficulties reaching the standard diploma. Thanks to their introduction, these young people can nonetheless obtain an official degree certifying their skills. This also has advantages for employers, as it improves the signalling capacity of the whole system, by being more precise at the bottom of the skill distribution (Di Maio et al. 2019).

The tension between efficiency and equality is a defining feature of collective skill formation systems. The experiences of the various countries covered in this book show that it is possible to reconcile these two objectives, but they also show that this is an incredibly delicate exercise. The room for manoeuvre, defined by the overlap between the interests of firms and governments, is extremely limited. This notwithstanding, creative policymakers have managed to identify the narrow paths that allow an expansion of the inclusiveness of collective skill formation systems. Inclusiveness remains limited, because of the dual quality of vocational training and the necessary involvement of labour market actors. However, it is being pushed to the limits.

14.7 Outlook

This book is about a very old institution that continues to impress for its ability to survive and adapt to structural economic and political developments. Modern collective skill formation systems go back to the early days of industrialization in Germany and in the surrounding countries. Their origins, however, are to be found even earlier, in pre-industrial systems of training controlled by the guilds and based on apprenticeships (Thelen 2004; Greinert 2005). Today's world is rather different. Yet the attractiveness of (partly) workplace-based vocational training remains intact, as the various contributions included in this book make abundantly clear.

This observation confirms the view that the shift to a knowledge economy, while representing a big challenge, will not mean the end of collective skill formation systems. However, constant adaptation is necessary, including in directions that remain to be uncovered. The ongoing labour market transformations and the loss of employment in the middle of the skill distribution represent a challenge for collective skill formation systems. But these systems seem capable of adapting by refocusing on the extremes: short degrees at the bottom of the skill distribution and higher VET at the top. In short, we observe an extraordinary capacity of collective skill formation systems to adapt to changing labour market conditions without giving up its defining features, e.g. the collaboration between employers and the state in the provision of vocational training.

While we can be reasonably optimistic with regard to the ability of collective skill formation systems to survive in the medium term, we are more agnostic in relation to the distributional consequences of both structural change and adaptation. Historically, collective skill formation systems have been praised for their capacity to integrate social groups at risk of being sidelined. Today, all the countries covered are making an immense effort in order to preserve this integrating function. The analyses of the various programmes and interventions discussed in this book, however, suggest that there are limitations to the extent to which the inclusiveness of these systems can be preserved.

Understanding where these limits lie and the extent to which they can be pushed back is a crucial question that will certainly attract substantial attention from policymakers and researchers alike over the next decades. Our contribution in this respect, is to highlight the importance of finding win-win solutions. Having employers on board seems a necessary condition for inclusiveness measures to be ultimately successful. This is an important condition, but not one that suppresses the possibility of preserving and enhancing the inclusiveness of these systems. True, employers will always want to retain some degree of selectivity, but this has not prevented the adoption of pro-inclusiveness measures in the past.

Win-win solutions in this field are elusive but not impossible. Creative solutions can generate new opportunities that, sometimes even unexpectedly, reflect the interests of employers and of the state, such as Austria's experience with public training workshops. Such examples tend to be rare, but they do exist. The task for both policymakers and researchers will be to identify win-win solutions where they exist. This will allow the continuing reconciliation of efficiency and equality in collective skill formation systems.

References

BMBF. 2016. *Berufsbildungsbericht 2016*. Berlin: Bundesministerium für Bildung und Forschung.

Bonoli, G., and P. Emmenegger. 2021. 'The Limits of Decentralized Cooperation: Promoting Inclusiveness in Collective Skill Formation Systems?' *Journal of European Public Policy* 28 (2): 229–47.

Bonoli, G., and A. Wilson. 2019. 'Bringing Firms on Board: Inclusiveness of the Dual Apprenticeship Systems in Germany, Switzerland and Denmark'. *International Journal of Social Welfare* 28 (4): 369–79.

Brown, P., H. Lauder, and D. Ashton. 2012. *The Global Auction: The Broken Promises of Education, Jobs, and Incomes*. New York: Oxford University Press.

Busemeyer, M. R., M. B. Carstensen, and P. Emmenegger. 2022. 'Orchestrators of Coordination: Towards a New Role of the State in Coordinated Capitalism?' *European Journal of Industrial Relations*, forthcoming. https://doi.org/10.1177/09596801211062556

Carstensen, M. B., P. Emmenegger, and D. F. Unterweger. 2022. 'Setting the Terms of State Intervention: Employers, Unions and the Politics of Inclusiveness in Austrian and Danish Vocational Education Institutions'. European Political Science Review. https://doi.org/10.1017/S1755773922000017

Culpepper, P. D. 2003. *Creating Cooperation: How States Develop Human Capital in Europe.* Ithaca: Cornell University Press.

Di Maio, G., L. Graf, and A. Wilson. 2019. 'Torn between Economic Efficiency and Social Equality? Short-track Apprenticeships in Denmark, Germany and Switzerland'. *European Educational Research Journal 18* (6): 699–723.

Durazzi, N., and C. Benassi. 2020. 'Going Up-Skill: Exploring the Transformation of the German Skill Formation System'. *German Politics 29* (3): 319–38.

Durazzi, N., and L. Geyer. 2022. 'Social Inclusion and Collective Skill Formation Systems: Policy and Politics'. *Journal of European Social Policy* 32(1): 105–116.

Emmenegger, P., and L. Seitzl. 2019. 'Collective Action, Business Cleavages and the Politics of Control: Segmentalism in the Swiss Skill Formation System'. *British Journal of Industrial Relations 57* (3): 575–98.

Emmenegger, P., L. Seitzl, S. M. Bajka, and C. Ivardi Ganapini. 2021. 'Collective Skill Formation Systems and the Knowledge Economy: Varieties of Going Upskill'. Paper presented at the 2021 Conference of the Society for the Advancement of Socio-Economics.

Esser, F. H. 2006. 'Vollzeitschulische Berufsausbildung: Bedrohung oder Herausforderung für das duale System?' In *Vollzeitschulische Berufsausbildung: Eine gleichwertige Partnerin des dualen Systems?,* edited by A. Zöller, pp. 91–8. Bielefeld: Bertelsmann–Verlag.

Goldin, C., and L. F. Katz. 2009. *The Race between Education and Technology.* Cambridge, MA: Harvard University Press.

Graf, L. 2013. *The Hybridization of Vocational Training and Higher Education in Austria, Germany, and Switzerland.* Opladen: Budrich UniPress.

Graf, L. 2018. 'Combined Models of Gradual Change: The Case of Academic Upgrading and Declining Collectivism in German Skill Formation'. *Socio-Economic Review 16* (1): 185–205.

Graf, L., A. Strebel, and P. Emmenegger. 2021. 'State-Led Bricolage and the Extension of Collective Governance: Hybridity in the Swiss Skill Formation System'. *Regulation and Governance.* Published online 16 August 2021. https://doi.org/10.1111/rego.12436

Greinert, W.-D. 2005. *Mass Vocational Education and Training in Europe: Classical Models of the 19th Century and Training in England, France and Germany during the First Half of the 20th Century.* Luxembourg: Office for Official Publications of the European Communities.

Hippach-Schneider, U., and V. Schneider. 2018. 'Eine Gefahr für die Leistungsfähigkeit der tertiären Bildung? Bildungspolitische Unterschiede zwischen Deutschland und der Schweiz'. *BWP 34*: 1–22.

Martin, C. J., and J. S. Knudsen. 2010. 'Scenes from a Mall: Retail Training and the Social Exclusion of Low-skilled Workers'. *Regulation and Governance 4* (3): 345–64.

Pilz, M., C. Ebner, and S. Edeling. (2020). 'University? No Thanks! An Empirical Study of Why German Apprentices with the Abitur Choose Not to Go to University'. *Oxford Review of Education 46* (6): 770–87.

Schulze-Cleven, T., and J. R. Olson. 2017. 'Worlds of Higher Education Transformed: Toward Varieties of Academic Capitalism'. *Higher Education 73* (6): 813–31.

Seitzl, L. 2020. *How Corporatist Economies Innovate*. Working Paper, University of St. Gallen.

Strebel, A., P. Emmenegger, and L. Graf. 2021. 'New Interest Associations in a Neo-Corporatist System: Adapting the Swiss Training System to the Service Economy'. *British Journal of Industrial Relations 59* (3): 848–73.

Thelen, K. 2004. *How Institutions Evolve: The Political Economy of Skills in Germany, Britain, the United States and Japan*. Cambridge: Cambridge University Press.

Thelen, K., and M. R. Busemeyer. 2012. 'Institutional Change in German Vocational Training: From Collectivism toward Segmentalism'. In *The Political Economy of Collective Skill Formation*, edited by M. R. Busemeyer and C. Trampusch, pp. 68–91. Oxford: Oxford University Press.

Trampusch, C., and P. Eichenberger. 2012. 'Skills and Industrial Relations in Coordinated Market Economies: Continuing Vocational Training in Denmark, the Netherlands, Austria and Switzerland'. *British Journal of Industrial Relations 50* (4): 644–66.

Wilson, A. 2021. 'A Silver Lining for Disadvantaged Youth on the Apprenticeship Market: An Experimental Study of Employers' Hiring Preferences'. *Journal of Vocational Education and Training 73* (1): 127–47.

Index